MOVED BY LOVE

MOVED BY LOVE

Inspired Artists and Deviant Women in Eighteenth-Century France

MARY D. SHERIFF

The University of Chicago Press
Chicago & London

The University of Chicago Press, Chicago 60637
The University of Chicago Press, Ltd., London

Paperback edition 2008
Printed in the United States of America

13 12 11 10 09 08   2 3 4 5
ISBN-13: 978-0-226-75287-7 (cloth)
ISBN-10: 0-226-75287-9 (cloth)
ISBN-13: 978-0-226-75288-4 (paper)
ISBN-10: 0-226-75288-7 (paper)

Published with the assistance of the Getty Grant Program.

Library of Congress Cataloging-in-Publication Data

Sheriff, Mary D.
Moved by love : inspired artists and deviant women in eighteenth-century France / Mary Sheriff.
p. cm.
Includes bibliographical references and index.
ISBN 0-226-75287-9 (cloth : alk. paper)—
ISBN 0-226-75288-7 (pbk. : alk. paper)
1. Arts, French—18th century—Themes, motives. 2. Creation (Literary, artistic, etc.) 3. Pygmalion (Greek mythology) 4. Héloïse, 1101–1164. I. Title

NX549.A1 S49 2004
700′.82′0944—dc21   2003001362

∞ The paper used in this publication meets the minimum requirements of the American National Standard for Information Sciences—Permanence of Paper for Printed Library Materials, ANSI Z39.48-1992.

For Keith

CONTENTS

List of Illustrations *ix*
Acknowledgments *xiii*

Introduction *1*

CHAPTER 1 **Enthusiasm: Reason's Masterpiece** *15*

CHAPTER 2 **The Artist and the Woman** *43*
Part 1: Just Like a Woman?
Part 2: Possession and Emulation

CHAPTER 3 **Deviant Spectators: Ignorant Girls and Women Who Know Too Much** *85*

CHAPTER 4 **Pygmalion's Enthusiasm and the Fires of Nymphomania, or The Psychology of Art and Desire** *125*

CHAPTER 5 **The Model Pygmalion and the Artist Galatea** *159*
Part 1: A Model for the Artist
Part 2: Playing Galatea

CHAPTER 6 **Inspired by Heloise** *201*

Conclusion: Closing the Circle, Opening the End *241*
Notes *247*
Bibliography *283*
Index *297*

ILLUSTRATIONS

FIGURE 1 Elisabeth Vigée-Lebrun, *Portrait of Madame de Staël as Corinne* 2

FIGURE 2 "Detailed System of Human Knowledge" 16

FIGURE 3 Gabriel-François Doyen, *Le miracle des Ardents (Miracle of St. Anthony's Fire)* 35

FIGURE 4 *Secours donnés Gabrielle Moler* 59

FIGURE 5 Michel Corneille II, *Sappho Performing Her Lyric Poetry* 67

FIGURE 6 Attributed to Elisabeth Sophie Cheron, *Portrait of a Woman as Sappho* 69

FIGURE 7 Charles Coypel, *Portrait of a Woman with a Lyre* 72

FIGURE 8 François Dumont, *Madame de Saint-Just d'Aucourt as Sappho* 73

FIGURE 9 Elisabeth Vigée-Lebrun, *Portrait of a Young Woman Playing the Lyre, the countess Fries as Sappho* 73

FIGURE 10 Elisabeth Vigée-Lebrun, *Self-Portrait* 75

FIGURE 11 Elisabeth Vigée-Lebrun, *Self-Portrait with Her Daughter Julie* 76

FIGURE 12 Jean Ranc, *Vertumnus and Pomona* 79

FIGURE 13 François Boucher, *Vertumnus and Pomona* 80

FIGURE 14 Augustin de Saint-Aubin after Jean-Baptiste Greuze, *A Young Woman Throwing a Kiss from Her Window* 81

FIGURE 15 Pierre-Imbert Drevet after Charles Coypel, *Portrait of Adrienne Lecouvreur* 83

FIGURE 16 Jean-Baptiste Chardin, *The Good Education* 87

FIGURE 17 Jean-Baptiste Chardin, *The Drawing Lesson* 88

FIGURE 18 Nicolas Ponce after Pierre-Antoine Baudouin, *The Cherry Picker* 90

FIGURE 19 Gianlorenzo Bernini, *Saint Teresa in Ecstasy* 93

FIGURE 20 Pierre-Antoine Baudouin, *La Lecture (Reading)* 95

FIGURE 21 Jean-Baptiste Chardin, *The Amusements of Private Life* 98

FIGURE 22 Jacques-Louis David, *Portrait of Madame Buron* 100

FIGURE 23 Emmanuel-Jean Nepomucene de Ghendt after Pierre-Antoine Baudouin, *Noon (Le Midi)* 101

FIGURE 24 Pierre Maleuvre after Sigmund Freudenberger, *The Boudoir* 102

FIGURE 25 Isadore Stanislas Helman after Nicolas Lavreince, *The Dangerous Novel* 103

FIGURE 26 Charles-André Van Loo, *The Spanish Reading* 105

FIGURE 27 Charles-André Van Loo, *The Spanish Conversation* 106

FIGURE 28 Antoine Watteau, *The Timid Lover* 111

FIGURE 29 Antoine Watteau, *Prelude to a Concert* 112

FIGURE 30 Jean Michel Moreau (Moreau le jeune) after Jean-Baptiste Greuze, *La philosophie endormie* 116

FIGURE 31 Jean-Baptiste Greuze, *The Lazy Italian Woman (La paresseuse Italienne)* 117

FIGURE 32 Étienne Jeaurat, *Woman Convalescing* 131

FIGURE 33 Jan Steen, *The Doctor's Visit* 132

FIGURE 34 François Boucher, *The Woman Tying Her Garter* 134

FIGURE 35 Gabriel de Saint-Aubin, *The Private Academy* 135

FIGURE 36 Pierre Parrocel, *Young Woman Reading before a Fireplace* 135

FIGURE 37 Jean-Honoré Fragonard, *The Powder Keg* (*Le feu aux poudres*) 136

FIGURE 38 Nicolas Bertin, *Anacreon and Amour* 137

FIGURE 39 Angelica Kauffman, *Sappho* 139

FIGURE 40 Antoine-Jean Gros, *Sappho Leaping from the Rock of Leucatus* 140

FIGURE 41 Jean Raoux, *Pygmalion* 160

FIGURE 42 François Lemoyne, *Pygmalion Seeing His Sculpture Come to Life* 161

FIGURE 43 Étienne Falconet, *Pygmalion* 167

FIGURE 44 Étienne Falconet, *Bather* 171

FIGURE 45 Étienne Falconet, *Menacing Cupid* 172

FIGURE 46 Emmanuel-Jean Nepomucene de Ghendt after Charles Eisen, *Pygmalion; ou, La statue animé* 180

FIGURE 47 *Sculpture* from *Iconologie par figures* 187

FIGURE 48 Gilles-Edme Petit after a portrait by Fenouil, *Portrait of Mademoiselle Sallé. The French Terpsicore* 190

FIGURE 49 Charles Louis Lingée after a portrait by Sigmund Freudenberger, *Portrait of Mademoiselle Raucourt* 195

FIGURE 50 Noël Le Mire after Jean Michel Moreau, *Pygmalion and Galatea* 198

FIGURE 51 Augustin Bernard d'Agesci, *A Lady Reading the Letters of Heloise and Abelard* 202

FIGURE 52 Charles Le Brun, *Le ravissement* 204

FIGURE 53 Noël Nicholas Coypel, *Rape of Europa* 205

FIGURE 54 François Boucher, *Toilet of Venus* 208

FIGURE 55 Jean-Baptiste Greuze, *The Broken Eggs* 210

FIGURE 56 Jean-Baptiste Greuze, *Young Girl Mourning Her Dead Bird* 211

FIGURE 57 Jean Massard after Jean-Baptiste Greuze, *The Well-Beloved Mother* 219

FIGURE 58 Jean-Baptiste Greuze, copy after? *The Dreamer* 221

FIGURE 59 Gilles Demarteau after François Boucher, *Young Girl Reading the Letters of Heloise* 222

FIGURE 60 Jean Massard after Charles Eisen, *Heloise in Her Cell* 224

FIGURE 61 Bernard Lépicié after Charles Coypel, *L'amour précepteur* 229

FIGURE 62 Herbert after Febvre, *La nouvelle Heloyse* 235

FIGURE 63 Jean-Honoré Fragonard, *Coresus Sacrificing Himself to Save Callirhoe* 243

ACKNOWLEDGMENTS

The National Endowment for the Humanities, the University of North Carolina Research Council, the Daniel W. Patterson Chair Fund, and a Reynolds Fellowship generously supported the research and writing of this book. I am also indebted to the UNC Research Council's Publication Fund for aid in obtaining photographs, rights, and permissions. Sincerest thanks to Dean Darryl Gless for supporting my scholarship and writing on my behalf at critical moments.

My participation in the seminar on enthusiasm organized in 1996 by Larry Klein and Tony La Vopa at the William Andrews Clark Memorial Library greatly aided the conceptualization of this project. I am indebted to the seminar participants for their astute questions and spirited exchange, and I thank the organizers for their careful and helpful reading of my work. I am also grateful to Régis Michel for inviting me to participate in the 1998 series, "Où en est l'interpretation de l'oeuvre d'art?" at the Louvre and for providing the opportunity to develop what became the final chapter of *Moved by Love.* I thank Régis Michel for his insightful comments and for providing a model of independent, engaged criticism. Presenting parts of this book at other venues refined my thinking about central issues, and I profited from discussions with faculty and students at the University of Aarhus, Denmark; the University of Georgia; the University of Oregon; the University of Illinois; the University of Iowa; the University of South Florida; the University of Uppsala, Sweden; and the University of Virginia.

I also profited greatly from close and careful readings of the entire manuscript, and for these I owe an enormous debt to Christopher Johns, Dorothy Johnson, and Keith Luria. Better colleagues are not to be found. Eric Downing's many helpful suggestions and ideas about chapter 4 greatly improved the manuscript, and I thank him for his subtle and expert reading. I am grateful to Kathleen Nicholson, Suzanne Pucci, and Paula Radisich for an ongoing exchange of ideas, and I could not have sustained this project without their enthusiasm, encouragement, and friendship. Also indispensable to this project was the support of Ann Bermingham and Lynn Hunt. I am indebted to their generosity and their counsel and grateful for the inspiration their work provides. William Ray has been equally forthcoming in his support, and I have benefited much from both his theoretical acumen and vast knowledge of eighteenth-century French culture.

I owe many thanks to my editor, Susan Bielstein, for her confidence in the project even in the face of my doubts and for her expert guidance in crafting a suitable introduction to the book. I am also grateful to Anthony Burton at the University of Chicago Press for all his help in the book's production and to Eileen Doyle at Art Resource for her efforts on my behalf. My sincerest appreciation also to my research assistants, who worked on every stage of the book: Samantha Baskind, Elizabeth Howie, Scott Karakas, Cathy Keller-Brown, and Debbie Selinger. Without their help I would still be writing chapter 5 rather than finishing the acknowledgments!

To Marsha Collins, Jane Burns, and David Gilmartin, much affection for many years of unflagging support and friendship and for the humor that makes things bearable even in the worst of times. And to my husband, Keith Luria, much love for everything.

INTRODUCTION

It has been nearly a decade since I traveled to Geneva to see the portrait of an inspired artist and deviant woman (fig. 1). Standing before a painting made in 1808 by Elisabeth Vigée-Lebrun, I gazed rapturously on the novelist Germaine de Staël shown in the guise of Corinne, the title character of Staël's immensely popular *Corinne, or Italy* (1806). Corinne is an improvisational poet, a performance artist feted throughout Rome for her prodigious talents and stunning looks. By 1806, the novelist who imagined Corinne was already renowned for her wit and intelligence, but never would she be hailed as a beauty.[1] Her portrait was bigger, bolder, and more in your face than I had imagined from the reproductions. And this monumental figure of a woman artist seemed sure to impress as it showed Staël/Corinne in an inspired state signaled in her upturned eyes, open mouth, and tousled hair. I was entranced. My cousin who came with me that day was not so taken with the image. "Boy is that an ugly picture" was her immediate response.

I have to admit that even now I can see her point. The picture doubly thwarts our expectations for it is not a showcase for beautifully painted feminine beauty. Vigée-Lebrun's mastery of color and paint handling is evident, but her composition lacks harmony. The awkwardly posed sitter seems bulky rather than grand, and the setting looks deliberately staged. The artist, moreover, has not idealized Staël's features, so both face and figure frustrate our desire to see a beautiful woman. The work even disappointed Staël, who commissioned a more idealized remake of the painting.[2] In my study of Elisabeth Vigée-Lebrun (*The Exceptional Woman: Elisabeth Vigée-Lebrun and the Cultural Politics of Art* [University of Chicago Press, 1995]), I imagined that some aspects of the portrait's "ugliness" suggested the painter's inspiration, for they separated Staël from the court lovelies Vigée-Lebrun so often flattered.[3]

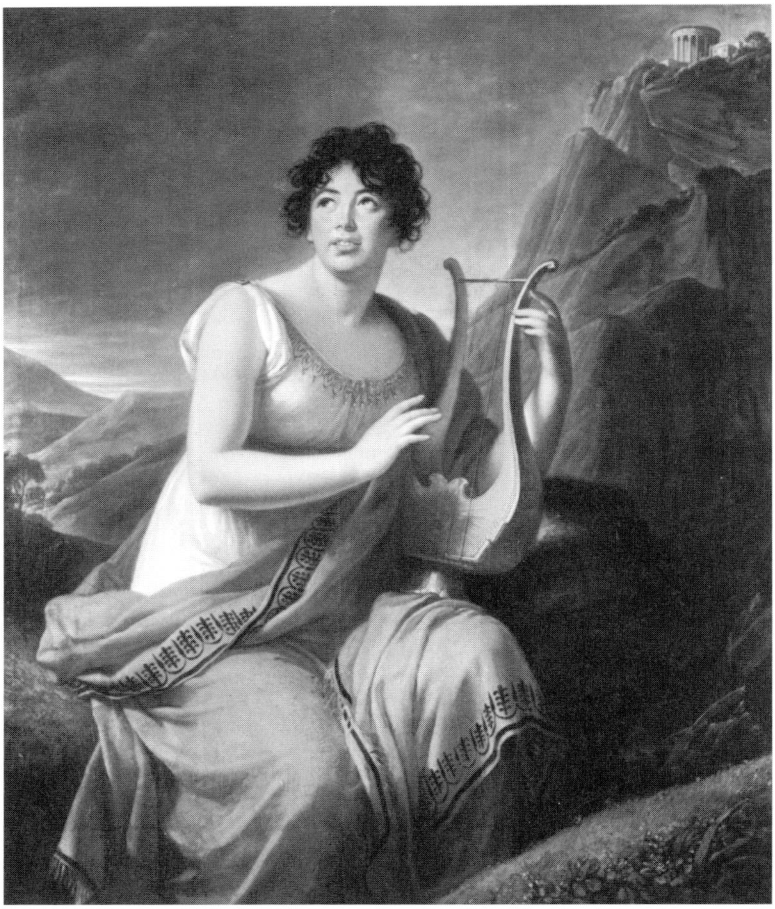

FIGURE 1. Elisabeth Vigée-Lebrun (French, 1755–1824), *Portrait of Madame de Staël as Corinne*, 1808. Oil on canvas, 140 × 118 cm. Geneva: Musée d'art et d'histoire. Photograph © Musée d'art et d'histoire, Ville de Genève.

In *The Exceptional Woman,* I concluded that the portrait of Mme de Staël as Corinne represented the inspired writer declaiming *Corinne.* The ideas I explore in *Moved by Love* lead me to another possibility: that in Vigée-Lebrun's painting we see Staël imagining, imagining a scene in which Corinne gives an inspired performance. So strong are Staël's imaginative powers, so intense is the passion that moves her to create, that we see her becoming Corinne. The ability to lose oneself in a character or fictive scene marked both great artists and ideal spectators in eighteenth-century France. Yet neither lost themselves entirely, for to do so would be to fall into a delirium, a madness. I now see the inspired Staël imagining Corinne, even projecting herself as Corinne, but at the same time, I see that in its particularized features and lack of conventional beauty, the portrait maintains a clear separation between Staël and the fictional character she imagines herself to be. And this point alone makes Staël an exceptional woman, at least for those eighteenth-century writers who posited the desire to lose oneself in fictions as a danger that imperiled women's health and prevented them from turning their fantasies into art.

To portray Staël imagining Corinne and to portray her in a way compelling enough for the viewer to feel her enthusiasm is the task I imagine Vigée-Lebrun set for herself. In painting an effective portrait, the artist had (at least in theory) to imagine herself as Staël filled with enthusiasm. But the artist goes one step further. In Staël's novel, Corinne never performs anything at Tivoli, the site Vigée-Lebrun indicates in her portrait by including the famous temple that stood there. The painter thus invents another moment in *Corinne* and imagines Staël as imagining that moment. There is a contagion of enthusiasm here, as the painter is inspired by the novelist and as her portrait of the inspired poet represents the enthusiasm of three artists: Corinne, Staël, and Vigée-Lebrun.[4]

In Vigée-Lebrun's painting, Corinne might well be imagined as singing of her sorrows, her passionate suffering, and the failure of love. An exceptional woman and a tragic heroine, Corinne suffers. In Staël's novel she falls hopelessly in love with Oswald, whom she imagines to be her soul mate. Yet Oswald is ruled by social convention, and he cannot take for his wife a woman who deviates so obviously from the norms of acceptable feminine behavior. Disappointed in love, Corinne remains full of longing and desire. She falls into a sort of lovesickness that eventually kills her after depriving her of talent and voice. Corinne is both moved and undone by love. I invoke the title of my book purposefully for here I analyze the myths and discourses in which love as desire, passion, or devotion motivates artistic production. When the discourses of art making intersect with those of erotomania, unrequited love can drive lovers mad, steal their talent, push them toward aberrant behavior, and induce cunning, but perverse, artifice. Although in her novel Staël describes the fate awaiting the deviant woman artist, this fate was not one the novelist herself ever met. And this is another critical point, another point at which Staël is not Corinne. In keeping Staël apart, Vigée-Lebrun tacitly separates her from the lovesick Corinne, who shares the fate of so many other women who die for want of love. That group included creative women, for example, Sappho, whom many depicted as jumping off the rock of Leucatus after Phaon abandoned her. Sappho, moreover, was one of the models for Corinne and an artist whom creative French women took as an inspiration well before Staël.

Although many in eighteenth-century France revered Sappho for her poetry, she remained a deviant woman. Writers figured her as either the heterosexual lover of Phaon driven to madness and suicide or the lover of other women, a tribade with "infamy" attached to her name. The example of Sappho, like that of Corinne, suggests that there were no unproblematic models for the inspired woman artist. In fact, both erotomania and wanton sexuality were often ascribed to inspired women. In her portrait of Staël, however, Vigée-Lebrun does not overtly mix the inspired state with sexual arousal, although the suggestion of heightened sexuality can (and will) slip into any image of inspiration because the pictorial conventions for representing enthusiasm overlap with those for showing sexual ecstasy.

In her painting, Vigée-Lebrun depicts Staël as a recognizable woman writer in the grasp of poetic enthusiasm, in the middle of her imagining. She keeps Staël separate from the beautiful, lovesick Corinne whom Staël may imagine but does not become. In many ways, this portrait is both the inevitable and the unexpected outcome of debates and theories I write about here. Inevitable because it figures strands of thinking long in the discourses that surrounded art making and viewing. Unexpected because it does so in relation to a woman. If unexpected, however, the outcome is not unprecedented, for there were always women to whom the discourse of creativity could apply if only as exceptions.

The idea of inspired creativity raises questions that have long engaged me. How have concepts of inspired creativity shaped art making and viewing in the period known as the Enlightenment, a moment when the apotheosis of reason supposedly reached its most intense and widespread expression? How did considerations of imagination, passion, and reason affect the production and consumption of visual images, in theory and in practice? How was imaginative, passionate, and inspired art understood in the age of reason? What were its dangers and pleasures, its purpose and import? To approach such questions, I have centered this study in the middle decades of the eighteenth century, in the 1750s, 1760s, and 1770s. And I have built its foundations on the *Encyclopédie, ou Dictionnaire raisonné des sciences, des arts et des métiers* (1751–65), the book of knowledge we take as central to the project of Enlightenment and imagine as proclaiming the supremacy of reason. But like the entries in the *Encyclopédie* and its *Discours préliminaire,* I also follow strands of thinking backward, deep into the seventeenth century, and even before. And some ideas lead me forward to the 1780s. In those years works by noted women, by Vigée-Lebrun, Vallayer-Coster, and Labille-Guiard, appeared together at the Salons and attracted substantial commentary. I examine the reception of these women's work in the context of the gendered discourse on creativity. In moving forward, I do not intend to explicate a prehistory of Romanticism nor find the roots of the so-called Romantic rebellion. My analysis rather points to the sheer persistence of certain cultural formations.

I began interrogating notions of artistic inspiration in my study of Jean-Honoré Fragonard, in which I analyzed his images of enthusiasm as well as his enthusiastic brushwork.[5] There it was already apparent that eighteenth-century theory associated artistic creativity with sexual arousal, and that this relation helped to represent the artist as a desiring, masculine, and male subject. From here my interest migrated to the question of how notions of creativity affected the fate of women artists and viewers, both fictional and real. Again I pursued the broader questions through the case study of a single artist, Elisabeth Vigée-Lebrun. *Moved by Love* takes a different tack, for it is focused not on an artist, but on the prevailing theories, myths, and paradigms of art makers and viewers. Here I analyze the ambiguous position of those whose work was "of imagination born": men and women, writers and painters, real persons and fictional characters, those who lived in the eighteenth century and those who died long before.[6] I am convinced that the issues central to the texts and images I consider are still pertinent today, reformulated, to be sure, but nevertheless fundamental to popular conceptions of art making and viewing. I will argue this case in due course.

My book has two prime movers, the mythical sculptor Pygmalion and the medieval writer Heloise, and the analysis runs between, around, past, and toward them. Each was figured in eighteenth-century France as an inspired artist. Both were moved by love, and both moved others through their love, even when it was represented by artists and writers distant from them in time and place. Pygmalion, like Heloise, is presented as a deviant in many versions of his story, at least up until the moment his artwork comes to life. By deviant I mean someone who in an obvious way diverges from the mores of a particular culture and time. I am especially interested in divergence from the norms prescribed for sexual practices, for men's and women's proper social and moral conduct, and for mental health. My study explores how such norms shaped paradigms of creativity and spectatorship and how this shaping, in turn, affected the arts of eighteenth-century France.

I argue that throughout the eighteenth century, French representations figured both inspired men and women as deviant. At the same time, the mythologies proposed in literature, theory, criticism, and the visual arts worked both to normalize and celebrate that deviance. Pygmalion's aberrant statue love, his confusion of reality and fantasy, his erotomania—all these are facilitated and "cured" through making and viewing art. Pygmalion not only becomes the model for the creative artist in eighteenth-century France, he also lives happily ever after with his Galatea. There were no such Hollywood endings for Heloise, just as there would be none for Corinne or Sappho. In the eighteenth century, Heloise remained both inspired artist and deviant woman. In this respect, she is like many of the other deviant women who move through this book, be they writers, readers, or mystics, artists, actresses, or dancers. I choose the word "deviant" not to brand these women anew, but to suggest the especially ambiguous position of inspired women as both artists and spectators.

In discussing my analytical practices, I take my inspiration from French philosopher Michèle Le Doeuff, specifically from the introduction to her work *The Philosophical Imaginary* (*L'imaginaire philosophique,* 1980). There Le Doeuff lays out some of the methodological propositions that guided her enterprise, stressing that what she offers is a retrospective description, a theorization, if you will, of her practice. She attaches to her propositions a "proviso" that they "do not encapsulate a method systematically deployed" and argues that her practice has, in fact, produced her propositions more than been guided by them. Designating her assessment as "a concluding appraisal," Le Doeuff sets for them the task of outlining "a programme for further work."[7] I offer my propositions in the same spirit and note that in the course of my chapters I will discuss theoretical notions that have a direct bearing on specific readings. From the start, however, I want to acknowledge several important studies that have especially helped me focus and shape my own analyses.

Joan DeJean's work on Sappho, on seventeenth-century French women writers, and on literary canon formation has been a continual stimulus for me, as have been the writings of Page duBois on Sappho herself and on issues of possession and inspiration.[8] Giulia Sissa's brilliant writing on oracles has much influenced me; it was invaluable in understanding the Pythia's import.[9] I could not have written the last chapter of this book without Peggy Kamuf's wonderfully suggestive analysis of Heloise, and other parts of this project would be unthinkable without Marie-Hélène Huet's work on the monstrous imagination.[10]

In the chapters that follow, I analyze the complicated gendering of creativity and spectatorship in eighteenth-century France by focusing on the varied ways that artists, critics, theorists, philosophers, and doctors both represented and responded to that gendering. My discussion does not take a direct line; it is not a narrative that has a nice beginning, middle, and end. Rather, the analysis jumps up and back in a kind of locomotion, returning to topics in different ways from different directions and different objects of analysis. In choosing the objects of analysis to be included in this book, I selected from my research those texts, myths, and images in which I found clustered together ideas of passion, inspiration, love, sexuality, artifice, disease, imagination, or possession. I pay close attention to these clusters, these knots in which some or all of these ideas come together, not always from the same direction, not always in the same way, not always in the same mix. The knots construct relations among these ideas in patterns that can be repeated, varied, and undone in other instances. My analysis attends to and unravels this network of ideas, and I elucidate the unstable position of both the "masculine" and the "feminine" as they twist and turn through the various patterns. I do not claim that my procedure is in any way original, although I have melded together a particular combination of strategies to address the questions specific to this study.

As well as attending to the intersections of ideas, I am also attuned to specific concepts and the points of agreement on them. I explore these not only across different fields of expertise but also between writers in the same field who might otherwise be unrelated to one another or even antagonistic in their thinking. I do not view every author or scientist with the specialist's eye, and my goal is not to chart direct influence or intentional meaning. Nor is this book a history of ideas. As I untangle knots, I try to understand and identify generalizations that thread through the culture, considering at all times that generalizations are never absolute, never uncontested, and never fixed. And that there are always exceptions.

At the center of my project stands the concept of enthusiasm, itself closely allied to both passion and imagination. If I were to follow the major strands of my project to find their beginning point, it might be in the ancient notions of enthusiasm explicated by the pre-Socratics, by Heroclitus, Empedocles, Democritus. Amatory, poetic, and religious enthusiasm, as well as diseases of enthusiasm, have their place in these early discussions.[11] Over centuries the strands split apart, separated, and came together again, but not systematically. General discussions of enthusiasm in eighteenth-century thought often attribute to Anthony Ashley Cooper, third earl of Shaftesbury the concept's rehabilitation.[12] Denis Diderot's 1745 translation of Shaftesbury's *An Inquiry concerning Virtue, or Merit* (*Principes de la philosophie morale; ou, Essai de M. S**** sur la mérite et la vertu. Avec réflexions*) might seem a formative moment in France, especially since Diderot seems to have been well acquainted with the Englishman's ideas. My investigation, however, shows that notions of poetic enthusiasm had early entered the French tradition, for example, in Nicolas Boileau's widely read translation of Longinus's *On the Sublime* (*Traité du sublime ou du merveilleux dans le discours*, 1674), in Abbé Jean-Baptiste Du Bos's influential work, *Réflexions critique sur la poésie et sur la peinture* (1719), and in Roger de Piles's central treatise on painting practice, *Cours de peinture par principes* (1708). Shaftesbury's writing undoubtedly had its influence, but in the case of poetic enthusiasm, it likely confirmed existing ideas more than established new ones. I do not intend here to write a history of enthusiasm in France but rather to show how concepts of enthusiasm entered into a variety of discourses.

In eighteenth-century France, theories of creative achievement presented enthusiasm as the force that moved the artist to create and the spectator to respond. But enthusiasm in the fine arts was at the same time intimately related to its sexual and religious forms, which in turn were tied to erotomania, melancholia, fanaticism, compulsion, and madness. Throughout the following chapters, I read together diverse images and texts that bear on the concept of enthusiasm or that have been in some way shaped by it. Many of the examples I discuss were celebrated and well known; others were more obscure. I find telling the appearance of enthusiasm in both sorts of examples. I argue that notions of enthusiasm affected artists—both men and women—and shaped a visual imagery of passion and inspiration, and I suggest the depth and breadth of this imagery.

Ideas about mental development and sexual difference often posed literature and the visual arts as potential dangers to women, whose sensitivity made them especially responsive to illusions. At the same time, both theorists and critics (Diderot is a good example) presented the ideal viewer as one who was passionately moved by the emotions and events depicted in paintings and texts. Since passion, imagination, and sensibility motivated both artistic production and reception, it would seem logical that women should be the better artists and viewers. But this was hardly thought to be the case. Art making and viewing, writers argued, also required the admixture of reason—a mental power thought stronger in the male sex. Thus when tempered by reason in the male body, the "feminine" qualities detrimental to a woman's mental, moral, and physical health could actually aid artistic achievement. Those widely considered great artists and spectators were often men who combined reason with sensitivity, imagination, and passion. Others anxious to link artistic achievement to masculinity pictured creative force as a productive male heterosexual desire, one vastly different from the deviant sexuality that often marked enthusiastic women like Sappho, Heloise, and the mystic Jeanne Guyon. Such constructions, however, could not effectively secure either art or the artist on the side of the masculine, for the feminine attributes remained fundamental to creative acts of making and viewing. I examine not only the contradictory ways texts and images presented women as artists, but also how women artists took advantage of the contradictions. Although the general conclusions that emerged from the entwining of art, philosophy, medicine, and religion worked to exclude women from the domain of art making, individual strands opened possibilities for some women to claim the domain as their own.

In chapter 1, "Enthusiasm: Reason's Masterpiece," I analyze the contradictory position of enthusiasm in French art theory of the seventeenth and eighteenth centuries and show how enthusiasm was related to or separated from imagination, passion, sensibility, reason, and melancholia. Drawing on the *Encyclopédie* as a summary of knowledge in these areas, I work out from its entries to explore the concepts in a broader cultural domain. I am particularly interested in the *Encyclopédie's* entry on enthusiasm, which clearly shows what is at stake in taking enthusiasm as the motor force of art making and viewing. Against all tradition, the entry not only posits a reasonable enthusiasm implicitly gendered as masculine, it also overtly devalues imagination's role in the creative process. This view of enthusiasm, however, could not be maintained, not even within the boundaries of this particular entry, for compulsion, passion, and sexuality inevitably make their way into the discussion.

Chapter 2, "The Artist and the Woman," proposes that the overlap between the categories of "artist" and "woman" posed special problems for eighteenth-century art theorists. The possibility of confusion led some authors—for example, the academician Antoine Léonard Thomas or the doctors Pierre Roussel and Edme-Pierre Chavot de Beauchêne—to argue away the similarities. Art theory and criticism, however, complicated such efforts in presenting enthusiasm as what allowed the male artist or spectator to become woman either by playing the part of a man changed into a woman (for example, that of the god Vertumnus transformed into an old crone) or by emulating the Pythia's possession. To emulate the Pythia was both to imitate a specific woman and to perform as a woman, since the sex had long been thought much more susceptible to possession, be it by Apollo, Jesus Christ, the devil, or their own imaginings. Although both the male artist and spectator could become woman either by a magical transformation or by taking the woman's part, "possession" by an actual woman artist (by which I mean an enthusiastic emulation of her work) many perceived as dangerous to the male practitioner. Writers like Nicolas Boileau Despréaux (hereafter Boileau) and Charles Batteux posed emulating a woman artist as a distinctly emasculating experience. Yet because the categories could not be effectively separated, and because the ancients had ordained some women—for example, the poet Sappho—as worthy of emulation, the discourse of enthusiasm created opportunities for women who could either identify with these exceptional models or pose themselves as becoming other through possession by or emulation of a great man.

The supposed effects of spectatorial enthusiasm on women and girls is the focus of the next chapter, "Deviant Spectators: Ignorant Girls and Women Who Know Too Much." Throughout the eighteenth century, art theory and criticism advanced the idea that art should move the spectator's emotions. At the same time, philosophers, doctors, and even art critics worried that women spectators would become too absorbed in illusions. Their more active imaginations and more easily aroused passions led women to mistake themselves for fictional characters. Philosophers, art critics, doctors, and theologians generally agreed that woman's active imagination should be controlled by limiting what could be imprinted on it. Thus many wanted to restrict women's free access to books, pictures, and spectacles. Although highly developed in women, the aptitude for becoming another—be it a woman or a man—was perilous and could easily arouse dangerous passions. In explicating the relation of women's reading and viewing to sexual deviance, I examine not only how these are represented in moral, medical, and philosophical discourse but also how they are pictured in erotic paintings—for example, those of Jean-Baptiste Greuze and Pierre-Antoine Baudouin, and in forbidden books like the anonymous *Thérèse Philosophe* (1748). While moralists warned against woman's imagination, artists and writers imagined its pleasurable effects and represented these effects in scenes of woman's solitary pleasure.

I continue this discussion of sexuality in chapter 4, "Pygmalion's Enthusiasm and the Fires of Nymphomania," which takes up art production in relation to the diseases of erotomania, lovesickness, and nymphomania. Here I explore the figure of the lovesick artist—the artist dominated by erotic enthusiasm—whose desire is channeled into creative acts and who is either cured or satisfied through art making. With its beginnings in ancient texts, this type persists from eighteenth-century versions of Ovid's Pygmalion, to Freud's theories of art making, to recent novels—for example, Barry Unsworth's *Stone Virgin* (1986)—based on Pygmalion and Freud. The lovesick or desiring woman artist in the eighteenth century had less attractive choices. Like the eighteenth century's Sappho, she might be pictured as driven to madness, suicide, or deviant sexuality, or like its Heloise, imagined as burning with an insatiable erotomania. In relation to these transgressive women, it is especially significant that the Pygmalion story turns on the rejection of a deviant female sexuality, represented by the Propoetides. These women suffer from an insatiable desire for sexual intercourse, a disease that in the eighteenth century would be called nymphomania or uterine furor. Moreover, the *Encyclopédie* tells us that the disease is called uterine furor, rather than venereal furor, because only women suffer it. Men could relieve the desire that drove women mad either through the sexual freedom society allowed them or through the remedies nature provided (e.g., spontaneous ejaculations and wet dreams). And in a similar way we find that the eighteenth-century Pygmalion and his imitators can use art to quell their irrational longings. Although Pygmalion exhibits the classic symptoms of lovesickness and erotomania, he is nevertheless cured of any disease. Still, the Pygmalion envisioned in eighteenth-century texts has much in common with the nymphomaniac. He suffers from delusions, he is fixed on a single object, he fears being distracted from his fantasies, his imagination runs amuck, he is compulsive, narcissistic, and in some stories ruled by madness and folly.

In chapter 5, "The Model Pygmalion and the Artist Galatea," I interpret specific works based on the Pygmalion theme, including paintings, sculptures, operas, plays, and philosophical tracts. Pygmalion emerges as a key figure in the eighteenth century, as the sculptor's story is repeated again and again in image and text, on the opera stage and at the fair theaters. Artists of all sorts adopted Pygmalion's story as their own; the theme became intensely self-referential, and in the hands of some creators used to advance particular aesthetic theories. Yet the lingering aura of disease and mania that surrounds Pygmalion suggests that even for the male artist there was never an unproblematic model. The artist was always in danger of slipping into madness, deviance, femininity. I end this chapter by suggesting that women found creative ways to use the Pygmalion theme. The dancer Marie Sallé and the actress Mlle Raucourt (Joséphe-Françoise Saucelle) took advantage of Pygmalion by inhabiting the part of Galatea in much the same way that women appropriated other allegorical, mythical, and historical types.

Where chapter 5 focuses on the mythical male artist Pygmalion, my final chapter, "Inspired by Heloise," highlights a historical woman writer whose legend and letters were enormously popular in eighteenth-century France.[13] Using Bernard d'Agesci's painting *A Lady Reading the Letters of Heloise and Abelard* (fig. 51 below) to open the discussion, this chapter explores how representations of Heloise and emulations of her writing condense religious, erotic, and poetic enthusiasm, sometimes mixing these with mania and illusion. Although both men and women emulated the work of this impassioned woman writer, eighteenth-century representations often presented her as suffering from an erotic obsession that borders on nymphomania, as a deviant woman in both her pursuit of knowledge and her passionate sexuality. *A Lady Reading the Letters of Heloise and Abelard* pictures the effects that reading Heloise could have on a woman, and here her ecstasy matches the writer's emotional state, and perhaps evokes a similar one in viewers. In this chapter, I once again take up notions of female creativity and spectatorship, specifically by analyzing *A Lady Reading* in conjunction with Diderot's Salon criticism. Although Diderot does not comment directly on this painting, he does take up the general question of how images of female pleasure affect both female and male viewers. I argue that *A Lady Reading* can be seen as representing a woman's enthusiasm in a positive way. And by a woman's enthusiasm, I mean both that of the depicted reader and that of Heloise whose writings inspired a passionate response. Although Heloise and her writings possessed many eighteenth-century readers, writers, and artists, our own obsession with Jean-Jacques Rousseau's *Julie, ou La nouvelle Héloïse* (1761) has nearly eclipsed the real woman whose name the novel invokes. In *Les confessions* (1782–89) Rousseau imagines himself not as an emulator of Heloise but as a new Pygmalion. He claims he invented his Julie in an overheated state, a state of lovesickness brought on by his troubled fantasy. It is with Rousseau, in *Les confessions* and *Pygmalion* (1762–63) that we can most clearly see how the femininity of enthusiasm could be unashamedly claimed for the creative male.

Moved by Love takes up artistic creativity in its varied complexity, showing the contradictory ways that eighteenth-century writers represented men and women as artists and spectators, allowing them to cross the sexual divide but at the same time endowing the fine arts with the crown of masculinity. For creative men, the unstable boundary between "artist" and "woman" made it necessary, and impossible, to insist on their masculinity. They could not place themselves firmly in one category without bending into the other. For women, the imbrication of sexuality, creativity, and disease simultaneously opened and closed possibilities. Creative women took advantage of those possibilities, and I emulate their strategies in my readings of texts and images.

I know that my readings cannot change the past, but I hope they will have some influence in the present. Interpreting images from perspectives other than those urged by the dominant cultural assumptions of a given time and place accomplishes two goals. First, it disrupts the repetition that reinforces those cultural assumptions and makes them seem inevitable. Such disruption is especially important when the assumptions that structure an image are still with us today, either in whole or in residue. And second, opening an image to other possibilities takes advantage of the contradictions that are evident in any discourse. It thereby pushes past the impasse of critique, which while revealing the assumptions that structure a representation, can inadvertently leave those assumptions in place. What I mean is that in its desire to unmask the oppression, injustice, or prejudice justified through cultural representations, a critique can silence other voices that viewed representations differently, or can unintentionally obviate the possibility of different understandings and, hence, of resistance. Strategic rereading does not so much rehabilitate an image or text as reclaim it as an object open to interpretation. The representation becomes less an ideal presented, a moral lesson proffered, or a justification for prevailing views and more a field of potential meanings. When we perform a specifically historical analysis, that field is not infinite, but limited by the possibilities that pertinent cultural discourses and visual conventions allow. Within those discourses and conventions, some eighteenth-century women found ways to unsettle prevailing assumptions, if only momentarily. I am inspired to repeat those moments, and I hope my enthusiasm moves readers to do the same.

CHAPTER 1

Enthusiasm: Reason's Masterpiece

What moves the artist to create, the spectator to respond? What mental faculties are engaged in making and viewing art? Who is capable of imaginative invention, and who is susceptible to artful illusion? These were fundamental questions about the arts in eighteenth-century France raised in the project we take as central to the Enlightenment itself—the *Encyclopédie, ou Dictionnaire raisonné des sciences, des arts et des métiers* (1751–65), edited by Denis Diderot and Jean Le Rond d'Alembert. Not only did its individual entries take up creativity, but the *Encyclopédie's* front matter addressed the issue in explaining how all knowledge devolved from human understanding.

Opening volume 1, subscribers would find d'Alembert's *Discours préliminaire de l'Encyclopédie* (1751) ready to aid their understanding. To that discourse, the Encyclopedists appended a "Detailed Explanation of the System of Human Knowledge" and illustrated it with a chart d'Alembert called an "encyclopedic tree," a tree that gathered the various branches of knowledge "under a single point of view" (fig. 2).[1] Rooted in Étienne Bonnot, abbé de Condillac's philosophy of mind, this tree grew from the premise that all knowledge came from a different aspect of the mind acting on sensation. "Either the understanding makes an enumeration, pure and simple, of its perceptions through memory, or it examines them, compares them, and digests them through reason; or it takes pleasure in imitating them and reproducing them through imagination."[2] Assuming that the action of different mental faculties produced different kinds of knowledge, the chart bracketed the offshoots of history, philosophy, and the fine arts (called poetry) into three separate columns, each headed by a specific mental power. History is the realm of memory and has as its branches the sacred, the civil, and the natural. Philosophy relies on reason, and in this account it is not a

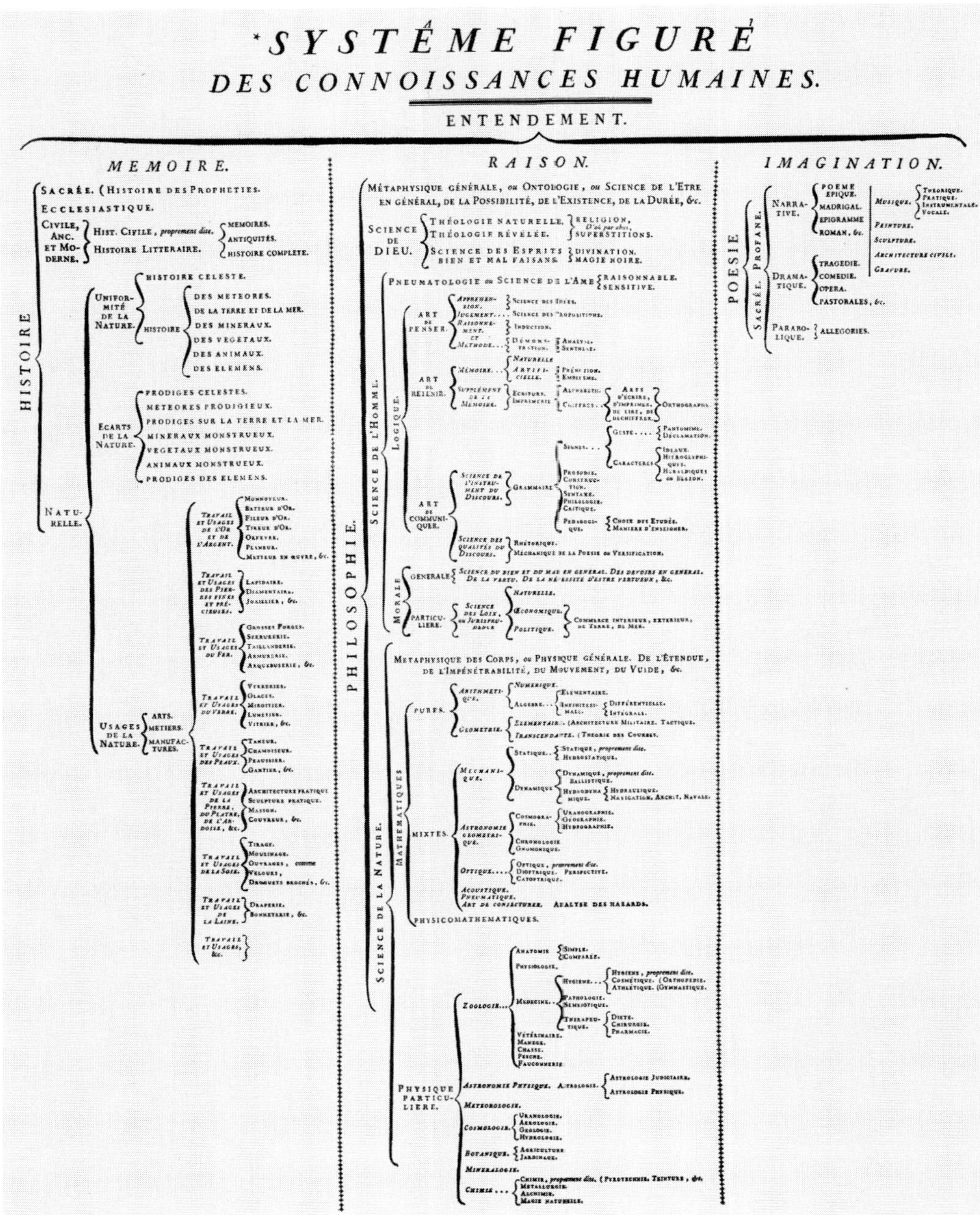

FIGURE 2. "Detailed System of Human Knowledge" from *Encyclopédie, ou Dictionnaire raisonné des sciences, des arts et des métiers* (1751–65). Edited by Denis Diderot and Jean Le Rond d'Alembert. Photograph courtesy University of North Carolina Photographic Services.

particular form of reflection but the sum of reasoned investigation in all fields. The fine arts—collectively grouped under the name Poetry—depend on imagination. Unlike historical fact and philosophical theory, knowledge in the fine arts is an imitation of nature created through the workings of imagination.[3]

Although at times it seems the different mental operations only create different sorts of knowledge, in the *Discours préliminaire* difference also implies hierarchy. When the discussion turns to "the general distribution of beings into spiritual and material," we find that history and philosophy are occupied with analyzing both spiritual (i.e., God and man's mind) and material beings, while imagination is limited to the material. And the *Discours préliminaire* further circumscribes imagination in outlining the "talents" of those who pursue the different branches of knowledge. Memory is the talent of the historian, who is concerned with facts; wisdom belongs to the philosopher; and artists have pleasure as their portion.[4] Pleasure in itself was certainly not a negative. Contemporary art theorists argued that the goal of art was to please and seduce, precisely by inducing attractive illusions or moving the emotions.[5] But pleasure separated from the goal of wisdom has a lesser position in the Encyclopedists' universe. When Diderot wanted to defend painting he did so by hailing those subjects that were both pleasurable and morally edifying. Pleasure, and especially pleasure derived from the imagination, also pushes art toward the feminine. In Condillac's philosophy, combinatory imagination—the basis of poetry and art—figures as a "coquette whose only desire is to please," who draws on her fancy rather more than on her reason and whose power ends where that of analysis begins.[6] Combinatory imagination is the only faculty in Condillac's account that bears the mark of sex, and it is figured here by the sort of woman who throughout the eighteenth century was known for her beauty and attraction but also for her inconstancy, self-absorption, and preoccupation with trivial things.

Although many entries throughout the *Encyclopédie* take up issues relevant to the fine arts, the article on enthusiasm raises most forcefully the question of creativity, commenting on its motivating forces, requisite faculties, and association with spectatorship. Louis de Cahusac (1705–59), an academician from Montauban, contributed that entry, and as a dramatist, poet, collaborator of Rameau, and author of a treatise on dance, he could claim some authority in the theory and practice of creative arts. In reading Cahusac's entry, however, it soon becomes apparent that his philosophy of enthusiasm breaks with the logic that supports the Encyclopedist's tree of knowledge. Even though he views enthusiasm as necessary to creative imitation and thus to the fine arts, Cahusac whisks it away from imagination's realm and places it under the domain of reason. Indeed, in his hands creative enthusiasm becomes "reason's masterpiece."[7]

Assigning enthusiasm to reason seems even more startling when we consult the entries cross-referenced in Cahusac's "Enthusiasm," in particular, that on "Genius," contributed by Jean François, marquis de Saint-Lambert (1716–1803), poet and member of the Académie française. Saint-Lambert casts enthusiasm not as reason's masterpiece but as imagination's transport. In the "man of genius," he observes, imagination recalls ideas with exceptional vivacity: "[I]n the heat of enthusiasm he orders [his work] neither according to nature nor the sequence of his ideas. He is transported into the situation of the characters he animates; he has taken on their character."[8] In contrast, the philosopher is governed by reason and must be scrupulously attentive, habitually reflective, and coldly analytical. There can be no excitement in his search for truth. Far from clarifying the concept of enthusiasm and fixing its definition, a reading of Saint-Lambert's account in tandem with Cahusac's entry shows how variable was its meaning. But such discrepancies are not necessarily at odds with the Encyclopedist's aims.

Although the *Discours préliminaire* points out that cross-referencing relates one entry to the next, it also allows that cross-referencing is not simply intended to elucidate one article by another.[9] In the case of enthusiasm, cross-referencing both links enthusiasm to genius and demonstrates how complex is the set of relations at work in each concept.

It is in terms of the so-called "unity of knowledge"—or what I call its connectedness—that the *Discours préliminaire* offers readers latitude in constituting their own knowledge, more latitude, in fact, than the systematic chart would suggest.[10] D'Alembert exhorts readers to find their own connections between the different entries, and when cross-references are not provided, to divine them from context. "Moreover, by the arrangement of the contents of each article, above all when the article is a bit extended, one cannot miss seeing that one article is related to another belonging to a different science, which in its turn is related to a third article, and so forth."[11] Sometimes a cross-reference is deliberately left out: "Often we have even omitted the reference to another article because the terms of art or science that it would have designated are explained in the individual articles, which the reader will find for himself."[12] Thus using the *Encyclopédie* actually allows the individual great freedom in her pursuit of knowledge, whether or not its editors actually intended this to be the case. In chasing down notions of creativity and spectatorship, I followed the links I found in Cahusac's entry on enthusiasm. As a result, I take up in this chapter reason, imagination, passion, and melancholia.

Using the entries in the way d'Alembert suggests, linking one to another, also leads the attentive reader to references outside the *Encyclopédie*'s volumes, since so many contributors explicitly cite or implicitly suggest other essays, books, and treatises. This process extends that of moving from entry to entry following the relations one finds there, and it is a practice tacitly sanctioned by both the *Discours préliminaire* and original *Prospectus* (1750). In the *Prospectus,* moreover, the editors make very clear that their *Encyclopédie* is not intended to replace all other books with its own abridgement of knowledge. This would, after all, have been an irrational aim since editors and contributors authored many of the texts that together made up the larger body of knowledge on which the *Encyclopédie* depended.

Like any other reader picking up the *Encyclopédie,* I did not find simple answers to my questions about creativity. I did, however, follow my own thread through the labyrinth of entries, citations, references, and links, both deliberate and inadvertent. Reading these entries encouraged me to seek relations across as well as within the fields of knowledge, to investigate the connections between theories of creativity and sexuality, between aesthetic treatises and medical, psychological, and moral discourse.

At the end of my reading, I concluded that Cahusac's enthusiasm only appeared to contradict the logic of creativity evident elsewhere in the *Encyclopédie.* It is not that his writing eventually reinforces the same general notions endorsed by other contributors but that the notion of creativity itself emerges as rife with contradiction. Cahusac explicitly argues that enthusiasm is reason's masterpiece but at the same time figures it as a compulsive, motivating force akin to passion. This contradiction, moreover, depends on the sexualizing of creativity and spectatorship evident throughout the discourse, and it suggests an unacknowledged desire to rescue the fine arts from those aspects of mind and body deemed feminine. As we shall see, this was easier said than done.

Throughout this chapter I explore enthusiasm by charting its contradictions. Although in mapping creativity I represent my particular point of view, this process is still consonant with the encyclopedic enterprise. As d'Alembert reminds us in his *Discours préliminaire,* the issues and practices a scholar positions at the center of things inevitably determine how she envisions the field of knowledge. He compares these maps of knowledge with maps of the world in which "objects are more or less distant and present a different appearance according to the point of view at which the eye is placed by the geographer constructing the map."[13] My vantage will place sexual difference at the center of things, and with this point of view, I offer chapter 1 as my reading of the *Encyclopédie.* I begin this reading with enthusiasm and pledge to use the volumes only as their editors intended, as a resource that "serves as much to guide those who find in themselves the courage to work for the instruction of others, as to enlighten those who are only teaching themselves."[14]

Enthousiasme, s.m. (Philosophie & Belles Lettres)

Like many a good academic today, Cahusac opens his entry on enthusiasm by insisting that no satisfactory account of his subject has yet been written. To demonstrate his point and introduce his analysis, Cahusac summarizes prevailing notions: "Commonly one understands by enthusiasm a kind of furor that seizes and masters the spirit; that enflames the imagination, elevates it, and renders it fertile. It is called a transport that makes one say or do extraordinary or surprising things."[15] And indeed, the tone and language Cahusac mimes are evident not only in Saint-Lambert's entry on "genius" but also in both general art treatises and works dealing with specific media. Abbé Jean-Baptiste Du Bos (1670–1742), for example, vaunted enthusiasm in his influential *Réflexions critiques sur la poésie et sur la peinture,* calling it "divine," and Roger de Piles was no less effusive in his *Cours de peinture par principes.* There he characterized enthusiasm as a transport, a fury of inspiration ("fureur de veine") that carried the soul to new heights. De Piles even coined the term "fureur pittoresque" so that visual artists could have their own special brand of divine madness.[16]

Cahusac, however, was not content to summarize the prevailing notion of enthusiasm. He located its origins in a failed search for origins, arguing that antiquity's "pedants" invented "fureur poétique" to explain the poet's vivacity when they found themselves incapable of discerning its true source. Although he does not name the Greek philosopher explicitly, Cahusac's entry leads its readers to Plato, whose *Phaedrus* contained the best-known statement of poetic furor or divine madness. The dialogue unfolds as a discussion between Phaedrus and Socrates, two self-proclaimed enthusiasts who discuss the nature of love. In his "Second Speech," Socrates argues that although the lover is out of his senses, madness is not invariably an evil. In fact, the greatest benefits accrue to humanity through a madness the gods bestow, an inspired state not to be confused with the insanity provoked by somatic causes. Divine madness embraces lovers, prophets, and poets. The famous characterization of poetic enthusiasm in the *Phaedrus* describes how it

> takes hold upon a gentle virginal soul, awakens and inspires it to song and poetry and so glorifying the innumerable deeds of our forefathers educates posterity. He who without the Muses' madness in his soul comes knocking at the door of poetry thinking that art alone will make him fit to be called a poet, will find that he is found wanting and that the verse he writes in his sober senses is beaten hollow by the poetry of madmen.[17]

It is in opposition to the Platonic tradition that Cahusac sets up his version of enthusiasm. After separating enthusiasm from physical madness and severing its connection with divine inspiration, he ties it, instead, to reason:

> Furor is only a violent onset of madness, and madness is an absence or limiting of reason, so when one has defined enthusiasm as a furor, a transport, it is as if one had said that it is a doubling of madness and consequently always incompatible with reason. It is reason alone, however, which gives birth to [enthusiasm] . . . Enthusiasm is, if one dares to say it, reason's masterpiece.[18]

If Cahusac dared to call enthusiasm reason's masterpiece, he was hardly alone in his desire to separate himself from Plato's *fureur poétique.* The abbé Charles Batteux (1713–1803), defender of the French classical tradition and professor of Greek and Latin philosophy at the College de France, had earlier called for a reconsideration of enthusiasm distanced from the "allegorical pomp and magnificence that clouds things for us."[19] In his *Les beaux-arts réduits à une même principe* (1747), Batteux decried the extravagant conceptions that seemed more the ravings of enthusiasm (in the sense of a furor or madness) than the work of rational beings. "The ideas that most authors give of it [enthusiasm] seem to come as much from an imagination itself astonished and struck by enthusiasm, as from a mind that has thought or reflected. Soon it is a celestial vision, a divine influence, a prophetic spirit; then it is a drunkenness, an ecstasy, a joy mixed with confusion and admiration in the presence of the divinity."[20] Batteux goes on to offer a reasonable definition of enthusiasm, locating it not in the heavens but in the human mind. Although Batteux finds the source of enthusiasm in the artist's acute powers of imagination while Cahusac locates it in reason, the two seem kindred spirits in both rejecting all *fureur poétique* and calling for a clearer definition of the concept. Indeed, Cahusac opens his entry on enthusiasm with this remark: "We do not have any perfectly satisfactory definition of this word; I believe, however, that searching for its true signification and fixing it if possible, is useful to the progress of the fine arts."[21]

Accounts of enthusiasm perhaps seemed unfixed because they mixed allegorical pomp with more reasoned analyses. For example, Roger de Piles, who figured enthusiasm as *fureur pittoresque,* also argued that it must be an "élévation surprenante, mais juste, mais raisonnable."[22] Moreover, he analyzed how artists could cultivate their enthusiasm, raise their thoughts by degrees, and fire their imaginations through studying the masterpieces of art and literature.[23] In describing this process, the French theorist cited the ancient writer Longinus, who in *On the Sublime* encouraged his readers to elevate their work by emulating the great authors.

Like his contemporaries, De Piles knew Longinus through the 1674 French translation, *Traité du sublime ou du merveilleux dans le discours,* which was the work of his friend Boileau (1636–1711). But more than a philosophy of emulation found its way into French art theory. Especially influential was Longinus's account of how great writing aroused the spectator's enthusiasm, which he describes as a spontaneous, passionate response to artistic effects.[24] Boileau, in fact, understood Longinus as urging a poetic strategy that aroused passion but was not conditioned by it.[25]

De Piles also made a place for the spectator's enthusiasm, which he distinguished from that of the artist. While the artist exercised a conscious and studied control over enthusiasm, enthusiasm seized the spectator emotionally aroused by the artist's work:

> But, because whoever contemplates a work rises to the heights he finds there, the mind's transport that belongs to enthusiasm is common to the painter and to the spectator, with this difference, however. Although the painter strives again and again to warm his imagination and to raise his work to the degree that enthusiasm demands, the spectator, on the contrary, without entering into any details, allows himself to be raised, suddenly and despite himself, to the level of enthusiasm to which the painter has drawn him.[26]

This account, moreover, ties the viewer's enthusiasm to that of the artist in a particular way, for the level of enthusiasm manifested in the artist's work determines the intensity of the spectator's response.

Drawing on earlier traditions, Cahusac also proposed that both artist and spectator experienced enthusiasm. "No one can see an interesting tragedy, a beautiful opera, an excellent piece of painting, a magnificent edifice, and so forth, without enthusiasm, and so the definition that I propose is equally applicable to the enthusiasm that creates and the enthusiasm that admires."[27] He claims that these two enthusiasms have the same character but argues that the spectator's enthusiasm is less lively than the artist's. At the same time, Cahusac suggests that in the moment of enthusiasm, the artist becomes a spectator who is transported suddenly and despite himself.

To explain the experience of creative enthusiasm, Cahusac presents his readers with an analogy that he admits is only imperfect. He compares the artist contemplating his mental conception with the amateur—the lover of art—who suddenly sees a new and stimulating picture. Asking readers to imagine themselves as enthusiastic artists by imagining themselves as enthusiastic spectators, Cahusac describes the experience: "Without expecting it, you see in the best light an excellent painting. A sudden surprise arrests you; you experience a pervasive emotion. Your gaze, as if absorbed, remains in a kind of immobility. Your entire spirit focuses on a mass of objects that occupy it all at once."[28]

Once the image has enthralled the amateur (and by analogy, the man of genius), the strength of creative fervor expressed within it—its "heat," as Cahusac calls it—speaks to the viewer. Falling under its influence, the viewer's senses are "animated by a lively fire." Soon, attention and reflection come into play as the art lover looks at the details; compares the poses; notices the contrasts, the light effects, the artist's touch. Attending to the characters, he identifies their emotions and correlates them to the action represented. A viewer's knowledge, sensibility, and judgment determine how much the work affects him. Cahusac summarizes the analogy: "But what you experience in this moment is an image (imperfect in truth, but sufficient for illuminating my idea) of that which passes in the mind of the man of genius when reason by a rapid operation presents him with a new and striking picture that arrests him, moves him, ravishes him, absorbs him."[29]

How should we, as twenty-first-century readers of the *Encyclopédie,* respond to Cahusac's image of enthusiasm? I have for a long time been taken with this image, which even after repeated viewing overwhelms me by the sheer mass of ideas it so elegantly combines. Or perhaps I should say especially after repeated viewing. For every time I come back to the image—and to the entry it summarizes—it presents me with a new picture of enthusiasm. Sometimes I find myself struck by a novel arrangement after I have reread Cahusac's entry and reconsidered how he explicates his image. At other times, it seems to grow more complex, especially after another *Encyclopédie* entry has made visible some connection that ties Cahusac's image to other images and to the body of knowledge. What I try to present here clearly and logically is an analysis that developed far less systematically, in fits and starts, as I forged new links and refused others.

From my present vantage, several ideas are especially intriguing. First, Cahusac's image presents enthusiasm as a lively emotion of the mind, a sudden surprise that begins by rendering the artist-spectator immobile and ends by arresting, ravishing, and absorbing him. In experiencing this emotion, Cahusac's artist appears as De Piles's spectator, a viewer who is "transported suddenly and without knowing it" by the sight of an excellent image. This nexus of ideas is intimately bound up, as we shall see, with writing about the passions. Second, it is reason that in this account generates and presents the artist's mental image, a point Cahusac stressed at the opening of his entry and repeated in every definition of enthusiasm. Enthusiasm is "a lively emotion of the mind produced by the sight of a new and well-ordered image that strikes it and that reason has presented to it."[30] And again: "Enthusiasm is that impetuous movement, whose effort gives life to all the masterpieces of the arts, and this movement is always produced by an operation of reason as prompt as it is sublime."[31] At the same time, reason seems suspended in the moment of enthusiasm and only comes into play later when the spectator has cooled enough to analyze the work. Here it is enthusiasm's linkage with reason and imagination that seems most pertinent. Finally, in Cahusac's analogy the artist is not just any spectator but an amateur, an art lover who has a passion for art. In this case, however, that passion transforms the artist into a Narcissus smitten by his own image, that is, by the image he has made.

Linking Enthusiasm and Passion

In presenting enthusiasm as a "lively emotion," Cahusac linked his image in complex ways to contemporary accounts that associated enthusiasm with passion. Condillac, for example, described the moment of enthusiasm as one in which "the passions agitate us so violently that we lose use of reflection, we experience a thousand different feelings."[32] There is, however, an evident rhetorical gap between this violent passion and Cahusac's "lively emotion." Moreover, if Condillac stresses that in moments of enthusiasm we suspend reflection, it is precisely reflection, or the ability to focus on things in succession, that Cahusac quickly restores to the spectator-artist who looks at the details, compares, notices, and attends to the various parts of the newly created image. What, then, is the nature of this emotion that can so easily turn to reflection?

One answer emerges in the *Encyclopédie* under the entry "Passions," for there we find that Cahusac's lively emotion corresponds closely to wonder (*admiration*), the first and simplest of the passions. The entry, moreover, relies on the classic statement offered in René Descartes's *Les passions de l'âme* (1649). There wonder is "a sudden surprise of the soul that makes it consider attentively those objects which seem to it rare and extraordinary."[33] Cahusac might have found wonder an appealing emotion because it had as its only object the knowledge of the thing wondered at. Indeed, as the *Encyclopédie* entry explains, wonder hardly merits the name of passion; it serves the intellect and produces curiosity, or "the desire to know better what we know only imperfectly."[34] Among the passions wonder is unusual because it never compromises reason.

For many eighteenth-century thinkers, the passions exercised vast power through their ability both to shape and pervert the human mind. Here is how the *Encyclopédie* summarized longstanding attitudes toward the passions:

> Let us say again that the passions excite in the body and above all in the brain, all the movements useful for their own conservation. In this way,

> the passions align the senses and imagination with them. If corrupted, this latter faculty continually works against reason. It does not represent things as they are in themselves, so that the mind can make a true judgment, but according to what accords with the present passion, so that the mind judges in its favor.[35]

From this account we can see how the dangerous alliance of passion and imagination could lead to fantasy, illusion, and even madness if one passion dominated the mind obsessively.

In categorizing the moment of enthusiasm as a demonstration of wonder, Cahusac seemingly sidesteps the dangers of less "reasonable" passions. Yet, the emotion the artist-spectator feels at the sight of the new tableau does not remain as simple wonder but morphs into a stronger passion as the spectator is arrested and absorbed. This characterization seems to shift wonder to the realm of astonishment, which for Descartes was an excess of wonder, a surprise that persisted so that all the animal spirits were driven to the site of the impression. And because these spirits did not pass into the other muscles, the entire body was immobilized, its movement arrested. The astonished person became a statue.[36] After Descartes, however, writers sometimes allied wonder and astonishment in more positive ways, associating them with enthusiasm. In his *Cours,* for example, De Piles noted how even the "true" could be insipid if represented in a work of art without enthusiasm. When coupled with enthusiasm, however, the true "transports the spirit into an admiration mixed with astonishment."[37]

Diderot's art criticism enacts the step from wonder to astonishment and from astonishment to uncontrolled enthusiasm as he analyzes Joseph Vernet's landscapes. Approaching Vernet's sixth painting or "site" (a painting that is yet to be identified) Diderot warns readers in his "Salon of 1767": "If you don't make an effort to conjure this site you will take me for a madman when I tell you that I cried out in wonder and that I remained immobile and stupefied."[38] He goes on to describe his enthusiasm as he stands before the site, suggesting how his uncontrolled emotions would be signaled involuntarily in gesture and expression:

> Without a doubt they would have been legible on my face. You would have been able to discern them in the tone of my voice, at one moment weak, at others vehement, hesitant, continuous. Sometimes my eyes and arms rose toward the heavens; sometimes they fell back at my side as if forced there by lassitude. I believe I shed some tears. You, my friend, who know so well enthusiasm and its intoxication, tell me whose hand took hold of my heart, alternately squeezing and releasing it, and provoking

> throughout my entire body the trembling that was particularly strong in the roots of my hair, which seemed to come alive and move? Who knows how long I remained in this state of enchantment?[39]

Diderot stresses not only the excessive wonder that has left him "immobile," he also dramatizes how reason and will are suspended, imagining that his passion must have been involuntarily (even automatically) expressed in a variety of physical signs. Enthusiasm, in effect, transforms him into an animated statue—one who can still feel while suspended in an "enchanted" state. At the same time, this animated statue resembles a madman who cries out involuntarily and whose immobility is described as "stupefaction." An undercurrent of danger clings to enthusiasm, and passion carried too far veers toward madness.

Reason for Desire

The passion of enthusiasm I have considered thus far relates primarily to the spectatorial function—that of the viewer responding to a work of art or that of the artist reacting to his own mental image. Although Cahusac presents his spectator-artist as filled with wonder, perhaps even astonishment, he does not suggest (as others would) that the artist imaginatively becomes his characters and feels their emotions. Nevertheless, passion must intervene again in Cahusac's account of enthusiasm since wonder and astonishment, while capturing the spectator, do not necessarily motivate the artist to act. To create, the artist must be moved, and in Cahusac's entry enthusiasm gets the job done: "The impulse that grabs him, fills him and leads him, is such that everything cedes to it, and it is the predominant sentiment."[40] Cast now as a compulsion of the mind, enthusiasm hardly seems the reasonable emotion Cahusac argues it is. We are certainly left to wonder how an operation of reason can produce this desire to create, which grabs the artist and demands obedience.

By insisting that reason produces this desire, Cahusac inverts Condillac's theory of mind in which desire eventually produces reason. Indeed, Condillac views desire, which grows out of pleasure and pain, as enabling all the mind's actions. In chapter 2 of his *Traité des sensations* (1754), the philosopher outlined how understanding could develop in a statue-man whose senses were limited to smell. "At the first smell our statue's capacity of feeling is entirely due to the impression made on its sense organ. This is what I call attention. From this moment it begins to enjoy or to suffer. For if the capacity of feeling is entirely taken up with a pleasant smell there is enjoyment [jouissance], and if it is entirely take up with an unpleasant smell, there is suffering [souffrance]."[41] Sensations of pleasure and pain lead to the passion of desire, and determine all operations of the soul.

> When [the statue-man] has noticed that it can cease to be that which it is, in order to return to being that which it was, we see desires born from a state of pain. It will compare this state of pain to a state of pleasure that memory recalls to it. It is by this artifice that pleasure and pain are the unique principle that determine all the operations of its soul, and will raise it by degrees to all the cognitions of which it is capable. In order to discern the progress it can make, it suffices us to observe the pleasures that it will have to desire, the pains that it will have to fear, and the influence of each according to circumstances.[42]

Long defined as a passion, desire is also a motivating principle that determines the degree and action of the faculties.[43] When the statue-man feels a "lack of pleasure" in his present sensation, the desire to return to a pleasurable one spurs "an effort to recall what it has ceased to be." Desire stimulates memory, and starting with memory, all the other cognitive functions, and thus even reason itself. The passions are indeed powerful precisely because they motivate the mind to act, and as we have already seen, they were capable of bending the mind in dangerous ways.

If at some points Cahusac attributes creative desire to reason, he seems in a complementary move to drain it of passion. He also characterizes the artist's compulsion to create as a desire to express. Once occupied with the striking picture it has created, the artist's mind wants to "spread outside of itself the lively impression the picture has made on it. The impulse that agitates it, fills it, and leads it is such that everything cedes to it, and it is the predominant sentiment."[44] This impulse, however, is not a passion, not even a sentiment, but a mechanical functioning of the mind that nature has programmed for expression as she has programmed the heart to pump blood: "But it is natural that the mind cannot experience sentiments without the quick and lively desire to express them; all its movements are only a continuous succession of sentiments and expressions; it is like the heart, whose machinery continuously opens itself to receive and to send."[45] The heart, usually viewed metaphorically as the seat of sentiment and love, Cahusac reduces to its mechanical operation in an analogy that tries to deny enthusiasm its passionate component. Yet in choosing the heart as his model, Cahusac simultaneously undermines his efforts to fix enthusiasm in reason's domain, for strong was the connection between the heart and sentiment.

From the connection of passion, imagination, reason, and desire, Cahusac's definition of enthusiasm emerges as unfixed, contradictory, and inconsistent as any that came before. We might say he has a desire—a passion—to separate enthusiasm from the dangerous passions, and this desire has motivated a set of irrational arguments, one contradicting the next. But even if Cahusac has a desire to separate passion and enthusiasm, his entry hardly achieves that end since his own discussion, like the entire discourse, relies on the language of motivation—of moving and being moved. No matter how much Cahusac wants to secure enthusiasm on the side of reason, the moment of absorption and compulsion is a passionate moment from which artists will emerge but to which they must return.[46]

Reason: Mother of Enthusiasm

The desire to link enthusiasm to reason knows no bounds in Cahusac's essay, and against all prevailing logic he makes his claim: "It is reason alone, however, that gives birth to enthusiasm."[47] Enthusiasm is "a lively emotion of the mind produced by the sight of a new and well-ordered image that strikes it and that reason has presented to it."[48] Figuring reason as the image-making mother of enthusiasm was indeed novel, and as we have seen, generated internal contradictions within the *Encyclopédie.* Reason, however, remains undefined in the entry, and although Cahusac never reveals how reason produces images, he relies on images to represent reason. Reason is, for example, a ray of light (*rayon de lumière*) and the emanation of a Supreme Being (*émanation plus ou moins grande d'un Etre suprème*). These two images, incidentally, Cahusac used earlier in his text to ridicule how the ancients figured "fureur poétique" taking it as "un rayon de lumière" and an "émanation sublime d'en haut." The repetition both underscores the connection Cahusac is trying to make between reason and enthusiasm and mocks his own enthusiasm for reason.

In representing reason through the same images used to picture ancient enthusiasm, Cahusac also uses figurative language familiar to the eighteenth-century reader. If we consult the general entry "Raison" in the *Encyclopédie,* we find reason again depicted as a ray of light and connected to the Supreme Being but combined with the specific function of knowing truth, a function distinct from that of making images. Reason is, for example, that "natural faculty that God provides mankind for knowing the truth." The word also refers to "the natural light that leads the faculty that we designate as reason."[49] The entry, moreover, is concerned with the sorts of truths we can know through natural reason, and the relation of those to the revealed truths of religion. Nowhere is there a hint that reason produces or presents images.

Cahusac, however, reinforces reason's position as a master faculty in giving it such wide-ranging powers: "The words imagination, genius, spirit, talent are only terms found to express different operations of reason; they are a little like the inferior divinities of paganism who are in the eyes of sages only convenient names to express attributes of a single God; only the ignorance of the masses allowed them to share the honors of divinity."[50] Aligning himself with the sages, Cahusac poses reason as the Jupiter of mental operations, implicitly accepting reason as masculine. It had been explicitly so throughout much of history, as we know from both ancient and Christian sources (e.g., Aristotle's opposition of female matter to the logos-creating male principle and Augustine's identification of reason, mind, and soul as male features). Readers of the *Encyclopédie* could find this assumption recapped in the entry "Femme," where they would be assured that in dividing the sexes, nature gave man force, majesty, courage, and reason, and woman, grace, beauty, finesse, and sentiment.[51] This is not to say that all eighteenth-century Encyclopedists, philosophers, or doctors believed that women lacked the ability to reason, and men, the capacity for sentiment. Rather, it is to point out that in general, individuals of the female sex were thought less generously endowed with the mental qualities that allowed good reasoning. Exceptions, moreover, did not disprove this general rule.[52]

While reason was usually imagined as masculine, or more "natural" to men, in no other authoritative account were imagination, genius, and talent assumed to express different operations of reason. Rather, reason and imagination were distinct operations of human understanding, as the *Encyclopédie*'s chart titled the "Detailed System of Human Knowledge" so clearly showed (fig. 2). There imagination, memory, and reason are bracketed below understanding in a version of Condillac's system, a system that defined understanding as "the collection or combination of mental operations. To perceive or to be conscious, to attend to, recognize, imagine, remember, reflect; to distinguish ideas, to separate, compose, and analyze them; to affirm, deny, judge, reason, conceive—all this is understanding."[53] Still, for Condillac and for many others, reason did "crown the understanding" for it acted as a control over the other operations, and especially over imagination.

The Forms of Imagination

Throughout the eighteenth century, French aesthetics, psychology, and medicine standardly attributed to imagination the task of making and presenting images. Condillac, for example, writes in his *Essai sur l'origine des connaissances humaines:* "Up to now I have taken the imagination as the operation that revives perceptions in the absence of objects; but now that I am considering the effects of this operation, I find no reason not to conform to standard usage, and I am even obliged to do so. That is why in this chapter I take imagination as an operation that, in reviving ideas, voluntarily makes combinations which are always new."[54] Although nothing in Condillac's definition would explain why a writer might want to transfer the image-making power from imagination to reason, exploring a bit further will help elucidate the problem. Like the passions, imagination was both dangerous and fundamental to human understanding. In its most basic function of reviving perceptions in the absence of objects, imagination was essential for the development of all higher thought processes. Yet reflection did not control this primitive sort of imagination, which operated without the intervention of will and easily led to error.

In the *Encyclopédie* entry on imagination, Voltaire—following Descartes's distinctions—called "passive" this primitive faculty common to both men and animals. "This *passive imagination*," he writes, "certainly does not need the help of our will, neither in sleep nor when we are awake. Regardless of will, it paints that which our eyes have seen; it hears that which we have heard and touches that which we have touched. It adds to those [sensations], it diminishes them; it is an interior sense that acts imperiously. Also, nothing is more common than saying that *one is not the master of his imagination*."[55] Far from depending on will, passive imagination creates will by its distortions: "[I]t pushes us toward or turns us away from the objects that it paints depending on the manner in which it represents them. The image of a danger inspires fear; that of a good, gives us strong desires."[56] Although Condillac did not develop the split between passive and active imagination, he, too, warned his readers that imagination could induce error since "as the senses act on the organ of imagination, that organ reacts on the senses."[57] Moreover, imagination was especially problematic because its power was uncontrolled and uncontrollable; it knew no limits: "It diminishes or even dispels our pains, and it alone can give our pleasures the spice that makes them worthwhile. But sometimes it is the cruelest enemy we have. It exacerbates our evils, gives us some we don't have, and finishes by sticking the knife in our breast."[58] It is important again to stress the intimate connection between imagination and the passions, a point that helps explain why Cahusac tries to present enthusiasm as a passion dominated by reason and separated from imagination.

If the problem of passive imagination turned on the issue of control, so did that of active imagination. Descartes believed that active imagination was closer to the intellectual functions because it was deliberately willed, but it could also be extravagant and dangerous if unchecked by reason. In active imagining, the mind painted its own images on the pineal gland, combining them to produce what Descartes called "chimeras" and "enchanted castles."[59] In other words, works of art, illusions, impossible beings, and fantasies. Voltaire tied active imagination to aesthetic and inventive processes in his *Encyclopédie* entry and highlighted its combinatory function: "Active imagination . . . brings together several distant objects; it separates those that are mixed together, composes them and changes them. It seems to create when it only arranges because it is not [in the power] given to man to make ideas; he can only modify them."[60] At the same time, however, Voltaire subdivides active imagination into "imagination de détail et d'expression" and "imagination d'invention."

Imagination d'invention could never go awry since by definition reflection ruled it. In poetry and painting, this sort of imagination creates the "ordonnance" (e.g., the composition or arrangement of forms and phrases), and in the sciences, it is that operation through which new instruments and machines are designed. Voltaire is quick to add that *imagination d'invention* acts only with profound judgment, and indeed, it seems to be the only sort of imagination not susceptible to disruption.[61] What I perceive in Voltaire's account, then, is an attempt to preserve one part of active imagination from the contamination of imagination itself. The status of imagination was for Voltaire a pressing concern because those who made "new combinations"—that is, artists—were thought to be dominated by this faculty. Thus Voltaire concludes his entry by locating unruly imagination primarily within its passive function: "When it is too ardent, too tumultuous, it can degenerate into dementia. But it is said that this illness of the organs of the brain is more often the fate of *passive imaginations,* limited to receiving the deep imprint of objects, than of those hardworking and *active imaginations,* which assemble and combine ideas, because *active imagination* always requires judgment, and the other sort of imagination is independent of it."[62] Here Voltaire shares Cahusac's desires, only he is more careful to say no more than the prevailing theories of mind allow.

In contrast to *imagination d'invention,* expressive imagination or "imagination de détail et d'expression" can veer toward the extravagant, the false, and the unruly. And this sort of imagination leads to enthusiasm, which Voltaire defines as an internal emotion that agitates the mind and transforms the author into the characters to whom he gives voice.[63] A lively and vivid imagination is essential for this process. In defining *imagination de détail et d'expression,* Voltaire seems inspired by a tradition that includes Cicero, Horace, and Aristotle, all of whom suggest the artist feels the emotions he represents. In the *Poetics,* Aristotle puts the problem in terms of the delicate balance between the affecting and the mad:

> So far as possible, one should also work out the plot in gestures, since a natural affinity makes those in the grip of emotions the most convincing, and the truest distress or anger is conveyed by one who actually feels these things. Hence poetry is the work of a gifted person, or a maniac: of these types, the former have versatile imaginations, the latter get carried away.[64]

Imaginative Projection

In what sense artists "became" their characters was, however, an open question in the eighteenth century, one complicated by the rhetoric of transformation and transport that often accompanied discussions of enthusiasm. Did artists actually feel the passions they represented or did they merely imagine and depict them forcefully enough to move the spectator? Here is how Batteux specifically characterizes the enthusiasm of painters: "If they wish to paint a battle; they transport themselves, same as the poet, into the middle of the melee; they hear the fracas of the arms, the cries of the dying; they see the furor, the carnage, the blood. They excite their imaginations until they feel themselves moved, seized, terrified."[65] The artist's enthusiastic delirium brings him to imagine not only that he actually sees the event before his eyes, but also that he is a character in the drama. And this drama is manly stuff, not the sort of subject accessible to soft, feminine heads.

Intense involvement in the imaginary, however, is dangerously close to the hallucination and error to which women, and not men, were prone.[66] Yet such hallucinations are necessary to the artist, who in them can become not only a warrior, but a lovesick woman, or even an animal or plant. Of such an artist Batteux writes, "[H]e forgets himself: his mind passes into the things that he creates. He is one after the other Cinna, Augustus, Phaedra, Hippolytus, and if it is La Fontaine, he is the Wolf and the Lamb, the Oak and the Reed. It is in these transports that Homer sees the chariots and the battle horses of the gods; that Virgil hears the frightening cries of the Phlegias in the infernal shades."[67] As an admirer of the classics, Batteux here seems to write under Aristotle's influence. Yet the classical tradition stemming from Boileau's translation of Longinus suggested only that the artist depicted the event so forcefully that he *seemed* to enter into it and to induce the spectator to do the same. What we find in much eighteenth-century theory is a slippage between seeming to feel the emotion and actually experiencing it. In the case of Batteux, I suspect that he writes for rhetorical effect. So keenly must the artist imagine a subject that he "becomes" the characters he creates.

In his *Réflexions critiques sur la poésie et sur la peinture,* Abbé Du Bos seems to be clearer on the point: "Of all the talents that give empire over men, the most powerful is not that of mental superiority and enlightenment; it is the talent of moving men and in seeming oneself moved and penetrated by emotions that one wants to inspire. It is the talent of being, like Catiline, *a simulator of all that one wishes,* that one would call if one wished, the talent of being a great actor."[68] At the same time, Du Bos demands that excellent actors or "declaimers" have a certain "sensibility of heart" that allows them to enter into the sentiments of their characters. Such actors can lend themselves easily to all the passion that they want to express. As he concludes, "All the orators and all the actors that we have seen succeed preeminently in their professions were persons born with the sensibility of which I have just spoken."[69]

The actor's sensibility would become the central issue in Diderot's *Paradoxe sur le comédien* (c. 1770), a treatise often read as posing the great artist as insensitive, as coolly imitating the signs of emotions she does not feel. David Marshall, however, has recently shown that Diderot does not entirely abandon the possibility that great art can arise from emotional turmoil.[70] Near the end of the dialogue the interlocutor designated as the Second, who has argued for the actor's sensibility, proposes a compromise. He accepts that most of an actor's performance stems from artifice but wishes "to reserve to the natural sensibility of the actor those rare moments in which he loses his head, when he no longer sees the spectator, when he has forgotten that he is in the theater, when he has forgotten himself, when he is in Argos, in Mycenae, when he is the very character that he plays."[71] In these moments the spectator sees the character's "real image" and hears the "true accents" of the passion that moves him.

What the Second has defined, of course, is the classic moment of enthusiasm. In response, the First allows that "a sensitive actor will have perhaps in his role one or two of these moments of alienation that contrast with the rest much more strongly if they are more beautiful."[72] At the same time, he forces the Second to admit that neither the spectator nor the actor entirely loses himself in the illusion; both recognize the difference between the real and its performed image. Not to recognize the difference was to fall into madness, which nearly happened to Rameau's nephew in Diderot's text of the same name (*Le neveu de Rameau,* written after 1761). Carried away with a scene, he plays all the different parts. "Here he is a young girl who weeps and he renders all her simpering, there he is a priest, he is a king, he is a tyrant, he threatens, he commands, he flies into a rage; he is a slave, he obeys. He relents, he wails, he complains, he laughs, never breaking tone, proportion, the meaning of words or the character of music."[73] The nephew was indeed lost in this performance. "He noticed nothing; he continued, seized by such a frenzy [aliénation d'esprit], by an enthusiasm so near to madness that it was uncertain if he would come out of it; if he should not be thrown in a cab and taken straight to the asylum."[74] The possibility remained that the artist's imagination would break free of reason's control, leaving artists prey to their own illusions. And this idea brings us to reconsider Aristotle's choice, for it is not only that the artist is *either* an actor *or* a madman; sometimes she is both.

Enthusiasm and Melancholia

The central importance of imagination and passion to the fine arts produced an uncomfortable overlapping between enthusiasm and madness even in aesthetic theories in which writers tried to differentiate one from the other. In characterizing false enthusiasm, Roger de Piles wrote: "[S]ome with fiery minds have taken the exaltation of their imagination for true enthusiasm although at base the abundance and vivacity of their inventions were only the dreams of a sick person."[75] False enthusiasm is generated by an imagination unchecked, which takes its own creations or phantoms for reality.

Sensationalist psychology, moreover, came to view insanity as either an extremely sensitive imagination or one uncontrolled by reason and reflection. Arguing that physically, imagination and insanity differed only in degree, Condillac wrote that insanity must "consist in an imagination that, without our being able to notice it, associates ideas in an entirely disordered manner and sometimes influences our judgments or conduct."[76] Diderot warns the painter Gabriel-François Doyen of just this peril in his "Salon of 1767." In the middle of his remarks on Doyen's *Le miracle des Ardents* (*Miracle of St. Anthony's Fire;* fig. 3) Diderot refers to his "Essai sur la peinture" and reiterates the point that all talent in the arts comes from "a particular temperament of reason and enthusiasm, of judgment and verve, a temperament rare and momentary, an equilibrium without which compositions are extravagant or cold."[77] Doyen is in danger of tipping the balance, and Diderot reads this near disequilibrium in his *Le miracle des Ardents.* "There's a danger Doyen should fear, namely, that excited by his work for *Le miracle des Ardents* . . . he does not exceed legitimate limits, that his head does not get too overheated, that he does not plunge himself into exaggeration. He's on the borderline; one step further and there he is in the middle of the disturbance, in the disorder."[78]

While Diderot seems to believe he can discern the borderline, the sculptor Étienne-Maurice Falconet (1716–91) admitted in his *Réflexions sur la sculpture* (read to the Academy in 1760) that sometimes it was difficult to distinguish enthusiasm from disorder. "If by the sort of error that fortunately we don't see too often a sculptor mistakes for enthusiasm

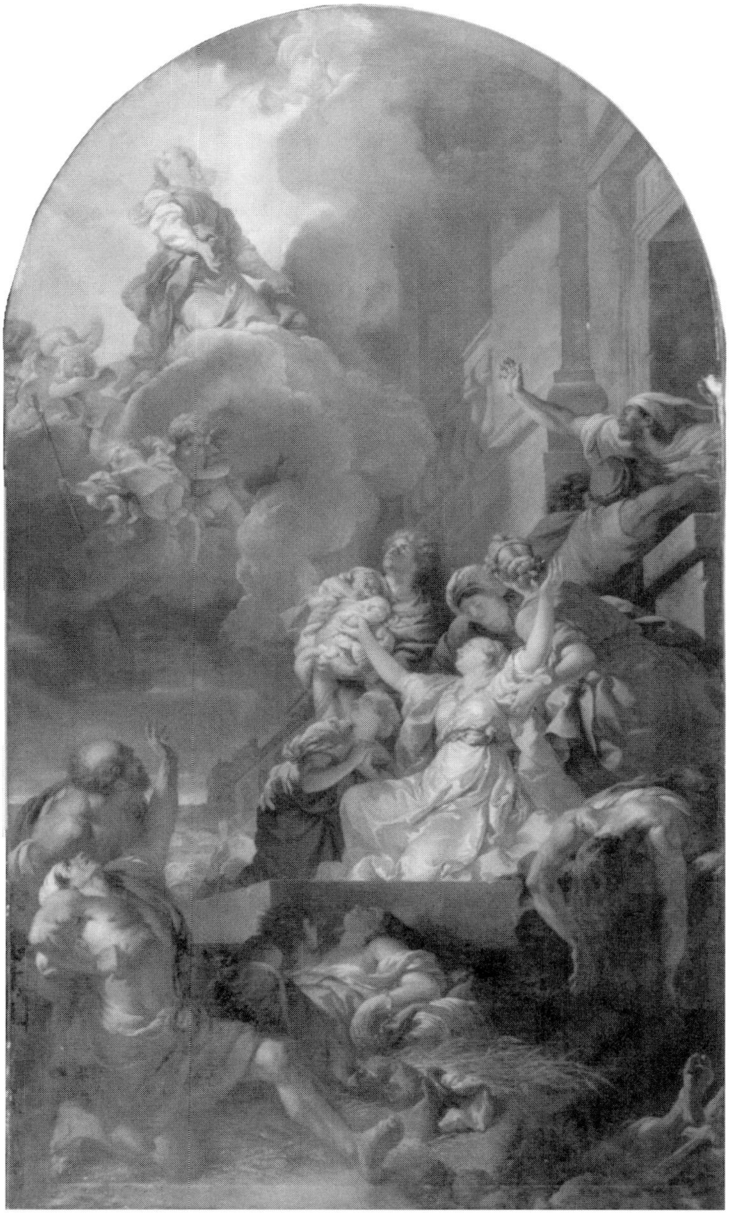

FIGURE 3. Gabriel-François Doyen (French, 1726–1806), *Le miracle des Ardents (Miracle of St. Anthony's Fire)*, Salon of 1767. Oil on canvas, 665 × 393 cm. Paris: Church of Saint-Roch. Photograph © Réunion des Musées Nationaux/Art Resource, NY.

and genius that unreasonable vehemence that carried off Borromini and Meissonier, then he must be persuaded that the same error, far from embellishing objects, depicts them untruthfully and represents only the imagination's disorder."[79] Borromini and Meissonier are no more deranged than Doyen, but Falconet presents them as having slipped into disorder, carried away by an unchecked imagination.

Although neither Diderot nor Falconet appealed overtly to the medical tradition, Du Bos in his *Réflexions critiques* made such a connection, if only implicitly. Du Bos associated the dangers of enthusiasm with an overheating of the blood. "I imagine that the blood of those who compose heats itself because the painters and poets cannot invent in cold blood. One well knows that they enter a sort of enthusiasm out of which they produce their ideas."[80] This enthusiasm—this warming of the blood—could result in a dangerously overheated imagination. Du Bos cites the example of Torquato Tasso (1544–95), who throughout the eighteenth and nineteenth centuries would be noted for his insanity. "Tasso gave birth to admirable images, he gave us Armida and Clorinda only at the price of the disposition he had toward a true dementia, into which he fell before the end of his life."[81] From the fate of Tasso, Du Bos concludes that the most favorable fermentation of the blood produces only chimeras in a brain composed of bad or badly disposed organs. The example of Tasso suggests again how difficult it was to keep things apart. Enthusiasm and imagination both mingled with real madness; indeed, either could fade into disorder. Tasso, moreover, had long been an example of a particular creative type—the melancholic.

Aristotelian natural philosophy had joined the Platonic conception of frenzy with a medical notion of melancholy and produced the "paradoxical thesis" that really outstanding men—poets, philosophers, generals, statesmen—were melancholics.[82] A theory of melancholia based on humoral science explicated the connection between genius, madness, and enthusiasm, positing that when heated, an excess of black bile could produce elation and brilliant thought; but it could also generate erotic fantasy, anger, desire, transport, and insanity. In theory there was a distinct line between the melancholic temperament and melancholy sickness, but the one was always in danger of turning into the other. The unpredictable black bile might heat up excessively, or suddenly increase in quantity and strength. Aspects of this theory lingered in both medicine and general opinion well into the eighteenth century, usually reconstituted in new theoretical frames.

Eighteenth-century medical discourse generally viewed melancholia as a disease in which the sufferer focused attention on a single thought or series of ideas to the point of obsession. In the entry "Mélancholie (Médicine)," the *Encyclopédie* defines its central feature: "the general and distinctive character is an individual delirium determinedly circulating around one or two objects, without either the fever of mania or the furor of frenzy."[83] This notion lasted through the eighteenth century, and the noted psychiatrist Philippe Pinel (1745–1826) wrote in his 1813 *Nosographie philosophique; ou, La méthode de l'analyse appliquée à la médicine:* "The character belonging to melancholy consists in general in a degeneration of the intellectual and emotional functions; that is to say that the melancholic is possessed by a single idea or a particular series of ideas with a dominating passion that is more or less extreme, for example, an habitual state of fright or of profound regrets."[84]

The fixation on a single idea, moreover, could have bizarre forms. Melancholics often imagined they were someone else: a king, a nobleman, even a god. Some fancied they had been metamorphosed into beasts; those suffering from *lycanthropie,* for example, imagined that they had been transformed into wolves. Others had singular delusions; a case reported in the *Encyclopédie* described a woman who perpetually kept one finger raised, believing she balanced the world on it.[85] But these were extraordinary examples, and often the delusions of melancholy were much less striking, bordering on the normal tricks of imagination.

While there was general agreement about the central definition of melancholia, the disease itself was—as one doctor put it—protean.[86] Among its common symptoms were profound sadness, disrupted sleep, extreme passion, mood swings, lustful behavior, a penchant for solitude, constipation, and a pasty complexion. Some pointed out that melancholia was both a disease and a temperament, and like the ancient writers tried to separate the two. Such a separation, however, proved difficult because melancholia had both physical and moral causes, and the melancholic temperament was attracted to precisely those things that pushed the mind and body toward disease. And as Pierre Pomme (1735–1812) argued in *Traité des affections vaporeuses des deux sexes* (1760), a melancholy temperament could be acquired; through habits of living a person could change his or her original constitution.

Indulging in strong drink, eating spicy food, excessive lovemaking—all these upset the nervous system, while leading a sedentary life slowed down the movement of fluids through the body.[87] Similarly, Nicolas Chambon de Montaux (1748–1826) in his *Des maladies des femmes* (1784) noted that when melancholy originated in either organic disease or a change in bodily functions, it soon invaded the mind. And too much exercise of the mind—and especially an imagination overly stimulated by spectacles, serious study, or novel reading—could invite the disease. By greatly increasing the activity of the brain fibers, such stimulation would exacerbate their mobility and thus have deleterious effects not just on the brain but also on the nerves and neighboring organs.[88]

Also extensive was the writing on the effects of study and creative work, and perhaps most influential of all was Samuel-Auguste-David Tissot's *De la santé des gens de lettres et des valetudinaires* (1768). Tissot concludes that when the brain is occupied for too long a time, its activity becomes too strong for its fibers and the brain is no longer its own master. This "ebranlement" continues automatically and reacts on the brain, making it re-experience the ideas in a sort of delirium. Because of this extreme exertion, some part of the brain becomes incapable of receiving new impressions from the senses, and so the brain no longer responds to exterior objects but only to its own inner disposition. Tissot gives as his example one Spinello, a famous Tuscan artist who painted an image depicting the fall of the rebel angels. Spinello gave such terrible features to Lucifer that the artist himself was seized by fear. All the rest of his life, Spinello believed he saw Lucifer continuously reproaching him for having shown the fallen angel as a hideous demon.[89] Tissot concludes the story by asking rhetorically how many others have so exhausted their minds that they have been cast forever outside the limits of reason. Again it is a matter of degree. Diderot, for example, sees a lesser version of the process that drove Spinello over the edge as marking all creative types when he defines a poet as "a man of strong imagination who is moved, even terrified, by the phantoms that he himself makes."[90]

Cahusac's Imagination

If in positing an "imagination d'invention" Voltaire tried to set aside an uncorrupted preserve within imagination, Cahusac took a more radical approach to the same problem. He protected the artist from dangerous imaginings by claiming that reason produced the image, without explaining how reason came to be an image-making faculty. Moreover, he simultaneously limited the fecundity of imagination, discounting combinatory imagination, that operation Condillac described as both feminine and productive.

Cahusac allows only that imagination works in conjunction with memory to revive sensations stored as signs. This operation of the mind, he tells us, is not particular to the creative talent but common to all:

> I speak finally, in the definition [of enthusiasm] that I propose, of a new painting; because it is not a question here of a cold and common operation of memory. There is no man to whom imagination does not recall often the different objects that he has seen, but these are only weak sketches that pass before his understanding as faint shadows, without surprising, affecting, or moving his mind, and they presuppose only some sensations previously experienced.[91]

The action of memory and imagination common to everyone Cahusac labels instinct's "apanage," a term that generally means territory or domain but etymologically refers to a portion of a domain accorded to younger members of the royal house because they are excluded from the throne. For Cahusac, this *apanage* is, needless to say, vastly different from "the most beautiful privileges of reason" that he intends to defend.[92] Already connected with immaterial light, Jupiter, and the Supreme Being, reason is now crowned king. Imagination, however, is more thoroughly cast out of the spiritual side of things. Figuring imagination as instinct's *apanage* ties it to the most primitive of imagination's functions, for instinctual imagination predates the ability to formulate signs and, hence, to remember. It is passive imagination, par excellence. As a part of instinct, imagination could not be controlled, could not conjure at will, and acted by chance when some object associated with a particular circumstance presented itself anew. As instinct, it is tied to the body and sensation. It is as far from creating new ideas as imagination can get.

Or is it? To underline his departure from tradition, Cahusac specifically asks his readers to notice that he has not used the word "imagination" in defining enthusiasm. He then goes on to characterize imagination as the canvas or "toile" that receives the idea forged by reason, and explains: "I see it in my hypothesis only as one of the secondary causes and as such . . . it is the canvas under the hand of the painter. The imagination receives the rapid sketch of the painting that is presented to the mind, and it is on this first sketch that genius distributes the colors."[93] In this account, genius is the natural aptitude to receive, to sense, and to render the impressions of the supposed tableau. Genius is here cast as a sort of sensibility; as such it is not the creative power or motor force but the instrument of production, the brush with which reason distributes the colors on its sketch. Although reason controls both genius and imagination, genius is an active principle through which the first sketch is completed. Cahusac reduces imagination to a receptive surface imprinted by reason's idea and colored by reason's brush. As a receptive material surface, imagination seems not to create or generate anything; it does not even partake in the image or idea itself, which already exists as a form of reason. Nonetheless, imagination is indispensable for the process of creation; it is the ground on which reason projects and genius paints. If in Condillac's scheme, the productive combinatory imagination is gendered as feminine, in Cahusac's scheme, imagination takes the role that philosophy has traditionally assigned the feminine.

Casting Out the Feminine

It is not simply that imagination is here rendered feminine by its passive role. Nor is it that this view of imagination reproduces those theories of reproduction in which woman provided the matter, and man, the form of a new creature. In a profound way, imagination is cast as the feminine because although it is an inscriptional space necessary for the reproductive process, it contributes nothing, not even matter, to the representation. Indeed, in Cahusac's account, imagination is that which must be expunged from the concept of enthusiasm to insure the productive workings of creative activity. I am taking my cue here from Luce Irigaray's reading of the form/matter distinction in Plato and Plotinus, which Judith Butler has further elucidated in her reading of Irigaray.[94] What particularly interests me is Irigaray's claim that in Western philosophy (beginning with Plato) the feminine survives as merely an inscriptional space. Both philosophers (Butler and Irigaray, that is) take up the question of reproduction and in particular focus on the Platonic explanation of how sensible representations—material bodies—are generated from forms. For me, Cahusac's logic—deliberately or not—runs along these ancient paths.[95]

Turning back to Cahusac, then, we can argue that instead of a feminine combinatory imagination that is a formative principle of ideas, Cahusac gives us imagination as the feminine, as the inscriptional site. At the same time, he installs masculine reason, which produces versions of itself through its projection onto imagination, as the sole progenitor of art. Imagination contributes nothing to reproduction. It is that which allows form to pass into sensible representation, but, at the same time, has no form of its own; it does not participate in the "nature" of form. In Irigaray's analysis, a similar logic constitutes the feminine as the impossible yet necessary basis of what can be imaged or figured.[96]

It is of particular interest that in claiming reason and repudiating imagination, Cahusac tries to move the creative arts toward the status of philosophy. Moreover, this move goes hand in hand with limiting to men the inspired creators he names, those whose enthusiasm has brought glory to France: Corneille, Racine, Molière, Quinault, Lully, Lebrun, Bossuet, Perrault, Le Nôtre.[97] In raising the status of the artist, in assigning artistic creativity to the eternally masculine, Cahusac takes the radical path of denying imagination. But denying imagination could hardly be sustained.

A return to his account of enthusiasm will show that separating the artist from the woman and art from imagination is not Cahusac's major aim, but only a necessary step toward his goal. His desire is to raise the status of the artist, which requires casting him as both reasonable and masculine.[98] In the *Encyclopédie,* Cahusac recounts his motivation for associating enthusiasm with reason:

> If *enthusiasm,* to which alone we are indebted for the beautiful productions of the Arts, has only reason as its primary cause, if we must always attribute the prodigious works that come from human hands to this ray of light, [whether it be] more or less brilliant, to this emanation of a supreme Being, [whether it be] more or less great, then all the

> prejudices detrimental to the arts are destroyed forever and the Artists triumph.[99]

He concludes that henceforth a musician can be thought sublime without being reputed a madman, and one can be an "excellent poet without ceasing to pass for a wise man." And if it was desirable to take the artist for a wise man, then on no account should he be confused with an overly sensitive woman.

Cahusac's entry, "Enthusiasm," is significant as an overt and failed attempt to control the dangers of imagination and passion and to align art making with reason. Whether he was conscious of expelling the feminine, whether he did so deliberately, or whether he himself was a misogynist are all irrelevant to my argument. My point is rather that because the feminine had already been thrown out of philosophy, because it had been disengaged from reason, and because it had been denied its role in the creation of things, Cahusac could not help but disavow femininity in his attempt to validate artistic creation by locating it in reason rather than imagination. In the next chapter, we shall see how the general aligning of different mental properties with differently sexed bodies in medicine, psychology, and philosophy created other dilemmas for those who would theorize the creative process. Those dilemmas were all the more problematic because the links between sex and inclination were neither universal nor absolute.

CHAPTER 2

The Artist and the Woman

PART I: JUST LIKE A WOMAN?

I write of the artist and the woman, and also of arms and the man. The potential for overlap between the categories "woman" and "artist" becomes evident when two realms of knowledge collide, when aesthetic theory runs into philosophical medicine. Despite the attempts of writers like Cahusac to relocate the creative process within the realm of reason, much art theory continued to emphasize the central importance of imagination, passion, and enthusiasm. Medicine, especially when mixed with philosophy, pictured the "normal" woman as endowed with a greater sensibility and a more active imagination than her male counterpart. These attributes made her more susceptible to the passions and more subject to both her own fantasies and the illusions of art. At the same time, a lively imagination, an ability to take on the passions portrayed, and the tendency to be moved by art all characterized the creative personality. Although "normal" women might seem to possess the mental qualities needed to create art, many physiologists were at pains to explain why they could not produce works of genius. Still, it remained possible to mix up the artist and the woman.

Those who based their physiology and psychology on sexual difference admitted that some members of one sex had minds more typical of the other, and some doctor-philosophers suggested that differences other than the sexual determined variations in mental faculties. Distinctions were never absolute, not even after the medicine of sensibility took hold in France. Theories of the artist's inspiration, moreover, allowed that creative personalities could cross the sexual divide and that those of one sex could imaginatively inhabit the bodies and minds of the other. When coupled with the unstable distinction between male and female minds, these potential overlaps had several consequences. Not only did they lead some to distinguish the woman's imagination from that of the artist, they also brought others to warn against the dangers of emulating women writers or painters and to pose manly things as the sublime subjects of art. Prime among those manly things were the furies of battle and the heroics of warriors.

Whose Sensibility?

Developed in the 1740s and 1750s, the medicine of sensibility established a physiological model that connected body and mind and gave a new foundation to old assumptions about the differences between men and women.[1] The *Encyclopédie* includes two entries under the term "sensibilité": a brief paragraph on sensibility as a moral faculty and a much longer entry that explains it as a concept in medicine.[2] Not only does the latter trace the concept's history, it also summarizes (and some have suggested vulgarizes) ideas advanced by a group of Montpellier doctors, many of whom contributed related articles. Among that group was Henri Fouquet, who authored the entry in the *Encyclopédie*.[3]

Fouquet defines sensibility as a property of all living bodies "that has certain aspects for perceiving the impressions of external objects and others for producing, as a result, movements proportionate to the intensity of those perceptions."[4] The different aspects he calls *le sentiment* and *la mobilité*. The first is a "purely animal intelligence" by which the organism distinguishes the usefulness or harmfulness of the physical objects encountered through sensation. The second is the mute expression of the sentiment, that is to say, the impulse that moves the organism toward or away from what it has sensed.[5]

Instead of describing the effects of sensation on a statue-man—the tack taken not only by Condillac but also by Charles Bonnet (1720–93) in his 1760 *Essai analytique sur les facultés de l'âme*—Fouquet begins with the human embryo, which is conceived as already "sensitive" because it moves and makes contact with stimuli. The embryo's sensitivity then becomes proof that sensibility is continuous with human life and inherent in the very substance of the nerves, which form the basis and essence of all the organs. The entry goes on to identify particular centers of sensibility in the human body—the head, the heart, the stomach and gastric region—and to note that sensibility determines the operations of the mind as well as the passions. It was this notion that Bonnet's work developed more fully. Bonnet argued for the union of mind and body through the sensibility of nerves and fibers, and he articulated how particular mental faculties depended on physiological processes.

For example, imagination—the faculty that recalls an image in the absence of sense perception—operates because ideas are attached to the movement of "des fibres sensibles." The disposition of the brain to repeat its movements explains how and why humans have the ability to imagine, since ideas arise anew as the brain fibers repeat the movements to which those ideas are attached.[6]

If sensibility determined mental faculties, as Fouquet claimed and Bonnet explicated, then the quality of an individual's sensibility would directly influence the mind. Sensibility, Fouquet argues, is the same in every human, but its effects vary not only according to the particular disposition of the organs but also according to age and sex. Children are more sensitive than adults, and women, more than men.

> The excess of sensibility that children have over adults explains the causes of the frequent convulsions and spasms that agitate them at the least illness, at the least emotion. As to women, their constitution approaches, as one knows, that of children. Women's passions are much livelier, in general, than those of men. Their great sensibility, which has one of its principle centers in the uterus, also throws them into the diseases that nature seems to have uniquely made for women, but which luxury and soft living have also given to men. I am speaking of the vapors.[7]

That women's passions were more easily aroused and more keenly felt than those of men was hardly a novel idea, but here it acquired a new scientific basis. Moreover, as Anne Vila's analysis of the literature has shown, doctors and moralists were as much concerned about controlling sensibility as analyzing its function in the human organism. Especially if excited through habits of living, an excess of sensibility could lead to illness, not only in women, but also in men made unnaturally susceptible to a woman's disease.

Too Sensitive

Vila has pointed out that as the debate on the vapors developed after 1756, the disease was more and more thought to be a woman's problem. By the time the Montpellier physician Edme-Pierre Chavot de Beauchêne (1748–1830) wrote his *De l'influence des affections de l'âme dans les maladies nerveuses des femmes* in 1783, he focused nearly entirely on women. Although he admitted that nervous diseases also struck men, their more active lifestyle reduced the number of cases to the point where they were not a pressing concern. Among women, however, the disease was so widespread that in Paris one saw a virtual epidemic.[8] Working from the medicine of sensibility, Beauchêne argued that woman's sensitive internal organs and more rapid movements of nerve and muscle fibers made her more susceptible to the effects of passion. Thus, woman's equilibrium was more easily upset, her functions more easily deranged. This was especially true for idle women living in the city because neither work nor exercise distracted their minds and so passions could quickly take possession of them. Their extreme sensibility made them more sensitive to outrage. The least subject ignited the "choler" of these women and sent them into transports followed by the vapors. Beauchêne warns particularly against the effects of anger, hate, and other violent or aggressive feelings that are "unnatural" to women. Born in their imaginations from the abuse of sensibility, these passions master women, "bringing on the ravaging and the violent convulsions that overthrow the economy of their constitution."[9]

An impassioned woman might fall into madness; at the least, she would behave irrationally, as did the sensitive painter Anne Dorothea Lisiewska-Therbusch (1721–82; known in France as Mme Therbouche) in a scene Diderot described in his "Salon of 1767." Of course, we do not know if Diderot is merely reporting a scene he witnessed or if he is embellishing one for rhetorical effect. He might even be making one up. Whether or not the scene actually happened, it still has a "truth to nature," given, that is, the discourse of sensibility. From the outset, the scene is tinged with its colors as the critic describes Mme Therbouche: "She is so sensitive to judgments that one makes of her works that a great success would drive her mad or make her die of pleasure. She's a child."[10] This sensitivity manifests itself in outbursts of passion that Diderot describes in terms of violent convulsions. He depicts the artist as unable to control her emotions when the Salon committee rejects her *Jupiter and Antiope* (whereabouts unknown):

> She fell into despair, she felt faint; weakness gave way to fury; she cried out; she tore out her hair, she rolled on the ground. She grasped a knife, uncertain whether she would strike herself or her painting. She spared them both. I arrived in the middle of this scene; she threw herself at my knees, imploring me to help her in the name of Gellert, Gessner, Klopstock, and all my Teutonic brothers in Apollo.[11]

A woman painter, of course, might be thought especially prone to such disruption. In theory, making art—and especially making a history painting like *Jupiter and Antiope*—required that the artist engage her imagination both in visualizing the scene and in conjuring her characters' emotions. In this case the scene would have an erotic character, and love was a passion to which women were thought particularly susceptible. Passion and imagination were also closely related. The passions could corrupt the imagination and make it act against reason; imagination (like the artwork itself) could raise passion through false illusions. Many believed women prone to the illusions of imagination; Condillac summarized a centuries old tradition when he wrote that women's brains were especially impressionable and so images could easily lead them astray. I develop these ideas in chapter 3.

In the new physiological model, woman's sensibility insured that she had a particularly active imagination. The *Encyclopédie*'s entry "Femme," for example, reports that the "delicacy of their organs" gave women a livelier imagination but rendered them less capable of attention. Women could perceive more quickly, but because they could not consider anything for any length of time, they never developed the powers of reflection necessary to good reason.[12] Later, Pierre Roussel (1759–1815) would make a similar claim in *Système physique et morale de la femme* (1775). Because woman's sense organs are active and sensitive, her perceptions are rapid and sensations imprint themselves easily on her imagination. Yet because in woman the variety of sensations was much greater than their duration, she was constantly distracted and never developed strong powers of reflection or reason.[13]

Although those who promoted the medicine of sensibility tied mental development to physiological properties that were often based on sexual difference, the generalizations derived from this theory were recognized as generalizations. For example, at the same time that Roussel carefully distinguishes the qualities of the female mind, he also admits that some men have a "delicate and soft" constitution and that these men develop the character and tastes of women. With their concern for individual temperament and variation, theories of sensibility certainly allowed for such possibilities. Roussel argues that "inclinations" and tastes are driven by the particular constitution. But he also admits that inclination can change constitution and concludes that whether exterior determines interior or vice versa, there is a rapport between them.[14] Thus even if Roussel does not develop the implications of this thinking, both chance (that is, particular configurations) and habit (the tastes one develops) have a profound effect on any individual, so profound that either can make a man like a woman. Following Roussel, Beauchêne makes a similar argument, admitting that "sometimes one finds among men individuals whose physical and moral constitution is more like women than is usual in their sex."[15] Such possibilities helped to destabilize the categories of "woman" and "man" whose boundaries seem both fixed and permeable in these treatises. Whether constitution led to habit or habit altered constitution, different degrees of sensibility led to different properties of mind.

At the same time that different constitutions could lead to different sensibilities, differences in mental development could be related to factors other than sexual difference. In *L'homme machine* (*Machine Man;* 1747), for example, Julien Offray de La Mettrie (1709–51) retains sensibility as a characteristic of the creative imagination and gives to artists and enthusiasts precisely those characteristics elsewhere attributed to woman. Although like the Montpellier Vitalists La Mettrie was trained as a physician, he explores in his work the radical philosophical implications of the developing physiology. In particular, La Mettrie uses the sensibility of matter to deny the existence of an immaterial and immortal soul, arguing that the potential for all thought and feeling lies in the body—in its material components. Needless to say, La Mettrie's position pushed to their limits developments in physiology and psychology. Other philosophers and physicians would find his conclusions too radical, too irreligious, too dangerous, and even those drawn to his ideas did not embrace them too openly.[16] Nevertheless, what interests me is how La Mettrie aligns the artists with a specific kind of imagination:

> Unless the imagination uses part of its muscles, so to speak, to balance on the brain's strings, in order to support itself for a while on an object that is about to flee and to prevent itself from falling onto another, which it is not yet the moment to contemplate, it will never be worthy of being called judgment. It will express vividly what it has felt vividly; it will form orators, musicians, painters, poets, and not a single philosopher.[17]

In this passage, the qualities that elsewhere belong to woman's imagination become characteristic of the artist, whose imagination is vivid and mobile but not capable of the concentration necessary for deep thought. In La Mettrie's conception, education alters the way imagination develops, and while assuming that the child's imagination is more sensitive and malleable than the adult's, he makes no distinction based on sexual difference:

> On the contrary, if from childhood the imagination is accustomed to restraining itself and not being carried away by its own recklessness, which only creates brilliant enthusiasts, if it has been accustomed to stopping and containing its ideas and turning them in every direction in order to look at all sides of an object, then the imagination will be ready to judge and, thanks to its reasoning, will take in the greatest range of objects, and its liveliness, which is always so promising in children and

> which only needs to be disciplined by study and exercise, will become only far-seeing perspicacity, without which little scientific progress can be made.[18]

A key issue here is how education affects the natural organization of the brain and the individual's constitution, which Le Mettrie took as of paramount importance. He follows his commentary on imagination with the claim that nature laid the foundations of logic "for all the human race, but some have profited from them, while others have misused them."[19] Le Mettrie's claims support those of writers who relate differences in the mind to differences in the body and constitution. As we have seen, doctor-philosophers like Roussel and Beauchêne all allow that "tastes" and "inclinations" can indeed change constitution—and what is education if not a shaping and disciplining of tastes and inclinations?[20]

Receptive but Not Productive

In using the quality of imagination to separate the artist from the philosopher and the enthusiast from the deep thinker, La Mettrie did not bring sexual difference into his picture. His analysis thus allows the possibility that women, too, could be either artists or philosophers. Moreover, this possibility also arises in other theorists who attribute to women the sort of imagination that for La Mettrie marks the artist. Yet this window closes just as quickly as it is opened, as doctor-philosophers seem to realize how near they are to defining women as imaginative creators. Beauchêne, for example, characterizes women as having a lively spirit that effortlessly produces the most wonderful images and animates them in the most seductive colors. Women, moreover, have all the graces of wit. Their bursts of imagination and exquisite sentiment compensate them for "that which is lacking in the profundity of their ideas, in the force of their reason, and in creative genius, which by right belong to man."[21] Here Beauchêne echoes Roussel, who in his assessment of woman's imagination referred to Antoine Léonard Thomas's treatise on women ("Essai sur le caractère, les moeurs et l'esprit des femmes dans les differents siècles," 1772). "It is said," begins Roussel about to paraphrase Thomas, "that her imagination, more lively than stable, lends itself little to those true and picturesque expressions that are the sublime of the arts of imitation. More able to sense than to create, she receives more easily in her mind the images of objects that she cannot reproduce."[22] This idea had been developed at some length in Thomas's essay, in a section devoted to the feminine imagination.[23]

Thomas offers the conventional wisdom that imagination rather than reason is the share of women. Women, he tells us, prefer the imaginary: "The real world is not sufficient for them; they love to create an imaginary world; they live in it and embellish it."[24] And in his assessment he draws on scientific evidence: sensations strongly affect women, whose imaginations are lively and represent sensations rapidly. He even holds them susceptible to enthusiasm; they arouse their imaginations, and their minds are "always very close to enthusiasm." This said, it would appear that such an imagination should advantage women in the fine arts, but this is not the case. Woman's imagination is not strong, but lively and light; it is adapted to feminine occupations, tastes, pleasures, and weakness. Where soft living and a sedentary life condition the female imagination, that of the poet nourishes itself on more manly things, "on the clime of the mountains, on the edges of the volcanoes, on the seas, on the battlefield, or in the middle of the ruins."[25] These are the sorts of dangerous venues that provoke passions deemed especially harmful to women, and it seems no mere coincidence that in his *Les beaux-arts réduits,* Batteux had already compared the artist's enthusiasm with the bravery that excited the hero on the field of combat: "The divinity that inspires the excellent authors when they compose is like that which animates the heroes in battle. In the one it is the natural audacity and bravery animated by the presence of danger. In the other it is a great fund of genius, a justness of exquisite spirit, a fertile imagination and, above all, a heart full of a noble fire that ignites itself easily at the sight of objects."[26] Although admitting there is an enthusiasm proper to all sorts of subjects, Batteux specifically described the enthusiasm of painters in this way: "If they wish to paint a battle, they transport themselves, same as the poet, into the middle of the melee; they hear the fracas of the arms, the cries of the dying; they see the furor, the carnage, the blood. They excite their imaginations until they feel themselves moved, seized, terrified."[27]

It is not only through the implicit subject matter of poets that Thomas puts art making out of woman's reach. He concludes his discussion by observing that although woman's imagination is lively, it resembles a "mirror that reflects everything but creates nothing."[28] Thus in Thomas's scheme, imagination is fecund when developed in the male poet but loses the ability to conceive art in the female mind. And here we come back to Cahusac's *toile,* but from another direction. Now it is not the imagination per se that does not create but only the imagination of women, which is feminine in receptivity, not productivity. Thomas thus reduces woman's imagination to an entirely passive function.

The Paradoxes of Art

If in Thomas's essay the bent of her imagination prevents the normal woman from making art, in Diderot's *Paradoxe sur le comédien* (c. 1770) she also lacks the skill to produce an artful imitation. Moreover, the sensibility that makes woman susceptible to real passion renders her less able to represent emotion in works of art. The central paradox of Diderot's text is usually taken to be that the least sensitive actor is best able to move the audience because he coldly represents the signs of an emotion he does not feel. But in my reading another paradox emerges as significant: Diderot's treatise posits woman's lack of ability in the imitative arts and then singles out a woman, albeit an exceptional one with an unwomanly constitution, as its most prominent example of a creative genius. It is worth noting at the outset that by denying the connection between art making and sensibility, Diderot tacitly begins to untangle the woman and the artist. Yet by admitting that different individuals have different levels of sensibility, Diderot leaves open the possibility that a particular woman could, indeed, be a great actor.[29]

As the two interlocutors in Diderot's *Paradoxe* debate whether or not sensibility is the essential characteristic of the great actor, the discussion comes around to the issue of woman.[30] The difference between men and women actors had already been taken up by Du Bos, who argued that "as women have a sensibility that is more sudden and more at the disposition of their will than the sensibility of men, as they [women] have, so to speak, more suppleness of heart than men, they succeed better than men at doing what Quintilian expects of all those who want to become declaimers."[31] And he continues: "So although men are more capable than women of applying themselves to a task and of close attention, although the education that they receive makes them [men] learn more easily than women all that art can teach, we have, nevertheless, seen for sixty years on the French stage a much greater number of excellent actresses than excellent actors."[32] In Diderot's *Paradoxe,* on the other hand, woman provides excellent proof of the position taken by the character designated as the First: that art is *not* the product of sensibility. Here is how the First states it just before bringing women into the discussion: "Great poets, great actors, and, perhaps in general, all the great imitators of nature whoever they are, beings gifted with fine imagination, broad judgment, exquisite tact, a very sure taste, they are the least sensitive of creatures."[33] Arguing that sensitivity is not a quality of great geniuses he adds: "Look at women; they surpass us certainly, and by a great distance, in sensitivity: there is no comparison between us in moments of passion! But as much as we are below them in action, so much are they below us in imitation."[34]

If women, in general, are far below men in imitative—and hence artistic—skill, the person Diderot chooses to exemplify the great artist in *Paradoxe sur le comédien* is the famed actress Mlle Clairon (Claire-Hippolyte Léris, 1734–1801). What acting, the First asks, was ever more perfect than that of Clairon? As a great actress, she is not an enthusiast, but she is an observer of the world, a skilled technician, a tireless worker, and a perfect imitator who has no "essence" of her own. In fact, the dialogue describes her as having no sensibility whatsoever, and in this she is indeed an exceptional woman. Clairon, moreover, goes about her work as a great artist would; she imagines an ideal type for her character, borrowing from history or creating "some vast specter in her mind." Through hard work and study she brings her imitation as close to the ideal as possible:

> If you were with her when she studied her part, how many times would you cry out, *That's right!* And how many times she would answer, *You are wrong!* It was the same with [the sculptor] Le Quesnoy when a friend grabbed his arm and cried, *Stop! You will make it worse by bettering it—you are going to spoil the whole thing!* "You see what I have made," replied the artist panting to the astonished connoisseur, "but you do not see what's in my head and what I pursue."[35]

The anecdote about Le Quesnoy (François Duquesnoy, 1597–1643) quoted here we also find in Diderot's "Salon of 1767," and it shows that the great artist does not slavishly copy nature but imitates an imagined ideal no viewer can see. But not only does Diderot imply that Clairon's art is the equal of Le Quesnoy's sculpture, he also suggests that sometimes it can even surpass that of writers like Voltaire. The First reports how, in hearing Clairon play one of his parts, Voltaire asked: "Did I really write that?"[36] Her conception, it seems, was stronger and truer than that of the poet, and the First explains this phenomenon by noting that Clairon's talent lies in

> imagining a mighty phantom and in copying it with genius. She imitated the movement, the action, the gesture, the entire expressivity of a being far greater than herself. She had found that which Aeschines, repeating a speech of Demosthenes, could never reproduce: "the roar of the brute." He said to his disciples, "If this affects you so strongly, what would have been the effect 'si audivissentis bestiam mugientem' [had you heard the roaring beast]?" The poet had engendered the monster. Clairon made it roar.[37]

It is an astonishing comparison, coming as it does on the heels of that between Voltaire's writing and Clairon's acting. Voltaire, like Aeschines, cannot reproduce the roar of Demosthenes; Clairon, however, can both imagine that roar and imitate it so well that her audience will hear it again. It is with this example that the First answers his seemingly rhetorical question: "Did Clairon know more about it than Voltaire?" Despite the sensibility that prevents many women from achieving greatness in the arts, some women do have the right sort of imagination and the talents necessary for artistic production. Like Clairon, and like all great copyists of nature, they are gifted with fine imagination, broad judgment, exquisite tact, and a sure sense of taste.

If writing on sensibility in medicine often took up the effeminate man, the exceptional man whose constitution and tastes are more like those of a woman, Diderot here highlights the exceptional woman, whose lack of sensibility enables her to become a great artist. At the same time, another of Diderot's writings, his 1774 *Sur les femmes* allows that a woman dominated by extreme sensibility, and in particular, the mystic, can also make inspired art. Unlike Clairon's acting, however, the mystic's writing emerges as a "natural" production, and she is taken not as an unwomanly woman, but as a figure for woman *tout court.*

The Role of Pythia

In Diderot's *Sur les femmes,* woman performs not as an actor who has mastered a part but as one who is literally seized by the emotion she displays: "The role of Pythia only belongs to a woman. It is only the head of a woman that can exalt itself to the point of sensing seriously the approach of a god, of agitating herself, tearing her hair, foaming at the mouth, and crying out, 'I sense him, I sense him, here is the god,' and of finding the proper language."[38] In proclaiming "only the head of woman can exalt itself," Diderot suggests that woman's transport comes not from an outside force acting on her, not from the vapors exuded by a god or a divine work of art, but from her own troubled imagination. While this transport can "find the proper language" to express itself, that language is accompanied by the physical gestures associated with madness: tearing the hair, foaming at the mouth, crying out. His comments on the Pythia, moreover, come in an essay that attributes woman's self-exaltation to an imagination stimulated by uterine sensibility:

> Woman carries within herself an organ susceptible to terrible spasms, disposing her to and raising in her imagination phantoms of all sorts. It is in the hysterical delirium that she returns to the past, that she throws herself into the future, that all times are present to her. It is from this

> organ belonging to her sex that comes all her extraordinary ideas . . . Nothing is more closely related than ecstasy, visions, prophecy, revelation, fiery poetry, and hysteria.[39]

By including fiery poetry in his list, Diderot allows that women can create moving works of art from their moments of ecstasy. The first example he cites is a mystic, the Prussian woman Anna Louisa Karsh (1722–91), who believed she saw God in the clouds when she raised her eyes toward a heaven on fire with lightening. Diderot goes on to explore her vision and its poetic expression, recalling that in the illuminated sky she sees God, who "with a sleeve of his black robe shakes the lightening that will strike the head of the impious one."[40] His next example is less specific, that of a recluse in her cell whose soul melts into the bosom of the deity; she is a woman who like the Quietist passively allows herself to be taken over by God's love. At night she "hears the celestial choirs," and when she speaks of her joys, she is convinced and convincing. In other words, it is through the visions and ecstasies related to hysteria that a woman could produce compelling images and poetic language:

> The woman dominated by hysteria experiences something indefinable that is infernal or divine. Sometimes she makes me shudder. It is in the fury of the ferocious beast that is part of her that I have seen it, that I have heard it. How much she felt! How she expressed herself! Her words were not those of a mortal woman. In her book *Torrents* Mme Guyon has some eloquent lines for which there are no models. Saint Teresa has said of devils, "How unfortunate they are! They do not love." Quietism is the hypocrisy of the perverse man and the true religion of the tender woman.[41]

The woman Diderot cites as writing those eloquent lines was Jeanne Guyon (1648–1717), a Quietist who preached both a passive acceptance of God's love and a renunciation of self. Like Marguerite Marie Alacoque (1647–90), whose mystical revelations in 1674 and 1675 provided the Devotion of the Sacred Heart with its most compelling images, Guyon described her devotion in prose motivated by passionate love.[42] And it is perhaps not a random choice that Diderot mentions her in relation to Saint Teresa. In her autobiography, Guyon describes a "conversion" experience activated by a pious brother of Saint Francis, who exhorts her to "seek God in your heart, and you will there find Him."[43] She goes on to figure this experience in terms that recall the famous vision of Saint Teresa, with Guyon playing the part of the mystic from Avila, and the pious brother, that of the angel who visits her: "Having said these words, he left me. They were to me like the stroke of a dart, which penetrated through my heart. I felt a very deep wound, a wound so delightful that I desired not to be cured."[44] The delightful effects continue into the night, and in recounting them Guyon first quotes the *Song of Songs* and then draws on its erotic imagery: "I did not sleep that whole night because Your love, O my God, flowed in me like a delicious oil and burned as a fire which was going to devour all that was left of self."[45]

For many eighteenth-century writers, the outpourings of Mme Guyon and Saint Teresa helped secure the tie between woman's nature and her tender sensibility, her inclination to love. In his conduct book, *Le nouvel ami des femmes* published in 1779, Pierre-Joseph Boudier de Villemert (b. 1716) describes the relation between women and religion in terms that were by then conventional and that Diderot would draw on. To him, women seem by nature more disposed to receive the impressions of a "divine fire" that warms the heart and is the soul of religion. He goes on to say that because religion's essence is love, the more a heart is *sensible,* the more it is prepared for the submission religion exacts. Yet this love has an excessive quality, especially in women who are extremely sensitive. Women are naturally inclined to abandoning themselves to love, and when religion fixes the tender sentiments natural to them and turns them toward God, they are capable of the greatest sacrifices. "Then there is no longer anything weak about women. Love makes them overlook anything painful; all is sweetened by the pleasure of loving. The celebrated Saint Teresa saw in the eternal suffering of the rebel angel no other torture than the absence of this pleasure; 'the unfortunate one,' she cried, 'he does not know love.'"[46] Although he quotes Saint Teresa, Boudier condemns Guyon as an inappropriate model for young girls, largely because Church and State condemned her mystic visions, while accepting those of Saint Teresa and Marguerite Marie Alacoque (who was later canonized).

Nothing is so displeasing, wrote Boudier, as a woman who assembles theologians at her house and forms a ridiculous sect. Women involved in such enterprises include Antoinette Bourignon (1616–80), a celebrated visionary who spread her dreams in nineteen volumes, as well as Mme Guyon, whom he calls a very rich, pretty woman who preached pure love and awakened the extravagances of Quietism. Boudier's conclusion is particularly striking: these women are worse than "filles galantes," indeed, they are "more shocking" than courtesans like Ninon des Laclos.[47] Their sexuality, ambition, and writing seem to be unregulated. Unlike Boudier, Diderot does not condemn Guyon. Rather, he treats her writings as an uncontrolled poetry that originates with uterine sensibility stirring the female imagination. It is only when imaginative vision—or madness—raises her outside herself that a woman can write with eloquence. And it is only woman who can play the Pythia.

Fureur Prophetique

Diderot's *Sur les femmes* reminds us that religious and poetic enthusiasm had long been part of the same family. Plato recognized their kinship in the *Phaedrus* when he attributed the poet's madness to the Muses and compared the artist inspired with the priestess at Dodona and the Pythia at Delphi, women who "in their right minds added nothing to society, but who when mad with the god's gift conferred splendid benefits on Greece."[48] Although the Pythia provided prophetic enthusiasm with its most important model, possessed women rarely conferred splendid benefits on Christian Europe. In fact, it was the Church Fathers who created a sexualized Pythia, possessed by an evil spirit. As Guilia Sissa has argued, for them "the woman who had prophesied in pagan Greece was just that: a female creature, an unsettling body."[49] After describing how the priestess received the vapor through her genitals, Origen asks: "In this was there not proof of the impure and vicious nature of this spirit?"[50] John Chrysostom implicitly compared the priestess with a bacchante, disheveled and foaming at the mouth after the evil spirit entered her vagina and filled her with madness.[51]

Good churchmen everywhere believed women easy prey for sorcerers and devils. In the 1486 *Malleus maleficarum,* Heinrich Kramer and James Sprenger reminded other witch hunters that "women are naturally more impressionable, and more ready to receive the influence of a disembodied spirit."[52] This statement punctuates a section that summarizes the misogynist doctrines of the Catholic Church along with many inherited from the ancients. Kramer and Sprenger also pointed out that all witchcraft came from carnal lust, which was insatiable in women.[53] Those demonologists skeptical about some aspects of the *Malleus* agreed with its authors on woman's nature. For example, in his rival treatise on sorcery, the physician Johann Weyer (1515–88) argued that devil worshippers sought out the weak and melancholic, which explained why women comprised a high proportion of those possessed. After all, everyone knew the daughters of Eve were congenitally weak and susceptible to mental disease.[54]

Treatises on religious enthusiasm—or the claim to be divinely, rather than satanically, possessed—depended on similar assumptions. I mention only one of those, Merit Casaubon's 1655 *Treatise concerning Enthusiasm,* written by the son of a Huguenot refugee in response to a French woman's biography, a biography the Catholic authorities approved. In his treatise, Casaubon (1599–1671) asked if "mystical theology" was "allowable or commendable in women, whom all men know to be naturally weaker of brain, and easiest to be infatuated and deluded"?[55] He concludes that to encourage a woman's mysticism was to exacerbate her natural susceptibility to illusions and to lead her toward madness.[56] In reading the life of Sister Katherine of Jesus, nun of the Order of Our Lady (published in Paris in 1628), Casaubon found that from childhood Katherine was not only devout but also given to mystical and enthusiastic behaviors. These included physical penance, voluntary chastisement, trances, and ecstasies. Although Catholic officials encouraged these behaviors, they eventually led to a general consumption of the body, which killed her. Casaubon attributes Katherine's visions and ecstasies not to divine or demonic possession, but to disease, to pure melancholia.[57] In claiming Katherine's case as the motivating force for his study, Casaubon poses his (anti-Catholic) treatise as a cautionary tale to those who would encourage women's enthusiasm.

One celebrated case in eighteenth-century France stirred the cauldron of religious enthusiasm, mental disease, and female sexuality: the *convulsionnaires* of Saint-Médard. The case began in 1727 with the death of a revered Jansenist deacon, François de Pâris, who was interred in the cemetery of Saint-Médard on May 3. His grave immediately became a site for pious devotion, and those who gathered there witnessed a variety of miraculous healings. Their reports quickly spread, and over the next three years the small group grew into a religious cult that attracted adherents from all Paris and beyond. Miraculous healings were soon only one manifestation of divine favor, as adherents were struck with convulsions, which they believed the Holy Spirit inspired through the intercession of François de Pâris. The manifestations continued into the 1760s, and the phenomenon fascinated many philosophers, including Voltaire and especially Diderot, who lived near the Church of Saint-Médard.[58] Writing about the *convulsionnaires* continued through the middle of the eighteenth century, and they later became prime examples of woman's psychiatric disturbance.[59]

Although little different at first from other such cults, that of Saint-Médard quickly became intertwined with a whole set of political and social concerns, as Robert Kreiser has so adeptly argued in his far-reaching study of the phenomenon.[60] In 1731, the crown took official measures to stifle activities at the tomb, but once pulled out of the cemetery, the cult flourished in monastic settings, particularly in the female orders and congregations.[61] And the majority of the adherents were women.[62] The movement, moreover, offered women a religious standing more elevated than the position they could find in mainstream Roman Catholicism or Jansenism, and within the group, women could attend all important services and assume ritual roles.[63]

Philippe Hecquet (1661–1737), the former dean of the Paris Faculty of Medicine, a mainstream Jansenist, and one of the most prolific writers on the movement, believed that a passion for recognition drove many of the women to sustain or artfully embellish their symptoms. As Lindsay Wilson has argued, Hecquet saw in these *convulsionnaires* a kind of self-seeking duplicity, and he likened their fraud to the most famous case of possession in the previous century—that of the Ursulines at Loudon. In his comparison, Hecquet portrays the *convulsionnaires,* "whose enthusiastic operations have appeared so extraordinary," as both "hysterical or vaporous" girls and frauds who, in luring others by their tricks, both made their profit and satisfied their vanity.[64] Here Hecquet figures the *convulsionnaires* as artful actors moved by ambition.

With the physical symptoms of possession already well established, it is easy to see how some could accuse the *convulsionnaires* of manufacturing their ecstasies through artifice. Primary manifestations of the convulsions were vocal; devotees cried out or muttered incoherently. In the midst of their inspiration, women would thrash on the floor screaming, trembling, and twitching, or they would contort their bodies into strange postures and expressions. In one common manifestation called the "tableau vivant," adepts acted out episodes in the Church's history. This varied menu of manifestations provoked Hecquet to ask, "What is the enthusiastic brain of a *convulsionnaire* not capable of imagining?"[65]

Most troubling to the authorities, however, were convulsions enhanced by "secours," or assistance administered by fellow participants known as "secourists." Those called the "petits secours" consisted of pressing or lightly striking the body; but the "grands secours," also known as "secours meurtriers," could include beating, piercing, hanging, dragging, pushing, and choking. Those subjected to this treatment—and remember, most of these were women—claimed not just that they alleviated pain, but that they were also pleasurable.[66] Some of the practices are illustrated in an anonymous print showing one of the most celebrated of all the *convulsionnaires,* Gabrielle Moulère (fig. 4). Gabrielle came from the lower ranks of society (her father was a cobbler by profession) and her entire family—mother, father, and four siblings—were active in the convulsionary movement.[67]

It was the *secours* that attracted the most attention from doctors, royal officials, and also philosophers. In an entry on "convulsion" from his *Dictionnaire philosophique,* Voltaire describes the *secours* as the fraudulent artifice of religious women:

> People had Sister Rose, Sister Illuminée, Sister Promise, Sister Confit come to their houses. They would flagellate themselves, and there would be no marks the next day. They would beat their stomachs, well armored in leather, well covered in hide, without harming themselves. They laid down before a roaring fire, their faces covered with pomade, without burning themselves.[68]

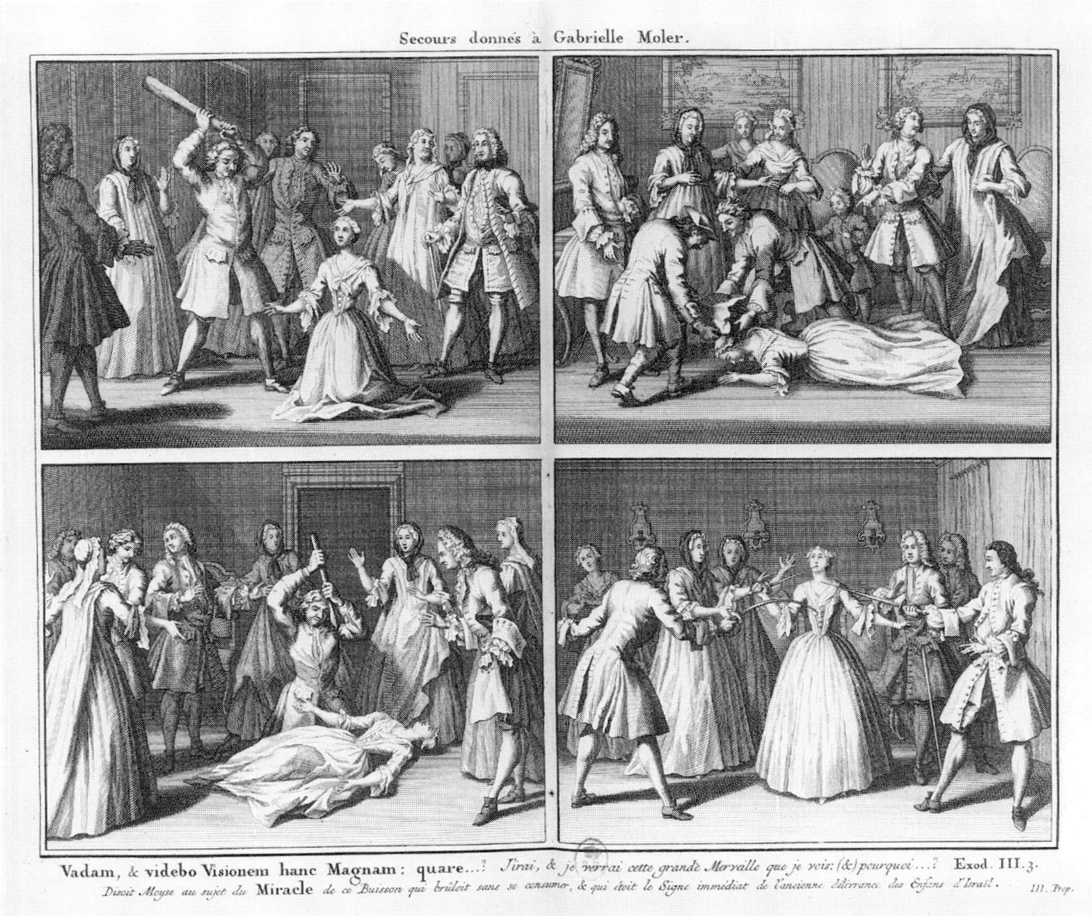

FIGURE 4. *Secours donnés Gabrielle Moler,* illustration from Louis-Basile Carré de Montgeron, *Continuation des démonstrations des miracles . . . Observations sur l'oeuvre des convulsions et sur l'état des convulsionnaires,* vol. 2 of *La vérité des miracles opérés par l'intercession de M. de Pâris* (1741–48). Photograph © Bibliothèque Nationale de France.

And he goes on to offer ironic praise for the women's deceptive arts: "[F]inally, as all the arts are perfected, they finish by forcing swords into their flesh and by crucifying themselves."[69] At the same time that Voltaire registers the convulsions as artful illusion, he also offers the adherents as a key example of fanaticism, which in his *Dictionnaire philosophique* he calls a gangrene of the brain, a nearly incurable disease: "I have seen the *convulsionnaires,* who in speaking of the miracles of Saint Pâris would excite themselves little by little without realizing it. Their eyes would glow, their bodies would tremble, fury would disfigure their faces, and they would have killed anyone who contradicted them."[70] Like artists, these women bring themselves to a state of enthusiasm, little by little, exciting their ardor as they recall the master's great works. Yet unlike most artists, they take their excitement to excess, crossing all boundaries of reason.

If some writers pictured these women as con artists, critics particularly focused on the *secours* as licentious and debauched, a charge that seemed credible because women called on their male *secourists* to press and pull their breasts or to pierce their bodies with swords or pins. We see such piercings in the images of Gabrielle Moulère (or Moler). On the bottom left a *secourist* prepares to push a spear into her upper body, and on the bottom right two helpers try to stab her in the breast and neck while she pushes a sword into her mouth. This last scene depicts the famous *secours des epées* of 1736 when, supposedly guided by supernatural forces, Gabrielle pushed a sword toward her stomach. Instead of piercing her body, the sword curved, and Gabrielle was unscathed. Later, she pushed the *epée* against her throat to similar effect, and she then pushed it down into her esophagus without injury. The print conflates all three aspects of the *secours,* which eventually became so widespread that it was one of the examples Voltaire cited in debunking the *convulsionnaires.*

Although Gabrielle emerged from the *secours* unscathed, she later suffered a fate far worse than Voltaire's barb. Her convulsionary activities led to imprisonment in the Bastille in 1738, and subsequently she was sent to the Salpêtrière where she died in 1748. Of this later incarceration her biographer lamented that she was sent to the place reserved for "monstrous impure women who devote themselves to being the public victims of the libertine's debauchery."[71] Gabrielle's imprisonment with "impure women" points to the most enduring charges leveled against the women who participated in the movement.

Moralists harped on the indecency of the *convulsionnaires,* which medical practitioners rooted in the female imagination. Hecquet, for example, concludes in his *Le naturalisme des convulsions dans les maladies de l'epidemie convulsionnaire* (1733) that the convulsions are "hysterical vapors, perhaps truly uterine, caused and sustained by passions of the soul, as philosophical physicians describe them, or by movements excited by objects that trouble the imagination, which in women is all the easier to rattle."[72] Similarly, in his *Lettre sur la convulsionnaire en extase; ou, La vaporeuse en rêve,* Hecquet compares the ecstasies experienced by Charlotte, a *convulsionnaire* in her fifties, with those symptoms displayed by the "jeunes vaporeuses lascivement histeriques." From this case and others, he diagnoses the *convulsionnaires* as suffering from a delirium that begins with an intoxication brought on by "the abundance of erotic fluids that are warmed in their entrails, troubling their brains by upsetting them with hysterical [uterine?] vapors."[73] The author concludes that a certain "erotomania" is mixed with the vapors, producing symptoms that he calls "criminal."[74] Thus uterine vapors are responsible at once for troubling the imagination, producing erotomania, and as Diderot argued, creating fiery poetry.

Diderot's *Sur les femmes* seems touched by the *convulsionnaires* as it reaffirms a link found in the analysis of older adherents—the connection between hysterical youth and devout old age. In affirming that all women are susceptible to hysteria, Diderot's remarks resonate with the central findings of the doctors who evaluated the women at Saint-Médard: "A woman who was hysterical in her youth becomes devout in old age, the woman in whom there remains some energy in old age, was hysterical in her youth. Her head still speaks the language of the senses though the senses themselves are mute."[75] In the later eighteenth and early nineteenth centuries, doctors like Pierre Roussel and Philippe Pinel used the *convulsionnaires* to debunk the idea that women had more rapport with divinity and were therefore its chosen interpreters. Their arguments turned on the similarity between the actions of those reputed to be prophets and the symptoms of "maladies convulsives."[76] From this similarity they concluded that women, far from being more inspired were simply more given to disease.

PART II: POSSESSION AND EMULATION

Divine inspiration, whether actual or feigned, marked the *convulsionnaires'* performance; similarly, the artist's creative act had long been conceived within a rhetoric of possession. Page duBois has pointed out that for the ancients, both poetic and prophetic enthusiasm often took the form of possession by someone or some being of a different sex. Poets from Homer to Hesiod claim that muses or nymphs inspired them, and in *Phaedrus* Socrates identifies a series of cross-sex enthusiasms that include the priestesses at Dodona, the sibyls, and the Pythia. The state of enthusiasm, of having the god or goddess in one, can connote a shifting of sexual identity.[77] DuBois, moreover, shows that emulation—the assuming of one poet's voice by another—can produce similar effects. She notes that in Plato's *Phaedrus*, Socrates (the character) assumes the mask of Sappho; his description of eros is "shadowed with allusion to Sappho." For duBois, to echo Sappho's response so deftly is "to become the lyric poet possessed by the lyric poetess, to blur once again the line between the sexes by dressing oneself in the words and images of the other."[78]

This emulation of Sappho that duBois identifies in Plato's *Phaedrus* is particularly interesting in the context of Longinus's *On the Sublime*, translated by Boileau as *Traité du sublime ou du merveilleux dans le discours*. There Plato emerges as the most accomplished of emulators:

> Further, this philosopher [Plato] has again taught us, if we do not neglect his words, that there is another path that can lead us to the sublime. What is this path? It is the imitation and emulation of the illustrious poets and writers who have come before us. We must always look toward this goal. Certainly we often see that the spirit of another

> transports us outside of ourselves just as a holy furor seized the priestess of Apollo on the sacred tripod. It is said that there is an opening in the earth from which comes a wind, an entirely heavenly vapor, that immediately fills her with divine force and leads her to pronounce oracles. Similarly, the great beauties that we notice in the works of the ancients are the sacred sources from which arise advantageous vapors that spread in the soul of their imitators, even animating spirits that are not naturally ardent, so that in this moment they are ravished and carried away by another's enthusiasm.[79]

The text positions Plato as both the classical source for the exaltation of enthusiastic possession—for the vision of the Pythia on her tripod—and an artist possessed by that which he emulates. Emulation here is conceived as possession and figured as the Pythia penetrated by Apollo's divine spirit. Although Longinus hinted at a sexual encounter, Boileau shied away from any such suggestion in his translation, rendering the action as "filling her with divine fire" rather than impregnating her.[80] But regardless of Boileau's translation, the relation of Pythia to Apollo was conceived as explicitly sexual in the eighteenth century.

Through descriptions of the Greek oracles, eighteenth-century writers associated both poetic and prophetic enthusiasm with possession and penetration. The sculptor Falconet summed up the issue as he envisioned the priestess receiving the god's pneuma through her vagina. In his translation of Pliny, Falconet pictures her at the opening of the sacred cave, nude and straddling a tripod. In this position nothing could hinder her enthusiasm when "the spirit of the god plunged itself into the entrails of the priestess."[81] Voltaire also offered a sexualized description of the Pythia's inspiration in his *Dictionnaire philosophique,* in which he asks, "[D]oes one first give the name of enthusiasm, of the agitation of the entrails, to the contortions of that Pythia who on the tripod of Delphi received the spirit of Apollo through a place that seems made only to receive bodies?"[82]

Pythia on her tripod remained a pertinent model for figuring the enthusiastic artist throughout the eighteenth century. Written for the students of the French Academy of Painting and Sculpture, Michel Dandré-Bardon's 1765 *Traité de peinture* recapitulates Boileau's translation of Longinus. On the point of inspiration, he compares the artist aroused by the works of past masters with the Pythia agitated by her god. The masterpieces themselves Dandré-Bardon calls "beneficial sources, from which come the happy vapors that warm genius. One is, so to speak, transported by their enthusiasm. So the priestess of Apollo was seized with a holy furor when she mounted the sacred tripod. The divine vapor gives off a sublime force, agitates her, and inspires her."[83] To be receptive to this power is to put oneself in the place of the Pythia, in the feminine position, in the place of the one penetrated and driven mad by the experience.

Alongside this model of emulation as possession, another was also available in Longinus's writing as translated by Boileau, one the French Academy also embraced. In this model emulation is more the rivaling and surpassing of past masters than the sexual possession by them, and it is cast as what we, after Freud, would call an oedipal conflict. Commenting on Plato's emulation of Homer, Longinus offers a second image that makes emulation a joust or duel. "Never, in my opinion, would [Plato] have mixed so much greatness in his treatises on philosophy, passing as he did, from a simple recitation to an expressive one to poetical writing, if he had not, so to speak, come with all his might as a new athlete to challenge Homer for the trophy, Homer who had already received accolades from everyone."[84] Possessing the artist sexually is here replaced by a rivalry in which one man challenges another, a paradigm that is not free from sexual desire.

It is tempting to view the construction of artistic inspiration as oedipal in the case of Homer but homosocial and homosexual in the case of the Pythia, since so many treatises directed toward male students urged them to seek inspiration in their esteemed male forebears. In either case, the transmission of enthusiasm seems to move from man to man. Even if one of those men takes a feminine position, women are eliminated from the transaction. In making this observation, I again refer to duBois, whose work analyzed how Greek philosophy passed from an older to a younger male lover, a paradigm she locates in Plato's *Phaedrus*.[85] Yet at the same time, one woman—Sappho—emerges as a general model for emulation, not in Plato, but in Boileau's translation of Longinus. There she is a key example of the sublime in writing, especially for those who would—like Socrates in Plato's *Phaedrus*—write or speak about love.

Sappho's Enthusiasm

Boileau's translation of Longinus poses Sappho as a model while discussing what makes writing great or sublime. It is particularly significant to my analysis that Sappho enters the account just as it outlines a process that calls into play the powers Cahusac would see as associated with reason:

> Let us consider whether we do not have another means of rendering writing great. I propose that because nothing happens in the world that is not always accompanied by certain circumstances, it will be an

> infallible secret for arriving at greatness if we know the way to choose the most worthy circumstances and to tie these together in a beautiful ensemble, like a body.[86]

The example of a great writer who can select and combine elements into a harmonious whole is Sappho, and the example of her work that he chooses is a poem representing love's frenzy, itself a type of enthusiasm. Longinus's text not only preserved the poem, but it also asked how Sappho excelled in depicting that passion. The answer repeats the criteria for making writing great.

> She brings together all the aspects of the accidental effects that follow and accompany this passion, but where her art principally appears is in choosing from all these accidents those that best indicate the excess and violence of love and in tying them together into a whole. In a word, one would say that she is not infatuated with a simple passion but that her mind is the meeting place of all the passions. And this is, in effect, what happens to those who love. We see, then, as I have already said, that all the great circumstances appropriately distinguished and brought together with choice makes the main beauty of her language [discours].[87]

Here the quality of Sappho's imagination is far from the disorderly workings of the female mind as outlined in eighteenth-century thought. And this difference is especially compelling given that Sappho writes about the disorder of love, an emotion that women in general, and Sappho in particular, were thought to know something about. But Boileau's translation of Longinus attributes Sappho's excellence not to her personal experience (in fact, he may ignore some of its salient aspects) but to her genius for selecting, relating, and forming a satisfying whole.

Boileau's disciple Batteux eliminates Sappho as the example of an artist who can synthesize various aspects of a subject into a satisfying whole. His model for this process switches from poetry to painting and from woman to man. Batteux replaces Sappho with Zeuxis, drawing on a story made famous by Pliny the Elder. He relates how the Greek painter solved the problem of fashioning an ideal figure for the temple at Agrigentum. Summoning all the young women of the town, Zeuxis examined them nude and selected from the group five models, each of whom had a particularly beautiful feature. After identifying and selecting these five "parts," Zeuxis united them into an ideal whole.

But the process of creating perfect beauty also requires the artist to conceive an idea, and Batteux argues that the enthusiastic artist is completely involved with what he imagines. As in many standard accounts, the artist forgets himself and in his imagination "becomes" the characters and objects he represents.

> Let us recall the example of Zeuxis. Nature has in its treasures all the traits from which the most beautiful imitations can be composed. These are like the studies in the sketchbook of a painter. The artist, who is essentially an observer, recognizes them, selects them from the mass [of other traits], assembles them. He composes in his mind a whole of which he conceives a vivid idea, which dominates him. Soon his fire is lit at the sight of the object. He forgets himself, and his mind passes into the thing that he creates.[88]

According to Batteux's model, Zeuxis must have fancied himself a womanly ideal, the goddess of perfect beauty. And this is indeed a seductive thought. Batteux does not seem to notice that Zeuxis' enthusiasm has turned the Greek hero from the model artist to the perfect woman.

Later eighteenth-century writers would figure Sappho not in terms of choice but in terms of passion.[89] Abbé Jean-Jacques Barthélemy (1716–95) brings Sappho together with the Pythia in his wildly popular *Le voyage du jeune Anacharsis en Grèce au IVe siècle de l'ère vulgaire* (1788):

> But with what force of genius she hurries us along when she describes the charms, the transports, and intoxication of love! What scenery! What warmth of coloring. Agitated like the Pythia by the inspiring god, she throws on paper her words that burn. Her sentiments fall like a cloud of arrows or a fiery shower about to consume everything. She animates and personifies all the symptoms of this passion, to excite the most powerful emotions in our soul.[90]

It would be easy to attribute to the narrator's enthusiasm this likening of Sappho and Pythia, so breathless is the description. But such a comparison also puts the poet back into the feminine position not only through imaging the encounter as heterosexual possession but also by occluding Sappho's reasonable construction of poetic effects. In a later passage, the young Anacharsis offers his own "vision" of Sappho as she abandons herself, without reserve, to the impression beauty has made on her "too susceptible heart":

> Methought I saw her languid, trembling, and as if thunderstruck; deprived of her understanding and her senses; alternately blushing and turning pale; yielding to the diversified and tumultuous emotions of her passion or, rather, of all the jarring passions of her soul. Such is the eloquence of sentiment.[91]

Here Anacharsis paints Sappho as an overly sensitive woman, even if the text later cites Longinus's account of her skill at selecting and combining poetic effects. Both her presence as a model for emulation and her elision with the Pythia disrupt the man-to-man transmission, be it from father to son, lover to lover, or artist to artist, that we most often find in the discourses of enthusiasm and the fine arts. What possibilities did Sappho offer for other women? What danger did possession by a woman present for the male artist?

Emulating Sappho

It is striking how many talented women in the seventeenth and eighteenth centuries readily identified themselves with a woman whose reputation as a tribade—a woman who had sexual relations with other women—could not be entirely effaced. In Sappho we find the only instance of a woman artist and great poet whom many believed crossed the border into a deranged state. Sappho, however, differs from Tasso and from the other enthusiastic male artists in this one important quality: she is also tinged with the color of sexual transgression. Why were women drawn to Sappho despite the "infamy" that clung to her name? Was possession by a tribade less scandalous than wrestling with a great male artist?

In her *Fictions of Sappho,* Joan DeJean has located part of Sappho's appeal for seventeenth-century women in the writer's cultivation of a gynosocial community. DeJean points out that Sappho "portrays both the composition and performance of her verse as an exchange among women, as the product of a female community whose members are united by bonds both personal and professional."[92] She contends, in fact, that Sappho represents the attempt to bypass male literary authority. Thus for Sappho, poetic inspiration is not figured as a male god penetrating a female priestess, nor as the enthusiasm of man for man, but as a gift handed from woman to woman. This aspect of Sappho was central to how some women imagined the poet, and DeJean gives credit for the modern reconstruction of Sappho to her seventeenth-century French emulators. Madeleine de Scudéry (1607–1701) particularly associated herself with Sappho and presented the Greek poet as an advocate of women's writing, progenitor of a female tradition, and defender of woman's mental prowess.[93] Here are the words Scudéry puts into Sappho's mouth in her 1642 *Les femmes illustres:* "Those who say that beauty is the share of women and that the fine arts, literature, and all the sublime and noble sciences accrue to men and that we can take no part in them are as far from being just as they are from being truthful."[94] This Sappho concludes that beauty in the female sex is the complement

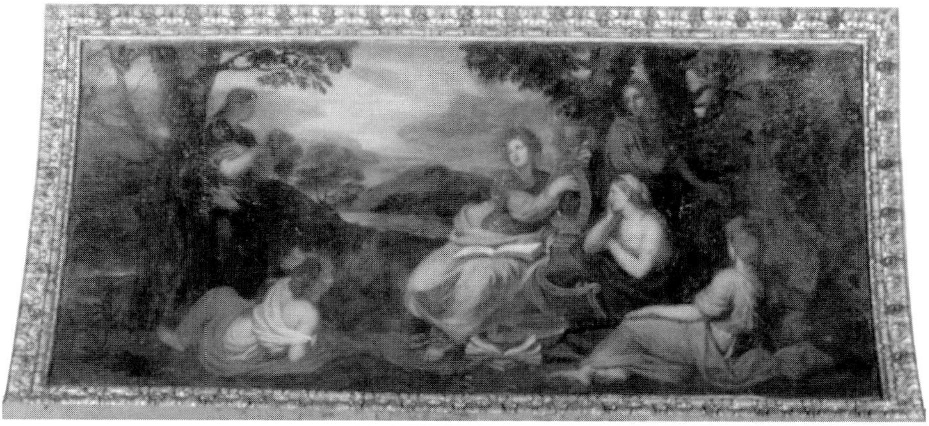

FIGURE 5. Michel Corneille II (French, 1642–1708), *Sappho Performing Her Lyric Poetry*, 1671. Oil on mounted canvas. Château de Versailles: Nobles' Room. Photograph © Réunion des Musées Nationaux/Art Resource, NY.

to valor in the male but that this quality does not contribute to either learning or the fine arts. If there is some difference between women and men, she contends, it is only in things of war.

Sappho's comments as imagined by Scudéry bring us back to the issues raised in the first part of this chapter, for to gain legitimacy in the arts and sciences, women had first to demonstrate that their minds were not lacking in either reason or judgment. Thus Sappho continues: "If our imagination shows us things as they are, if our memory operates as it should, how can our judgment be in error? When it is lively, the imagination mirrors things so faithfully; when it is illuminated, the mind penetrates things so profoundly; and when it is just and cultivated, our memory instructs us by example so powerfully that it is impossible for judgment not to be formed."[95] Scudéry thus places her Sappho squarely in the middle of the debate over woman's mental powers and creative talent.

Despite any scandal associated with her name, Sappho also proved a suitable model for women in the official culture of Old Regime France. Consider, for example, four paintings the crown commissioned from Michel Corneille in 1671 to decorate the Nobles' Room in Queen Marie-Thérèse's ceremonial apartments at Versailles (fig. 5). Each of the four images takes as its central theme a famous woman known from antique sources, and each depicts her engaged in making art or philosophy. Lala of Kuzikos cultivates painting; Aspasia discourses with the Greek philosophers. Penelope weaves a tapestry, and Sappho recites her lyric poetry. Three of the paintings show women artists appealing to other women, and Corneille represents Sappho seated in a landscape amid a group enchanted by her song. Although together the four images might be read as transforming the female figures into allegories for the arts, they seem more in the tradition of praising exceptional women. Moreover, the room's decoration places its allegories elsewhere. On the ceiling, for example, Corneille depicted Mercury and Minerva with Eloquence, Poetry, Geometry, and the Sciences, the last pictured as allegorical women. In the corners of the room, four large, muscular male figures stand as allegories for vigilance, immortality, trade, and diligence.

Corneille made this cycle of famous women to decorate a room Marie-Thérèse used as antechamber to her apartment, a place where visitors would wait for the queen to receive them. A similar emphasis on famous women also marked the decoration of the Queen's Guardroom, in which the works not only have martial themes but also show *femmes fortes,* that is, heroic women. Its imagery includes Claude Vignon's *Arpelia Rescuing Her Husband,* as well as several subjects by Antoine Paillet (1626–1701): Artemisia, ruler of Halicarnassus, battling against the Greeks on Xerxes' ships; Zenobia fighting against Emperor Aurelian; Hypsicratia, concubine of King Mithridates IV, following him to war; and Cloelia on horseback with her companions. The iconography is continued in the four overdoors, which are painted to represent trophies and weapons. These works, however, are important for more than their subject. They were completed in 1673 by Madeleine de Boulogne (1646–1710), one of the few—perhaps even the only—woman to execute such decorative work at Versailles. Taken together, the decorations for these two antechambers suggest that the iconography appropriate to queenship included references to women's military exploits and their civil rule, as well as to their achievements in philosophy, art, and literature. These decorations remained in the rooms through all of the transformations and changes in the Queen's apartments, which Marie Leszczynska began as early as 1730 and Marie-Antoinette continued in the 1770s.

Other women throughout the seventeenth and eighteenth centuries chose Sappho as a particular model and had themselves pictured in her guise. The Musée des Beaux-Arts in Rouen, for example, holds the portrait of an unknown woman as Sappho attributed to the *academicienne* Elisabeth Sophie Cheron and dated to 1670–1680, when allegorical portraiture was at the height of its popularity (fig. 6). Despite her specific features and individualized face, the sitter remains unidentified. Sappho, however, can be recognized from the laurel crown, lyre, scroll, and dress decorated with musical notation.[96] But who could this Sappho be? Although the sitter's traits do not correspond with those in other images of Mme de Scudéry, earlier speculation named her as the subject of this portrait. And this identification still has something to recommend it, especially if we bear in mind the variability of any individual's portrayal. Whether or not this portrait represents Scudéry, however, we need to recognize her influence on it, for she established Sappho as a model for women, promoted her reputation, and knew

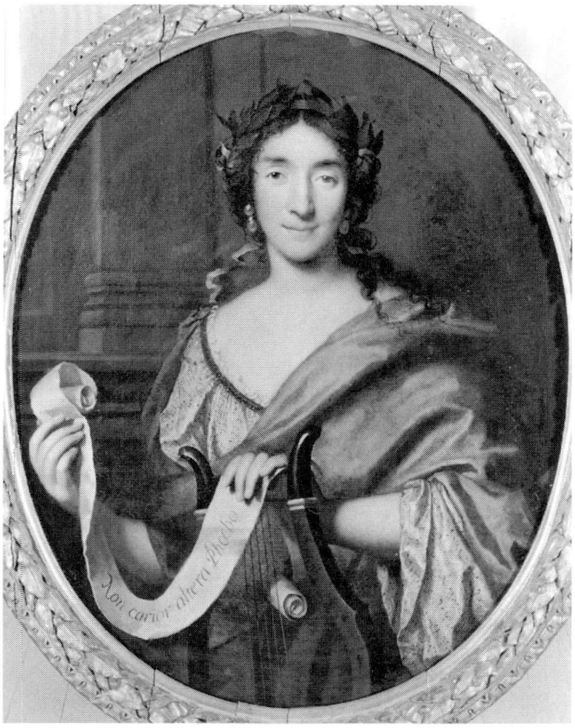

FIGURE 6. Attributed to Elisabeth Sophie Cheron (French, 1648–1711), *Portrait of a Woman as Sappho,* c. 1670–80. Oil on canvas, 88 × 73.3 cm. Rouen: Musée des Beaux-Arts. Photograph © Rouen, Musée des Beaux-Arts. Photograph: Didier Tragin/Catherine Lancien.

better than anyone how the poet had been represented in the past. Scudéry, in fact, compiled the first modern biography of Sappho, which challenged Ovid's canonical representation of the Greek poet on at least one key point.

In the *Heroides,* Ovid pictures Sappho as the distraught lover of Phaon who in despair over losing his affection throws herself off a cliff and into the sea. Sappho's love for Phaon was a significant point in her biography, and some French writers during both the seventeenth and eighteenth centuries tried to "normalize" Sappho's sexuality by stressing this heterosexual romance.[97] But to normalize her in this way was to pathologize her in another, for the story of her suicide pictures Sappho not as a lyric poet worthy of emulation but as a woman who has lost her reason. This image of a Sappho mad for love owes much to Jacques Ferrand's *Traité de l'essence et guérison de l'amour* (*Treatise on Lovesickness;* 1623), which points out that the forlorn poet leaps into the sea because Phaon has abandoned her. Ferrand takes this Sappho as proof that lovesickness strikes women more frequently and more grievously than it does men.[98] Nevertheless, he has a more complicated and contradictory view of Sappho. He presents her poetry as a touchstone for identifying the symptoms of love and contends that she is as experienced in the art of diagnosis "as our Greek, Latin, and Arab physicians, in light of the fact that they mentioned no indisputable signs that this lady did not already know."[99] And while presenting Sappho as distraught over a man, Ferrand also places her among the tribades. Indeed, he splits Sappho into the heterosexual mad woman and the tribade poet-diagnostician.[100]

Scudéry moves Sappho in a different direction by maintaining a belief in her heterosexuality while undercutting the story of her madness. She contends that Sappho never hurled herself from a cliff and revises the legend by explaining that Sappho's relatives circulated the fiction to account for why Sappho, when she retires to the land of the Amazons, leaves a will disposing of her worldly goods.[101] Uncertainty surrounded the figure of Sappho into the eighteenth century and emerges in Voltaire's brief comments on Sappho's enthusiasm. These comments leave in doubt the reality of her leap, but contrast her feverish writing with Ovid's wit. "Ovid speaks of love only with 'esprit'; Sappho expresses the enthusiasm of this passion; and if it is true that it cost her her life, enthusiasm in her mind became dementia."[102] Voltaire seems unsure where to place Sappho: is she a model for representing enthusiasm passionately or is she an example of a woman whose enthusiasm has run amuck?

Equally equivocal is Barthélemy's account in *Le voyage du jeune Anacharsis.* We have seen that Barthélemy brings together Sappho the madwoman and Sappho the enthusiastic poet through figuring her as the Pythia. Although conflating these may help "normalize" the poet's sexuality, Barthélemy knows of Sappho's reputation and feels compelled to explain it. How is it possible, he asks, to reconcile the sentiments of Sappho's poetry and the honors given her, with her supposedly infamous morals? Barthélemy leaves the question unresolved. Sappho's reputation might be deserved, but one could also attribute it to the scandal that dogs all talent: "When I read some of her works, I dare not acquit her, but she had merit and enemies, and I dare not condemn her."[103] As the abbé well knew from his own day, slander, and especially sexual slander, followed prominent women.

Barthélemy, however, goes on to explain how later commentators misconstrued Sappho's history and misread her poetry. He claims that after the death of her husband, Sappho devoted herself to poetry and inspired the women of Lesbos with a taste for it. Thus far the history fits with the image of Sappho forming a community of women. But the abbé goes on to explain that she loved them to excess because she could not do otherwise, just as she could not but express her tenderness with all the violence of passion: "Your surprise at this will cease when you become better acquainted with the extreme sensibility of the Greeks and discover that among them the most innocent connections often borrow the impassioned language of love."[104] The Greeks emerge as extremely sensitive—a characteristic that eighteenth-century writers often attributed to women. This trait, however, was not confined to Sappho as a Greek woman but extended throughout the entire culture and even to Plato himself. In a moment that now seems deeply ironic, Barthélemy uses Plato's Socrates as his example of "extreme sensibility" and argues that there was no less "purity" in Sappho than in Socrates, as Plato describes him. Thus Barthélemy traffics in a more general repression of the homosexual elements of Greek culture, seeing in them only homosocial arrangements of friendship and artistic transmission. Such blindness, however, might have been useful to the women of his time. Casting doubt on what was for many the most troubling aspect of Sappho's deviance may very well have allowed women to identify publicly with the Greek poet.

And identify they did. DeJean has shown how Sappho attracted seventeenth-century French women, and we have seen how she was honored even in the queen's ceremonial apartments at Versailles. Gill Perry has written on the importance of Sappho for English women in the next century. Perry argues that many were attracted to Sappho because her poetry both celebrated and revealed a woman's experiences and emotions. Women like the actress, writer, and poet Mary Robinson (1758–1800) used Sappho "to construct a mythology of their lives that acknowledged female creativity and a woman's capacity for artistic production."[105] And we can also find women in eighteenth-century France presenting themselves as Sappho, although some of these portraits—for example, Charles Coypel's *Portrait of a Woman with a Lyre* (1740–45; fig. 7)—await further explication. More securely identified, however, is François Dumont's miniature of Mme de Saint-Just d'Aucourt as Sappho holding a lyre (1797; fig. 8), which shows the sitter crowned with laurel and leaning against a tree. Her expression, as well as the lyre's placement, hints at a pleasurable inspiration. And Elisabeth Vigée-Lebrun, the painter who revived the allegorical portrait in late eighteenth-century France, shows Countess Fries as Sappho crowned with laurel, holding her lyre, and searching for inspiration (1793–94; fig. 9).[106] This tradition reached its climax only at the beginning of the nineteenth century when Mme de Staël associated her poet Corinne with Sappho and Vigée-Lebrun depicted the novelist as this Sappho-Corrine in an allegorical portrait made in 1806 (see fig. 1 above).[107]

Dangerous Emulation

While reputed sexual deviance in a woman artist might be tolerated if there was a shade of doubt, what seems to have been as problematic was a man who seemed possessed by a woman artist or a woman artist who overtly challenged (emulated?) her great male predecessors. That

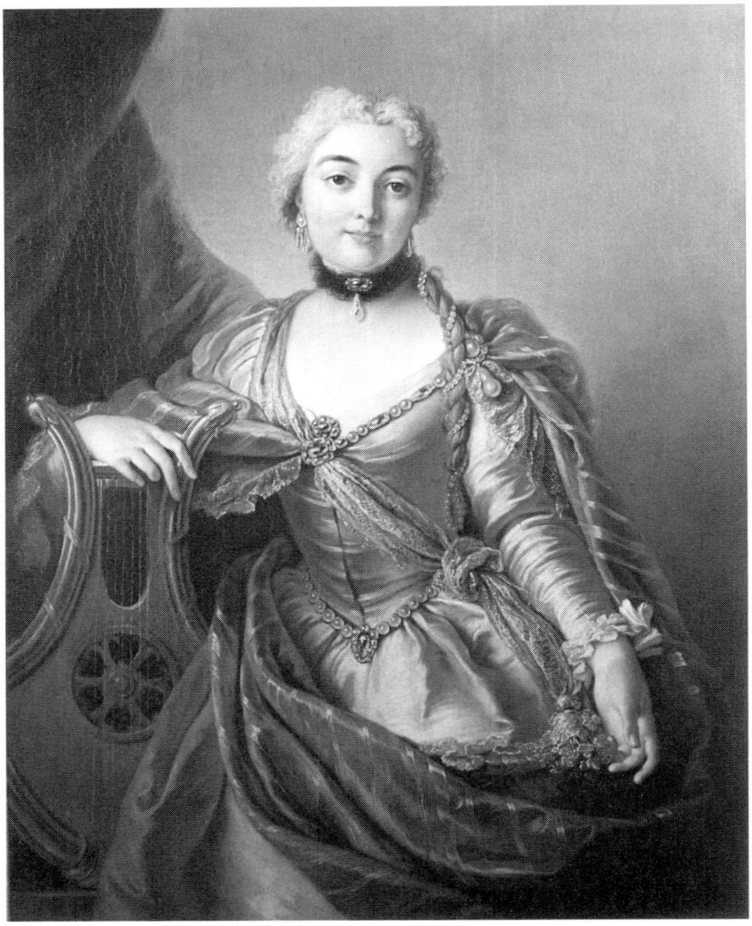

FIGURE 7. Charles Coypel (French, 1694–1752), *Portrait of a Woman with a Lyre,* c. 1740–45. Oil on canvas, 39 3/4 × 35 inches. Norfolk, Va.: Chrysler Museum of Art. Gift of Walter P. Chrysler, Jr. Photograph: Courtesy Chrysler Museum of Art.

Longinus recommends Sappho as a model for great writing suggests that he does not fear, at least in this case, emulating or imitating an actual woman. Although this fear does not seem to have entered into Longinus's theory of great writing, we can find it in the work of his translator Nicolas Boileau. Boileau is especially significant here because his vision of literary history and theory of poetry provided the foundation for the French canon of literature established by the middle of the eighteenth century. It also found its way into the *Encyclopédie.*[108] In his *Discours préliminaire,* d'Alembert relies heavily on Boileau for his history of literature, noting that "in his *L'art poétique,* Despréaux [i.e., Boileau] made himself the equal of Horace at the same time that he modeled his work after him."[109]

As DeJean has shown, Boileau's attacks on women intellectuals and women's writing set the standard for future hostility. Boileau dismisses the seventeenth-century writer Mme de Scudéry in his work *L'art poetique,* warning that only those who want to produce frivolous novels

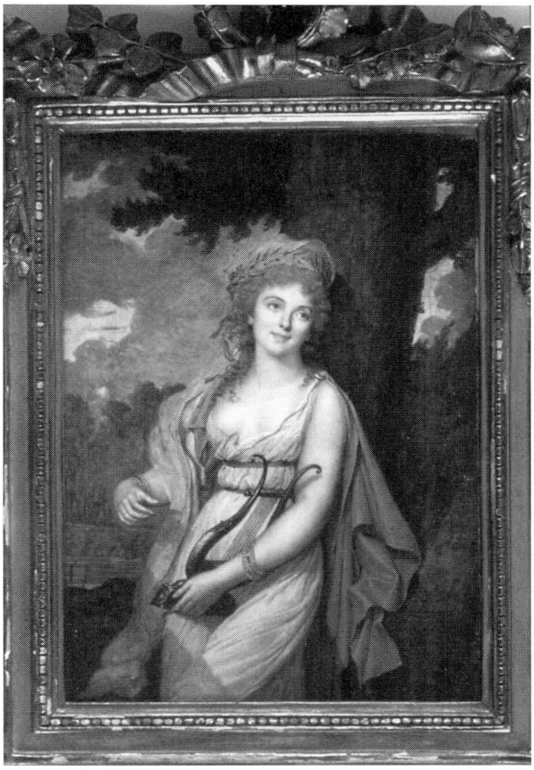

FIGURE 8. François Dumont (French, 1751–1831), *Madame de Saint-Just d'Aucourt as Sappho,* 1797. Miniature on ivory, 20.3 × 14.1 cm. Paris: Musée du Louvre. Photograph © Réunion des Musées Nationaux/Art Resource, NY.

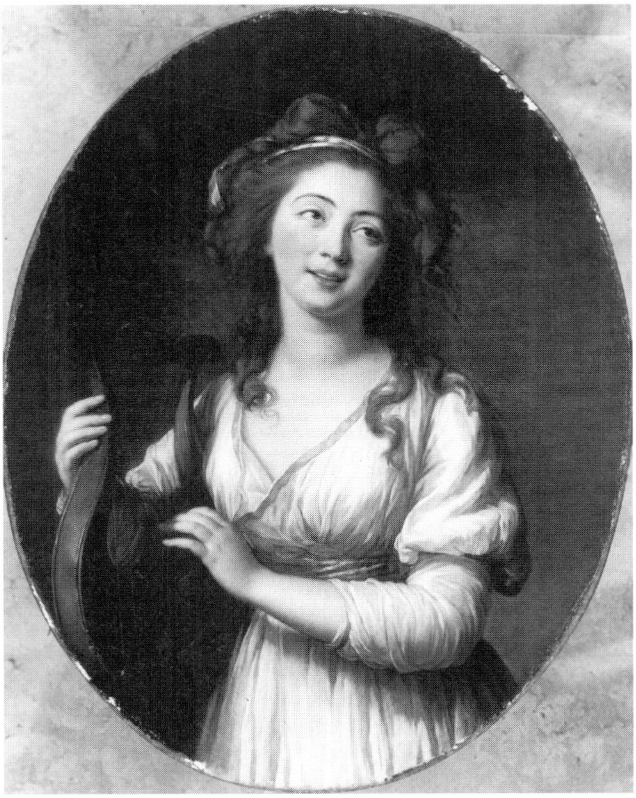

FIGURE 9. Elisabeth Vigée-Lebrun (French, 1755–1842), signature copy, *Portrait of a Young Woman Playing the Lyre; the countess Fries as Sappho,* c. 1793–94. Oil on canvas. Cincinnati, Ohio: Cincinnati Art Museum, Gift of Emilie L. Heine in memory of Mr. and Mrs. John Hauck. Photograph courtesy Cincinnati Art Museum.

should imitate her work. And in a more sustained assault (*Dialogue des héros de roman*, 1664–66), he accuses her of inventing a heroic model that threatens to weaken the male fiber on which the state relies. Rather than models of manly action, she creates flabby, effeminate heroes lacking in vigor.[110] Do not listen, he says, to this other Sappho—for that was the name Scudéry gave herself—she is not a model for emulation, she can only lead to the male body's corruption. Refusing to cross swords with Scudéry, Boileau rather condemns her by raising the specter of male effeminacy. And that specter would be increasingly powerful as medical theory propounded the idea that those who emulated the habits of woman would develop an unmanly constitution.

In emulation of Boileau, Batteux also tried to expunge from the French canon all literature deemed dangerous to civic virtue—especially the prose fiction of women writers. DeJean argues that in his *Cours de belles-lettres* (the 1747 companion to *Les beaux-arts réduits à un même principe*) Batteux completely ignores prose fiction, and if he mentions other sorts of women's writing, it is only to excoriate female authors. He deems Marie de Rabutin-Chantal, marquise de Sévigné (1626–96), a model not for men of letters but for "overly tender mothers"; and the poet Antoinette Deshoulières (ca. 1634–94), a woman whose work weakens the moral fiber through an Epicureanism "entirely opposed not only to Christian morality but also to that vigor of the soul, to that male force, that is the foundation and the support of true integrity."[111] As we have seen, Batteux allowed that male artists could become the fictive women they imagined; at the same time, he cautions them to avoid at all costs possession by an actual woman's writing.

Boileau and Batteux both warned against the emulation of women because possession by their writing could render the male artist effeminate. When Elisabeth Vigée-Lebrun wanted to portray herself as the emulator/challenger of Rubens, however, she did so in a way that neither robbed her of femininity nor him of his masculine authority. She did so indirectly in a self-portrait that pictured her as Rubens's beloved (1783; fig. 10). The artist repeated this strategy in another self-portrait, showing herself as the emulator of Raphael by appearing as the woman he loved, his Fornarina (1789; fig. 11).[112] This displacement might seem necessitated only by the artist's desire to merge herself with a specific idealized female figure invented by each of her predecessors. We might say she figures herself as the woman who inspired the portrait, not as the artist who made it. Yet her choices can also be seen as a savvy move to render more acceptable her competitive emulation of great male painters. In representing herself as the master's beloved, Vigée-Lebrun presents her emulation less as a contest and more as the sexual possession of a priestess by her god. For while no one doubted that the Pythia could

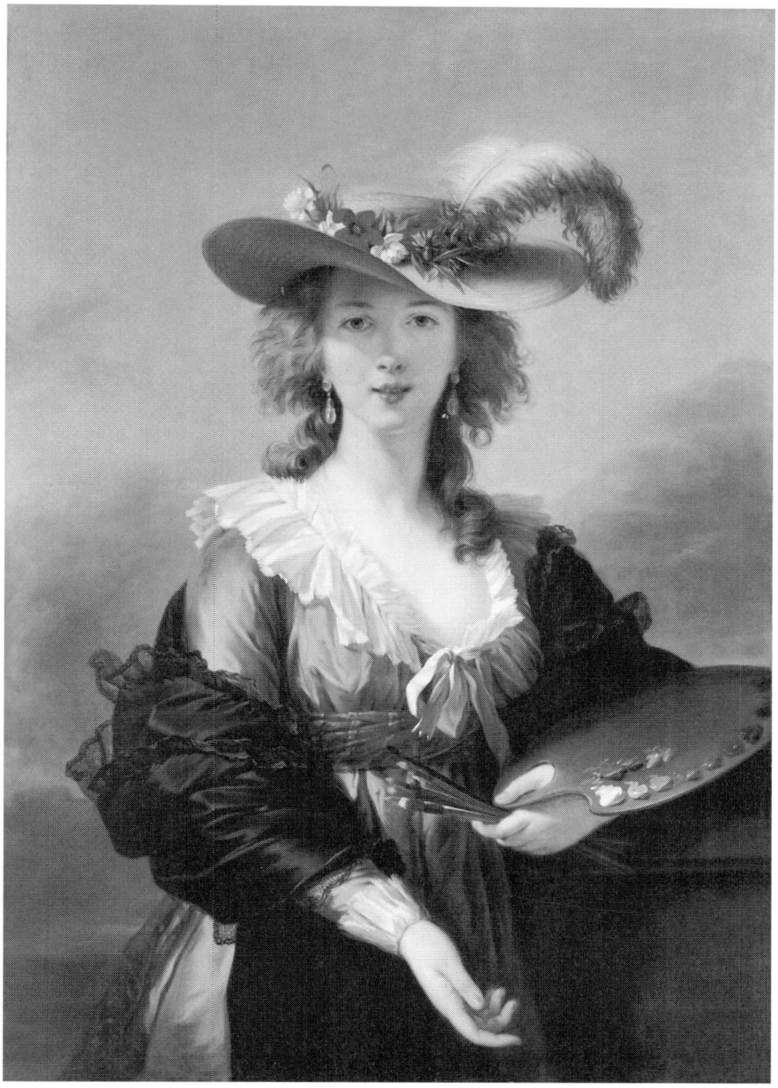

FIGURE 10. Elisabeth Vigée-Lebrun (French, 1755–1842), *Self-Portrait*, 1783. Oil on canvas, 96.8 × 70.5 cm. London: National Gallery of Art. Photograph courtesy National Gallery of Art.

be penetrated by a male pneuma, many believed women incapable of inhaling those sublime vapors emanating from the great masterpieces of art. Vigée-Lebrun could be—and was perceived as—the new Rosalba, but never was she viewed as actually challenging Raphael or Rubens.

In 1783, Vigée-Lebrun presented a particular sort of problem to conservative critics since she positioned herself not only as an emulator of the great masters but also as a history painter. Although some pamphlets from the Salon present women's emulation of (and rivalry with) men in a positive way, they either consider emulation as an abstract possibility or as limited to the lesser genres. For example, *Le véridique au sallon* compares the work of still life painter Anne Vallayer-Coster (1744–1818) with that of male artists who practiced the same genres: "At the Salon

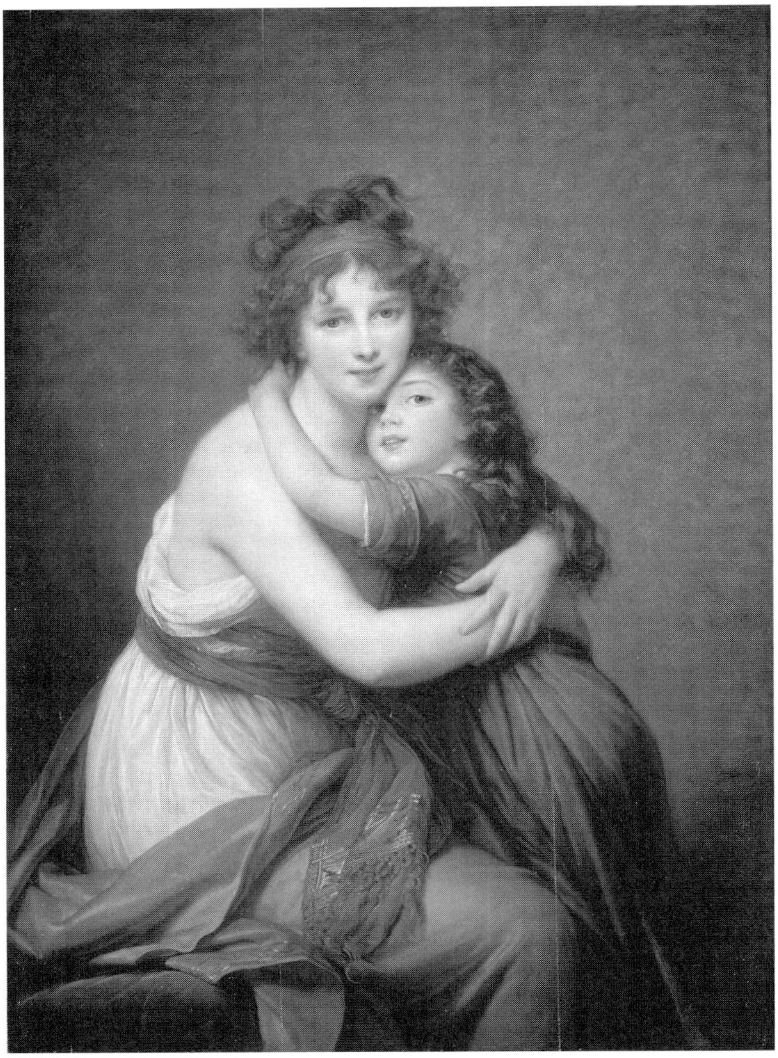

FIGURE 11. Elisabeth Vigée-Lebrun (French, 1755–1842), *Self-Portrait with Her Daughter Julie,* 1789. Oil on wood, 130 × 94 cm. Paris: Musée du Louvre. Photograph © Erich Lessing/Art Resource, NY.

we see this able painter [Vallayer-Coster] battle Monsieurs Duplessis and Roslin with her portraits, Monsieur Lépecie with her *Anxious Cook,* Monsieur Sauvage with her depiction of the attributes [of art] and finally with Monsieur Van Spaendonck."[113] Referring to Van Spaendonck and Vallayer-Coster, critics repeatedly call them "two celebrated *émules.*"

The pamphlet *Apelle au sallon* poses emulation as an abstract possibility for women: "Encourage your women with flattering tokens of esteem, Apelles said to me; if they were admitted into your schools, they would be your *émules,* and you would often see them equal you."[114] The "if" here is significant. Since there was little or no chance that women would ever be admitted into the Academy's schools, perhaps the comment suggests that women are excluded because men fear competition. Although Apelles claims it would be possible for women to equal men, there is no hint that they might surpass them, and nowhere does the writer suggest that men might come to emulate women. It is assumed that men are the more accomplished, more educated artists, and thus they are the ones women strive to equal or rival. I do not mean to imply here that male artists did not, in fact, compete with women, nor do I mean to suggest that men never imitated aspects of their work. Rather, my point is that normative constructions of masculinity made it very unlikely that they could admit doing so. That critics felt the need to warn against emulating Vigée-Lebrun, moreover, suggests that artists were tempted to imitate this popular and successful portraitist.

The warning comes at the Salon of 1787 in a pamphlet that finds her emulation of Rubens presumptuous despite her attempt to dress it up with a feminine face. In the pamphlet, *L'ombre de Rubens au sallon,* Rubens himself—or at least his ghost—draws the differences between her work and that of his true emulator Van Dyck. The text is constructed as a dialogue between Rubens's shade and another viewer simply designated as an Englishman. Rubens characterizes Vigée-Lebrun's talent as "charmant, gracieux, séduisant" but finds her color especially false, noting that "this talent has the character of her sex and hides under this seducing charm the greatest dangers for those who would want to follow this manner."[115] Here it is an artful seduction that characterizes both the woman and her art, and to be captured by this seduction is dangerous for any artist. The Englishman, who before hearing what Rubens had to say found her work beautiful and well made, admits that he is astonished: "I tell you frankly that my seduction had been absolutely complete: you have opened my eyes."[116] To which Rubens replies, "She has seduced quite a few others. Go look at Van Dyck, my student, that's the best antidote [*contrepoison*] that you can take."[117] This critic does not see that Vigée-Lebrun is possessed by Rubens, but that others must fear being possessed by the woman, emulating her seductive but poisonous charms. Vigée-Lebrun thus joins those women, those sirens, whose art could both seduce men and lead them to destruction. To emulate woman was, by the end of the century, a dangerous business.

Becoming Other

Although emulating a woman proved dangerous for the male artist, there were other ways he could safely become woman. Most theories of art making demanded a certain amount of imaginative projection into the character portrayed, and such projection anticipates the spectator's response. As Du Bos outlined in his *Réflexions critiques,* art pleases precisely by moving the spectator's passions. Viewers responded to fictional events as if they were real, experiencing the emotions they imagined to move the characters portrayed. For Du Bos, the principle merit of art lay in imitating objects that excited real passions so that the copy of the object aroused a copy of the passion.[118]

This is precisely the process Diderot's Salon reviews describe as he is both the enthusiastic viewer and the enthusiastic artist inspired by the work of another. At the exhibition Diderot is a literal spectator—one who sees with his eyes—as well as an artist—one who imagines how he will recreate the visual image in writing. And he is called upon, as he tells his readers, to recreate a variety of visual images produced by different brushes. To do his job adequately, he must enter imaginatively into all sorts of situations: "To describe a Salon to my satisfaction and yours, do you know, my friend, what it is necessary to have? All kinds of taste, a heart sensitive to all charms, a mind susceptible to an infinity of different enthusiasms, a variety of styles to respond to the variety of brushes."[119] Having described the task that faces him, Diderot challenges his readers: "Tell me, where is this Vertumnus?" What he hopes, of course, is that his writing will show him to be that god.

To identify with Vertumnus is to invoke a character in Ovid's *Metamorphoses* well known from eighteenth-century French painting. A god of the orchards and gardens, Vertumnus tries to woo the nymph Pomona, a woman who like so many of Ovid's protagonists has scorned the other sex. To gain entrance into her garden, Vertumnus assumes a variety of disguises but fails to reach his goal until he hits on the one that opens Pomona's gate and eventually her heart—that of an old woman. As the story reaches its climax, however, Vertumnus transforms himself back into a handsome god, reconciling Pomona to his manly self.

It was traditional in France to show Vertumnus not as a virile god but as an old woman, and examples include works by Nicolas Bertin (1706; Versailles: Grand Trianon) and Clément Belle (1772; Versailles: Petit Trianon) as well as the stunning version by Jean Ranc (fig. 12) painted between 1710 and 1720. It is also as an old woman that Boucher's Vertumnus seduces Pomona in the three versions of the story he painted between 1749 and 1763 (fig. 13).[120] As Vertumnus, Diderot too will transform himself into a woman when necessary to achieve his ends. His readers, however, can rest assured that as soon as he has won their hearts, he will turn back into a man.

Becoming woman was a standard part of Diderot's repertoire, as we see in his entry on Jean-Baptiste Greuze's *A Young Woman Throwing a Kiss from Her Window* shown at the Salon of 1765 (fig. 14). Mme de Grammont commissioned the painting as a New Year's gift for her lover, the duc de Choiseul, and what a seductive present it was! The image shows a young woman in her négligé leaning out of a window. One hand is caught as it releases an invisible kiss; the other as it fingers a

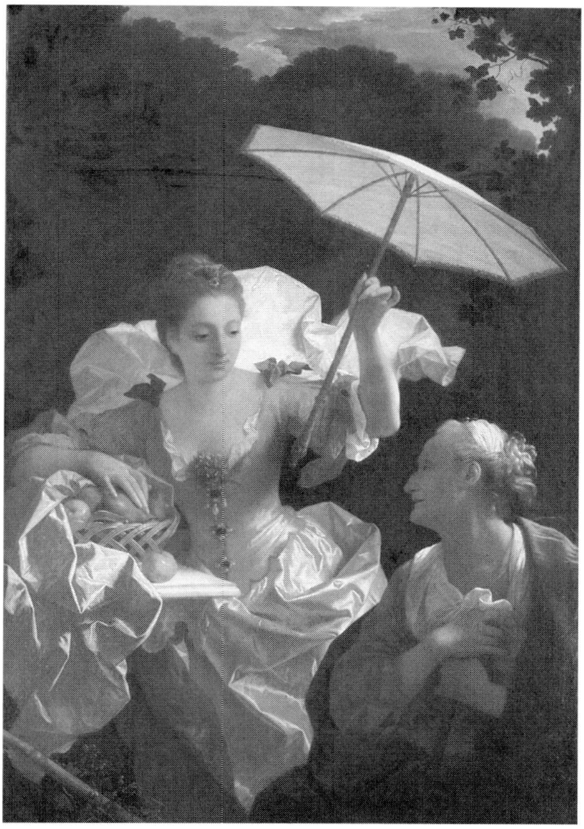

figure 12. Jean Ranc (French, 1674–1735), *Vertumnus and Pomona,* c. 1710–20. Oil on canvas, 170 × 120 cm. Montpellier, Musée Fabre. Photograph © Giraudon/Art Resource, NY.

letter—presumably a love letter just delivered—that rests on the window ledge. Reaching out over the painted ledge, this voluptuous creature sends her greeting to both an imagined lover below and the actual viewer who happens to be standing in front of the painting. As a gift to Choiseul, the painting suggests that in him both lover and viewer coincide.

Diderot is charmed by the work and begins to set and narrate a scene: "Imagine a window facing onto the street. At this window a green curtain partly open; behind this curtain a charming young girl coming out of bed and not having the time to dress. She has just received a note from her lover. This lover is passing beneath her window, and she throws him a kiss."[121] From describing the scene, the critic moves to exclaiming over the voluptuous woman, who would seem to be the ideal figure now dismembered into component parts: "Such a face! Such a mouth! Such lips! Such teeth! Such a bosom! We see this bosom, and we see it all even though it is covered with a thin veil. The left arm . . . ."[122] At this point of building excitement, the critic represents his passion through broken sentences and ellipsis.[123]

After signaling his passionate involvement with the work, Diderot switches from describing the woman as an object that arouses passion

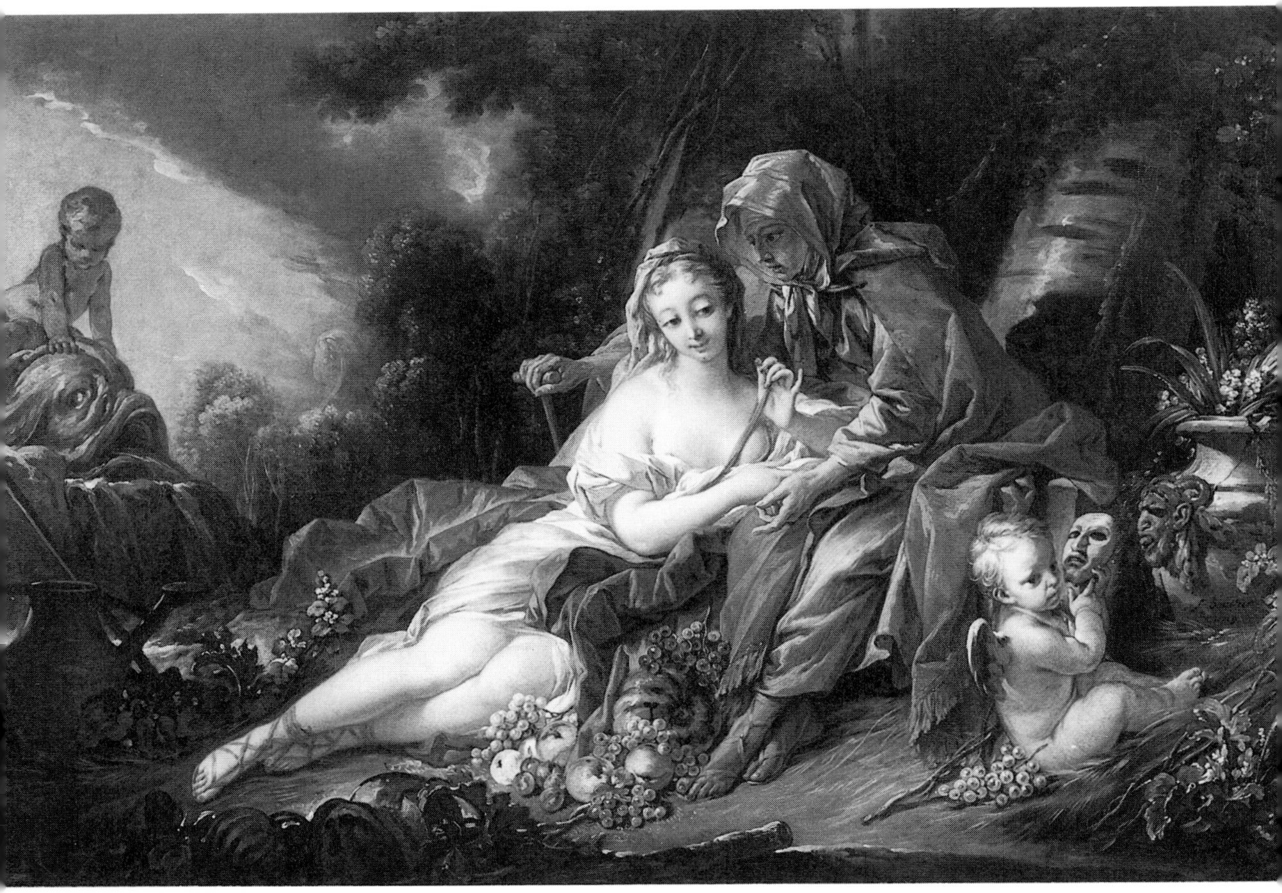

FIGURE 13. François Boucher (French, 1703–70), *Vertumnus and Pomona,* 1745. Oil on canvas, 86.84 × 136.21 cm. Columbus, Ohio: Columbus Museum of Art, Museum Purchase, Derby Fund. Photo courtesy Columbus Museum of Art.

to taking on her emotion as his own: "She's intoxicated, she's beside herself, she no longer knows what she's doing, nor I, almost, what I'm writing . . . ."[124] But the operative word here is "almost," and Diderot recovers much of his sang-froid as he extols the beauty of Greuze's execution. In doing so he dismembers Greuze's work part by part, but always in relation to the painted body. "And the subtlety of the curtain's shadow on her arm, of the shadow of those fingers on the palm of her hand, of the shadow of this hand and arm on her breast!"[125] In the end, however, Diderot's intoxication again overcomes him as the viewer-critic identifies with the woman and her desire. Indeed, the same sensuality courses through their veins. "And the voluptuous limpness that reigns from the tips of her fingers and that you follow from there into all the rest of the figure; and how this limpness carries you away and slithers into the veins of the spectator as he sees it slithering in this figure!"[126] Like enthusiasm, *volupté* is contagious; like the woman at the window, the spectator is transported. He enters into her emotion, or rather, it enters into him, turning him voluptuously limp.

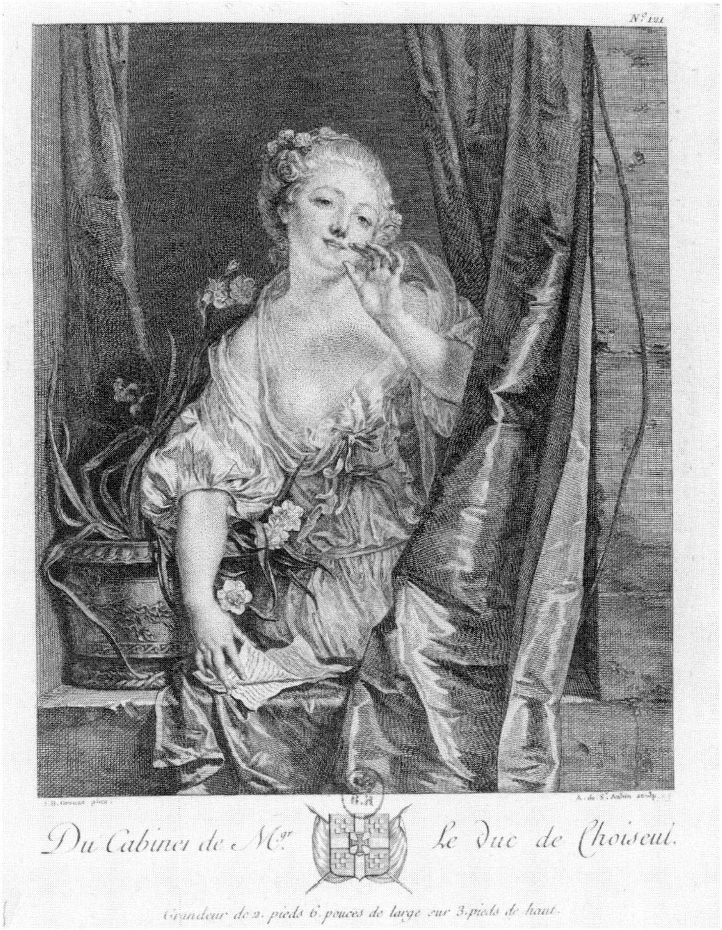

FIGURE 14. Augustin de Saint-Aubin (French; 1736–1807) after the 1765 painting by Jean-Baptiste Greuze (French; 1725–1805), *A Young Woman Throwing a Kiss from Her Window,* 1771. Engraving. Photograph © Bibliothèque Nationale de France.

In relation to fictive or painted women, it seems that the writer can become a woman while remaining a man. In the case of Greuze's *Woman at the Window,* heterosexual desire secures Diderot's position as a man, while at the same time a part of him enjoys merging with a woman's languorous state. It is the sort of troubled position that Diderot tries to explain at other points in his writing about art, for example, in describing the dynamics of the spectator.

If the critic's skills include becoming woman, the spectator's task is to divide himself into feminine and masculine sensibilities. In the "Salon of 1767," Diderot makes this point by suggesting that the spectator enjoys the work of art by simultaneously identifying with the painted figure and retaining his own subjectivity. The example is particularly interesting because in identifying with the painted figure, the spectator—here an imagined abbé—becomes not the painted figure, but a famous tragic actress, Adrienne Lecouvreur (1692–1730). The commentary is staged as an imaginary conversation between Diderot and an abbé as they gaze on a series of landscapes. The landscapes correspond to paintings by Joseph Vernet (1714–89), although Diderot writes the descriptions as though they were real terrain the two had just entered. At the fourth site, Diderot and the abbé discuss why spectators take pleasure in seeing represented events they would find tragic in real life. The discussion here reprises Du Bos's central argument in the *Réflexions critiques.* Aesthetic pleasure requires the combination of empathy and reasoned distance—we must be able to experience vicariously the character's plight and at the same time recognize that we are seeing an illusion.

Lecouvreur enters the conversation as the abbé realizes the wisdom of Diderot's position and paraphrases the theory:

> " Ah, I understand now" . . . What, Abbé? "I play two roles. I am doubled; I'm Lecouvreur and I remain myself. It's the Lecouvreur part of me that shudders and suffers and its myself *tout court* who experiences the pleasure. " . . . Very good, Abbé, and there is the limit for the imitator of nature. If I forget myself too much and for too long a time, the terror is too strong; if I don't forget myself at all, if I always remain whole, it is too weak.[127]

Diderot argues here for an ideal spectator of mixed sex—half woman, half man—and mixed sensibility—half enthusiastic actress, half distanced observer. The abbé understands that the spectator must be carried away and lose himself as Lecouvreur did in the tragic roles she played. At the same time, he must maintain his sang-froid, must make the reasoned judgment that he is not in actual danger. The self-possessed spectator then is also inhabited by a Lecouvreur possessed by her tragic role.

We see Lecouvreur in the role of Cornelia (from Pierre Corneille's 1642 play *Le mort de Pompée*) in a well-known portrait made by Charles Coypel and engraved by Pierre-Imbert Drevet about 1730–31 (fig. 15).[128] The portrait shows the actress in a part she made famous: she played Cornelia fourteen times at the Comédie Française between 1721 and 1727. And it shows her at a specific moment, interpreting a scene from act 5 in which Cornelia swears on her husband's ashes to revenge his death.

It is difficult to see in this portrait the actress merging herself in the part. The portrayal gives little sense of her actual performance; its expression (eyes turned upward to heaven) and costume are conventionally theatrical. Yet we must keep in mind that in making this work a specific *portrait,* the artist was bound to keep the individual actress from dissolving into the fictional character. We know from contemporary accounts, however, that spectators did indeed perceive Lecouvreur

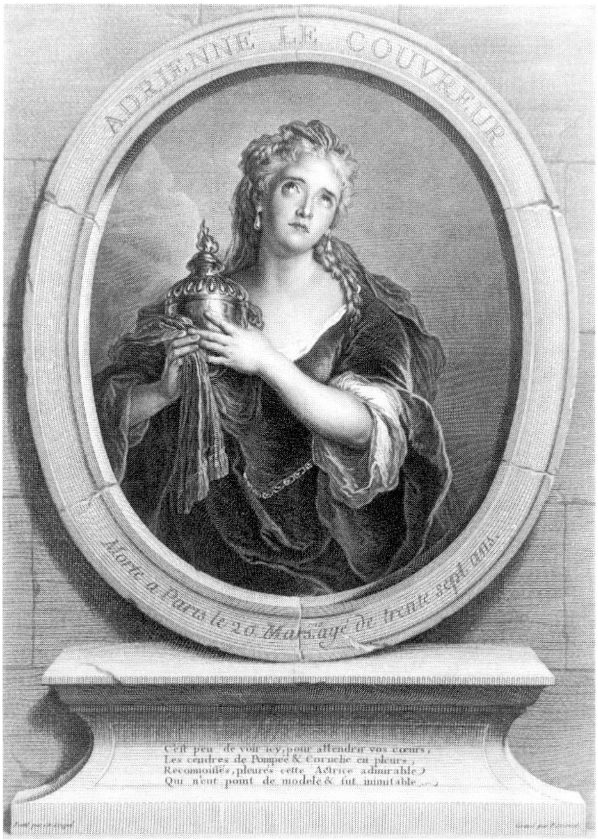

FIGURE 15. Pierre-Imbert Drevet (French, 1697–1752) after the c. 1730 painting by Charles Coypel (French, 1694–1752), *Portrait of Adrienne Lecouvreur,* 1730–31. Engraving, 40.5 × 28.6 cm. Ackland Art Museum, The University of North Carolina at Chapel Hill, Bruton Emmett Collection. Photo courtesy Ackland Art Museum.

as losing herself in her role. A critic for the *Mercure de France* explained: "[S]he has the marvelous weakness of allowing the role to overtake her, and in so doing she mistook false for true, thus communicating her own pleasure to the audience so that it too was pleased by the sweet charm of its own deception."[129] Although Adrienne Lecouvreur was not the ideal actor Diderot would tout in his *Paradoxe sur le comédien,* she was perfect for a role in his Salon pieces.[130] There she represents that part of the spectator caught up in the fiction beheld, that part able both to experience and to transmit pleasure.

Throughout the discourses of sensibility, imagination, and enthusiasm, there is evident equivocation when it comes to defining the qualities of woman and artist. On the one hand, some texts are shaped by a desire to separate the "normal" woman from the artist, and on the other, many writings allow that the "exceptional" woman can make great art. Women who aspired to creative work capitalized on the equivocations and took advantage of the "exceptions," no matter how potentially problematic. And the exceptional woman was problematic indeed; she was often sexually transgressive—as was Sappho—or a powerful woman outside the bounds of respectable society—as was the actress Clairon. Exceptional women also proved dangerous models for men's artistic emulation, as was the case for the writer Scudéry and the painter Vigée-Lebrun. Imitating their works effeminized the male artist, just as imitating woman's lifestyle and taste effeminized the "normal" man and left him unnaturally susceptible to the vapors. This dynamic held women's work outside the canon of masterpieces, for such work was not an acceptable model for emulation. That male artists could not easily admit to borrowing from women or emulating them also had added benefit—woman's work could provide a source of artistic invention that one never had to acknowledge. One could steal from women and not fear Prometheus's fate.

At the same time that women artists proved a dangerous (and convenient) model, male artists could metaphorically and imaginatively become "woman." Either they took over Pythia's tripod to inhale the divine vapors emanating from the works of other men, or they projected themselves into the women they imagined and portrayed. And the male spectator could safely become woman for the duration of his aesthetic experience. Perhaps this imaginative activity posed little threat because most often this becoming woman entailed projecting oneself into a woman as imagined by another man. In effect, through the figure of woman one man could commune with another. Such becoming woman also posed little threat because the "normal" man had adequate powers of reason and reflection; he could remain himself and play Lecouvreur at the same time. The female spectator, however, was not always so gifted, and as a "normal" woman she was less able to keep her projections under control. The illusions of art held special perils for women, whether they were the producers or the beholders of those illusions. In contrast to that of her father or brother, a woman's imagination was more likely to refuse the bit of reason. And if some creative men—actual and mythical—reaped wondrous rewards from confounding the real and the imaginary, forbidden pleasures and degrading punishments awaited the woman who fell prey to such confusions.

CHAPTER 3

Deviant Spectators: Ignorant Girls and Women Who Know Too Much

Philosophers, doctors, and theologians might agree on little else, but many found common ground on the question of woman's imagination. There was no doubt about it: to insure the smooth workings of the social order female fantasy had to be carefully controlled. But this was easier said than done, especially since a woman's power of reason was rarely strong enough to take on such an arduous task. To many, the obvious solution was to regulate what could be imprinted on a woman's imagination by controlling her access to both knowledge and culture, especially in the form of books, pictures, and spectacles.[1]

Although "experts" did not imagine that women experienced the enthusiasm that generated sublime works, they believed them ready to imagine themselves the characters in books, pictures, and plays. As we have seen, the process of becoming another had long been connected to the enthusiasm of the artist and spectator. Yet entering into a fictional character or scene could very well lead to a woman's undoing, for what passed into her imagination by way of reading, looking, or listening could easily arouse dangerous passions. Thus moralists, philosophers, and doctors deemed many kinds of spectatorship perilous for women. At best, a woman would jeopardize her modesty or damage her reputation through such reading or looking; at worst, she would fall into a dissolute life or a fatal illness. At the same time, a woman's enthusiasm might be more properly channeled if edifying stories and pictures occupied her imagination and conventional religious training led her toward virtue.

Promoting Virtue, Protecting Innocence

Eighteenth-century conduct books, such as Barthélemy-Claude Graillard de Graville's *L'ami des filles* (1761), stressed that anyone who did not guide a girl's reading material was inviting certain ruin. *L'ami des filles* recommended, for example, that young women be encouraged to take up the best historians of their own country and then those of other European peoples. But such "serious" reading could also have its dangers, for it could overtax the mind and exhaust a girl's resources. To provide young women with amusement, poetry could be judiciously added to her reading.[2] Advice manuals never proposed that girls and women be kept completely ignorant, only that their reading be carefully regulated. One popular publication, Pierre-Joseph Boudier de Villemert's *Le nouvel ami des femmes; ou, La philosophie du sexe* (1779), even claimed that to forbid all study to women was to treat them as did Mohammed, who denied them a soul only to render them more voluptuous. Although Boudier de Villemert argues that women should not take up the abstract sciences, he encourages them to read history and know something about the arts so they can make witty conversation.[3]

Throughout the eighteenth century, writers on women's education would also recommend religious reading, and they often appealed to François de Salignac de La Mothe Fénelon's 1693 *De l'education des filles.*[4] Fénelon, in fact, advises that parents encourage their daughters to read religious texts: "To make them better understand the mysteries, the actions, the maxims of Jesus Christ, one must lead young ladies to read the Gospel [l'Evangile]. One must prepare them early to read the word of God, just as one prepares them to receive through communion the flesh of Jesus Christ."[5] In 1749, the artist Jean-Baptiste Chardin pictured this practice in *The Good Education* (fig. 16), which represents a young girl reciting the Gospel.[6]

Chardin sets *The Good Education* in a modest, though comfortable salon where a young woman—it is unclear whether she is a mother or governess—is educating a little girl. Although in the Salon commentaries there is some confusion as to the relation between the woman and the girl, the *livret* makes clear the nature of her reading: she is learning her Gospels.[7] This edifying scene takes place before a window where we see a mature, but still youthful, woman holding an open book on her lap atop a piece of needlework. Having abandoned her embroidery, the teacher looks toward her pupil who stands facing her with bowed head, lowered gaze, and hands clasped in front of her waist. The composition levels out the difference in height between adult and child, and they face one another directly. Silhouetting the figures against a blank and darkened wall further emphasizes their encounter. This strategy isolates the teacher's gaze upon the student, and the light streaming through the window underlines that gaze, following it from left to right. The teacher's look thus seems connected to the shaft of light, as if the good education

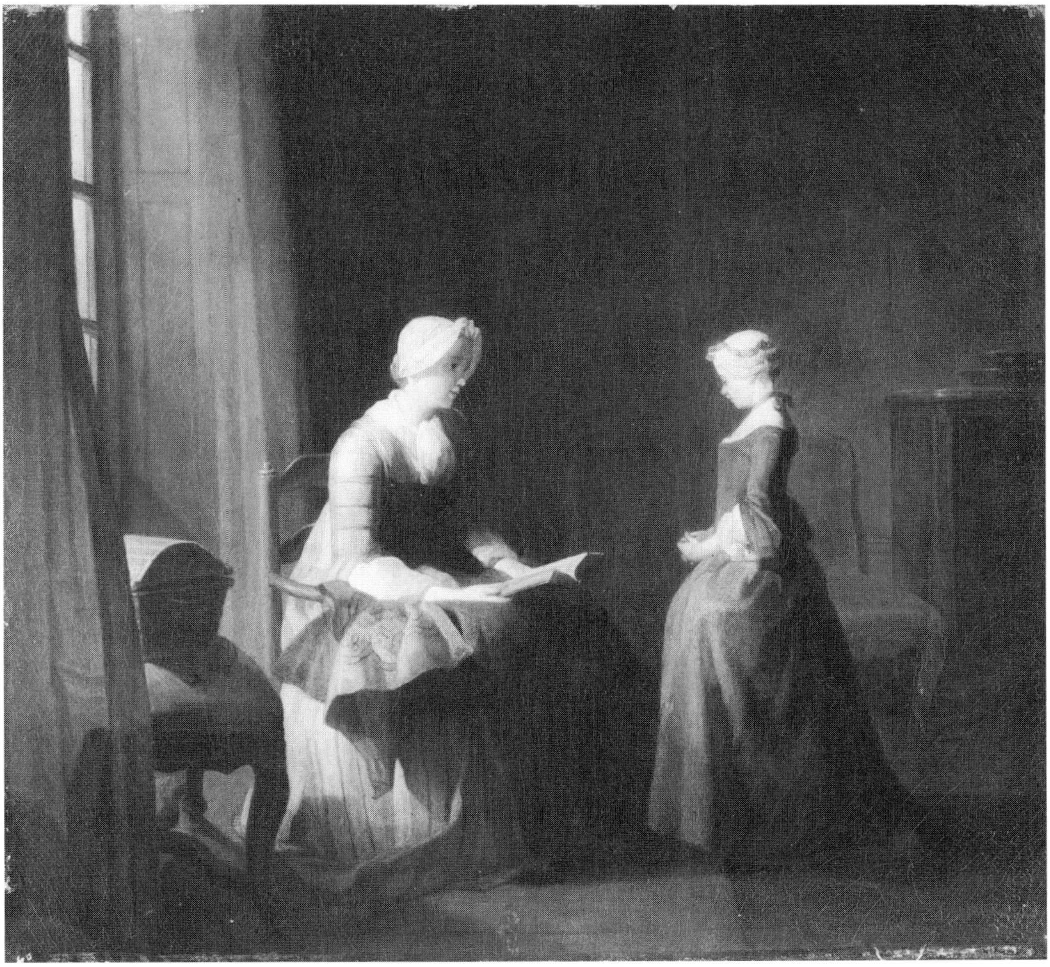

FIGURE 16. Jean-Baptiste Chardin (1699–1779), *The Good Education*, 1749. Oil on canvas, 41 × 47 cm. Sweden: Wanås Collection. Photo courtesy Nationalmuseum Stockholm.

she proffers through the Gospels will illuminate, perhaps even sanctify, the young girl.

The restrained and sober exchange we see in *The Good Education* emphasizes the mental process at work, and the scene suggests the serious labor of memorizing rather than the pleasures of imagination. In his comments on the painting, one critic saw in the young girl's expression the effort of reciting from memory for she stands with lowered eyes before her teacher. The instructor's "pedantic" air he attributed to her insistence that the child repeat her lessons.[8] Indeed, repetition and memorization seem to imprint the correct sentiments on her mind. In the little girl's upright posture, deferential attitude, and careful grooming, the image suggests not only that she is disciplined but also that she is modest, and both virtues are implied through the lowered head and eyes.

The significance of *The Good Education* is deepened when we view it alongside the work listed in the Salon *livret* as its pendant: *The Drawing*

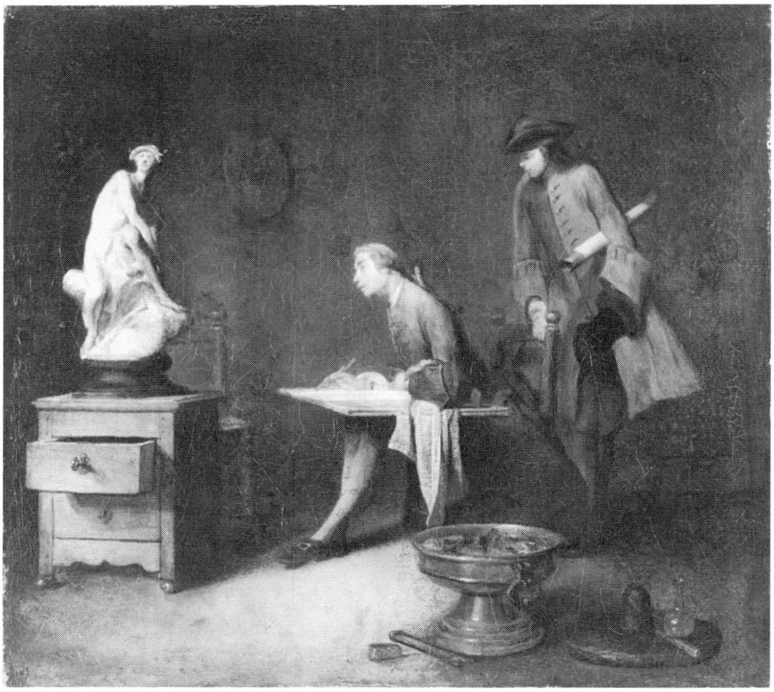

FIGURE 17. Jean-Baptiste Chardin (1699–1779), *The Drawing Lesson,* 1749. Oil on canvas, 41 × 47 cm. Sweden: Wanås Collection. Photograph courtesy Nationalmuseum Stockholm.

Lesson (1749; fig. 17). In this work we see a young artist drawing after a piece of sculpture, Jean-Baptiste Pigalle's *Mercury* of 1744. In contrast to the young girl who learns her Gospels, the artist raises his gaze, all the better to look closely at the object he studies. The figure standing behind him could be another student, as some critics suggested, but the relation between the two is not clear. He looks over the draftsman's shoulder, but neither interferes nor directs, nor seems to comment on the work in progress. For his part, the draftsman gives no sign that he notices the other figure. Far from simple repetition, the artist's task is to translate a three-dimensional object onto a two-dimensional surface.

In *The Drawing Lesson,* Chardin's purpose may have been to say something about the concentration and imagination needed to make art, or even about the tasks appropriate for an apprentice. When *The Drawing Lesson* is paired with *The Good Education,* however, the works together suggest what is appropriate for minds that inhabit differently sexed bodies. In his lesson, the young man not only practices drawing but also mythology (he studies the figure of Mercury), anatomy, and the science of perspective. He is groomed to participate in the making of culture as he trains to be an artist. For the little girl, reading and memorizing the Gospels encourages not only a particular sort of mental discipline but also the assimilation of moral principles and religious belief. Such an education was designed not only to give women the fundamentals of their faith but also to restrain their imaginations and instill a sense of modesty.

While appropriate historical or religious reading could help shape a woman's mind, reading novels and mystical writings were suspicious activities, especially for young girls. Since the seventeenth century, moralists, philosophers, and even some literary critics harped on the dangers of reading novels or romances, and they found women especially vulnerable to their effects. As Joan DeJean has shown, Boileau engineered the most vicious and long-lasting assaults. In his *Satire on Women* (1694), for example, he depicts the corruption of a virtuous woman inspired by reading Mme de Scudéry's novel *Clélie* and presents novel reading as a contagious disease that corrupts female readers, and with them all of French society.[9] That the novel developed in the hands of women writers was, of course, an additional reason for its denigration. Despite Pierre-Daniel Huet's defense of the novel as educational for young women in his 1670 *Traité de l'origine des romans,* suspicion of novel reading remained high.[10]

Eighteenth-century advice manuals and volumes like *L'ami des filles* or Jean-Baptiste Drouet de Maupertuis's *La femme faible* (1733) or Madeleine Darsant de Puisieux's *Conseils à une amie* (1749) all presented to readers the fatal consequences of indulging in love stories. Here, for example, is what a woman would learn about reading a romance in *La femme faible:* "You have drunk this poison with pleasure; it has passed from your imagination to your mind, from your mind to your heart, from your heart to your reason."[11] Such reading finally corrupts everything. *L'ami des filles* even includes a cautionary tale, the story of Olimpe, whose friend lends her a romance. The novel inflames her internal fires, whets her appetite for more novels, and leads her to mistake sex for love. Giving herself to the first comer, Olimpe ends up in the "infamous traffic" of prostitution.[12]

Images, too, could have their effect, especially if they were suggestive or erotic. Diderot opens his comments on Pierre-Antoine Baudouin's paintings at the Salon of 1765 with these remarks: "A nice young man, who is good-looking, kind, witty, a bit libertine. But what is that to me? My wife has passed her forty-fifth year, and he won't get near my daughter, neither he nor his compositions."[13] The critic here implies that Baudouin's works are dangerous for women, especially daughters, and goes on to characterize as "libertine" Baudouin's *Peasant Girl Quarreling with Her Mother* and *The Cherry Picker* (fig. 18). Known through Nicolas Ponce's engravings, the first shows a mother catching her daughter just as she was about to give herself to a lover now fleeing up a stairway, and the second uses a crude symbol—two cherries dangling beneath a pointed finger—in a scene of veiled sexual proposition. Neither is

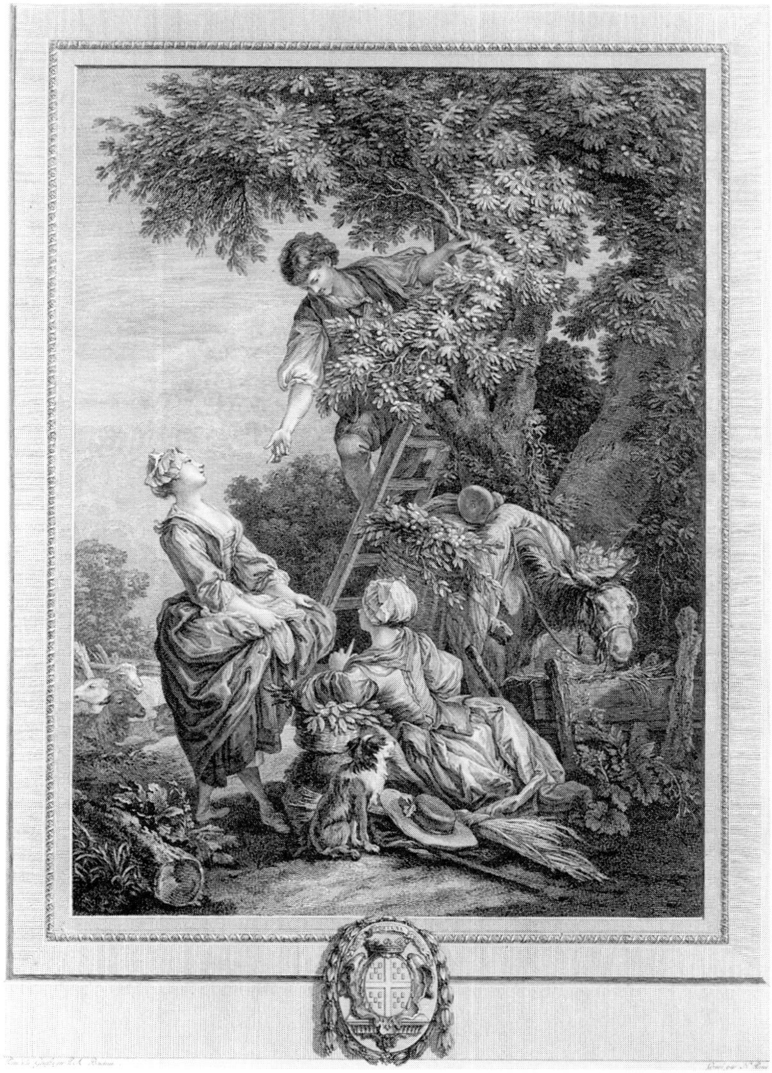

FIGURE 18. Nicolas Ponce (French, 1746–1831) after the painting by Pierre-Antoine Baudouin (French, 1723–69), *The Cherry Picker,* shown at the Salon of 1765. Etching and engraving. Widener Collection. Washington, D.C.: National Gallery of Art. Photograph © 2002 Board of Trustees, National Gallery of Art, Washington, D.C.

overt in its depiction of sexual encounter; neither shows a lascivious display of the body, and both would have circulated openly. It is these works, moreover, that Diderot claims attracted all the young girls who studied them attentively: "At the Salon there were many little paintings by Baudouin and all the young girls, after having cast a distracted eye on some other paintings, finished their tour at the place where you see his *Peasant Girl Quarreling with Her Mother* and *The Cherry Picker.* It was for this window bay that they reserved all their attention. At a certain age one would rather read a libertine book than a good book, and one would rather stand before a smutty picture than a good one."[14]

In the middle of his commentary on Baudouin's work at the next Salon in 1767, Diderot addresses artists on the dangers—to them and to society—of making indecent paintings. "Artists, if you are keen to make your works last, I advise you to stick to decent subjects. Everything that preaches depravation is marked for destruction, and the most perfect works much more surely so."[15] What attacks these works is "probity, virtue, morality, and scruple," and Diderot warns artists that "the petty superstitious minds will sooner or later get their hands on indecent works."[16] But what is their scruple? The fear that indecent works corrupt good women and innocent sons and daughters. Addressing his comments to fathers and husbands, Diderot asks:

> Who among us, possessing a masterpiece of painting or sculpture capable of inciting debauchery, would not attempt to hide it from the sight of his wife, his daughter, his son? . . . Which of us would not declare in the depths of his heart that talent could be better used, that such a work should not be made, and that there would be merit in destroying it? What is there to choose between a painting and statue, however perfect it might be, and the corruption of an innocent heart?[17]

The Protean critic here becomes a man with petty scruples, a reasonable man who admits he would not blame the "decent, barbarous" one who dashed to pieces a great but indecent work of art. Given that this commentary is placed in the middle of Diderot's discussion of Baudouin, it would seem related to that painter's work, which in the previous Salon Diderot pictures as riveting the attention of young women. Diderot stresses that he is concerned particularly with daughters, even with his own daughter: "I can't pretend that a wicked book or indecent print that by chance is brought to my daughter wouldn't be sufficient to set her to dreaming and lead to her ruin."[18]

Diderot fears that in her daydreams his daughter might imagine herself the heroine of a wicked book or indecent print. A similar fear had already been set out in Condillac's psychology, where even reading classic literature—like the works of Tasso—could endanger a young woman's sanity, for

> their minds, which are too little occupied with educational things, avidly seize upon fictions pandering to the passions natural to their age. In them they find material for the most beautiful castles in Spain. They exploit those materials with even more pleasure as their desire to please, and the gallantry that they are shown supports them unceasingly in this taste. Then it takes only a slight disappointment to turn the head of a young girl, to persuade her that she is Angelica or some other heroine who has pleased her, and makes her take for Medoro every man who approaches her.[19]

But it was not only reading love stories and romances that imperiled women, as Condillac was quick to point out. Reading works like the autobiography of Saint Teresa of Avila (1515–82) put them in as much danger as a novel that transported them to Cythera. Condillac warned that novels were dangerous for women, "whose brains are very impressionable," and so were devotional books. "These books can sometimes turn a woman's brain until she is made to believe that she has visions or converses with angels or even that she is already with them in heaven."[20] The mystic Teresa herself provided a prototype for the young woman reader engrossed by a chivalric romance. This aspect of her life she recounts with regret her in autobiography: "I thought there was nothing wrong in wasting many hours, by day and by night, in this useless occupation, even though I had to hide it from my father. So excessively was I absorbed in it that I believe, unless I had a new book, I was never happy."[21] In the very next section Teresa goes onto describe how she also became interested in her appearance and aware of her power to attract.

Devotion Materialized

Devotion, sexuality, and reading came together in Saint Teresa's image as well as in her name. The most famous representation of Saint Teresa's ecstasy is surely Gianlorenzo Bernini's sculpture (fig. 19) completed in 1652.[22] For twentieth-century interpreters, the expression of Saint Teresa and the nature of her ecstasy have seemed clear. Here is Jacques Lacan's well-known assessment: "[Y]ou only have to go and look at Bernini's statue in Rome to understand immediately that she's coming, there is no doubt about it."[23] Perhaps Lacan is so sure because so many others had already interpreted the sculpture in this way. Accounts of travelers from the late eighteenth and early nineteenth centuries offered the same conclusion, although in language a bit more veiled. The artist Elisabeth Vigée-Lebrun, for example, puts it delicately, and at the same time shows the disapproval necessary to demonstrate her own modesty: "I don't know if it is necessary to say that one sees in the Church of Santa Maria della Vittoria the famous *Saint Teresa* of Bernini, whose scandalous expression cannot be described."[24] Without similar social constraints, Stendhal in *Promenades dans Rome* can joke about the possible mix-up of sacred and profane love:

> Saint Teresa is represented in the ecstasy of divine love. It is the most vivid and the most natural expression. An angel holding an arrow in one hand seems to bare his chest to pierce it to the heart. He looks at her with a tranquil expression and smiles. What divine artistry! What voluptuousness! Our good monk, believing that we did not understand it, explained the group to us. "È un gran peccato [i.e., It's a terrible

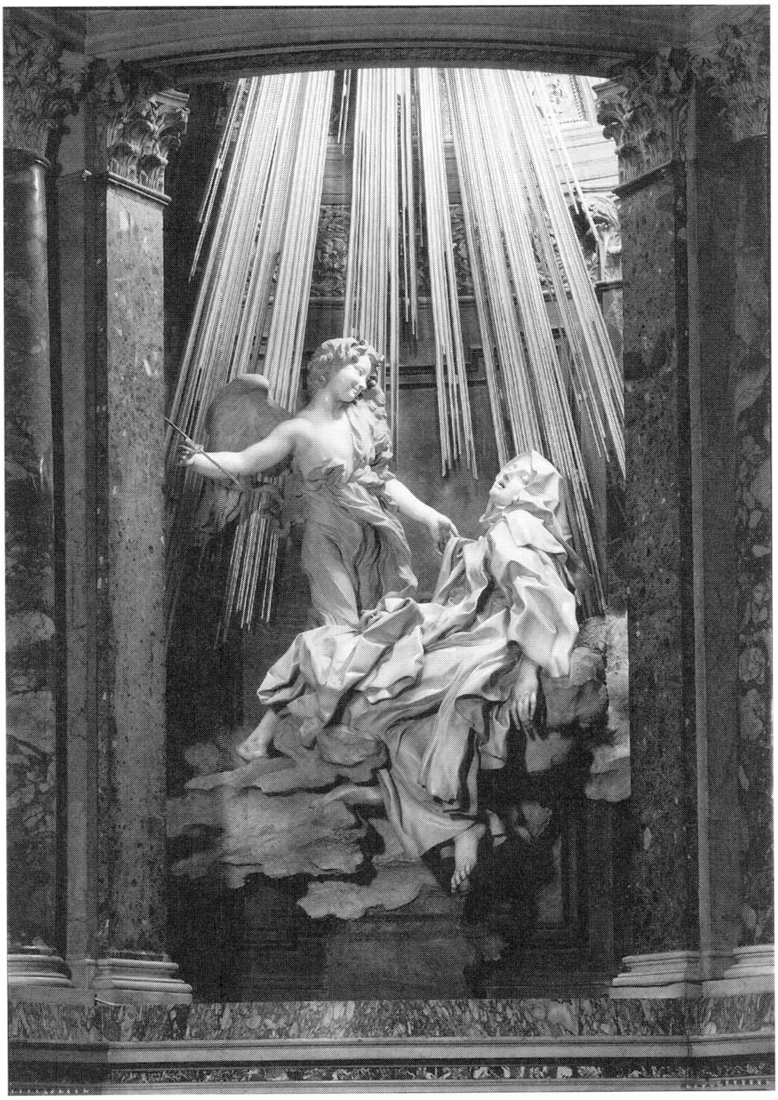

FIGURE 19. Gianlorenzo Bernini (1598–1680), *Saint Teresa in Ecstasy,* 1647–52. Marble, 3.5 meters in height. Rome: Santa Maria della Vittoria, Coronaro Chapel. Photograph © Scala/Art Resource, NY.

> shame]," he told us, "that these statues can easily convey the idea of a profane love." We forgave Bernini all the harm he has done to the arts. Has the chisel of the Greeks made anything equal to the head of Saint Teresa? In this statue Bernini has succeeded in translating the most passionate letters of the young Spanish woman.[25]

Although Stendhal can joke about the confusion, mistaking Saint Teresa's sacred love for the profane variety had been no laughing matter for those who analyzed the ecstasies at Saint-Médard. In his *Lettre sur la convulsionnaire en extase; ou, La vaporeuse en rêve,* Hecquet was at pains to prove that the convulsions experienced by Charlotte, an older woman, were not the *ravissement* of a Saint Teresa, not a divine ecstasy in which the soul was fixed on spiritual objects. He advanced his argument by contrasting the symptoms of divine ecstasy with those of hysteria. Divine *ravissement* showed none of the extraordinary movements in the muscles of the arms, legs, chest, or lower belly common to the fits of both hysterics and *convulsionnaires*.[26] Despite the attempts to differentiate their symptoms, however, the ease of confusing spiritual and sexual ecstasy fueled erotic and pornographic literature, and in particular, *Thérèse Philosophe*. It is no coincidence that the mystic from Avila shares her name with the eponymous heroine of the eighteenth-century novel.[27]

Published anonymously in 1748, *Thérèse Philosophe* was well known to eighteenth-century readers and, as Robert Darnton has shown, dominated the bestseller list until the end of the Old Regime.[28] In the novel's first section, "Dirrag and Eradice," an unscrupulous confessor, one Father Dirrag, seduces a gullible Mlle Eradice by leading her deliberately to confuse spiritual and sexual ecstasy.[29] Indeed, it seems this is not the only time that Dirrag has performed this miracle of transformation, for he takes as his special province "the self-proclaimed *Dévotes*, enthusiasts, quietists, and fanatics."[30] Mlle Eradice indeed fits these models: "She was dominated by a passion for distinguishing herself from her companions . . . This passion, joined to a great fund of tenderness, made her choose the path of the *Dévotes* as most appropriate to her project. She loved God as one loves a lover."[31] Eradice, moreover, thinks only of satisfying her immoderate desire to perform miracles. Consumed by this passion—and undoubtedly others—she is easy prey for the libidinous confessor who trains her in the "spiritual exercises" that will bring her to holy rapture.

Father Dirrag warms up for these exercises by flagellating Mlle Eradice and then proceeds to penetrate her with what he calls the "cord of Saint Francis," which is, of course, nothing else but his erect penis. (Indeed, the scene mixes up the Jansenist *convulsionnaires*, Jesuit spiritual exercises, and the Capuchin obsession with the cord that bound Saint Francis's habit). In seducing Eradice, Dirrag encourages her to experience orgasm as religious exaltation, to confuse bodily pleasure and spiritual *ravissement*. At the moment of her climax, Eradice cries out that she is feeling celestial happiness and that her mind is completely detached from matter.[32] She later tells her friend Thérèse that she has seen paradise unveiled and has experienced angelic bliss. Thérèse, however, is not taken in. With Eradice's connivance, she has witnessed the so-called spiritual exercises and recognized them for what they are.

Looking at Books

The confusion between sexual and religious enthusiasm becomes a question of reading in the visual arts. There the saintly Teresa whose

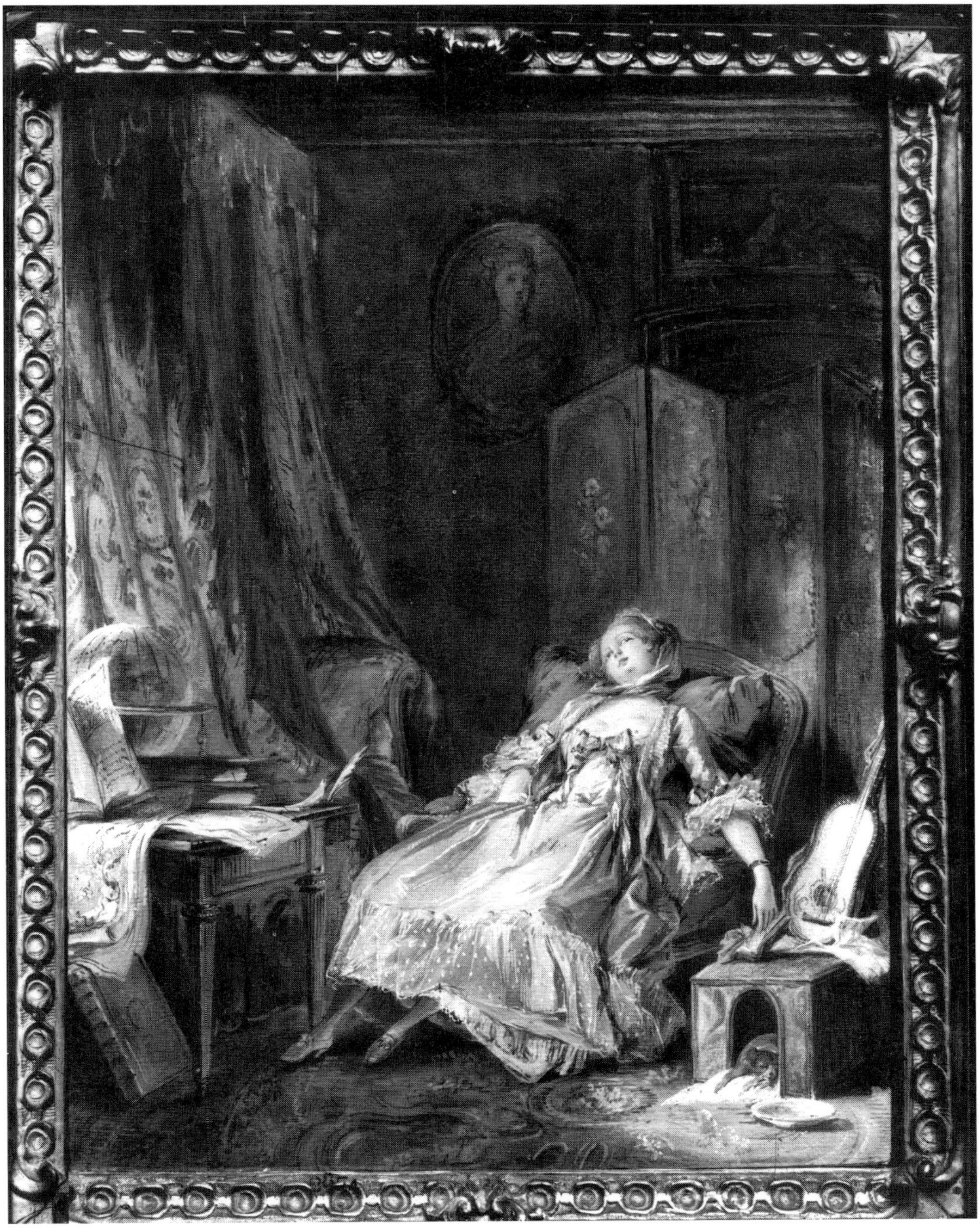

inspiration comes from on high is transformed into a masturbating woman whose hand has slipped down low. When attached to the female figure in eighteenth-century France, versions of Saint Teresa's pose often appeared in erotic or pornographic paintings and prints, for example, in Baudouin's *Reading* (*La Lecture*, c. 1765; fig. 20). Like Bernini, Baudouin marks woman's ecstasy on her collapsing body; her head is thrown back

FIGURE 20. Pierre-Antoine Baudouin (1723–69), *La Lecture (Reading)*, c. 1765. Gouache. Paris: Musée des Arts Decoratifs. Photograph courtesy Union Centrale des Arts Décoratifs.

and to the side and her left arm hangs limply. But in Baudouin's image no angel's dart pierces her soul, no confessor's cord penetrates her body. Rather, she has aroused herself, and we can see that her hand lingers beneath her skirt at the point where we imagine her legs parting. What has provoked this reader to self-stimulation is the small book—presumably a novel or romance—that slips from her grasp. The book might contain an explicitly pornographic tale, a libertine adventure, or even just a love story, for any of these could set women on a reckless course. Yet Baudouin's reader is not an ignorant girl in the first throes of erotic longing. Libertine images like *Reading* often expressed the pleasures, rather than the dangers, of self-stimulation. Her surroundings show her to be a woman of means at her leisure in a private, intimate space ruled by the cupids who frolic above her door in simulated bas-relief.

Alone in her boudoir, this reader swoons with delight. Baudouin's image suggests her abandonment not only through her expression and pose but also through her costume. The bodice of her uncorseted gown is loosened and pulled down beneath her breasts, and her skirt is raised up to reveal nicely turned ankles. Only her head is modestly covered. This deshabille is matched by the room's physical disarray. We see papers falling over the edge of her writing desk, books propped up on the floor, sheet music lying on the doghouse, and the curtains of her day bed suggestively parted. Baudouin renders the room in a *beau désordre* that we can imagine extending to the reader's unruly imagination as well. The work is hardly subtle, and sexuality spreads to every aspect of the image. The dreams of her little lap dog—the constant companion and sometime erotic partner of fashionable ladies—seem as sweet as those of his mistress as he snoozes in his satin lair.[33] Perched atop the doghouse are not only the book she still touches but also a guitar and sheet music. The guitar refers simultaneously to a fashionable woman's musical accomplishments, to an instrument of seduction, and to the shape of the female body. Indeed, the guitar is set upright, leaning against the screen, so that its curving form will parallel that of the woman who sits alongside it. Perhaps as a stringed instrument, it also suggests the vibrations she has set into motion with her fingers, twanging the cords of her delicate nervous system.

Despite this display of sexuality, however, Baudouin contrives to give his viewers the pleasure of forbidden looking. While the woman and her bed chamber are opened up, the room itself is closed off, for a fashionable screen decorated with painted roses blocks the door and seems to insure his reader's privacy. Adjacent to the left corner of the screen, Baudouin hangs a woman's portrait. Is this the reader's image adorning her room, or that of some friend or ancestor? This painted onlooker might suggest the voyeur who typically hides behind screens in eighteenth-century plays and pictures, but her head is turned away and her eyes look beyond the reader. Does she gape in disapproval, mocking the modest woman shocked by this reader's display? Or is she there because her looking away makes our gazing seem all the naughtier?

Looking carefully around this private space, the voyeur sees a fashionable room gotten up in the latest style, replete with signs of both love and learning. To the right of the bed alcove and prominent in the composition is a writing table with its pen and inkwell, and on the table are large, leather-bound books. These are not novels but learned tomes, perhaps even some volumes of the *Encyclopédie.* Before we open these books, however, more needs to be said about fiction reading, about the enthusiasm it provoked, and the dangers it brought. As we shall see, the question of reading turned on the content of what was read and the site of reading as well as the bent of woman's imagination.

Reading Women

Reading causes an obvious transgression of moral and religious codes in Baudouin's image of a woman masturbating, but eighteenth-century viewers saw in other "ingeniously veiled" works, which may seem to us perfectly innocent, the possibility of transgression or at least the dream of love. Here I am borrowing a term from *L'ami des filles* who especially warned against works in which "indecency is ingeniously veiled." The subtly erotic works might be even more dangerous than overtly pornographic ones since they can catch one unawares. At least one contemporary viewer was on record for seeing such dangers in Chardin's *The Amusements of Private Life* (fig. 21) exhibited at the Salon of 1747.

The painting shows a woman seated comfortably in an armchair, her back resting against a pillow. The chair's straight lines and rather meager proportions make it significantly different from the wide, curving one in which Baudouin's reader splays herself. Indeed, Chardin's entire image seems more spare than sensuous, and no collapsing swoon suggests that his reader is overcome with pleasure. Her costume is modest, perhaps excessively so, and Chardin fastens down her garments so the only flesh we see is that of hand and face, although the sides of her bonnet even shield her cheeks. We know that this reader's fingers have not strayed, since she holds the book in her left hand while she grips that wrist with her right. And we can infer from her crossed ankles and knees seemingly pulled together beneath her skirt that her legs are not secretly open. Beside her sits the type of small spinning wheel aristocratic ladies used, and it signifies an acceptable female pastime. But what private amusement is depicted, since Chardin does not show her either spinning or reading? She has put her book aside, but from the way she inserts

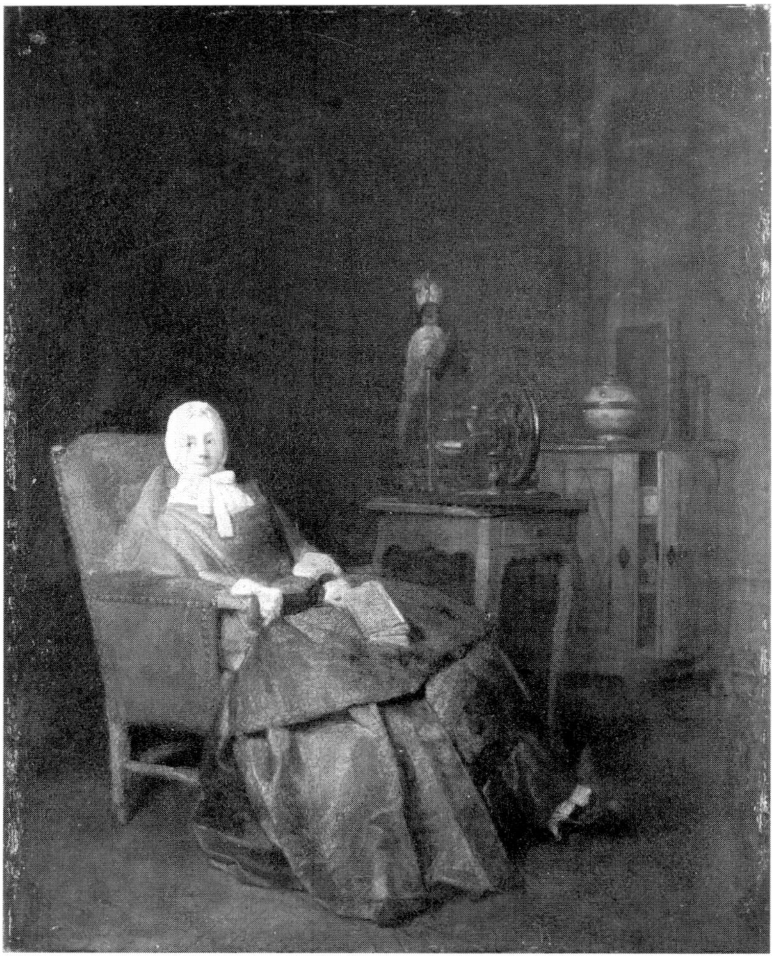

FIGURE 21. Jean-Baptiste Chardin (1699–1779), *The Amusements of Private Life,* Salon of 1747. Oil on canvas, 42.5 × 35 cm. Stockholm: Nationalmuseum. Photo courtesy Nationalmuseum Stockholm.

a finger into its pages we can assume she is holding her place and will soon take up the story where she left off. Her head is turned slightly to the right, and although she looks out of the picture, she makes no eye contact with the viewer.

The reader's look was the giveaway for one contemporary critic who had this to say in the *Observations sur les arts:*

> It represents a woman seated nonchalantly in an armchair and holding in one hand a novel, which rests on her knees. From a sort of languor that dominates her eyes, which she fixes on a corner of the painting, one surmises that she reads a novel and that the tender impressions that she has received make her dream of someone that she would like to see arrive.[34]

And perhaps to this observer other signs also suggested this reading: the spinning wheel abandoned for the book shows that this lady has given up the work appropriate for occupying women's time and has turned instead to the pleasures of imagination. The distaff that forms the strongest vertical line of Chardin's composition was long a recognized phallic symbol; and to spin, a pun on sexual intercourse. The cabinet slightly ajar lends a note of disarray to an otherwise carefully laid out and sparely furnished scene. The reader is placed, moreover, near the curving table legs, which themselves mimic the female body, and her finger placed in the book might also be construed as suggestive. How easy it is to slide from the hint of a love story to imagining a full-fledged sexual image, at least when a woman reads.[35]

I do not mean to imply that all images of women with books intentionally represent frivolous fantasy or overt sexual transgression, although here I am especially interested in those that do, for they have a particular relation to the discourse of enthusiasm. It must be said that the visual arts also represented other sorts of relations between women and books, some of them distant from the issues raised here. Consider, for example, the case of portraits in which the sitter presumably has some control over her representation.

Portraits of women holding, or even seated near, books are rare in seventeenth-century France, and despite a definite increase, they are not particularly common in the next hundred years either. It hardly bears repeating that during this time women were generally considered unfit for learning and as a group had lower rates of literacy than men did. Men much more often than women are shown reading, holding, or sitting near books. Part of this difference can also be explained by the professions portrayed, professions that included many men but few, if any, women. Books identified authors, philosophers, magistrates, scientists, clerics, and so forth. Among those women sitters portrayed with books, a high percentage belonged to religious orders and for them the book could be both a marker of profession as well as a sign of devotion. Elite women who were by and large the subjects of portraits usually had no "profession," and they were most often shown with flowers, letters, sheet music, children, miniatures, pets, ribbons, or if in allegorical disguise, with an appropriate attribute. Some, like Mme du Châtelet, whose portraits show her with books and astronomical instruments, are obvious exceptions.[36] After the mid-eighteenth century, and especially in the 1780s and 1790s, women sitters who are neither authors nor nuns appeared much more frequently with books, although these portraits still only constitute a modest share of the overall production.

Given the widespread notions about reading women, one might well ask how artists could veer away from any suggestion of impropriety. They could, for example, avoid that languid look the critic found evident in Chardin's *The Amusements of Private Life*. Careful attention to the pose,

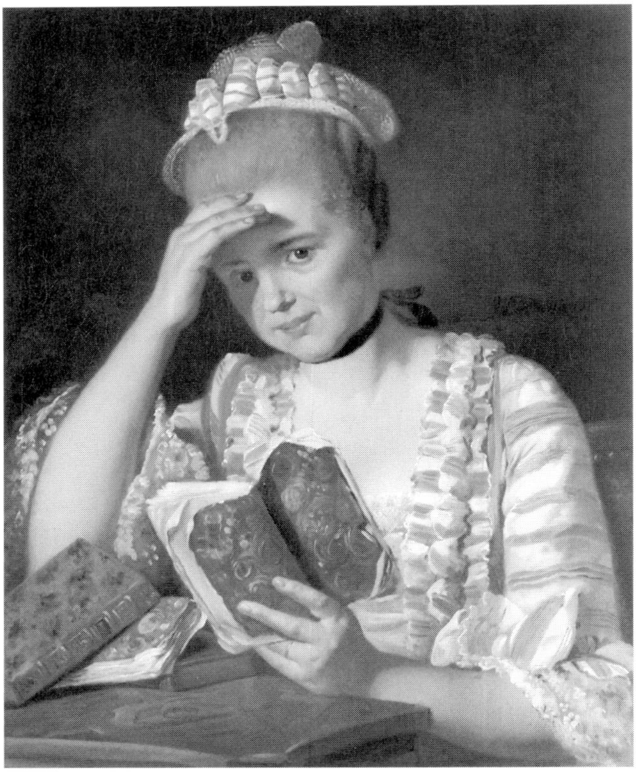

FIGURE 22. Jacques-Louis David (French, 1748–1825), *Portrait of Madame Buron*, 1769. Oil on canvas, 66.3 × 55.5 cm. Restricted gift of Mrs. Albert J. Beveridge in memory of her mother, Abby Louise Spencer (Mrs. Augustus Eddy), 1963.205. Chicago: The Art Institute of Chicago.

costume, and accoutrements would also help reduce the chances of an immodest reading. In his *Portrait of Madame Buron* (1769; fig. 22), for example, the young Jacques-Louis David depicts an aunt for whom he had great affection, and thus I assume he did not "intend" any salacious meaning to be attached to her portrayal. Mme Buron is seated at a simple desk holding a brochure in her left hand. She threads her fingers through that brochure in such a way that the viewer can see a sentimental ring, which suggests her legitimate status as someone's wife. Not only do we notice that the book she holds is well thumbed—its edges and soft cover are obviously bent and curled—but the three other books forming a still life next to her look equally used. Here we see the young artist experimenting with the sort of arrangements that eighteenth-century painters used to render their images more picturesque. Although this piling hints at a *beau désordre,* nothing else is out of place in either the room or the woman's demeanor and clothing. Her dress is modest, her coiffure as carefully regulated as her expression.

It almost seems that Mme Buron has been combing through her texts—doing research, if you will—taking up one book and putting another down, for all are within easy reach. As she looks up from her reading, her right hand is raised to shade her face, and she gazes at the viewer with a frank and appraising look that seems appropriate for her unidealized face. Not only is there no hint of deviance in that look, but Mme Buron does not even smile or try to charm the viewer. Rather, her serious expression suggests that she has just paused in some important passage to look up at something or someone that has attracted, or distracted, her attention. The expression is one I think I know. It is the expression I imagine I have when my husband walks into my study just as I am finally getting to some significant point in my work.

Locating the sitter at a desk or table in a straight-backed chair seems to help secure the woman reader's propriety. Erotic reading, we might say, preferred certain locales—the boudoir, the garden, the bathing room—and certain pieces of furniture—sofas, divans, daybeds, and easy chairs. Baudouin, for example, situates a masturbating reader outdoors in an engraving designated *Noon* (*Le midi*) and included in his series "Times of the Day" (engraved by Emmanuel-Jean Nepomucene de Ghendt; fig. 23). In this case, the artist likens the fervor of the reader's passion to the heat of midday. He might even allude to the common

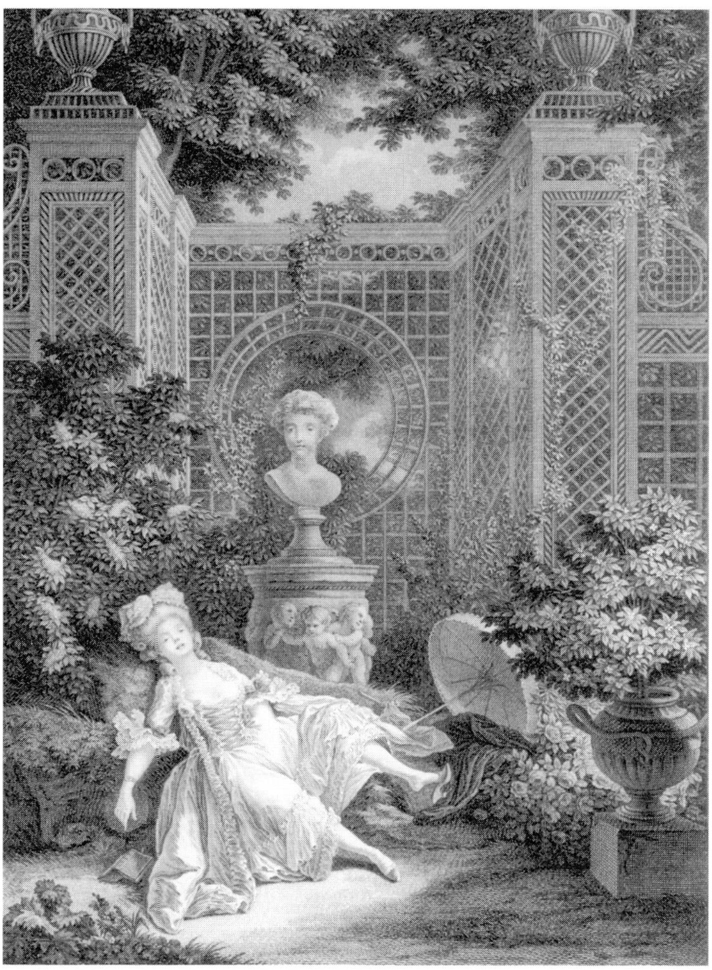

FIGURE 23. Emmanuel-Jean Nepomucene de Ghendt (1735–1815) after Pierre-Antoine Baudouin (1723–69), *Noon (Le Midi)*, c. 1765. Etching and engraving. Photograph © Bibliothèque Nationale de France.

notion that people from warmer climes, from the Midi, were of hotter temperaments and more inclined to sexual passion. In *Noon* he shows us a woman who reads not in her boudoir but in a garden niche, an area marked off as private by the trellis and foliage that enclose it at the back and sides. The woman displayed out of doors appears to have even less control than the reader in her boudoir, a point that perhaps suggests the woman's "natural" state. The book has dropped entirely out of her hand, and she raises one leg off the ground, her shoe dangling from her foot as if some rocking motion is in progress. Equally significant is that the scene takes place beneath the watchful eye of a classicizing statue—the bust of a man looking down at her pleasure. And the bust rests on a sculpted pedestal that itself shows a putto seeming to gape at her immodest display. This cupid appears to rush toward our reader as his two companions hold him back, keeping him captive in the stone base. Is it the spectacle of an aroused woman that has brought the stone voyeurs to life?[37]

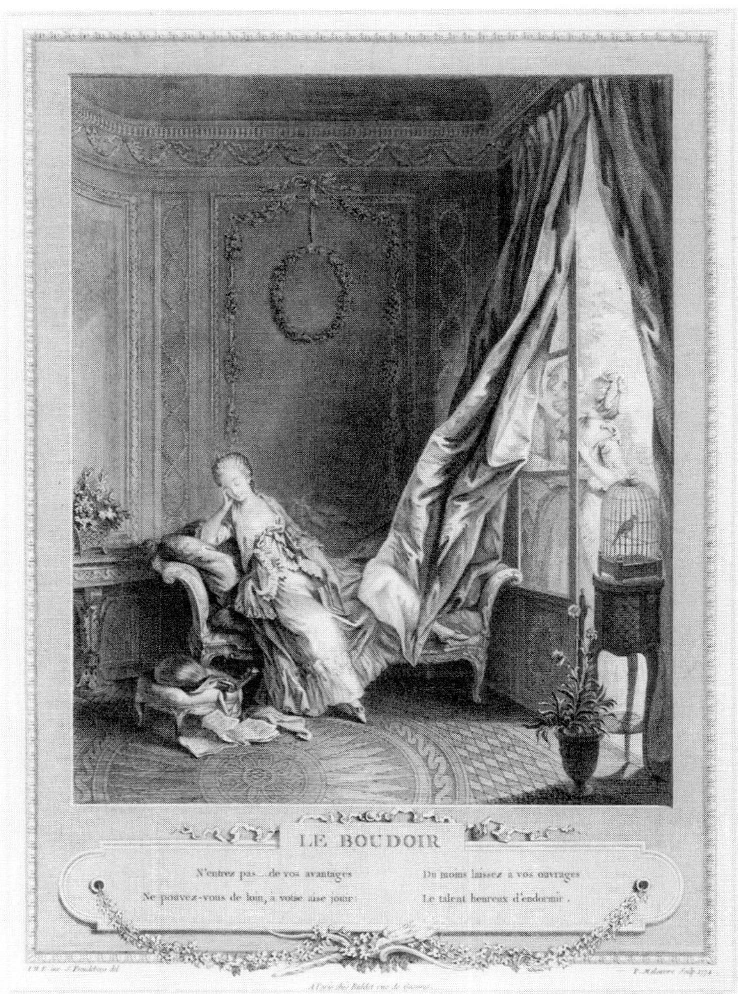

FIGURE 24. Pierre Maleuvre (French, 1740–1803) after Sigmund Freudenberger (French, 1745–1801), *The Boudoir.* Etching and engraving, 1771. Washington, D.C.: National Gallery of Art, Rosenwald Collection. Photograph © 2002 Board of Trustees, National Gallery of Art, Washington, D.C.

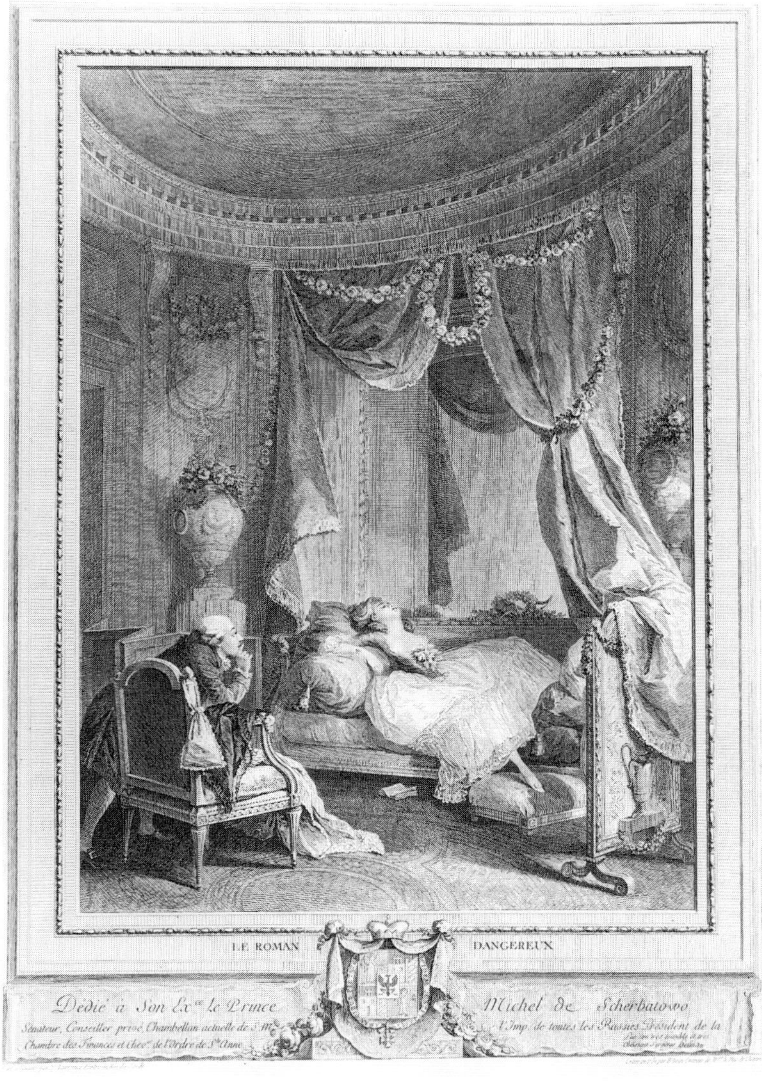

FIGURE 25. Isadore Stanislas Helman (1743–c. 1806) after Nicolas Lavreince (1737–1807), *The Dangerous Novel*. Etching and engraving, 1781. Photograph © Bibliothèque Nationale de France.

The boudoir is likewise presented as both a privileged place of voluptuous reading and daydreaming, and a private space vulnerable to the voyeur in prints like *The Boudoir* (1771), made by Pierre Maleuvre after a painting by Sigmund Freudenberger (fig. 24) and *The Dangerous Novel*, engraved by Isadore Stanislas Helman after Nicolas Lavreince (fig. 25).[38] In *The Boudoir* we see a young woman who has fallen asleep on her daybed, book in hand. The erotic nature of her reading and dreaming is suggested in her pose—her legs are wide apart with her hand holding her book at the critical point between. At the open French doors, a couple has stopped to peer in at the scene; perhaps they have approached the boudoir from a tryst in the garden.[39]

If *The Boudoir* takes as its title the private space fit for voluptuous reading, *The Dangerous Novel* draws our attention to what is read and shows a reader splayed on her day bed in erotic abandon. But where is the dangerous object that has caused this excitement? We see that it has been discarded under the day bed, and that the reader—believing she is alone—has succumbed to her imaginings. She seems singularly unaware of the man who has sneaked into her boudoir, who with fingers to lips asks some accomplice not to give him away. Whether he is there to watch or to actuate her fantasies is not entirely clear, but it is obvious that we, the real viewers, are invited to play our part in his game. Erotic readers, in fact, are often represented as observed. This strategy emphasizes not only the pleasure and imagination of the reader depicted but also that of the fictive voyeur and, by extension, that of the actual viewer. Such a construction highlights the similarity between reading erotic texts and viewing erotic pictures, since both stimulate the imagination and invite the viewer to fancy herself as part of the scene.

The Romance of the *Salonnière*

Given that genre paintings titillated their viewers with both overtly erotic and ingeniously veiled scenes of transgressive reading, what are we to make of Mme Geoffrin's attachment to Carle Van Loo's *The Spanish Reading* (Salon of 1761; fig. 26)? The image shows two young ladies and their governess in a woodland setting enthralled by the novel a young man is reading aloud. The novel's title is clearly legible, and we see that it is *Zayde,* a *romance espagnole* published in 1670 under the name of Jean Regnauld de Segrais (1624–1701). A tale of both true and misguided love, *Zayde* engages the young ladies who have reached the age of awakening desire, and their interest in the story is contrasted to the apparent disregard of the youngest sister standing near the governess. Her attention is instead directed toward a pet bird released from its cage, which she watches intently. The bird, however, is far from free; a tether has checked its flight.

The woman who commissioned Van Loo's *The Spanish Reading,* Marie-Thérèse Rodet, known as Mme Geoffrin (1699–1777), was not an ordinary patron. She presided over one of the leading intellectual salons in Paris from 1740 until her death in 1777. Her group included members of the Encyclopedist circle, among them Diderot and d'Alembert. Geoffrin, moreover, instituted her "Mondays" for artists, and as Paula Radisich has shown, artists, dealers, and amateurs met there to examine and study art from the standpoint of connoisseurship. Radisich reminds us that Geoffrin's collection included only works by living artists and that she had a significant role in their production. Geoffrin in fact claimed: "I began my collection of art in 1750. They were all made under my eyes."[40] Radisich's careful analysis of both Geoffrin's involvement in the

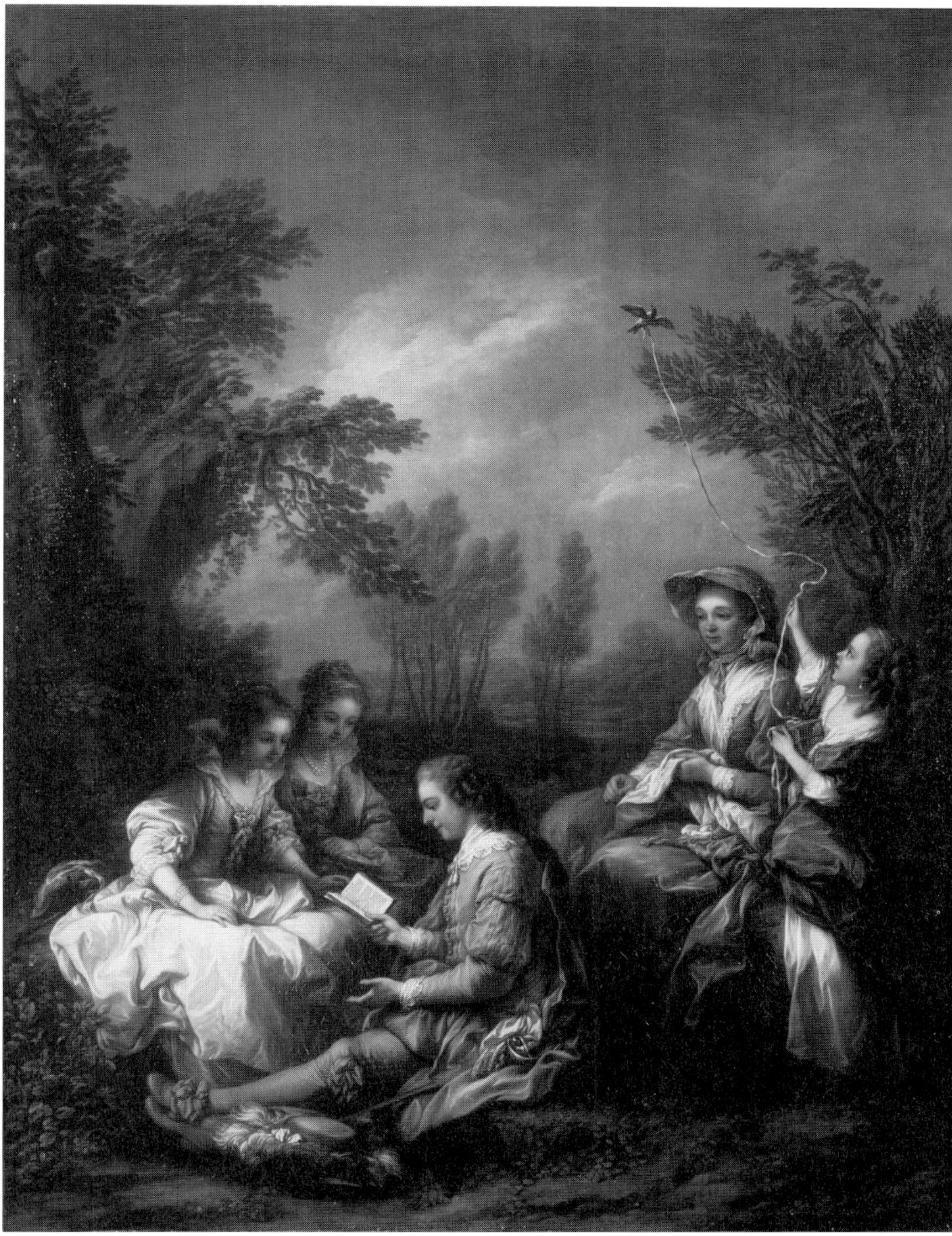

works she commissioned and her relation to artists allows us to see the possibilities of a woman's patronage in the public sphere. And it also reminds us that Geoffrin presents an exceptional case; her bread and butter was patronage, whether of intellectual life or the arts, and she held a place in the public sphere available to only a handful of self-made women.

FIGURE 26. Charles-André Van Loo (called Carle Van Loo; French, 1705–65), *The Spanish Reading*, Salon of 1761. Oil on canvas, 164 × 129 cm. St. Petersburg: Hermitage Collection. Photograph © Scala/Art Resource, NY.

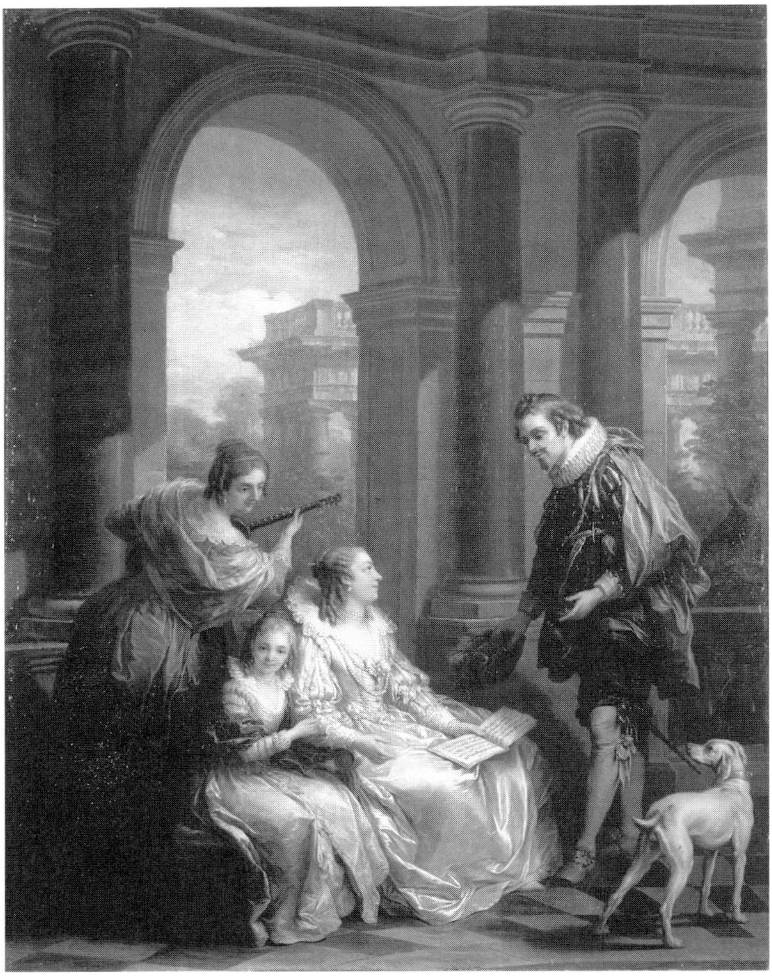

FIGURE 27. Charles-André Van Loo (called Carle Van Loo; French, 1705–65), *The Spanish Conversation,* Salon of 1755. Oil on canvas, 164 × 129 cm. St. Petersburg: Hermitage Collection. Photograph © Scala/Art Resource, NY.

The Spanish Reading and its pendant *The Spanish Conversation* (Salon of 1755; fig. 27) were arguably the most celebrated paintings in Geoffrin's collection as well as the costliest.[41] *The Spanish Conversation* shows two women and a young girl making music on an open portico. One woman with a stringed instrument looks down at the sheet music that the other woman holds open across her knees, while the young girl, arm entwined in that of the seated woman, looks out at the viewer. Their play, however, has been interrupted by a gentleman who approaches the seated woman, doffs his hat, and seems to engage her in conversation. His left hand gestures as if he is in the middle of some point, and the woman gazes at him intently. All the figures are dressed in what would have been called Spanish costume, as they are in *The Spanish Reading.*

We know that these pendants had a particular significance for Mme Geoffrin. In her important work on the Republic of Letters, Dena

Goodman has pointed out that when Geoffrin sold her art collection to Catherine the Great in 1772, she used the proceeds to set up her protégé Julie de Lespinasse (1732–76), in whose salon the Van Loo paintings reappeared as engravings. What fascinates Goodman is that these works show activities that dominated the salon: conversation and reading aloud, and that Van Loo, especially in *The Spanish Reading,* shows the attentive listening that was of special import to Mme Geoffrin.[42]

Given the general discourse on novels and their effects on women, this might seem a surprising interpretation of *The Spanish Reading.* Attentive listening could be dangerous, and here is how one critic—who took the governess for a mother—interpreted the painting when it appeared at the Salon:

> A young man dressed in Spanish costume reads a novel that holds his eager attention and that of those gathered there. It is a love story. Two young women listen with a pleasure that is painted on their faces. The mother who is on the other side of the reader and behind him suspends her work so that she can also listen. But her attention is entirely different from that of the girls. We read in it her thoughts and the mix of the pleasure she takes from the book and the fear that it will perhaps make a dangerous impression on young hearts.[43]

The young man reads a novel *espagnole,* and thus the image might suggest that the young women have so projected themselves into the story that they imagine themselves as Spanish heroines, and the young man reading, as a hero or love object. They are, in Condillac's words, building castles in Spain. The fantasy dress matches the fantasy that the work is producing in their heads; we see not what they are, but what the reading has made them become—at least imaginatively. We can easily hear another critic expounding on that dangerous impression, denouncing the novel and ranting on about woman's imagination. But the more moderate observer quoted above gives the painting something of a moral lesson, for it pictures the mother's proper response to novel reading.[44] In this account, hearing the story both pleases and troubles the mother who, while enjoying the tale, fears for the impression it will make on tender hearts. Given the prevailing sentiments about novels and about woman's impressionability, it is most believable that a diligent mother hearing a love story would be pleased as a woman and apprehensive as a parent. The Salon commentary accounts for many features of *The Spanish Reading,* and it also accords well with contemporaneous ideas. It is a fully viable interpretation of the image. At the same time, it is not an interpretation that can account for Mme Geoffrin's investment in the painting.

The idea of costuming the figures *à l'espagnole* apparently came from Mme Geoffrin, as reported in *L'année littéraire.*[45] I raise this point because it shows the patron taking a part in the conceptualization of Van Loo's works. Mme Geoffrin was known for such interventions, and Diderot quipped in his 1765 commemorative essay on the artist:

> Madame Geoffrin had from him [Van Loo] several easel paintings at a high price. The one called *The Conversation* enjoyed great success for its novelty and always kept its reputation; *The Reading* had less success. Madame Geoffrin presided then over these works, and there were everyday scenes that would make you die laughing. Rarely in agreement on the ideas and the manner of executing the works, there was trouble, then reconciliation, one laughed, one cried, one made injurious comments and flattering ones. It is in the midst of all these changes that the painting was advanced and finished.[46]

We do not know, however, the extent of her participation in *The Spanish Reading,* but I like to think it was substantial and that it at least included choosing the novel *Zayde* depicted in the work.

Whether the book was chosen to harmonize with the costume or the costume was chosen to harmonize with the book, selecting *Zayde* and making that title evident opens further possibilities for interpreting the image. By the time Van Loo painted his composition, *Zayde* was recognized as the work of its true author, Marie-Madeleine Pioche de La Vergne, comtesse de La Fayette (1634–93).[47] Thus in Van Loo's painting women are associated not only with reading novels but with writing them as well. Still, I don't think that *Zayde* would have been an attractive choice only for this reason. More important for the work's connection with women in general, and Mme Geoffrin in specific, was the preface that accompanied *Zayde,* Huet's *Traité de l'origine des romans.* In this preface Huet (1630–1721) answers Boileau, that most tenacious attacker of women, and Huet's search for the novel's origin reinstates Madeleine de Scudéry as the finest writer of contemporary prose fiction.

As Joan DeJean has pointed out, Huet's preface was the first public inscription of Scudéry's name in literary history and the first lauding of her novels as contributing to the national glory.[48] Just as significant for my purposes, however, is that Huet also defends novels, or romances, which he defines as "fictions of amorous adventures written artfully in prose for the pleasure and instruction of readers."[49] He posits an educational mission for the novel not only because it demonstrates vice punished and virtue rewarded but also because it teaches young minds about the passion of love so they can guard against it when it is criminal and know how to conduct themselves when it is honest. Nothing polishes the mind so much as a good romance. Novels, for Huet, are silent instructors that in an agreeable manner inform young people how to live.[50] But what does this defense of the novel have to do with Geoffrin's salon and its activities?

We might associate the novel's educational purpose with one function of Geoffrin's salon. As Dena Goodman points out, women educated themselves through salons, where they heard authors read from their latest writings and listened to discussions of new ideas.[51] This aspect of the painting could have appealed to Geoffrin, whom one can imagine fancied herself as the governess overseeing the entire process of reading, listening, and learning. Indeed, Radisich has argued that some works the *salonnière* commissioned, such as Hubert Robert's painting *The Swans of the Abbey Saint-Antoine* (1773; Paris: private collection) can be understood as portraits of Geoffrin even if she is not directly portrayed in them. The *Swans* is one of three works representing the gardens of the Abbey of Saint-Antoine, a place where Geoffrin regularly took her retreats. While she appears as an identifiable figure in the two other works (*Madame Geoffrin's Walk at the Abbey Saint-Antoine* [1773], Paris: private collection; and *Madame Geoffrin Taking Lunch with the Sisters of the Abbey Saint-Antoine* [1773], Paris: private collection) in the *Swans* her legendary kindness and charity are depicted through the aged woman who bends over to feed the birds. This subtle invocation of Geoffrin's virtues points to her modesty.[52] The *salonnière* knew how to veil her cultural power under the widow's clothing and modest, self-effacing demeanor she habitually wore. She could play the good woman while actually performing beyond the limitations imposed on her sex. As Goodman has argued, "the salonnière's art was based on selflessness that allowed her to manage the egos of others without imposing her own. Her virtues were negative virtues, 'female' virtues, such as modesty."[53] Geoffrin's modesty thus generates her power as a cultural mediator and as ruler of men.

If we return to Huet's preface, however, we find that its explication of the French woman's effect on the language of *politesse* could have struck much closer to home. DeJean has shown that the activities of a salon emerge in Huet's argument as what make France's novels superior to those written in other countries. In the course of his treatise, Huet notes that in Italy and Spain women are nearly recluses; they are scarcely seen, and they do not converse with men. Freedom, on the other hand, characterizes the exchange between men and women in France, and a uniquely French genius—the art of gallantry—he cites as the origin of the novel and the cause of its success. "But in France, women living under their own good faith, and having no defense but their own heart, made it [the heart] into a rampart stronger and more secure than all the keys, all the grills, and all the vigilance of duennas. Men were therefore obliged to lay siege to this rampart in proper fashion [par les formes]."[54] The "forms," DeJean argues, were verbal, the language of politeness, "the linguistic code devised by women in the salons and carried over by Scudéry into the novel."[55]

Returning to our focus on Geoffrin's salon, we might say that in France the *salonnière* who regulated the forms of conversation replaced the duenna or, in the case of *The Spanish Reading,* the governess. And the little girl with her tethered bird who is placed beside the governess reaffirms the idea of gentle control. Just as the child both enables and limits the bird's ascent, so the *salonnière* not only facilitated the wit of her guests, she also regulated their flights of fancy. Indeed, the abbé Ferdinando Galiani (1728–87) commented on the centrality of such a figure when he wrote to Louise Tardieu d'Esclavelles d'Epinay (1726–83) about the gatherings available to him in Naples: "[B]ut our Fridays are becoming Neapolitan Fridays and are getting farther away from the character and tone of those of France, despite all our efforts . . . There is no way to make Naples resemble Paris unless we find a woman to guide us, organize us, *Geoffrinise* us."[56]

The emphasis on a social interaction between men and women and on polite conversation also ties *The Spanish Reading* more closely to its companion piece, *The Spanish Conversation.* The latter resembles a *fête galante* in the manner of Antoine Watteau, who was also known for his use of historical and theatrical costume. In fact, both of Van Loo's works seem to take their cue from Watteau's figures and fêtes. Compare, for example, the young man in *The Spanish Reading* with the seated gentleman in *The Timid Lover* (c. 1716; fig. 28) and note how Van Loo's young girls show the same attention as Watteau's smitten beauty. The music making on an open portico we see in *The Spanish Conversation* recreates a motif Watteau used in several works, for example, his *Prelude to a Concert* (c. 1716; fig. 29). In addition, Mary Vidal's study of Watteau and conversation has located much of the form and import of his imagery in this social practice. Vidal notes how Watteau's keen observation of conversational relationships recalls Scudéry's definition of conversation as "the bond that holds society together and the greatest pleasure of refined persons."[57] She convincingly shows that conversation provides an interpretive key to Watteau's work and that the development of conversation in art depended on the preeminent role aristocratic women played in seventeenth-century culture. Huet's preface and the argument

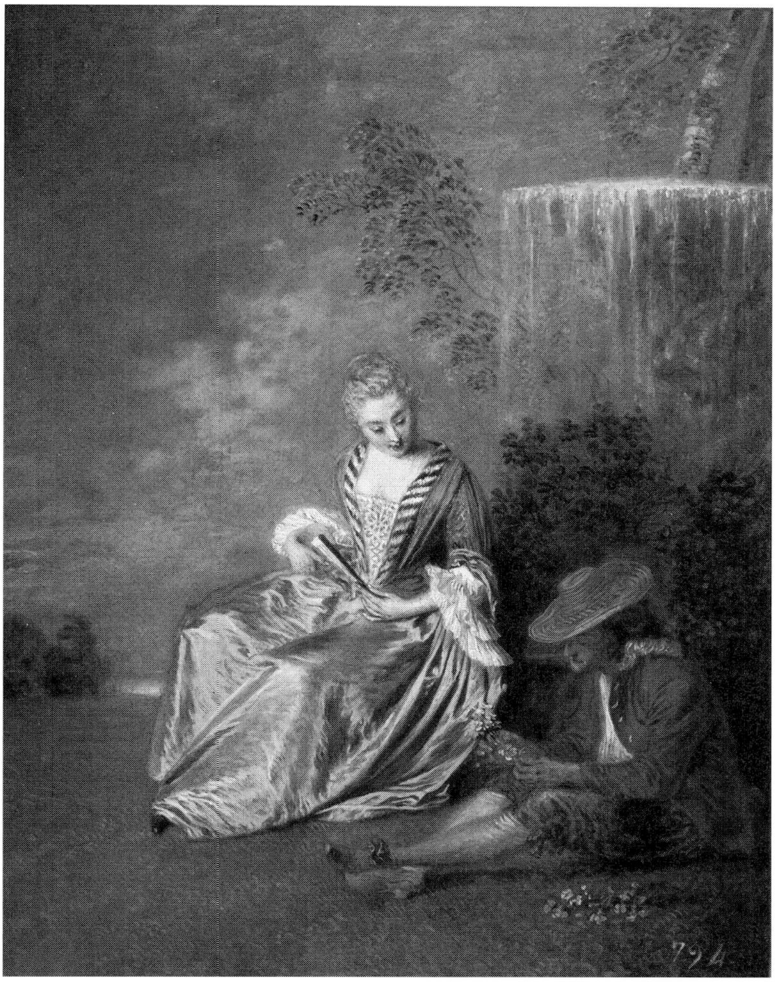

FIGURE 28. Antoine Watteau (French, 1684–1721), *The Timid Lover,* c. 1716. Oil on canvas, 41 × 32 cm. Madrid: Palacio Real. Photograph © Scala/Art Resource, NY.

it makes is doubly linked to Van Loo's pendants—through both the picture's invoking of Watteau's fêtes and its inclusion of *Zayde.*

We still cannot be certain how Mme Geoffrin understood Van Loo's *The Spanish Reading* with its young women enjoying the novel *Zayde.* What we can know, however, is that by including *Zayde* in an image intended for Mme Geoffrin's salon, Van Loo constructs a lineage of women who are cultural mediators, even if he never meant to do so. From the salons of the *précieuses,* the art of conversation moved into novels authored by women and then into those authored by men. It traveled to Huet's treatise on the novel and into the paintings of Watteau. All these converge on Van Loo's pendants and from there make their way into the eighteenth-century philosophical gatherings Geoffrin bequeathed to her protégé Julie de Lespinasse, the youngest representative of that lineage. In the case of *The Spanish Reading,* woman's cultural authority is hidden in a genre scene that shows an activity deemed questionable

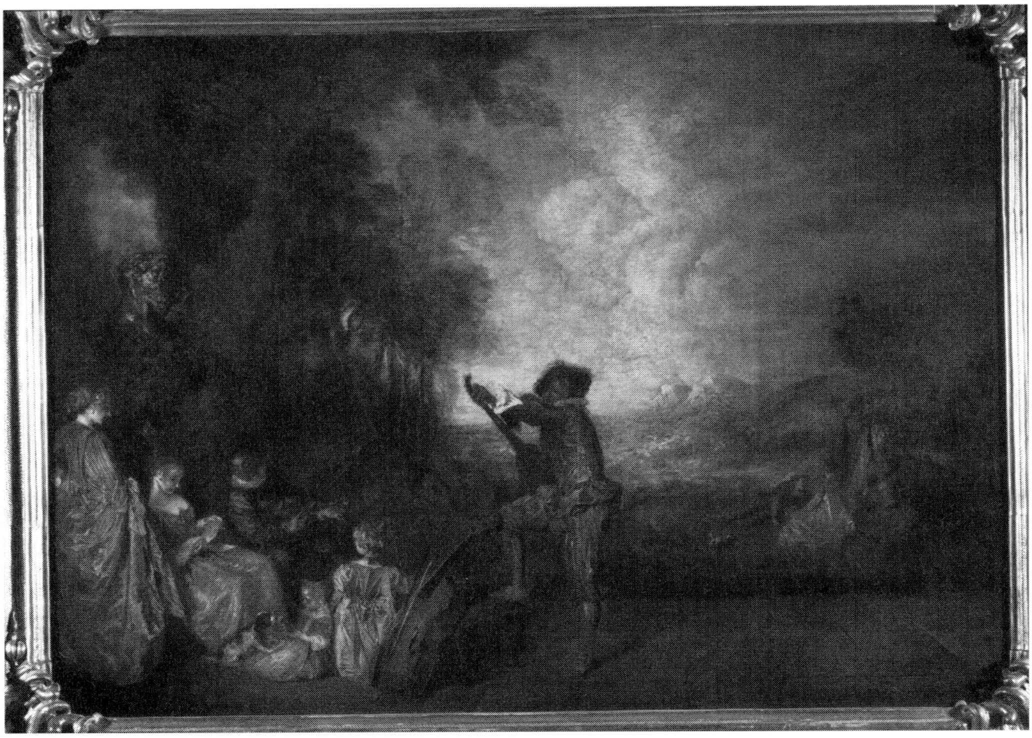

FIGURE 29. Antoine Watteau (French, 1684–1721), *Prelude to a Concert*, c. 1716. Oil on canvas, 66 × 91 cm. Berlin: Schloss Charlottenburg, Staatliche Schlösser und Gärten. Photograph © Erich Lessing/Art Resource, NY.

for young women. In the minds of many, were not Geoffrin's enterprise and the knowledge it generated just as dangerous?

The *Femme Savante*

Writers have found ways to associate woman's knowledge with her sexuality ever since man imagined the story of Eden. In that garden, the serpent tempts Eve to pluck an apple from the forbidden tree of knowledge, and then she seduces Adam into eating it. Because Eve dared to grab for knowledge, mankind fell from paradise and shame marked human sexuality. In images showing the expulsion from the garden, we see Eve pointedly covering her genitals.[58] For Eve's daughters in eighteenth-century France, to display either sexuality or knowledge violated modesty.

In his study of novels, medical texts, and obscene writing, Jean Mainil has pointed out that since the seventeenth century sex played a privileged role in the unsayables of woman's knowledge. He argues that the popularization of medical knowledge made the problem of the *femme savante* especially pressing, since so much of it dealt with issues of reproduction and sexuality, about which women were just too curious.[59]

Even Jacques Ferrand in his *Treatise on Lovesickness* warned that scientific writing could be as dangerous as pornography:

> With the sense of hearing must be associated the reading of lewd and immoral books as well as those works that discuss sperm, human reproduction, and several hidden diseases concerning male impotency and female infertility, which the physicians are inclined to treat in rather crude, but necessary terms.[60]

While Ferrand fretted over the effects of such books on both sexes, Fénelon specifically advocated that women be separated from scientific knowledge in his *De l'education des filles:* "[F]or their sex one must have a modesty about science nearly as delicate as that which inspires a fear of vice."[61] That many heeded Fénelon's advice is suggested in *Les conversations d'Émilie* published by Louise Florence Pétronille Tardieu d'Esclavelles, marquise de Lalive d'Épinay (1726–83) in 1782. There the author contrasts the education she would offer young women to that of her youth: "I would not allow myself to fix the limits of knowledge for persons of our sex; perhaps it is not even necessary to have a general rule in this regard . . . during my childhood, it was not customary to teach girls anything." "Above all," she continues, "one never spoke to us of reason, and science was deemed out of place in persons of our sex."[62] But if women's scientific learning was proscribed, that does not mean women obeyed the prohibition. Indeed, it is precisely because so many did not obey that moralists railed against them.[63]

It was not only scientific knowledge that was "out of place" for women. The notion that modesty must generally shield women from learning as fiercely as it protected them from vice reappeared throughout the eighteenth century in conduct books for young ladies and in the writings of women who, like Mme d'Épinay, refuted the idea. And one did not have to wait until near the end of the century to find women contesting this notion. In 1727, the *salonnière* Anne Thérèse de Marguenat de Courcelles, marquise de Lambert (1647–1733), analyzed the shame attached to woman's knowledge in the course of protesting women's exclusion from serious study. In thinking about why knowledge seemed shameful for women, she concluded in her *Réflexions nouvelles sur les femmes* that since Molière wrote *Les femmes savantes* (1672), "shame has been attached to women's knowledge, as much shame as is attached to the most forbidden vices."[64]

Lambert was hardly the only writer in the eighteenth century to focus on the devastating effects of Molière's satire for women's learning; it became common to suggest that he had made of it a vice. Yet the commonplace is especially interesting since the way Molière associated female sexuality and learning was by and large outdated in the mid-eighteenth century. In *Les femmes savantes,* Molière's targets are the Cartesiennes, and to a lesser degree, the *précieuses,* especially those who denigrated conjugal love in favor of a spiritual and rarified friendship. Molière makes woman's knowledge shameful by savagely ridiculing women who not only have pretensions to learning but who also scorn the legitimate sexual pleasures of marriage for the delights of knowledge. Molière's *femme savante,* Armande, exhorts her less enlightened sister, Henriette: "Marry yourself, my sister, to philosophy, and give sovereign empire to reason, subjugating to its laws the animal instincts whose gross appetites lower us to the level of beasts."[65] Learning replaces or substitutes for sexuality, which suggests a link between them.

Eighteenth-century materialism challenged the implicit split between body and mind on which Molière's comedy operates. Consider, for example, André François Boureau-Deslandes's materialist tale, *Pigmalion; ou, La statue animée* (1741) in which Galatea's animation demonstrates the inherent sensibility of matter.[66] In this tale, woman's learning and sexuality are intertwined, and each proves difficult to control. Pygmalion has at first a properly intellectual relation with his beloved, whom he begins to educate once she has come to life. He explains to her that one receives ideas and knowledge through the senses and eventually presses a kiss on her mouth. "What are you doing," she cries, "what are the unknown movements I feel? Speak. Stop. Don't stop, I give in to your transports, but what name do you give to them?"[67] This Galatea quickly develops a taste for the act Pygmalion names as pleasure, and the greatest of all pleasures. She lies down on a bed and invites Pygmalion to repeat his caresses. He obeys, and in a witty evocation of Descartes, Galatea reasons, "Now I cannot doubt that I live. What you call pleasure succeeds in convincing me of my being and persuading me of its reality."[68] Having made this discovery, the statue calls pleasure the true queen to which all must be sacrificed.

Pygmalion tries to teach his ideal woman that pleasure must be regulated and that need must go hand in hand with appetite, but it is not at all clear that she learns that lesson well. Moreover, when Pygmalion wants to marry her, the statue responds coldly: "[A]re we assured that we will always please one another?" and tells him to forget formal oaths and pledges. They will be together as long as they give one another pleasure.[69] Here Pygmalion's statue is not an ignorant girl but a woman who has learned too much. She thinks freely and insists on freely disposing of her sexuality. Such a woman was not, to be sure, every man's cup of tea. Although the story ends with the narrator calling on Venus to bless the union and assuring the reader that Pygmalion will always please Galatea, the text raises the specter not only of woman's inconstancy but also of her insatiable desire for sexual pleasure.

Despite the writings of materialists like Boreau-Deslandes, the upper strata of society absorbed Molière's satire not as a specific critique of Cartesian dualism but as a send up of female pretension.[70] At the same time, some moralist critiques in the eighteenth century implied—as had Molière—that too much learning took women away from their traditional duties. Roussel, for example, argued that in directing too many vital forces to their heads, women retarded the action of all other organs and deprived them of vital fluids. As a result, their organs would wither like tender saplings planted in an arid terrain under a blazing sun. Roussel concluded that by pursuing a reputation in science or the arts, women deviated from their natural destiny to please and reproduce.[71] At the same time, some moralists implied that woman's attachment to book learning created an atmosphere of sexual and intellectual license that propelled them beyond the bounds of acceptable female behavior.

The connection between sexual and intellectual license could be used in covertly erotic images in which the appetite for knowledge implied a promiscuous imagination. We see this exchange in *Philosophy Asleep* (*La philosophie endormie*; fig. 30), a print made by Jean Michel Moreau after a painting by Jean-Baptiste Greuze. We can infer from the image that the young woman has fallen asleep while reading. Her right arm rests on an open book and holds her place, while her left arm seems still to support the chin of a small dog napping on her lap. Already the alert viewer might be suspicious. Like Baudouin in *Reading*, Greuze includes in his painting the pet that writers and artists often cast as a surrogate lover. He seats his woman next to a writing desk that holds closed and open books, a globe, and a pen and inkwell. On the floor around the "sleeping" woman the artist has strewn more books, as well as her discarded embroidery and an object that could be either her seal or some tool used in needlework. In describing the woman, I put "sleeping" in quotation marks because her pose, expression, and accoutrements suggest it is not so much her sleep as the nature of her dreams that attracts the viewer's gaze.

The title *Philosophy Asleep* is not original to the painting but comes from the later print of the work dedicated to Mme Greuze. Like so many other titles and legends attached to eighteenth-century engravings, this one provides an interpretation of the work, transforming the painted woman into the allegorical figure of Philosophy and characterizing her as "endormie." The qualifying "endormie" suggests that this Philosophy is lethargic, even indolent, and through an association with the verb *endormir*, that she has been bored or put to sleep by her reading. But should we take the engraving's title as the privileged interpretation for the painting, using it to understand this portrayal as a moralizing

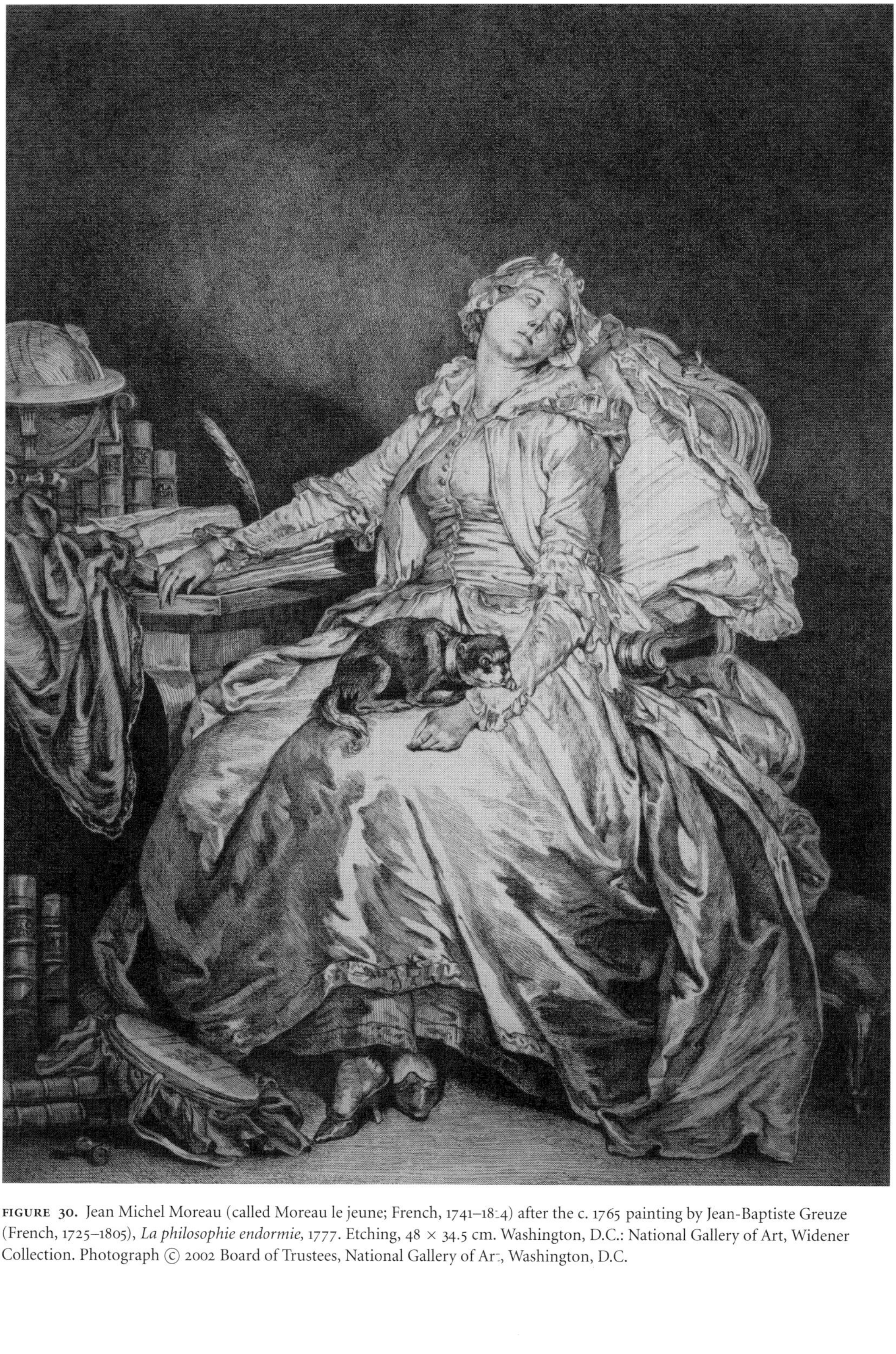

FIGURE 30. Jean Michel Moreau (called Moreau le jeune; French, 1741–1814) after the c. 1765 painting by Jean-Baptiste Greuze (French, 1725–1805), *La philosophie endormie*, 1777. Etching, 48 × 34.5 cm. Washington, D.C.: National Gallery of Art, Widener Collection. Photograph © 2002 Board of Trustees, National Gallery of Art, Washington, D.C.

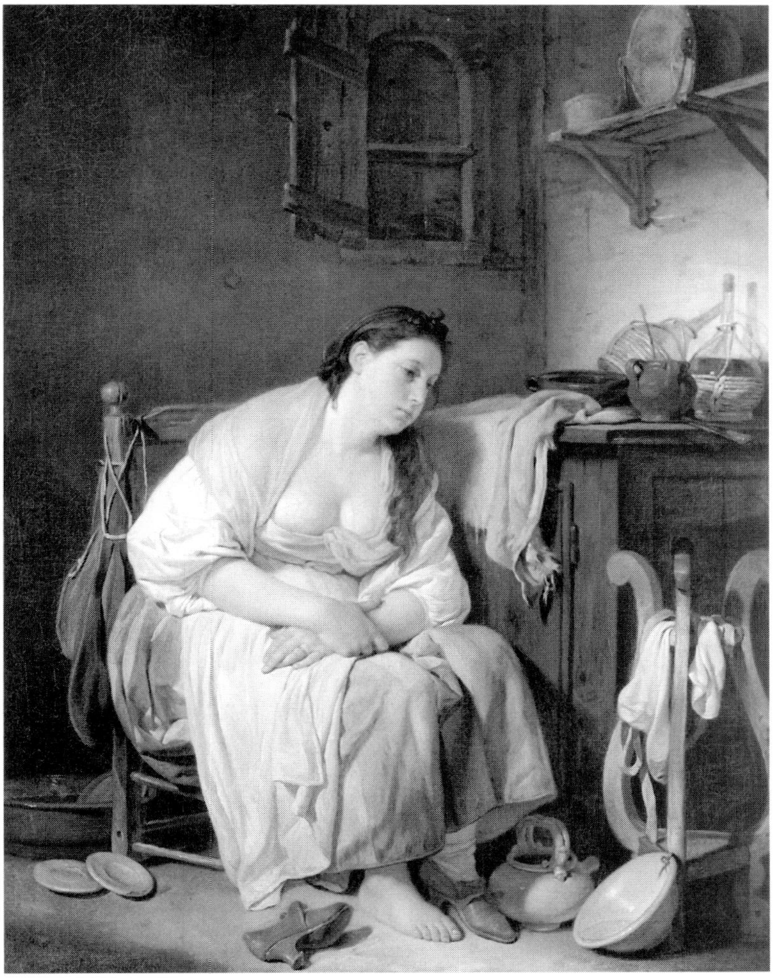

FIGURE 31. Jean-Baptiste Greuze (French, 1725–1805), *The Lazy Italian Woman (La paresseuse Italienne)*, Salon of 1757. Oil on canvas, 25.5 × 19.688 in. Hartford, Conn.: The Wadsworth Atheneum Museum of Art, The Ella Gallup Sumner and Mary Catlin Sumner Collection Fund. Photo courtesy The Wadsworth Atheneum Museum of Art.

allegory for laziness?[72] Perhaps. But other readings are equally possible, especially since we know how Greuze earlier imagined a lazy woman in *The Lazy Italian Woman* (*La paresseuse Italienne,* Salon of 1757; fig. 31).

The Italian woman's sloth is expressed in the disarray of her surroundings as well as in her careless dress, listless pose, and blank expression—the expression of a woman too lazy even for thought. Indeed, she seems to lack the energy for dressing herself, and we see that although her left foot is properly shod, her right lacks the stocking she holds in her left hand and the shoe that lies on the floor in the foreground. She doesn't even seem to notice that she has not pulled up her bodice and is exposing her breasts to the viewer. Although this woman is available to the viewer's gaze, her sluggish body and mind suggest neither sexual energy nor desirable innocence nor languid desire.

The figure represented in *Philosophy Asleep* is meticulously groomed and dressed, and although we can imagine that she is asleep, her pose suggests none of the lassitude evident in *The Lazy Italian Woman.*[73] Her body is marked by a particular sort of tension evident in the sharp turn of her head and the long line of her neck. And her head falls onto her right shoulder in a way that bespeaks a voluptuous abandon rather than an indolent sloth. There is, one could say, more than a whiff of Saint Teresa's ecstasy in her pose. On the other hand, her dress is modest, especially for Greuze, revealing neither breasts nor ankles, and the viewer must be content to see her long, vulnerable neck. Yet the work clearly has an erotic charge, evident not only in her vulnerable state and lap dog but also in the artist's handling of the sensuous surfaces that arouse the viewer's touch. The erotically charged pose, moreover, gives a particular cast to the woman's expression, which suggests that thoughts are moving behind the closed eyes. Her facial muscles have not relaxed, her mouth has not fallen open, and there is no slackness to her features. Certainly her sleeping state leaves the viewer free to look, makes her vulnerable to his gaze. At the same time, it renders her lost in her dreams and thus inaccessible to the viewer who can only project her own desires onto the painted image. Do we see this woman just as she is aroused by her dreams? Can we imagine that she will convulse, gasp, and sigh in her sleep? Or in other words, does this young woman dream like Diderot's sleeping d'Alembert, her mind excited by reading science or philosophy?

In posing these possibilities, I am comparing Greuze's sleeping woman and a character in Diderot's *Rêve de d'Alembert* (*D'Alembert's Dream*; 1769).[74] In that text, the dreaming philosopher's mind works over the problem of reproduction and generates the idea of an "infinite succession of animaculae" and a world ceaselessly ending and beginning.[75] In this state, d'Alembert babbles about the human condition, his materialism evident as he proclaims that there is nothing beyond the physical necessities of "eating, drinking, living, making love, and sleeping." He calls out for Mlle de Lespinasse, who as a character in the dialogue has been at his side throughout his dream, and it is through her report to Dr. Bordeu that we learn of d'Alembert's hallucination.[76] She describes what followed his rambling thoughts on generation: "Then his face became flushed. I wanted to feel his pulse, but I didn't know where he had hidden his hand. He seemed to experience a convulsion. His mouth was half open, his breath gasping; he let out a deep sigh, then a weaker and deeper one. He turned his head to the side and fell asleep."[77] As commentators have often observed, d'Alembert's ideas about generation excited his imagination and led him—unconsciously, of course—to masturbate. Here we see materialist philosophy taken to the logical conclusion that follows from its connection of body to mind.

Diderot seems to have anticipated d'Alembert's dream in his "Salon of 1767," in his commentary on Joseph Vernet's landscape paintings. In his remarks on the seventh painting or "site," Diderot takes up the question of dreaming: "Dreaming is quite an odd state. No philosopher that I know has successfully described the true difference between dreaming and waking."[78] In dreaming, moreover, we find that male sexual arousal cannot be controlled: "You see a beautiful woman; her beauty strikes you. You are young; immediately the organ of pleasure expands. You are asleep, and this rebellious organ is aroused; immediately you see the beautiful woman again, and perhaps you ejaculate voluptuously."[79]

To my mind, Greuze's *Philosophy Asleep* represents a doubly immodest woman as much as it depicts one who is bored by intellectual labor. A return to Baudouin's reader, moreover, shows that she, too, is inclined toward both mental and sexual stimulation. Notice especially the emblems of learning evident on her writing table—the weighty tomes, the globe, the maps, the papers. Contemporary sources lead us to believe that no one would expect to find these in the typical woman's boudoir. As Nicolas Le Camus de Mézières (1721–93?) envisions it in his architectural treatise, *The Genius of Architecture* (1780), the boudoir is no place for heavy reading: "The boudoir is regarded as the abode of delight; here [the woman] seems to reflect on her designs and yield to her inclinations."[80] He compares the room to a lady of fashion—both are ready to be decorated—and the other rooms in the woman's apartment are, in fact, for purposes of adornment—for dressing, bathing, and making the toilette.[81] The boudoir, however, is specifically for love and should be decorated with both natural scenes and amorous subjects drawn from mythology, so that "the burden of the whole is this: that enjoyment is close at hand."[82]

Libertine images such as *The Boudoir* and *The Dangerous Novel* celebrated the boudoir in a way that pushed even further the associations of Le Camus des Mézières. Women, of course, did not necessarily use the boudoir in the way that artists suggested, nor did they reserve it only for lovemaking, licit or otherwise. Rochelle Ziskin describes the boudoir of Mme Dangé, a financier's wife, in her hôtel on the Place Vendôme as a semiprivate space for receiving a few friends. It opened off the more public salon and was furnished with a sofa and chairs.[83] We also know that women's apartments had studies, offices, and even libraries, even if Le Camus de Mézières made no provision for these in his ideal home. The boudoir Baudouin imagines seems to confuse the functions of different spaces, picturing a room reserved for pleasure as also housing books and instruments used for study.

That Baudouin places objects of learning in the boudoir not only draws our attention to them but also suggests that they have some symbolic import. Especially begging attention is the book propped up so that we can read the title, *Histoire de voyages.* Is this travel literature—a genre immensely popular in the eighteenth century—included to underscore that the reader is subject to fantasy? That because she is not able to visit exotic places, she allows her imagination to wander? Such an interpretation would surely highlight the activity on the other side of the scene where she is taking herself to Cythera.[84] But reading the story of a voyage also represents a desire to know about other places, about their geography, history, and customs. The maps and globe that accompany the books on her table also suggest that knowledge, as much as fantasy, is at stake here. Joan DeJean has reminded us, moreover, that for French writers such as Montesquieu, travel was the beginning of philosophical and religious doubt.[85] Baudouin's work, then, comments on the relation between woman's sexual and intellectual appetites as much as it shows the results of erotic reading. His reader is not only a passionate and deviant spectator, she is also a curious woman, a woman who knows too much.

Thérèse Philosophe

The most notorious *femme philosophe* of the eighteenth century certainly ended up both knowing too much and avoiding her reproductive destiny, although not to the detriment of her health. That woman was Thérèse Philosophe, whose story *Le nouvel ami des femmes* listed among those works that have ruined women, books that have scorched their souls with bad philosophies and terrible writings.[86] The novel is an account of Thérèse's education, both philosophical and erotic, and materialist philosophy blends with sexual encounter throughout the story.[87]

Actually there are two privileged, deviant women in the novel, each of them a *femme philosophe.* One, of course, is Thérèse herself, and the other is Mme C***, a pretty young widow who nearly lost her life giving birth to a child who died three months later. For most of the novel, the preferred sexual practice of both women is masturbation, either alone or with a partner. Section two of the novel is, in part, an apology for masturbation as both a release for sexual longing and a method of birth control that safeguards a woman's health.[88] What is of particular interest to me is the positive confluence in these fictional women of the passionate spectatorship that induces masturbation and the intellectual appetite that prompts clear reasoning. In these claims, *Thérèse Philosophe* transgresses the norms of acceptable sexual behavior.

From the start, Mme C*** is presented as an intellectual woman. Here is how Thérèse describes her: "Mme C*** had much wit; she was firm in the opinions that she adopted only after mature reflection. She read a lot and loved to converse on the most abstract subjects."[89] She has a particular friend and confessor, the abbé T., and together they advise Thérèse on the necessity of therapeutic masturbation, which she undertakes to good effect. They also discuss moral philosophy, religion, and metaphysics, and Mme C*** is described as shepherding Thérèse's thinking and reasoning. Topics discussed in this section range over a wide spectrum of philosophical issues, including sexuality, religion, and nature, as well as moral justifications for both masturbation and coitus interruptus. Later, Thérèse will reflect on her experiences, noting, "Perhaps for the first time in my life, I began to think."[90] Thinking, reading, and self-stimulation go hand in hand for Thérèse, as they do for Mme C***, who describes to the abbé how the erotic novel, *Histoire de Dom B.... portier des Chartreux* aroused her: "Reading your awful Portier des Chartreux has set me all on fire. Its portraits are so striking. They have an air of truth that charms."[91] In this comment Mme C*** takes into account the novel's artistry and sees it as enhancing the erotic effects. What the novel portrays, it represents with an air of truth, allowing the reader more easily to envision the fictive scene as a real one, all the better to enter it imaginatively. As many have already pointed out, such scenes are directed to the actual readers of *Thérèse Philosophe,* inviting a similar response to the irresistible truth that it, too, conveys.

As her adventures come to an end, Thérèse has clearly established beliefs, which she puts into play in her relation with a count who falls in love with her but will not marry.[92] About to leave Paris for his country chateau, he proposes that Thérèse accompany him. He offers her a portion of his income if she will become his companion and perhaps in time his mistress. Thérèse agrees to the arrangement because she believes that she and the count can make each other happy, even without sexual intercourse. Their love grows as the count caters to her taste for moral and metaphysical issues. He eventually proposes coitus interruptus, but Thérèse still fears pregnancy and is satisfied with her own pleasures. In the end, they make a wager. He bets his entire library of erotic books and pictures that she cannot refrain from masturbating for two weeks. If she loses, she will agree to coitus interruptus. Thérèse accepts the bet and loses, seduced into masturbation not only by his erotic books but especially by the exciting images of Priapus and Venus. Her loss, however, is a happy one, for she and the count continue their relation and renew their pleasures without a problem, without a worry, and without children for the next ten years.[93]

The scene in which Thérèse loses her bet with the count shows her an enthusiastic consumer of visual images, even if her viewing experience is prepared by five days of erotic reading. Indeed, the novel—and especially in its illustrated versions—is about looking as much as it is about reading, not only for its many scenes of voyeurism but also for its description of how viewers project themselves into pictures. On the fifth day of her erotic reading, another hour of this activity proves too much for Thérèse, and she falls "into a kind of ecstasy." Lying on her bed she spies two paintings, and here is how she describes looking at the *Feast of Priapus*: "I set about imitating all the poses I saw. Each figure inspired in me the feeling that the painter had given it. Two athletes in the lefthand part of *The Feast of Priapus* enchanted me, transported me by the conformity of the diminutive woman's taste with my own. Mechanically, my right hand went to where the man's hand was placed."[94] Clearly Thérèse is excited by the identification of her "taste" with that of the woman in the picture. She continues admiring the work part by part, much in the way Cahusac's enthusiastic artist admired the new image that reason had created. Yet the result is cast in a different light.

Turning to the second picture, the *Love Affair of Mars and Venus*, it is Venus's sensuality and the prospect of her pleasure that arouses Thérèse, and she both imagines herself as Venus and mimics the goddess in tableau vivant. In her moment of enthusiasm, Thérèse literally becomes the image she sees, and the scene reads as a parody of spectatorial theories:

> What lasciviousness in Venus's pose! Like her I stretched out with graceful abandon. My thighs slightly apart, my arms voluptuously opened, I admired the striking attitude of the god Mars. The fire that appeared to animate his eyes, and especially his lance, passed into my heart. I slipped under the sheets. My buttocks rocked pleasurably as if to carry forward the crown destined for the conqueror.[95]

Thérèse Philosophe does not present its ideas on pleasure and metaphysics for general consumption; rather, they are meant only for an enlightened few. At least this is the wisdom of Abbé T, who tells Mme C*** it is unwise to reveal to fools wisdom they could not appreciate and might misuse. Such wisdom should be available exclusively to those who know how to think, and according to Abbé T., this type of man or woman is rare. Robert Darnton has pointed out that the novel itself is addressed to what he calls a "champagne-and-oyster" readership, a salon society. And although Darnton assumes that the work was written primarily for men, it seems to me that its strong advocacy of birth control (among other things) suggests the work was equally addressed to women.[96] And indeed, Abbé T.'s comments imply that the wisdom of *Thérèse Philosophe* should be available to those who are freethinkers, men and women alike.

Darnton further argues that *Thérèse Philosophe* challenged many accepted values of Old Regime France, a point that is particularly interesting given that she is not presented in the novel as an aristocratic woman or a wealthy one, that is, belonging to the class potentially freer in their loving and living. Even if Thérèse eventually chooses what might be the least transgressive of the sexual acts described in the novel, she presents in her living arrangements a woman who disposes of her own body and mind, pursues her sexual and intellectual pleasures, and achieves happiness. Darnton argues that Thérèse was not entirely a fiction, that there were in the mid-eighteenth century independent, libidinous women who represented a powerful threat to the existing social order. Among those Thérèses, he names the "salon lionesses" Claudine Alexandrine Guérin, Mme de Tencin (1682–1749) and Julie de Lespinasse (1732–76).[97]

The latter existed as both a real person and a fictional character in Diderot's *Rêve de d'Alembert,* which is coincidentally the only "legitimate" philosophical work of the period to condone, even advise, female masturbation. The topic emerges in the last section entitled "Conversation between Mademoiselle de Lespinasse and Bordeu." In their discussion of solitary acts, Bordeu claims these at least give pleasure. He goes on to argue that they are harmless but not useless; masturbation both fulfills a need and provides a pleasant sensation. To prove their utility, Bordeu poses this problem to his interlocutor:

> "You have a judicious daughter, too judicious; innocent, too innocent. She is at the age when her amorous instincts are developing. Her mind is troubled; nature does nothing to help it. You call me. I perceive immediately that all the symptoms you fear come from the excess and retention of the sexual fluids. I warn you that she is threatened by a madness that is easy to prevent but is sometimes impossible to cure. I tell you the remedy. What do you do?"[98]

Rather than answer, Mlle Lespinasse poses her own questions: Has Bordeu given this advice to mothers, and what did they say? "All of them, without exception," Bordeu answers, "took the right line, the sensible line."[99] Every one, in other words, introduced her daughter to the pleasures of Venus. Female masturbation is presented in the *Rêve de d'Alembert* as what *preserves* female reason. Here Doctor Bordeu speaks not the opinions of his medical colleagues, but the lessons of *Thérèse Philosophe.*[100]

In holding, reading, or listening to books; in looking at paintings, engravings, and illustrations, women could not escape the cultural discourses that surrounded their spectatorship. Theirs was neither the enthusiasm that generated great art nor the spectatorship that appreciated it. Yet in the face of warnings and threats, women picked up novels in increasing numbers and educated themselves in literature, history, the arts and sciences, as well as in theology and religion. And there is reason to believe they enjoyed libertine books and pornography. They picked up books and looked at images despite warnings not to—despite fears for their modesty, reproductive capacity, and mental health. They continued to read and look despite the prospect of ridicule, the shame of a ruined reputation, the ranting of moralists, and the threat of nymphomania.

CHAPTER 4

Pygmalion's Enthusiasm and the Fires of Nymphomania, or The Psychology of Art and Desire

Be she a reader or a viewer, the woman spectator provided eighteenth-century artists and writers with a charged example of imagination's power. Such women appeared regularly in two complementary venues—erotic art and moralizing tracts—each concerned in one way or another with the dangerous liaison between sexuality and imagination. Nowhere was the threatening power of woman's fantasy so clearly laid out as in the writings on nymphomania, a disease whose ultimate cause was a deranged imagination and whose final effects were madness and even death.

But before turning to that disease, it must be said that men's sexual desire and imaginative activity were also tied together. La Mettrie, for example, posited a relation between the male imagination and the male genitals, as this remark suggests:

> Why does the sight, or the mere idea, of a beautiful woman cause singular movements and desires in us? Does what happens then in certain organs come from the very nature of those organs? Not at all, but from the intercourse and sort of sympathy of those muscles with the imagination. All we have here is one spring, excited by the ancients' "bienplacitum" or the sight of beauty, exciting another one, which was very drowsy when the imagination woke it. And what can cause this except the riot and tumult of the blood and spirits, which gallop with extraordinary rapidity and swell the hollowed-out organs?[1]

Although La Mettrie appeals to men's common experience to prove the relation between imagination and genitals, mind and body, others would find that connection potentially dangerous, especially if it brought on masturbation. The *Encyclopédie* entry "Manstupration" summarized the perils of habitual practice as described by the good doctor Tissot in his 1760 treatise *L'onanisme.* Tissot argued that normal sexual relations fulfilled natural urges but imagined desires solicited masturbation. Succumbing to these desires brought on further lascivious thoughts—and further masturbatory activity.[2] Habitual male masturbation drained the body of its vital fluids, which both enervated the physical organs and led to mental disease. In extreme cases, death ensued.

The *Encyclopédie* entry relied on Tissot but also pointed out that therapeutic masturbation could augment the outlet for sexual tension nature provided for men in wet dreams and other spontaneous ejaculations.[3] To be sure, male masturbation led to deadly results if frequent and driven by imagination and passion. Still, the *Encyclopédie* entry admits: "Masturbation that is not frequent, not prompted by an impulsive and sensual imagination, and that is, in the end, determined by need, is not in any way harmful and, therefore, is in no way wrong. At least not from a medical point of view."[4] This conclusion differed significantly from the account of female masturbation contained in the entry on *fureur utérine* or *nymphomanie.* There, self-stimulation was deemed particularly harmful for women since it inevitably brought on a kind of madness to which no man was subject.

Nymphomania

The *Encyclopédie* defines nymphomania, or *fureur utérine,* as a delirium, a disease of the venereal appetite that drives women to use every possible means to try to extinguish the uncontrollable ardor that devours them.[5] Frequent sexual intercourse was not the defining feature or symptom of nymphomania, but rather, the illness was one of insatiable desire. The *Encyclopédie* presented this account of woman's susceptibility: delicate nerve fibers located in her genitals are particularly sensitive to vibrations that physical or mechanical contact sets into motion. Once excited, these vibrations travel to the brain, prompting it to imagine representations of lascivious things. As the genital organs react on the brain, so the brain reacts back on the genitals. The brain releases a nervous fluid, which when sent to the genitals, stimulates more vibrations, and these in turn travel back to the brain releasing more erotic imaginings. This vicious cycle between woman's genitals and brain disrupts the proper workings of her imaginative functions. As a result, imagination veers out of control and fixes on erotic things.[6] Soon she is prey to insatiable desire and, of course, nymphomania.

This circuit, moreover, explains how dangerous was the relation between reading and masturbating, bringing together physical and mental stimulation. The assumed connection between a woman's genitals and imaginative function meant first that the "normal" excitability of the genitals would be increased by external, physical causes: for example, by touching, coitus, or any action that could stimulate orgasm. And second, that once her brain was affected, a sick woman's distress was not relieved, but only worsened, "by the normal remedy of love, which is orgasm."[7]

Nymphomania, moreover, was not simply a woman's disease dependent on her physiological makeup. It was a woman's disease that had no male counterpart, as the *Encyclopédie* explained: "If observation had provided examples of men affected with this type of uncontrollable desire pushed to the same extreme, one would have called the resulting derangement of the physical functions *fureur vénérienne,* a name that would have conveyed this sort of delirium considered in both sexes; but men are not subject as women are."[8] The author goes on to argue that morals did not impose on men the same constraints that restricted women, so they could satisfy their urges through extramarital or premarital intercourse without fear of losing either their modesty or their good reputations.[9] Moreover, the male organs of generation are constituted differently; because men can experience involuntary ejaculations and wet dreams, they have a natural means of stifling the need for copulation.

This account, however, did not exclude the possibility that men also suffered from some sort of sexual mania. The article "Satyriasis" at first seems to outline a man's disease that corresponds to nymphomania in women. Satyriasis is marked not only by frequent and long lasting erections, but by "a violent appetite for venereal pleasures, which degenerates nearly [presque] to furor."[10] But "nearly" is the operative word here, and reading further we learn: "Men are the only ones subject to satryiasis, properly speaking, but women are not exempt from diseases characterized by insatiable desires for venereal pleasures: the need is the same in both sexes, as are the sins. Women are punished even more than men. Diseases of this kind progress further in women and are much more violent."[11] The entry goes on to cite as cause for their greater distress women's more excitable imaginations coupled with the constraints that law and education impose. In women, venereal illness advances and "soon it is to the point of deranging the reason of these unfortunate sufferers."[12] Concluding its discussion of women's greater distress, the article describes the disgusting acts to which the sex is driven and refers the reader to the entry on "fureur utérine."

Not only did the *Encyclopédie* entry "Fureur utérine" label nymphomania an illness that had no exact male counterpart, it distinguished uterine furor from mere lovesickness or erotic melancholy, also tied to sexuality. The entry on melancholy listed among its causes not only the passions, but more particularly disappointments in which either the romantic or sexual appetites were not satisfied. Such disappointments were often followed by a "melancholic delirium."[13] In associating melancholy with lovesickness and erotic longing, eighteenth-century writers were revamping a very old tradition, one that had already been set out by the ancients, expanded by the neo-Platonists, and explored by doctors such as Jacques Ferrand in his 1623 treatise on lovesickness. Although nymphomania had for its immediate object the sexual act in general, erotic melancholy sought only to be with some person hopelessly loved.[14] Nevertheless, the two syndromes were related for women: unrequited love could bring on insatiable desire, and the passions developed from reading novels could induce a woman to fixate on any love object that chance put in her path. Just as there was no drawing a firm line to separate a melancholy temperament, the disease of melancholia, and melancholic genius, so lovesickness could easily glide into a more dangerous and disruptive erotic disease.

The problem of woman's sexual deviance came into clearer focus in 1771, when D. T. Bienville published his *La nymphomanie; ou, Traité de la fureur utérine.* For Bienville, true nymphomania combined an insatiable desire for sexual intercourse with delirium. Again, woman's susceptibility lay in her sensitive organs, which received livelier impressions and inflamed themselves more easily than those of men.[15] Lest his audience think he was tilting at windmills, Bienville was at pains to stress the reality of the threat. "The disease I treat is not a chimera; not only does it currently exist in the sex [i.e., women], it is every day making very rapid progress."[16] Indeed, he claimed that every woman was susceptible at one time or another to an obsession with those things that carried "the infernal flame of lubricity." Women with a naturally ardent temperament were especially at risk, but nymphomania could strike young girls who had never known love, prostitutes (*filles débauchées*), married women, and young widows. As Bienville put it, "In a word, all of them."[17]

Because all women were naturally at risk, they easily endangered themselves by unwise practices. According to Bienville, women exacerbated their "natural fire" and increased the risk of contracting the disease by reading "lascivious novels" that at first only disposed the heart to tender sentiments but ended by inspiring the grossest impropriety. They abused wine, alcohol, and chocolate, foods long known to inflame the passions. They secretly masturbated. He goes on to describe how the nymphomaniac was continually absorbed in her own thoughts and feared being distracted even for a single moment.[18] Like the melancholic given to study, she sought repose and silence. Perhaps she found these in the private boudoir and secluded garden, the favorite sites of erotic reading.

If no woman was immune to nymphomania, the disease posed the threat of becoming a contagion. Bienville tells us how women, usually servants but sometimes companions or governesses, introduced other women to the pleasures of Venus.[19] Although throughout Bienville's treatise the nymphomaniac is presented as having a primary heterosexual desire, sexual encounters with other women could function as an alternative method of gratification akin to or associated with masturbation. Even more directly than Bienville, Tissot (following Ferrand) had earlier linked tribadism to female masturbation and through masturbation to nymphomania. Arguing in his treatise on onanism that masturbation led to nymphomania, Tissot added to manual sullying, another sort he called "clitoridienne" whose origin he traced back to Sappho and to the Roman women condemned by Juvenal. With other doctors, Tissot believed these women used a "monstrous clitoris" to mimic the virile function in sexual relations. He noted that although this form of self-pollution had not gotten a lot of attention, it was "frequent" in contemporary society.[20]

Masturbation held a privileged place in the discourse on nymphomania, and Bienville envisioned his treatise as a supplement to Tissot's *Onanism,* which did not fully explore the practice in women. For Bienville, masturbation not only led to nymphomania, it was also the regular practice of all nymphomaniacs, not just those without other means of gratification. Predictably, Bienville tied masturbation to imagination, which stood as nymphomania's ultimate cause. An obsession with "disgusting" desires increased the progress of nymphomania; lascivious representations exhausted the imagination and finally it became so saturated with them that the sick woman dreaded any return to normalcy. To emphasize the important role imagination played in nymphomania, Bienville devoted his concluding chapter to the relation between them. There he showed that imagination brought on nymphomania because it demanded masturbatory practices, which aided the disease's progress by further inflaming imagination and binding women to forbidden pleasures. In this section he cites the sad case of one Julie, who dissimulates her "deadly mania for masturbation of which the imagination is the artisan."[21]

No one doubted that the female imagination crafted nymphomania. It was not easy to tell, however, in just which women imagination had created the disease. The difficulty in recognizing the nymphomaniac and distinguishing her from the "normal" woman made the disease particularly threatening and conveniently necessitated the surveillance and control of all women. This was especially the case since only in the very last stages of the disease did a victim show the horrible symptoms—the rickets and curving spine that Tissot described and the total madness that Bienville depicted so effectively in his cautionary examples. In its early stages, the disease had far more subtle symptoms that could easily be overlooked or misdiagnosed. These included a loss of color in the complexion and a general languor of body and expression.[22]

Sometimes a woman in danger remained invisible to the father and mother who feared for their daughter, the husband suspicious of his wife, or the ordinary doctor who wanted to know his patient's state. At least Bienville says as much. In discussing how women presented themselves to others, and especially to those in authority, he points out that they are careful to hide their filthy penchants. A woman's very nature, moreover, exacerbated the problem of detection. Moralists had long characterized woman as given to deception and artifice, and in Bienville's hands nymphomania is a disease that mirrors the wiles of its female host. Warning of nymphomania's dangers, Bienville wrote: "[I]t nearly always hides itself under a deceptive exterior of apparent calm, and often it is already dangerous even if one has not already perceived its beginnings, let alone its main progress. Sometimes the sick woman struck with nymphomania has a foot on the precipice without being aware of the danger; [nymphomania] is like a serpent that glides imperceptibly into her heart."[23] Bienville continually stresses not only the deceptiveness of the disease but also the deceptiveness of the sufferer. Although there are moments when women may wish to reform, more often they are preoccupied with the means of hiding their state from everyone else.[24] Patients feign, deceive, dissimulate, and in a sense his entire discussion praises women's artistry. Art here does not hide art, as eighteenth-century aesthetic theory demanded; rather, it hides nature, or what is most frightening about woman's nature. In this account, woman is a perverse artist whose performance is designed to sustain an abominable disease that could lead to delirium, melancholy, mania, and even death. In her artistry the nymphomaniac is both like and unlike the *convulsionnaire.* In that famous case, doctors found the symptoms of possession manufactured or embellished artfully, while in the case of the nymphomaniac, the act of "normalcy" artfully hid the obsession with erotic desires. In both instances, however, woman's artifice was on display.

Women on the verge of nymphomania could present an interesting subject for the artist. Take, for example, the shut-in Étienne Jeaurat depicted in *Woman Convalescing* (fig. 32) exhibited at the Salon of 1769. The title of this work scarcely fooled a discerning viewer like Denis Diderot. "This is a woman convalescing?" he asked. "Ah! Monsieur Jeaurat, you do not know the peril of her state; she is sicker than you think."[25] Nymphomania here masquerades as something else, and the woman

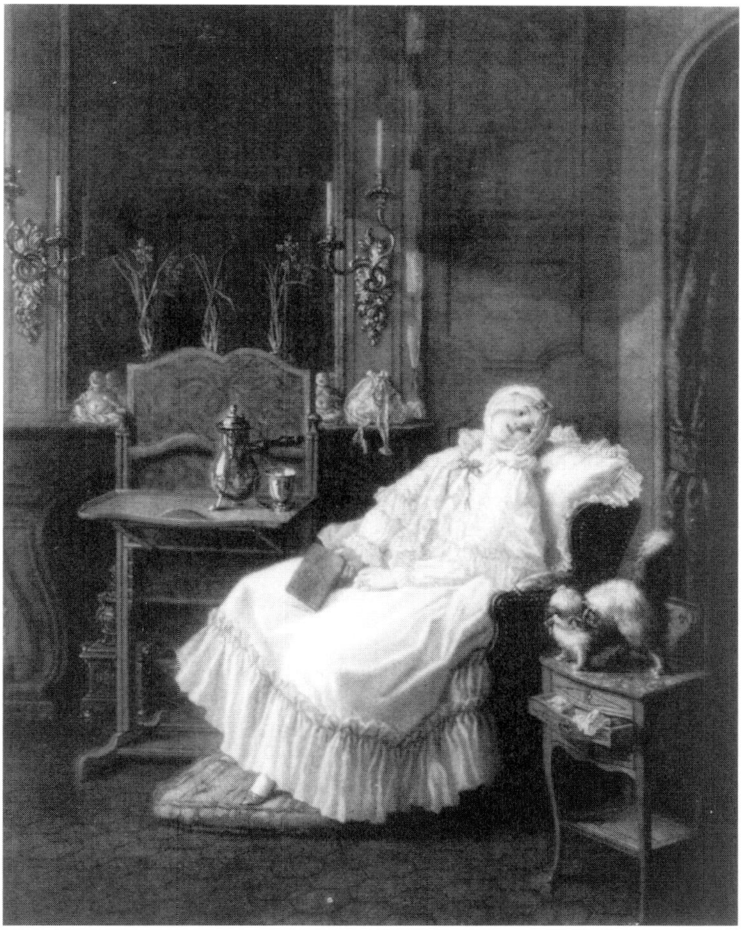

FIGURE 32. Étienne Jeaurat (French, 1699–1789), *Woman Convalescing*, Salon of 1769. Oil on canvas. Private collection.

assumes her role as a seemingly proper lady. She is carefully bundled up in a frilly bed coat and scarf, and her ankles are discretely covered. Neither woman nor room is in the obvious *beau désordre* that we find in Baudouin's *Reading,* and the bed alcove is far less evident. Indeed, the room seems carefully arranged with the symmetrically placed sconces on the mirror, the balanced *magots* sitting on the mantle, and the three vases in which long-stemmed flowers stand at attention. Like Baudouin's reader, however, the convalescent reclines in her chair, head supported by a pillow, with another cushion under her feet. The two painted women share a similar pose and expression with heads thrown back, eyes rolled up, and a smile playing on their lips. But the scene of masturbation is definitely underplayed in Jeaurat's image. The convalescent's left hand grasping the closed book and her right hand free of encumbrance both rest visibly in her lap.[26]

Now Jeaurat's convalescent might be suffering from a simple case of lovesickness, a malady often represented in the seventeenth-century

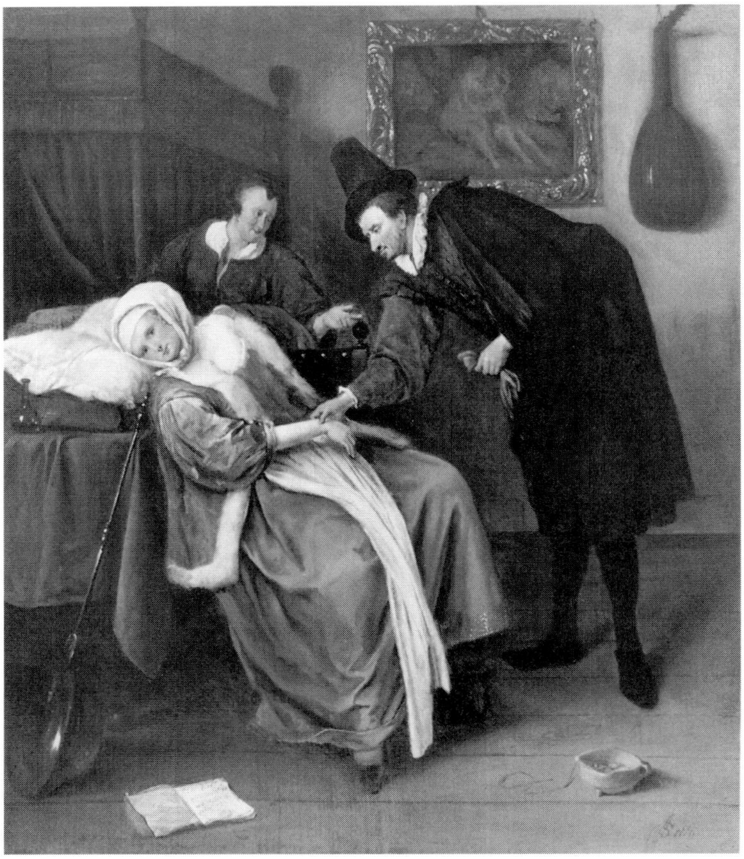

FIGURE 33. Jan Steen (Dutch, 1626–79), *The Doctor's Visit*, c. 1663. Oil on panel, 44.5 × 37.1 cm. Cincinnati, Ohio: Taft Museum of Art, Bequest of Charles Phelps and Anna Sinton Taft. Photo courtesy Taft Museum.

Dutch paintings that filled eighteenth-century French collections. In that tradition, analyzed recently by Laurinda Dixon, we see ladies languishing in poses similar to the one Jeaurat chooses, for example, in Jan Steen's *The Doctor's Visit* (c. 1663; fig. 33) or Gabriel Metsu's *Sick Lady and the Doctor* (c. 1665; Hermitage: St. Petersburg).[27] Sexuality is indicated in these Dutch examples by erotic images on the wall or the visible presence of a bed. There are, however, differences between the seventeenth-century Dutch works and those made in eighteenth-century France.

In the earlier paintings, doctors or servants attend the women represented, and there is often evidence of a "real" lover—a letter, a portrait, and so forth. None of the Dutch women appears to be masturbating, nor is any of them reading. The erotic prints displayed on their walls more cue the viewer to the nature of their disease than suggest its origin in the illusions of art. Like Baudouin's swooning reader, Jeaurat's convalescent shows signs—beyond her reading—that she is exalting her imagination. Note that she is positioned near the fireplace and that a chocolate server and cup are near her. Her tastes imply that the convalescent is given over to pleasures like chocolate drinking, which moralists found dangerous because they enflamed the passions. Her ecstatic expression hints at discrete masturbating. The chocolate, the reading, the masturbating lend a particular glow to her position near a fireplace.

All Ablaze

Through the metaphor of fire, nymphomania connects not only to the passions and sexuality but also to enthusiasm. In fact, Bienville figures nymphomania as a fire and uses related tropes to convey that disease's causes and effects. Referring to those struck with nymphomania, he calls it a "fire that devours them," "a fire that could suddenly ignite itself with greater force." He speaks of the inflamed atmosphere that surrounds nymphomaniacs, describes "the burning heat" that they experience. When the young Julie, suffering from nymphomania, casts her look on a young man, her eyes are "full of fire," and miming this young girl's imaginings, he writes, "My soul is devoured by a thousand desires that nothing can moderate. I burn with a fire that is a thousand times more violent than the most terrible fever."[28] No wonder Baudouin chose a masturbating woman, a blossoming nymphomaniac, to exemplify the day's hottest hour!

So widespread was the association between fire and female sexuality that the fireplace puns on the woman's sexual organs. In François Boucher's *The Woman Tying Her Garter* (1742; fig. 34), the artist rhymes visually the woman's splayed legs with the widely set jambs of the fireplace in which we see flames sparking. And in *The Private Academy* (fig. 35), Gabriel de Saint-Aubin asks us to look there, between the jambs of the fireplace, for he compares the nude model's genitals with that opening by associating the cartouche at the center of the mantel with the model's pubic triangle. Such images bring into focus the fireplaces we see in Jeaurat's *A Woman Convalescing* and in other images of women with books, such as Pierre Parrocel's *Young Woman Reading before a Fireplace* (1735; fig. 36).

Parrocel's image shows the back view of a seated woman reading before a fire. She could be a housemaid, a governess, or the mother of the child standing nearby. The relation is not at all clear. It is evident, however, that she is oblivious to his presence, and even from the back view Parrocel conveys that she is engrossed in what she reads. Not only is the woman's head bent toward her book, but she grasps it with both hands. Her right arm moves around the book and supports it from behind, while her left hand holds the top of the left page, with fingers visible over the edge. It is a rather tight embrace, and there is no doubt as to the nature of her reading. Parrocel places a small cupid figurine

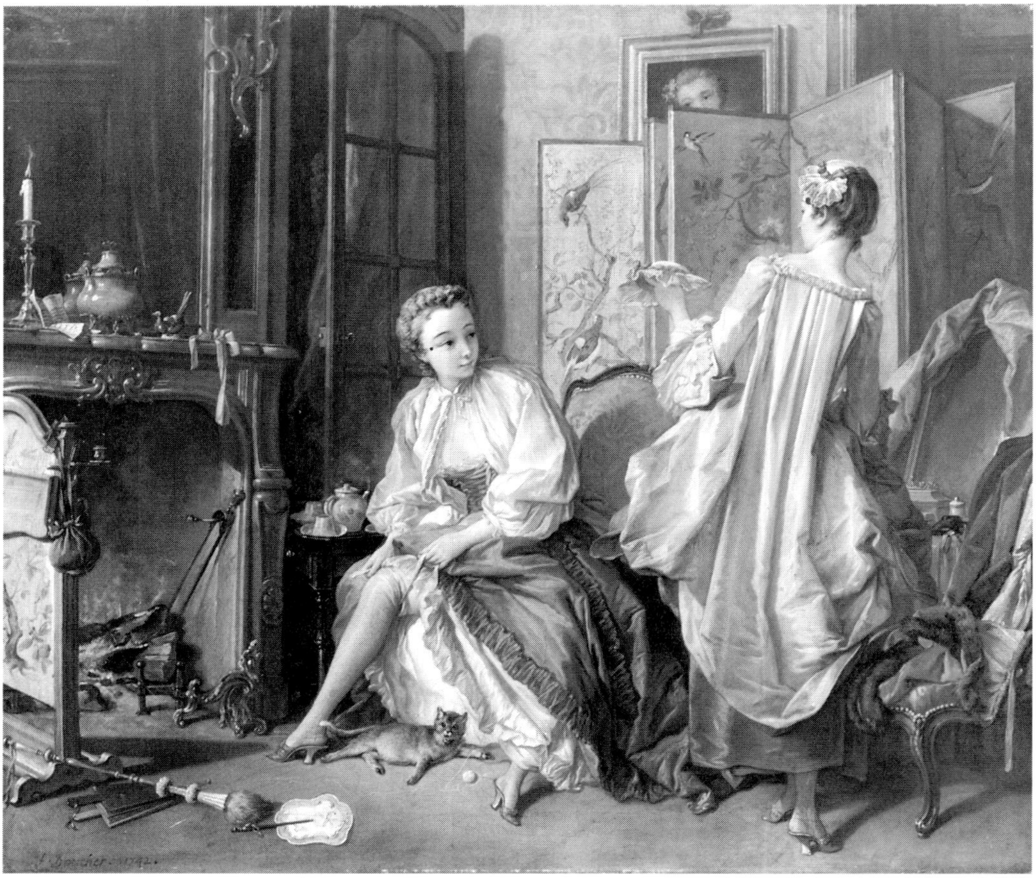

FIGURE 34. François Boucher (French, 1703–70), *The Woman Tying Her Garter*, 1742. Oil on canvas, 52.5 × 66.5 cm. Madrid, Fundación Colleción Thyssen-Bornemisza. Photograph © Museo Thyssen-Bornemisza, Madrid.

on the mantelpiece and among the cards lying on the floor is the ace of hearts, a traditional symbol of love. Obviously this woman is reading a romance that fans her flames in the same way the bellows lying near the hearth could be used to keep the fire alit. How long before the book leads to a crime worse than ignoring the child? How long before her hand slips beneath her skirt? How long before she falls ill from her activities?

Although "fire" might characterize woman's true nature, it was neither proper nor modest for her to be burning. It was primarily immodest women in libertine books and pictures who were thus shown or signified. The general conception of the woman "inflamed" is perhaps most clearly displayed in Jean-Honoré Fragonard's *The Powder Keg* (*Le feu aux poudres,* before 1778; fig. 37). In this work a putto holds a lighted torch between a young woman's legs, seeming to ignite her genitals. With her drapery gathered up at her waist and down at her bosom, she lolls back seductively, deep in her dreams or reveries, which we can presume to be erotic. A smile lingers on her lips, and she seems pleased by the attention of this putto and his companions. Yet this work is especially pertinent because it also plays on fire as the (implied) artist's creative enthusiasm

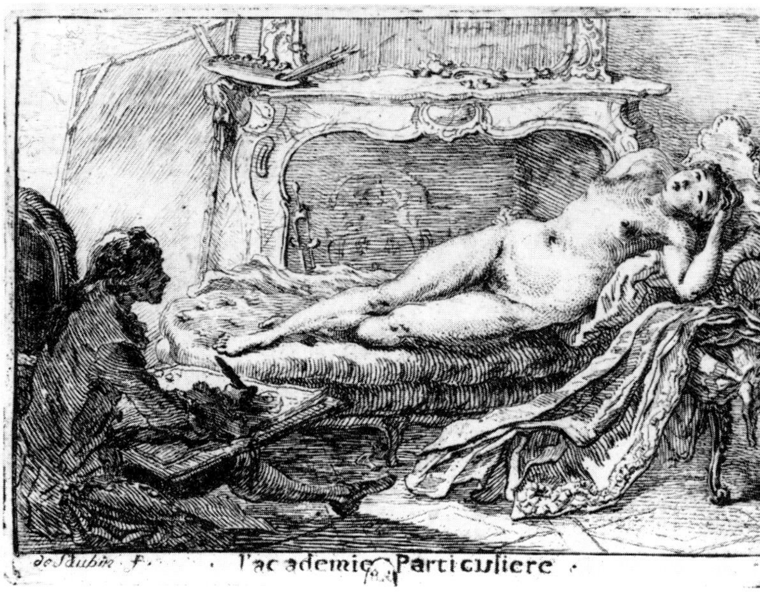

FIGURE 35. Gabriel de Saint-Aubin (French, 1724–80), *The Private Academy*, Paris: Photograph: Bibliothèque Nationale de France.

FIGURE 36. Pierre Parrocel (French, 1670–1739), *Young Woman Reading before a Fireplace*, 1735. Oil on canvas, 36.5 × 47 cm. Stockholm: Drottlingholm Palace Nationalmuseum. Photograph courtesy Nationalmuseum Stockholm.

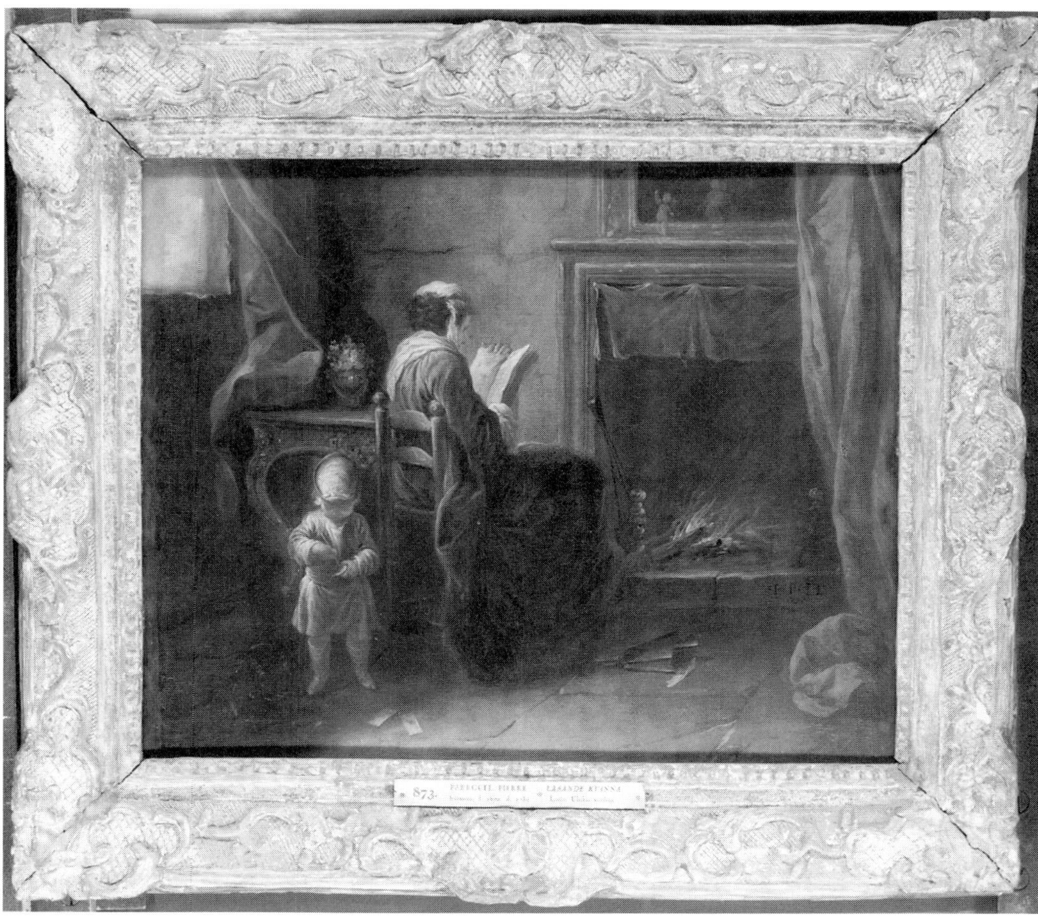

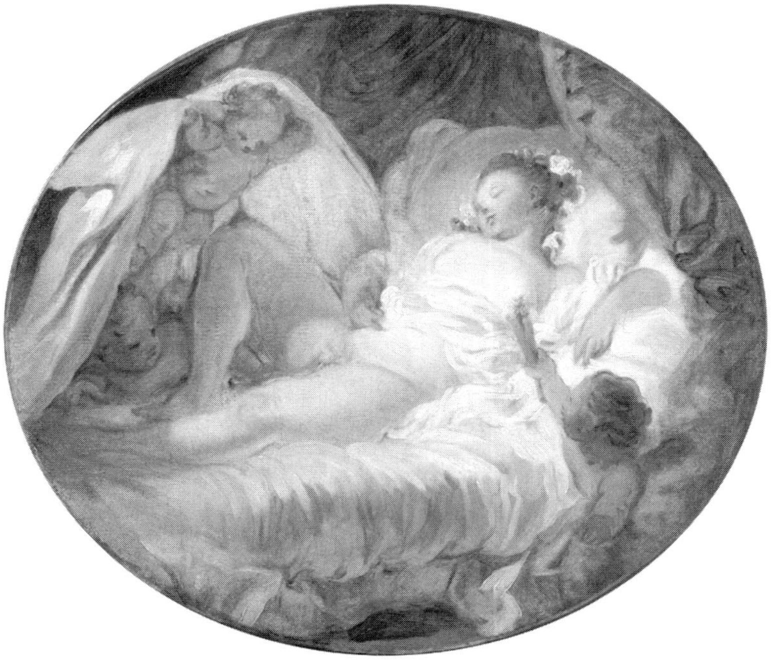

FIGURE 37. Jean-Honoré Fragonard (French, 1732–1806), *The Powder Keg (Le feu aux poudres)*, c. 1778. Oil on canvas, 37 × 45 cm. Paris: Musée du Louvre. Photograph© Réunion des Musées Nationaux/Art Resource, NY.

and passion. *The Powder Keg,* in fact, trades on the doubled meaning of fire as male sexual desire and as creative energy, or enthusiasm.

As explicit in connecting the fires of desire and enthusiasm is Nicolas Bertin's undated *Anacreon and Amour* (fig. 38). The subject is drawn from the life of the Greek poet Anacreon, well-known and loved in the eighteenth century for his erotic and graceful poetry. We see in Bertin's picture the results of Anacreon's kindness to Cupid, who arrived cold and wet at his door asking for shelter. As the young god of love dried himself at the fire, he decided to test his bow to see if it had rusted. In the process he hits Anacreon with an arrow. Although the roaring flames we see in an eighteenth-century fireplace might simply be there to situate the story, Bertin has put them to other use. They play off the much smaller flame that lights Anacreon's working desk where we see the artist sitting before books, papers, and a scroll bearing the title of his most famous work.[29] The flaming arrow that pierces his side is lined up visually with the pen in its inkwell, and the obvious suggestion is that Love's fire will inspire Anacreon's poetry. Indeed, struck with Cupid's arrow, the poet's eyes fall on the god himself. The poet in love with Love is thus inspired to write more verse. The sensuality of the scene is increased by the slender, nearly nude Anacreon, typical of the young, libidinous male gods who appeared in other of Bertin's mythological love scenes.[30] This Anacreon is shown as a desirable and desiring male body inflamed, indeed inspired, to write of love.

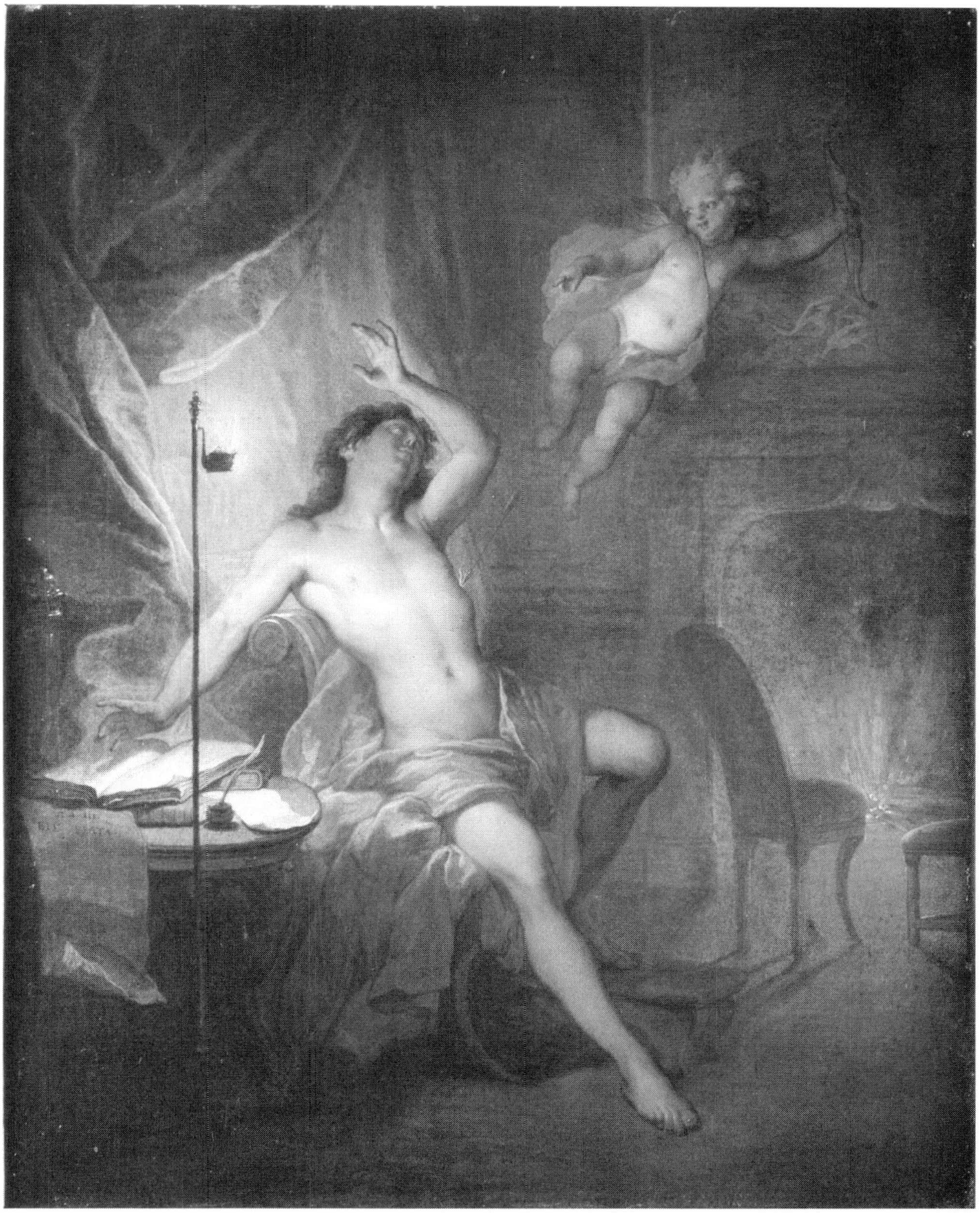

The Sketch and the Finished Work

FIGURE 38. Nicolas Bertin (French, 1667?–1736), *Anacreon and Amour,* c. 1715–20. Autun, Musée Rolin. Oil on canvas, 46 × 37 cm. Photograph © cliché S. Proust, courtesy Musée Rolin, Autun, France.

Because enthusiasm was the fire that motivated the artist to create, that emotion left its traces in the action, the play, the physical touch of the brush. When touch was considered a true index, the touching most apt to signify enthusiasm was that associated with the sketch. A sketch-like technique—evident in both Bertin's *Anacreon* and especially in Fragonard's *The Powder Keg*—was widely perceived to be close to the "hot" stages of inspiration, as Diderot was to remark in his "Salon of 1765": "The sketch usually has a fire that the painting does not. It is the heated moment for the artist, the purest verve without any mixing of the affectation that reflection puts into everything."[31] If the sketch-like technique indicated the "fire" of enthusiasm as creative energy, when used to represent an erotic scene of a woman sexually aroused, it both suggested her ardor and expressed the passion of the male artist.

As the academic theorist Claude Henri Watelet (1718–88) made clear, the artist's touch was at once an imitative sign tied to the object represented and an expressive sign, linked to how the artist saw and felt in making the representation.[32] Thus the touch was to resemble or be appropriate for the object represented, and in the case of Fragonard's *The Powder Keg*, the "fire" of the sketchlike technique depicts female ardor. Yet the touch also "expressed" how the artist "felt": here it suggests that the fires of genius and love have inflamed him. The idea that the artist would be sexually as well as creatively on fire after contemplating a mental image obviously inflects the way enthusiasm might be understood to pervade paintings like those of Fragonard and Bertin.

At this point it might be useful to compare how women artists represented Sappho, that other ancient poet whom passion inspired. Women who made images of Sappho inspired by love did not overtly show either Sappho or themselves as enflamed or fired by passion. Passion is toned down to a sweeter, more decorous sensibility in both Angelica Kauffman's *Sappho* (1775; fig. 39) and that of Marie Guillemine Benoist (1768–1826) shown at the Salon of 1795 (current location unknown).[33] In each case the artist depicts Cupid gently touching Sappho's shoulder as he inspires her poetry. Sappho sits calmly, and her image is rendered in a carefully finished paint handling. No woman painter in the eighteenth century represented a passionate Sappho burning with the fires of love and enthusiasm; none showed ardent sexual desire motivating her art. Although filled with touching sentiment, Kauffman's Sappho, like that of Benoist, seems distant from the image of the poet Barthélemy felt empowered to write in his *Voyage of the Young Anacharsis*.[34]

Sappho remained a privileged example of a woman who transformed her passion into art, but it is important to keep in mind that although women took her as a model, she remained suspect as a tribade, as a woman of transgressive sexuality. The passionate Sappho did become popular in late eighteenth- and early nineteenth-century painting, but men executed the extant works. More significant, however, is that instead of showing her passion transformed into art, these artists preferred to show it leading to her suicide. Jean-Joseph Taillasson (Salon of 1791; Brest: Musée des Beaux-Arts), Pierre-Narcisse Guérin (c. 1800; St.

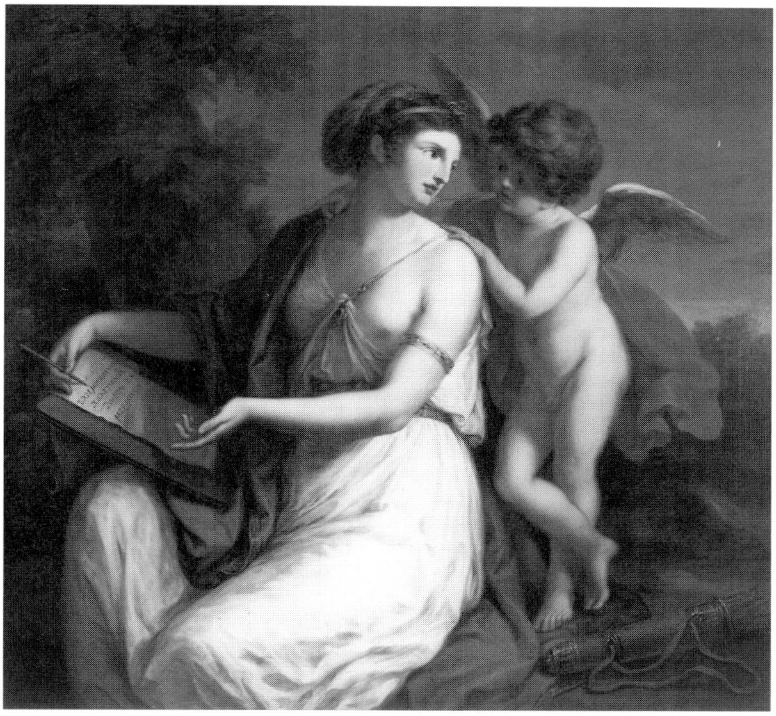

FIGURE 39. Angelica Kauffman (Swiss, 1741–1807), *Sappho,* 1775. Oil on canvas, 52 × 57 1/8 inches, SN329. Bequest of John Ringling, Collection of The John and Mable Ringling Museum of Art, The State Art Museum of Florida. Photograph courtesy the Ringling Museum of Art.

Petersburg: Hermitage), and Antoine-Jean Gros (1801; Bayeux, Musée Baron Gérard; fig. 40) all show the Sappho who in despair over losing her man leapt from the rock at Leucatus.

Where's the Ass?

Although the relation between a man's imagination and his genitals could lead to masturbation, disease, and death, a sexually excited imagination was not inevitably harmful to him. Many imagined a positive relation between male sexuality and creative imagination, even if sexual excitement was not the only requirement for making great art. Diderot makes this clear in his "Salon of 1767" when he points out that passion makes only sketches, which thrive on enthusiasm and genius, but paintings demand prolonged study and technical experience. This distinction explains why sometimes a student can make a great sketch but cannot produce an adequately finished work.[35] The issues, however, are both complicated and sexualized as the critic exemplifies his thoughts through a tale whose salacious humor he heralds with this remark: "If you send these pages to any women whose ears have not been broken in, advise them to stop here, or to read what follows only when they're alone."[36]

The main character in the anecdote is a youthful Charles de Brosses (1709–77), who visited prostitutes with his friend the naturalist Georges

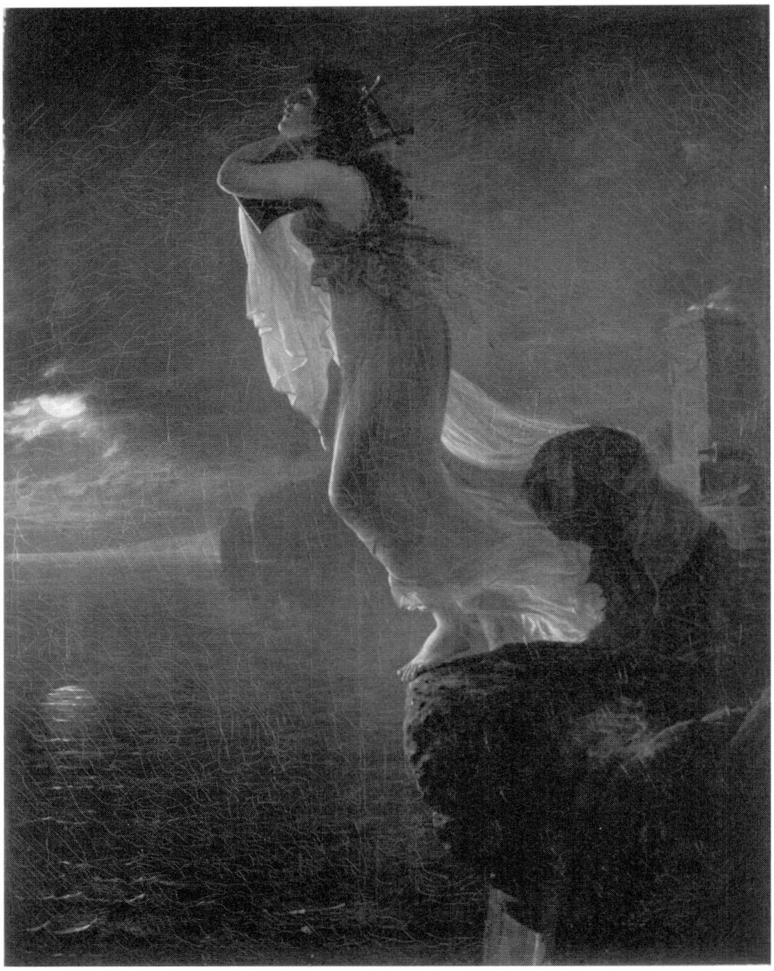

FIGURE 40. Antoine-Jean Gros (French, 1771–1835), *Sappho Leaping from the Rock of Leucatus*, 1801. Oil on canvas, 122 × 100 cm. Bayeux, Musée Baron Gérard. Photograph © Réunion des Musées Nationaux/Art Resource, NY.

Louis Leclerc, comte de Buffon (1707–88):

> One evening when they were with some prostitutes and in the intimate dress worn in a house of pleasure, the little *président* [de Brosses], who is scarcely taller than a Lilliputian, unveiled before their eyes an asset so astonishing, so prodigious, so unexpected that everyone cried out in admiration. But having admired it greatly, they began to reflect. After circling the marvelous little *président* several times in silence, one of them said to him: "Monsieur, that's beautiful, no doubt about it, but where's the ass to pump it?"[37]

The story continues on with a comparison between a sketch and de Brosses's impressive asset, so proudly on display:

> My friend, if someone presents you with the rough draft of a tragedy or comedy, take a few turns around the man, and say to him, like the

> prostitute to the *président* de Brosses: That's beautiful, no doubt about it, but where is the ass? If it is a financial project always ask, where is the ass? To the draft for a novel or speech, where's the ass? To the sketch for a painting, where's the ass? Perhaps the sketch attracts us so strongly because being somewhat indeterminate it leaves more to our imagination, which sees in it anything it pleases.[38]

Here the sketch is the work of ardent burning youth, a time of life when both men and women were commonly thought to be most easily aroused. The male genitals, presumably in an erect state, are compared to the sketch, and sexual arousal, to the excitement of conceiving a great idea. A prodigiously large penis is like a sketch, not only because it is susceptible to enthusiasm but also because it gives free rein to the viewer's imagination. It is the promise of pleasure for both the artist/customer and the spectator/prostitute. But to make this "sketch" into great art, its possessor needs the right "ass"—the "ass" standing for hard work, prolonged study, and technical skill.

The *président* may reveal his prodigious asset, but it is the prostitute who unveils truth, and it is she Diderot asks us to emulate in her skeptical challenge. As a professional, this savvy whore does not simply imagine the pleasure such an instrument might bring, but after observing and reflecting, asks the practical question: "Where's the ass to pump it?" Rather than losing her head over the "sketch," she wants to know if the *président* has what it takes to finish the job. And because she has looked him over before posing her question, we can infer that she has her doubts. The prostitute emerges as a woman whose emotions do not interfere with her analytical processes, a woman who dispassionately observes, a woman who reasons, a woman who knows how to control her fantasy and how to wield the gaze. One can only imagine that such a woman would dampen a young man's enthusiasm.

The prostitute intrudes again in the discourse of art making when the enthused artist is figured as a passionate Pygmalion. Pygmalion was moved to make his ideal woman after he lost his desire for the real thing, for the women Venus transformed into the first prostitutes. But does Pygmalion reject these desiring women because they are lascivious or because their presence in his story can deflate male pretense grown large?

Pygmalion's Enthusiasm

The mythical artist Pygmalion easily slipped into the discourse of enthusiasm, and in his *Encyclopédie* entry Cahusac invoked his achievement in describing the artist's compulsion to create: "So without anything able to distract or stop him, the painter seizes his brush and the canvas is colored, the figures arranged, the dead revived; the chisel is already in the hand of the sculptor and the marble comes to life."[39] And indeed, many statues did come to life in eighteenth-century France. They appeared on the stage in vaudevilles and ballets and in the new genre of monodrama. Animated statues peopled philosophic treatises, scientific writings, poems, and panegyrics. Painting and sculpture, porcelain and book illustration represented their metamorphosis. Most of these statues were the work of Pygmalion, whose invasion of French arts and letters spanned the entire century. In chapter 5, I will analyze some of these representations in detail. Throughout the eighteenth century, many were taken with the sculptor-king Pygmalion who, rejecting real women, made himself an ideal one. He was mad enough to fall in love with his stone virgin and fortunate enough to see her animated. His story is one of a peculiar enthusiasm, a mad love, a deluded imagination, all heated up by his creative and erotic fires.

The best-known version of Pygmalion's story, the one that shaped all the others, was the tale Ovid told in his *Metamorphoses*, a text writers translated throughout the eighteenth century. There, Ovid described how a Cypriot sculptor named Pygmalion fell in love with a maiden he carved from pure, white ivory. Unlike the beauty Zeuxis made, Pygmalion's ideal was not composed by combining the most perfect features in real women. He would never have allowed those lascivious wretches—for that was his opinion of the sex—into his workplace as Zeuxis had done. Pygmalion, we know, had sworn off women, hardened to the fair sex by the obscene Propoetides and their wanton ways. Ovid makes a particular point of distinguishing Pygmalion's artful creation from her living semblables: "Meanwhile with wondrous art he successfully carves a figure out of snowy ivory, giving it a beauty more perfect than that of any woman ever born."[40] By emphasizing the difference between Pygmalion's sculpture and those creatures of "woman born," Ovid not only proclaims the ivory superior to the flesh; he also compares and separates artful male creativity from "natural" female reproduction.

It is the sight of his ideal creation, his brainchild, that touches Pygmalion and moves him, "And with his own work he falls in love."[41] Now dependent on an object of sensation, Pygmalion kisses and caresses his masterpiece; he fondles it, speaks to it, and decks it in jewels and finery. His courting of the statue parodies the rituals of love poetry and makes his ardor seem perverse and more than a little mad. He imagines, moreover, that the statue—called Galatea only in later reworkings of the story—returns his affection. In giving the statue no name, Ovid's text reveals that Pygmalion engages not another subject but his own passion reflected back to him through his art. In Ovid's tale, Venus endows Pygmalion with the confidence he needs to believe in his own ability to animate matter—this is his gift from the gods, his divine inspiration. When he next kisses the statue and caresses her breast, he feels the ivory softening and warming under his touch, a sensation he had hitherto experienced only in his imagination. We learn little about Pygmalion and his statue after she comes to life, only that their relation is carnal, and Ovid tells us that nine months later the infant girl Paphos is born.

Ovid's *Metamorphoses* includes Pygmalion's tale among those stories that Orpheus narrates, and there it has a complex relation to themes of art, desire, and misogyny.[42] Eighteenth-century authors and artists who reworked Pygmalion's tale abstracted it from this complex narrative web and emphasized those aspects that resonated with Enlightenment aesthetic discourse. As retold in eighteenth-century France, Pygmalion stories confirmed that erotic desire was part of the creative process. So much was this the case that in Boureau-Deslandes's materialist tract, *Pigmalion; ou, La statue animée* (1741), the sculptor fears working on the statue of a goddess or a heroine after he has rejected women:

> He feared arousing himself and igniting in his heart fires that he would not then have been able to extinguish. How, in effect, to represent a beautiful woman, to give life to her eyes and grace to her flesh tones; how to characterize a perfect smile, a noble carriage of the head, that marvelous undefinable something that renders the entire physiognomy lively, without himself being touched? The imagination of the painter or the sculptor sketches, the heart finishes and perfects.[43]

Pygmalion here stands as both creator and spectator; once his imagination has sketched and contemplated the desirable object, the sculptor catches fire. Unable to extinguish the flames, he is compelled to complete the work and destined to fall under its spell.

Artists often chose the Pygmalion story to represent their profession in eighteenth-century France, taking as an imaginary ancestor not a rational creator but a desiring lover. Although writers, composers, and painters also identified their art with his animating power, Pygmalion's creative act sometimes specifically represented sculpture when paired with the tale of Apelles and Campaspe, a standard emblem for painting. One might say that the century opened with a pairing of Pygmalion and Apelles as the presiding geniuses of sculpture and painting. In 1700, Antoine Houdar de La Motte's *Le triomphe des arts* showed Painting as the story of Apelles and Campaspe, and Sculpture as that of Pygmalion and Galatea. Sculptures also linked the two themes. At the Salon of 1743, Lambert-Sigisbert Adam (1700–59) showed a terracotta sketch representing Pygmalion and Galatea, and two years later he exhibited another of Apelles painting Campaspe, which the *livret* listed as pendant to his *Pygmalion*. Reprising those sketches as finished works, the sculptor Étienne Falconet (1716–91) exhibited the same subjects as companion pieces fifteen years later at the Salons of 1763 and 1765.

The pairing of Pygmalion and Apelles highlights the role of erotic desire in art making. In recounting what happened when Alexander the Great brought his favorite mistress Campaspe to sit for his court artist Apelles, Pliny's *Natural History* tells us that in watching the portrait making, Alexander noticed that the artist had fallen love with his model. Out of a high regard for Apelles and satisfaction with his work, Alexander gave his concubine to the painter.[44] Both this story and that of Pygmalion show the artist favored—one by the ruler, the other by a divinity—and in both cases that favor is manifested as the satisfaction of libidinal desire. If casting the enthused artist as Pygmalion tacitly supported a vision of art making that put passion—the artist's narcissistic passion for his own work—center stage, the gesture seems far removed from the view of enthusiasm as reason's masterpiece. Yet there is a deep connection between the two. As I have argued in chapter 1, figuring enthusiasm as reason's masterpiece worked to secure the artist on the side of the eternally masculine, posing (masculine) reason and not (feminine) imagination as what generates images and excites the desire to create. The Pygmalion story in an allied gesture invests reproductive power in the male creator and repudiates female sexuality. In each case such a move was necessary because in so many ways the artist/Pygmalion resembled a woman.

A Mad Desire Satisfied, or Deviance Overcome

In giving life to his Pygmalion, Ovid added the explicit elements of art and animation to earlier versions of the tale in which Pygmalion is a Cypriot king, but not a sculptor, who makes love to a statue of Venus that remains a work of art. Ovid's invention, however, did not completely obscure his source material. Christian writers reanimated the old Cypriot king in castigating his sinfulness. This Pygmalion they saw as an idolater blinded by passion who violated a statue of Venus. Clement of Alexandria (ca. 150–215) underscored how erotic statues aroused vile desires and argued that Venus was not a goddess, but a woman who instituted prostitution on Cyprus.[45] The abbé Géraud de La Chau's need to refute this tradition in his 1776 *Dissertation sur les attributs de Vénus* suggests that it remained viable.[46] La Chau challenged the Church Fathers, asking if there was any reason to believe that Pygmalion, king of Cyprus, had assaulted the statue. Whether or not the story was believable, the idea that erotic statues (like titillating books and salacious painting) could corrupt viewers or promote lustful desires was alive and well in eighteenth-century France.[47]

In his "Salon of 1767," Diderot warns against lascivious sculpture, specifically targeting the copy of *Venus with the Beautiful Buttocks* on the grounds of Versailles. What Pliny (and other ancient writers) would repeat as evidence of sculpture's power, Diderot restates as insult.

> Those who people our public gardens with images of prostitution hardly realize what they are doing. So many sordid inscriptions unceasingly scribbled on the statue of the Venus of the Beautiful Buttocks in the gardens of Versailles; so many dissolute acts avowed in these inscriptions, so many insults made by debauchery even against its own idols; insults that mark wayward imaginations, an inexplicable mixture of corruption and barbarity, these are sufficiently instructive about the pernicious impression made by these sorts of works.[48]

The work Diderot condemns copies a famous erotic sculpture from antiquity thought so seductive that it drove young men—both heterosexual and homosexual—to try to copulate with it, the former approaching it from the front, and the latter, from behind. These men left the stains of their "insult" on the statue, which Diderot compares with the "marks" retained by the wayward imaginations of those incited to such acts. In aligning sexual desire for the sculpted Venus with depravity, moreover, Diderot invokes a longstanding tradition that categorized such deviance as a lovesickness or erotomania.

The seventeenth-century physician André Du Laurens (1558–1669), for example, culled from antique texts—both literature and medical writing—examples of those stricken with desire for a statue and repeated their cases in his *De maladies mélancholiques et du moyen de les guérir* (1613).[49] Following Du Laurens, Ferrand discussed many of these same examples in his *Treatise on Lovesickness* (1623), a work that had its influence into the nineteenth century. There Ferrand locates lovesickness in a depraved imagination and exemplifies its symptoms in Alkidias's love for a statue. In his account, a depraved imagination causes lovers not only to idealize inordinately a living object of desire but also to imagine inanimate things as appropriate love objects.

Ferrand argues that fascination with an inanimate object can lead not only to a loss of reason but also to despair, citing as his example a young Athenian who "became insane for love of a marble statue and killed himself."[50] Related to a depraved imagination, statue love takes its place with other sorts of melancholia; in Ferrand's hands these stories of desiring viewers are no tribute to the artist. Rather, they attest to imagination's power and potential for disorder. Ferrand's most comprehensive list of statue lovers comes in book 11, where they are one category of lovers "blinded by lasciviousness." There he includes

> those mentioned by Aelian and by Philostratus in his *Life of Apollonius* who were so enamoured of marble statues that they slew themselves for grief when the Athenian Senate refused to sell them those beautiful idols of their soul. Xerxes fell in love with a tree and Alkidias of Rhodes with a statue of Cupid sculpted by Praxiteles, Charicles with a statue of the Cnidian Venus, Narcissus and Eutelidas with their own shadows.[51]

What Ferrand finds "depraved" about these loves is that they offer no possibility for mutual affection, and perhaps this is why Ovid's Pygmalion, despite his obvious narcissism, does not figure among Ferrand's examples.[52] Ovid cures his Pygmalion of statue love by imagining that his work becomes a living woman who returns his affection. The sculptor's passion effects both a material transformation and a uniting of art and nature.

There is no doubt that before the miracle of animation Pygmalion suffers from lovesickness, and in Ovid's story his statue love does not seem reasonable. In detailing how Pygmalion makes love to his creation, Ovid retains the element of mad passion, which was at the core of the Pygmalion material he transformed, but did not obliterate. Later French classics that drew on the *Metamorphoses,* and in particular the *Romance of the Rose,* emphasized even more completely how abnormal and transgressive was Pygmalion's love. What that narrative is most intent on elaborating, as Kenneth Gross has argued, is "the phase *preceding* the event of animation, the dead statue's provocation in the sculptor of a 'suicidal madness.'"[53] And in eighteenth-century representations, Pygmalion is cast as suffering from a mental derangement. In Rameau's 1754 "Pigmalion, acte de Ballet," it is a "mad ardor"; in Boureau-Deslandes's *Pigmalion; ou, La statue animée,* it is a "strange passion," and "folly unleashed." In a travesty of Pygmalion's story, *Brioché; ou, L'origine des marionnettes* (1753), it is Folly and not Love who animates the statue.[54] Given the images of Pygmalion available in eighteenth-century France and the concepts of imagination and melancholia circulating at the time, it is hardly surprising that versions of Pygmalion showed his insane courtship before they resolved his dilemma through Galatea's animation.

Pygmalion's story, however, is part of a larger thematic in which art making depends on a condemnation of woman's imagination and sexuality, aspects of which are then appropriated by the male creator. Nowhere is this process more evident than in the treatment of

Pygmalion's lovesickness. Taken to represent the artist endowed with a *fureur poétique,* Pygmalion in his madness is actually quite close to the woman stricken with *fureur utérine.* Those writers and artists who drew their inspiration from Ovid tell us or show us that Pygmalion's masterpiece fires him with love. He imagines it returning his kisses, yielding to him, speaking to him. He imagines that it responds to him, just as a nymphomaniac imagines her Adonis returns her desire. Indeed, Bienville noted how the imagination of the woman struck with *fureur utérine* would transform the object that obsessed her—an ordinary young man—into an "Adonis."[55] In mentioning Adonis, he is, of course, invoking an idealized construction of myth and art. It is merely coincidental that Adonis is born from the incestuous coupling of Myrrha, Pygmalion's great granddaughter, with her father.

Not coincidental, however, is that what gives both artist and nymphomaniac ideas are art works—visual images or other sorts of representations. Bienville cites looking at erotic images as among the props the nymphomaniac uses to stimulate her imagination. Women, in fact, exacerbated their propensity to nymphomania by looking at lascivious pictures and sculptures. Woman's imagination, it was well known, confused reality and fantasy. Is Pygmalion so different in this regard? Pygmalion's confusion, however, has a different outcome in eighteenth-century versions of his story. His is not the story of insatiable desire but the fantasy of that which is *fulfilled.* And if the *Encyclopédie* tells us that men have opportunities for sating their desires that women do not, the Pygmalion story shows us that making art can lead to satisfaction. Not only does Galatea come to life, but in many instances she is the perfect, compliant, and obedient woman who expresses a total love for Pygmalion. In Antoine Houdar de La Motte's ballet, for example, Galatea sighs: "Ah! I feel that the gods who have given me life have only given it to me for you." And when Pygmalion says that the first movements of her heart have been to love him, Galatea adds, "And my first concern is to please you. I will always follow your rules."[56] In getting the woman he made for himself, Pygmalion also fulfills the desires of the Tissots and the Bienvilles to control women by compelling them to control themselves, by compelling them to restrict the workings of their imaginations.

If Ovid's tale posits a male creativity that depends on monopolizing desire, that monopoly is consolidated through repressing the potential nymphomaniac. A return to Ovid will make it clear how this dynamic structured his Pygmalion story right from the start. As the tale opens, Pygmalion has vowed celibacy and turned away from real women, disgusted and horrified by their lewd behavior. The particular women in question are the Propoetides, and their story moves us from the tale of

Hyacinth, set in Sparta, to that of Pygmalion, set on Cyprus, a location famous in antiquity for its sacred prostitution. As best we know, Ovid invented the Propoetides to explain why Pygmalion scorned women, but he also associated them with the prostitution for which Cyprus was famous. He imagines that Venus punishes the Propoetides for not believing in her divinity, making them forever subject to venereal pleasures. The goddess of love transforms them into prostitutes and strikes them, it seems, with a kind of nymphomania, an insatiable desire for sexual pleasure. Indeed, this is what the abbé de La Chau implies in his *Dissertation sur les attributs de Vénus,* claiming that the ancients believed her vengeance caused *fureur utérine.*[57] The Propoetides eventually turn to stone, their faces hardened when shame or modesty leaves them. Their fate is thus opposed (and compared) to that of the other woman, the one brought to life by the sculptor's touch.

The Propoetides, most importantly, are women "with the faults which in such full measure nature had given the female mind," as Ovid tells us.[58] It is those vices that also link Pygmalion's story with that of another animator, Prometheus; and some eighteenth-century writers easily conflated the two. Consider, for example, Voltaire's humorous poem, "L'Origine des Métiers" (1764), which is based on those versions of the story (including Voltaire's 1760 opera *Pandore*) in which Prometheus is a sculptor.[59] The poem opens by reminding its readers that Prometheus had fashioned with his own hands, animated, and married a statue of white marble named Pandora. Although Voltaire diverges from Hesiod's telling of Pandora's history in obvious ways, he, too, names her as the first woman.[60] And like the Biblical Eve, Voltaire's Pandora is the mother of all humans. Pandora not only makes Prometheus the first husband, she also transforms him into the first cuckold. As the verse unfolds, Pandora has it on with Mars, then Neptune, then Mercury, then Vulcan, and so forth. Because all humans are born from her different infidelities, all have different tastes and occupations: hence the title of the poem, "L'Origine des Métiers." The work concludes by proclaiming that although Pandora's métier is common, it is the sweetest—and the one all Paris honors. Pandora, of course, practices the métier of prostitution, the same profession that Ovid assigns to his Propoetides.

The hunger for sex that Voltaire uses as the basis for his humorous poem softens the condemnation of women found in Hesiod's account of Prometheus in both *Works and Days* and *Theogony.* In those texts, Prometheus is not himself a sculptor, but the one who steals the animating fires of heaven and brings them to earth. These tales also relate the origin of woman in a negative light. Before Prometheus's theft, only men inhabit the earth, reproducing themselves with nymphs or other demigods. Having been robbed by Prometheus, Zeus evens the score by sending to earth a counterpart to fire, a beautiful evil: woman. Zeus directs Hephaestus to mold the creature from mud, mixing lies and deceitful words with the wet earth. Although Pandora, the first woman, appears as a chaste virgin who incites love at first sight, what she conceals is, in Jean-Pierre Vernant's words, "the spirit of a bitch and the temperament of a thief."[61] In his brilliant analysis of the myth, Vernant concludes that "woman can compensate for fire and provide the balance because she herself is a kind of fire, which will burn men alive by consuming their strength day by day."[62] Women for Hesiod "roast" their husbands by their appetite for food and hunger for sex.[63]

Those other hungry women, the Propoetides, were not forgotten in the eighteenth century. On the stage they appeared in the Pygmalion story as women scorned. In La Motte's version, a Propoetide burns for Pygmalion's love, telling him: "My fires are ignited again by your scorn; my life is tied to the pleasure of seeing you."[64] Her ardor for Pygmalion is set against the sculptor's desire for his statue, and both seem equally hopeless as the story opens. By its end, however, Pygmalion's desire is satisfied, while the Propoetide is turned to stone. The libretto explains their different fates as devolving from contrasting attitudes toward Venus—Pygmalion invokes the goddess's power, while the Propoetide questions her divinity. Nevertheless, the juxtaposition of the man whose sexual desires, no matter how irrational, are satisfied, and the woman whose longings are not, resonates again with the discourse on sexual disease. This is especially the case when we consider that in other stage versions of Pygmalion's tale, the scorned woman is not turned to stone but doomed to burn with unrequited love. Social and physiological constraints prevent women from relieving their suffering, and they fall ill or turn to compulsive prostitution. Men, on the other hand, can satisfy their desires both by making love and making art.

The representation of woman as fundamentally a creature driven by her desires would have been familiar to many eighteenth-century French readers. It confirmed the reports of medical authorities who observed that women had the physical capacity to act on their desires repeatedly. Although writers on nymphomania did not explicitly name the Propoetides, they did view nymphomania as a sort of prostitution and cited other ancient models for debauched women to make the point. Tissot, for example, noted that because women did not lose fluid in the sex act, each had the potential to be a Messalina.

As a woman out of control, the Roman Messalina became a negative example invoked in cautionary tales. Along with Semiramis and Coelia, she brought together nymphomania and prostitution, for her excesses were understood as a prostitution by compulsion, a disease and not a profession. These women are linked with nymphomania in the *Encyclopédie:*

> It was undoubtedly from the effects of this sort of delirium carried to excess that Messalina was tired, exhausted, even satiated by the crudest pleasures to which she prostituted herself without limit and with the most infamous bestiality. It is also perhaps as true that because of this disease Semiramis, queen of the Assyrians . . . fell into the most shameful and excessive dissolution, to the point of giving herself to a great number of soldiers . . . Martial mentions Coelia's enormous debauchery, which by all appearances could only be the effect of a *fureur utérine,* since she was not a prostitute by profession. Otherwise there would have been nothing remarkable in her excesses.[65]

These historical examples fit the paradigm of the disease proposed by Tissot, who defined it as a libidinous rage, a continual and insatiable desire for copulation.[66] The ability to copulate repeatedly marks every woman as a potential prostitute or nymphomaniac, just as the mental and physical equipment for making art marks every man as a potential Pygmalion. Indeed, in the Pygmalion story we see that woman's potential for libidinous rage is not limited to the Propoetides, it erupts again in Pygmalion's great granddaughter Myrrha.

In the *Metamorphoses,* Myrrha's tragedy follows directly Pygmalion's triumph and is related to it in several significant ways. Not only is Myrrha descended from Pygmalion's mating with his statue, but she—like the sculptor—is overcome by strong desires. And like those of Pygmalion, Myrrha's desires are incestuous. In the original case, the sculptor develops a passion for the girl he has created, or fathered, as tradition would have it.[67] Reversing the positions of creator and created, Pygmalion's great granddaughter develops an incestuous desire for her father. Love's madness drives Myrrha, and she unwillingly capitulates to desire. Her story ends in tragedy as Myrrha finally tricks her father into copulating with her repeatedly. Ferrand includes Myrrha among those unnatural lovers who "engaged in lewd and foul relationships with their fathers, mothers, brothers, or with dumb beasts."[68] Through Myrrha and her incestuous love the *Metamorphoses* suggests that erotic disorders persist in the artist's bloodlines—and manifest themselves in his female progeny.

The Psychology of Desire and Art

It is tempting to argue that the myth of Pygmalion had a special resonance in eighteenth-century France since its various components—creativity, desire, erotomania—could so easily be configured to express prevailing paradigms of artistic production. Yet in another sense, embracing Pygmalion as the model artist runs against the current that sought to rationalize the production of art and to place art making on the side of reason. Little is rational or reasonable in Pygmalion's story. Moreover, to argue that Pygmalion has a "special" relation to the eighteenth century is to ignore all the evocations of the sculptor that came before, and the many that came after. If one part of my project is to historicize the Pygmalion theme and present it as a complicating factor for a period that considered itself the age of reason, another is to suggest why we should be interested in those complications, why we should care how eighteenth-century writers configured artistic creativity and woman's place in it. Beyond antiquarian or academic interest, the problem still has import for us today.

Although it would be foolish to pinpoint an originary moment, it is arguable that modern configurations of sexuality, gender, and aesthetics crystallized in eighteenth-century France (and elsewhere). This is not to suggest that individual ideas were radically new. As I have argued, some notions—for example, that of woman's impressionability—had a long history prior to the eighteenth century even if Enlightenment science and philosophy gave them new form and justification. Aspects of the new configuration are evident in Pygmalion stories and pictures, which taken together form a rich archive of images. A look at later Pygmalion myths, and especially those that color our own common notions of artistic production, suggests the continued power of the sculptor king and his repudiation of real women. But if Pygmalion has force today, it is because Sigmund Freud reconstituted this configuration of ideas in his analysis, or rather his mythology, of creative work. Stephen Owen has remarked that "the myth of Pygmalion giving life to stone raises a possibility that haunts art: the work of art might be nothing more than the bare image of the artist's craving and the cravings of the audience."[69] If this possibility "haunts" anything, it is the Kantian notion of an aesthetic appreciation free of all interest, appetite, and desire. Friedrich Nietzsche effectively belittled this notion in the third book of *The Genealogy of Morals* (1887) in which he cites the example of Pygmalion. He points out that while

> our aesthetes never get tired of throwing into the scales in Kant's favor the fact that under the magic of beauty men can look at even naked female statues "without interest," we can certainly laugh a little at their expense:—In regard to this ticklish point, the experiences of *artists* are

more "interesting" and at any rate Pygmalion was not necessarily an "un-aesthetic man."[70]

The persistent repetition (and citation) of the Pygmalion myth in various forms suggests a continuous belief in the erotic nature of art making, a belief reinforced in Freud's psychoanalysis and reiterated still today. As others have long pointed out, in this view of art making, male erotic desire generates art. Looking forward from Ferrand and back from Freud brings into clearer focus the traditions and mythologies that had long surrounded art making in the West and suggests both their tenacity and infinite potential for creative metamorphosis.

In recent years there has been an interchange between Freud's theories and the Pygmalion myth as critics and interpreters have used psychoanalytic concepts to elucidate different versions of Pygmalion's story.[71] But Freud, too, had his fling with statues in *Delusions and Dreams* (1907), a text that treats a fictional narrative—Wilhelm Jensen's 1903 novella, *Gradiva*—as if it were a case history. Although in his account Freud certainly recognizes a difference between the fictive and the real, his handling of the one as if it were the other has a special resonance with Pygmalion's treatment of an ivory statue as an actual lover. Jensen's novella, moreover, takes another confusion of the fictive and the real as its subject, for in *Gradiva* a young man is obsessed with a sculpted woman. That man is an archaeologist, Norbert Hanold, who as the story opens has no interest in the opposite sex but becomes increasingly involved with an antique bas-relief that depicts a young woman walking.

What at first intrigues Hanold about his walker is that her "realistic, simple maidenly grace" seems to impart life to the relief. His obsession begins as a desire to know if the artist reproduced the manner of walking from life, and he eventually decides the relief represents a young Pompeiian woman hurrying across the cobblestones. He calls his stone woman Gradiva, which is translated from the Latin as "beauty in walking." Through a series of dreams, delusions, and encounters with what he takes as Gradiva's reincarnation, Hanold convinces himself that the young woman, though she belonged to the first century A.D., still lives. As the story unfolds, we find that the girl he has mistaken for Gradiva is actually his childhood friend Zoë Bertgang, who after perceiving his fantasy, consciously plays the part of Gradiva to free him from it. What finally shocks Hanold from his delusions is touching the hand of his Pompeiian woman, only to encounter warm, living flesh, a flesh that speaks, calls him by name, and proclaims him mad.

After the fateful touch, Hanold realizes that he had been "utterly foolish and irrational to believe that he had sat with a young Pompeiian girl, who had become more or less corporeally alive again."[72] Yet he remains perplexed because clearly some Gradiva does live. Hanold is finally enlightened when Zoë explains all, telling him that she was startled to learn his "head harbored an imagination so magnificent as here in Pompeii to consider me something excavated and restored to life."[73] Freud points out that Zoë Bertgang plays the role of analyst; it is she who leads Hanold to recognize his fantasies and delusions. The two rediscover their childhood love, and the story ends predictably with their marriage. Jensen recasts the statue lover's erotic melancholia as Hanold's delusion, and in his story the archeologist is cured of his obsession not when his bas-relief comes to life but when a real woman reveals herself as the actual object of his desire.

Freud interests himself in *Gradiva* because he believes it reinforces the findings of psychoanalysis. Specifically, he argues that the novel not only presents dreams as wish fulfillment constructed from psychic material but also exemplifies his own theory of the unconscious and elucidates the role of repression in psychic life. In the case of Hanold's obsession, Freud explicitly separates himself from the psychology that would label it an erotomania.[74] For Freud, Hanold suffers from the repression of a childhood attachment.

> And now the discovery dawns upon us that the young archaeologist's phantasies about his Gradiva may have been an echo of his forgotten childhood memories. If so, they were not capricious products of his imagination, but determined, without his knowing it, by the store of childhood impressions which he had forgotten, but which were still at work in him.[75]

The antique bas-relief awakens the slumbering eroticism in him and activates his childhood memories. Yet a resistance to eroticism means that these memories can become active only in the unconscious, the unconscious expressed in dreams, delusions, and art.

In *Delusions and Dreams,* the issue of art making emerges as significant, for Freud must avoid the charge that he, like Pygmalion and Hanold, has taken art for life.[76] Thus, he contends that "even if our inquiry should teach us nothing new about the nature of dreams, it may perhaps enable us from this angle to gain some small insight into the nature of creative writing."[77] Freud concludes that although the artist is by no means a psychoanalyst, he works over the same material and reaches the same conclusions with different methods:

> He directs his attention to the unconscious in his own mind, he listens to its possible developments and lends them artistic expression instead of suppressing them by conscious critique. Thus he experiences from himself what we learn from others—the laws which the activities of this

> unconscious must obey. But he need not state these laws, nor even be clearly aware of them; as a result of the tolerance of his intelligence, they are incorporated within his creations. We discover these laws by analysing his writings just as we find them from cases of real illness.[78]

Taking Freud at his word, we must conclude that the unconscious desires of both Ovid and Jensen are incarnate in their fictions. And we can also include Freud in this group, unless, of course, we believe in the strict separation of imagination and reason, fiction and science.

Freud justifies treating a novel as a case history by imagining a theory of the creative process in which the artist projects his own psychic organization in the characters he creates. Thus in *Delusions and Dreams* we find a double coincidence with the Pygmalion theme. Not only does the case concern a (fictional) man obsessed with a piece of sculpture, but Freud's analysis also meditates on the artist's psychology: that of Jensen, who wrote the novel, and that of Hanold, the character who particularly interests Freud. It is through Hanold that we have a first glimpse of the artist's psychic world, and in describing him Freud defines what we might call a Pygmalion complex:

> Of this hero [Hanold] we are further told that he was pre-ordained by family tradition to become an archaeologist, that in his later isolation and independence he was wholly absorbed in his studies and had turned completely away from life and its pleasures. Marble and bronze alone were truly alive for him; they alone expressed the purpose and value of human life. But nature, perhaps with benevolent intent, had fused into his blood a corrective of an entirely unscientific sort—an extremely lively imagination, which could show itself not only in his dreams, but in his waking life as well. This division between imagination and intellect destined him to become an artist or a neurotic.[79]

For our purposes, it is significant that Freud not only sees a similar psychic pattern in the artist and the neurotic, but also that he defines this pattern as a withdrawal from life and its pleasures combined with both an obsessive fixation on ideas and a lively imagination. This indeed describes the figure of Pygmalion as he is developed throughout the eighteenth century and before (although admittedly Pygmalion was not "pre-ordained by family tradition" to become a sculptor). But of additional interest is that Freud's position on the relation of imagination and intellect seems quite equivocal. On the one hand, he suggests that neurotic symptoms and poetic creativity devolve from the forced separation of imagination and reason, and on the other, he implies that the two are distinct, categorizing a lively imagination as an "entirely unscientific" corrective that can burst into waking life. In the end, Freud concludes that through both his intellectual obsessions and imaginative fantasy, Hanold "was one of those whose kingdom is not of this world."[80]

What it means for the artist to be "not of this world" is made clear in *Totem and Taboo,* which Freud first published in 1913.[81] There he links the artist to the primitive, the neurotic, the hysteric, and the narcissist, who all exteriorize their own psychic organizations: "Primitive man had immense belief in the power of his wishes. The basic reason why what he sets about by magical means comes to pass is, after all, simply that he wills it."[82] Freud contends that from this belief in magic developed a general overvaluation of all mental processes, which he calls the principle of the "omnipotence of thought." He sees this principle at work in obsessional neurotics whose symptoms are determined not by experiential reality, but by thought. These neurotics are, like Norbert Hanold or Pygmalion, "not of this world," and in their realm only "neurotic currency" is legal tender: "that is to say they are only affected by what is thought with intensity and pictured with emotion, whereas agreement with external reality is a matter of no importance."[83]

Freud then turns to what for me is the most important link in this series connecting art with the omnipotence of thought: "In only a single field of our civilization has the omnipotence of thoughts been retained, and that is in the field of art. Only in art does it still happen that a man who is consumed by desires performs something resembling the accomplishment of those desires and that what he does in play produces emotional effects—thanks to artistic illusion—just as though it were something real."[84] Here again Freud might be describing a Pygmalion complex in which desire is satisfied through the artful creation of an ideal woman. For even if the myth locates satisfaction in the actual animation of the statue, in Freud's view it is the process of making art that itself satisfies the artist. The artist may be subject to delusions, he surely overvalues his mental processes, but in the end he can satisfy his desires, if only through imagination. And what is Galatea if not a substitute for, an imaginative representation of, the sex Pygmalion has foresworn?

Freud posits art as a "substitutive satisfaction," in specific, a sublimation of the sexual urge. In his later *Civilization and Its Discontents* (1930), he argues that civilized man fends off suffering through sublimation, which he defined as a displacement of libido, a shifting of instinctual aims so they cannot be frustrated by the external world. Although sublimation cannot give a subject complete protection from suffering, its intention is to make him independent of the external world by seeking satisfaction in internal processes, such as psychical and intellectual work. Freud's prime example of a sublimated pleasure is the artist's joy in creating, in giving body to fantasy.[85] What is of particular interest is that sublimation "normalizes," even universalizes, the link between art and desire, so much so that Freudianism urges us, like other mythologies of art, to see the intimate connection between the two.

Freud's artist, however, occupies a contradictory position. On the one hand, he is a neurotic, even a hysteric, who mixes up what he imagines and what is real; on the other, he finds the relief that restores his reason in satisfying the desires that, if repressed, could lead to neurosis. What is critical to note is the obvious: the artist Freud describes here is male, and it is male desire that is sublimated into art making. In *Civilization and Its Discontents* women represent the "interests of the family and of sexual life," which at first civilization requires. But soon, as Freud explains: "[t]he work of civilization has become increasingly the business of men, it confronts them with ever more difficult tasks and compels them to carry out instinctual sublimations of which women are little capable."[86]

In his *Essay on Femininity* (1933), Freud makes woman's inability to sublimate an inborn and indelible inferiority, as Sarah Kofman has pointed out.[87] This inability may also explain why, according to Freud, "women have made few contributions to the discoveries and inventions in the history of civilization."[88] Kofman argues that because Freud denies woman the capacity to sublimate her libidinal energy into social or cultural life, the only remedy he leaves her is to take refuge in neurosis.[89] Here we have a familiar constellation of ideas—men can sublimate libido into art making (or other cultural work), while women, unable to sublimate, fall victim to disease. The artist is like the neurotic, the hysteric, and the woman, but unlike them he is saved from his fate by a capacity that in general belongs to the male sex. Through the science of psychoanalysis, Freud (inadvertently?) repeats ideas about art making that have long held sway in the Western imaginary.

This Freudian view of art making still holds power in the popular imagination today. Consider, for example, Barry Unsworth's *Stone Virgin,* a novel published in 1986 and billed as a "brilliant, ironic, sublime version of the Pygmalion legend."[90] Here the modern artist Litsov so thoroughly satisfies his sexual instincts in making art that he has lost interest in his wife Chiara except as a servant or model. Indeed, she bitterly complains about her fate: "Stuck there on the island to assist his talent, cook and clean for him, strip to be his model, stand or sit or lie while he cut me up into fragments. Was that enough? It was enough for *him.* All his sex went into those bits of metal."[91] We might be tempted to say that Litsov suffers from repressed desire, but the sculptor displays few, if any, symptoms of the psychic distress that point to repression. There are no delusions, no dreams, no obsessive-compulsive behaviors, that is, beyond making art and isolating himself in its imaginary world. In *Stone Virgin,* Litsov has so thoroughly sublimated, so thoroughly satisfied his erotic desires in making art that he cannot enjoy a "normal" outlet. He is like Pygmalion in that he has given up real women for the metal ones he creates. Although Litsov never turns back to women of flesh, in the novel other characters find that both sorts of ladies arouse their desires.

Stone Virgin proposes that events surrounding a work of art, especially erotic events, can be embedded in the work and that the sensitive observer—in this case, an art restorer—can perceive them, if only vaguely and as hallucinations. In contrast to Litsov, it is the art restorer, Simon Riakes, whose sexuality is aroused by stone women but who satisfies himself with those of flesh and blood, in specific, with the wife Litsov ignores. The statue that arouses Riakes's desire, however, is at the center of the novel, which traces his response to the Renaissance Madonna he is commissioned to restore. The process of restoration does more than reveal the sculpture's virginal surface; it releases a miasma of desire and violence that has adhered to the work. His proximity to the miasma on one level seems to account for the restorer's hallucinations and sexual visions. But on another, the narrative attributes those delusions to a mental disorder, to a neural discharge in the temporal lobe of the brain. The restorer muses: "He had been dubbed ill; an anticonvulsant had been prescribed for him, as if he were subject to fits; his visions had been dismissed as the result of a malfunction."[92]

Nevertheless, we know from the narrative with its backward and forward movement through time that sexual desire has left its residue on the sculpture. The primary erotic event narrated and repeated in variation throughout the novel is the Renaissance artist's sexual enjoyment of the model/prostitute, Bianca, who poses for the figure of the Blessed Virgin Annunciate. Art making arouses his lust for the model, and that lust is both satisfied by and imprinted on his art. Unlike Pygmalion, however, this artist comes to a tragic end when he is falsely accused and convicted of murdering Bianca.[93] In a series of flashbacks that trace the history of the sculpture, Unsworth's story recounts other sexual encounters that the sculpture both witnessed and absorbed. Thus in *Stone Virgin,* the Renaissance artist, the modern sculptor, and the sensitive restorer are among the figures who play out the imbrication of art and desire that emerges as the central theme of this new *Pygmalion.*

At the same time, *Stone Virgin* comments on this theme in a way that is entirely modern. The woman whom the restorer tries to metamorphose into his ideal vision, the sculptor's wife Chiara, comments acidly on his fantasy of making her an ideal woman, of imagining her his Madonna/prostitute:

> You go at once into a dream about women. I knew it from the first time we met. I saw it on your face that day we met on the path and I had been planting the seedlings. Simply it was a person doing some work in the garden, but that could not be enough for you, could it? I saw you then beginning to make a shape for me . . . Now because I have failed to be the Madonna, you want to turn me into Jezebel . . . I am *myself,* not your distortions.[94]

Like both Zoë Bertgang and Diderot's prostitute, Chiara here punctures male fantasy. At the same time, however, that male fantasy dominates the novel, as it dominated the theory and representation of art making in eighteenth-century France. In the concluding image of the restorer's tale, we see that Chiara's protest has changed nothing. The novel ends with Raikes imagining Chiara as Venus rising from the waters: "Raikes watched the pale gold, glistening form emerge, saw the bright swirl of water around it, the flashing ripples made by the thrust of the thighs, saw the lineaments of flesh emerge from the heart of light."[95] And like Pygmalion, he remains immobilized before his vision.

CHAPTER 5

The Model Pygmalion and the Artist Galatea

PART I: A MODEL FOR THE ARTIST

As the motivating force for making art and the passion aroused in its beholding, enthusiasm held an intermediary position in eighteenth-century theory, linking together the creative process and the aesthetic experience. By merging these two aspects of enthusiasm in the mythical sculptor, eighteenth-century Pygmalion images also connected art making and viewing with the satisfaction of a man's desire. Take, for example, Jean Raoux's 1717 *Pygmalion* (fig. 41) and François Lemoyne's 1729 *Pygmalion Seeing His Sculpture Come to Life* (fig. 42). Each painting shows us the sculptor-king as an impassioned spectator stunned by the miracle of animation. With Venus, Cupid, or both soaring into the scene, these painted *coups de théâtre* recall what a theater audience might actually have witnessed. Those attending Antoine Houdar de La Motte's 1700 ballet or the 1754 performance of Jean-Philippe Rameau's opera, for example, would have seen Cupid fly onto the stage brandishing his torch before the statue.[1] The action that precipitates the statue's animation and the manner in which she comes to life are significant aspects of each Pygmalion story or image.

Ovid's text never suggests that the metamorphosis happens in a sculptor's studio, nor that the statue remains on a pedestal amid other works of art. In his account, the statue's transformation begins when Pygmalion returns home from a festival where he has made his offering to Venus. Although we presume the goddess of love has brought about the miracle, neither she nor Cupid act directly on the statue. Ovid's tale relates Galatea's animation to the sculptor's lovemaking. "When he returned he sought the image of his maid, and bending over the couch he kissed her. She seemed warm to his touch. Again he kissed her, and with

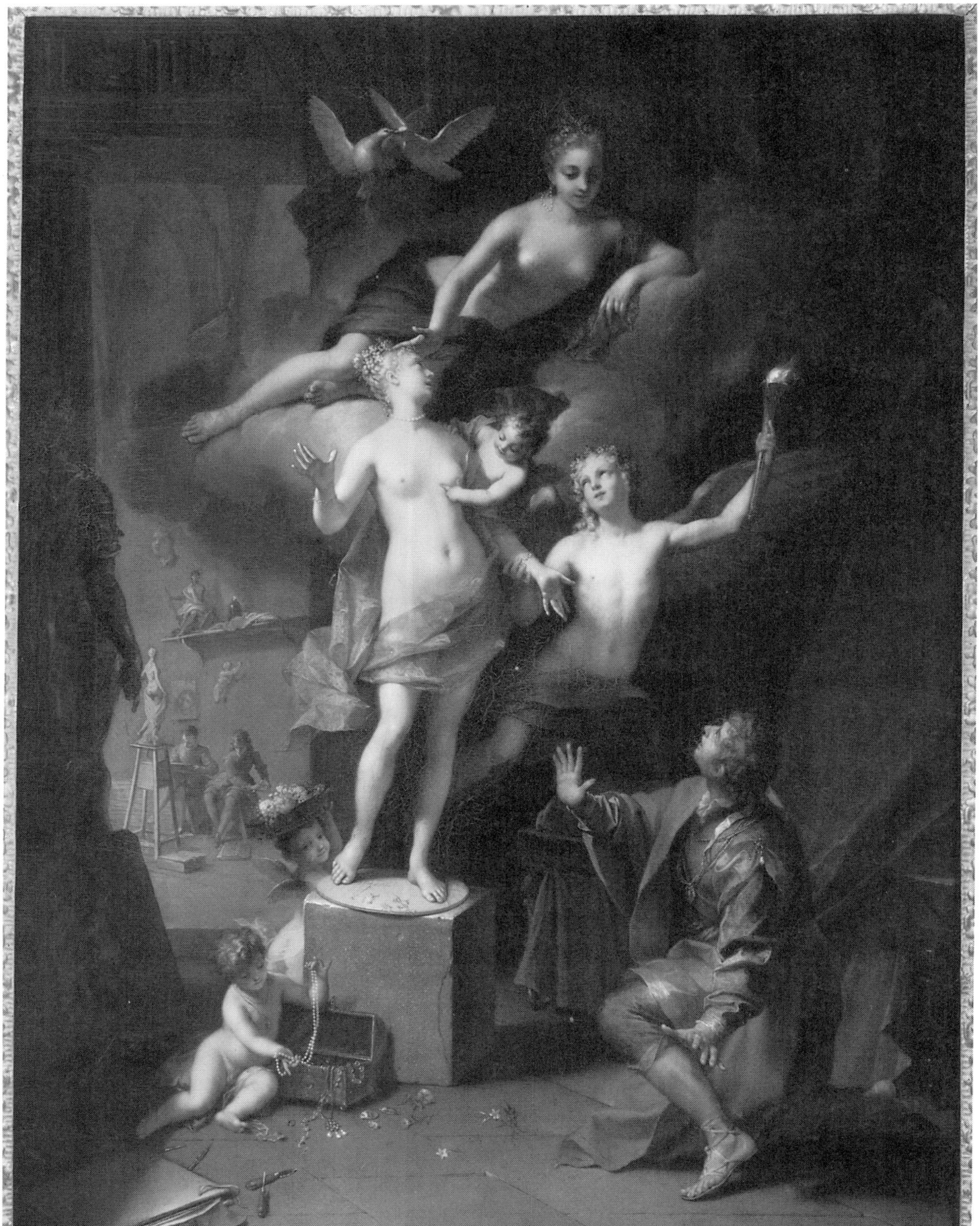

FIGURE 41. Jean Raoux (French, 1677–1734), *Pygmalion,* 1717. Oil on canvas, 134 × 100 cm Montpellier: Musée Fabre. Photograph: Cliché Frédéric Jaulmes. Reproduction forbidden without authorization.

his hands also he touched her breast. The ivory grew soft to his touch and, its hardness vanishing, gave and yielded beneath his fingers."[2]

Where touch belongs to Pygmalion in Ovid's tale, in both Raoux's and Lemoyne's *Pygmalion* touching Galatea seems to be the privilege of divine beings. Looking at Raoux's painting, we can surmise that the

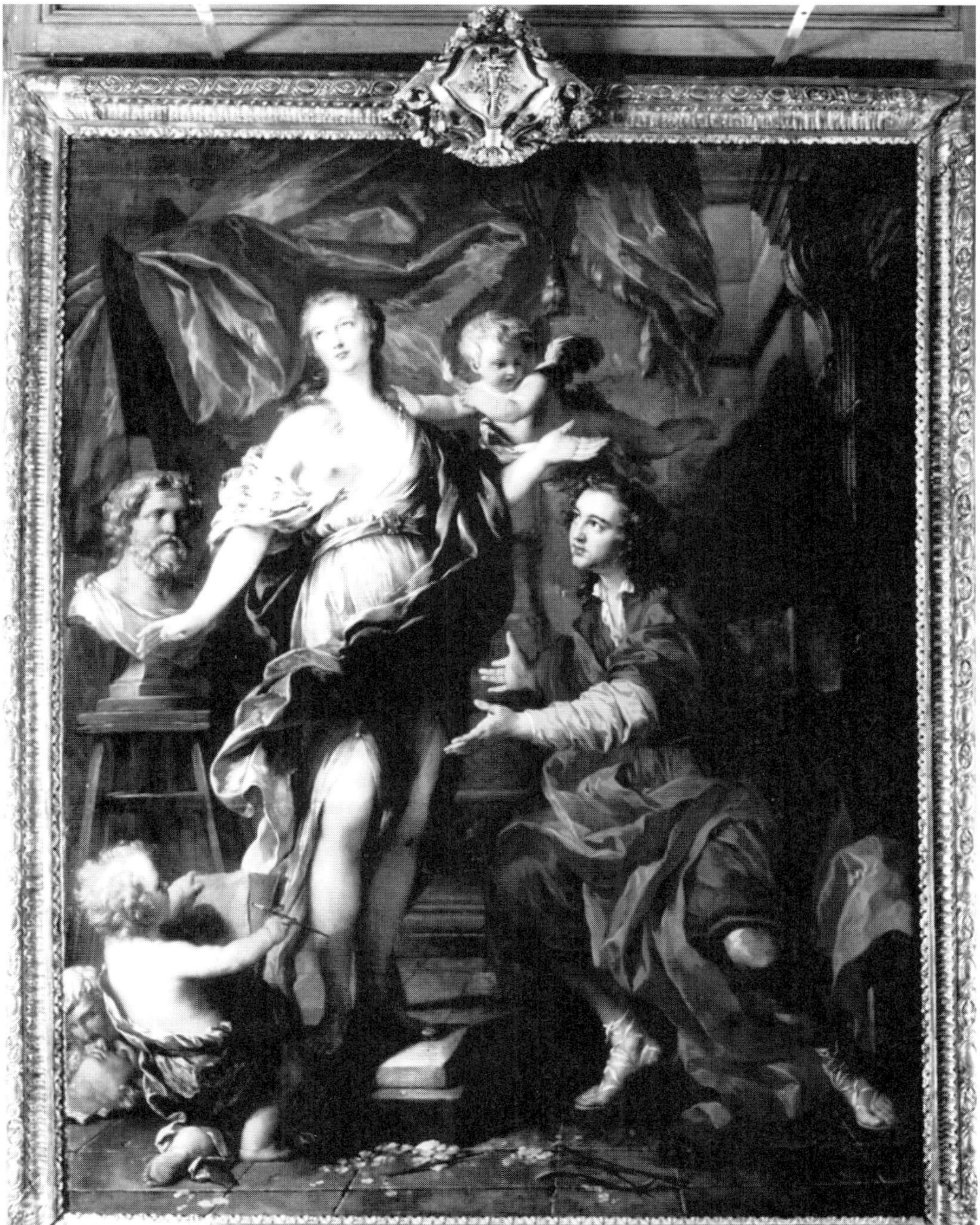

gods have already laid a hand on Galatea, who seems more than half alive. The statue appears flushed around her neck and shoulders, and the pink tone intensifies the impression of blood flowing to her upper body, which has taken on the color of flesh. Her feet, ankles, and lower calves are portrayed as hard stone: they share the green tinged

FIGURE 42. François Lemoyne (French, 1688–1737), *Pygmalion Seeing His Sculpture Come to Life*, 1729. Oil on canvas, 212 × 168 cm. Tours: Musée de Beaux-Arts. Photograph courtesy Patrick Boyer, Atelier d'Antan.

whiteness of the round base and show the shiny surface of highly polished marble.[3]

With one hand Raoux's Cupid holds high his torch, and with the other he grips the statue's wrist, as if to take the pulse of a living being whose heart now beats. At the same time, Cupid gauges the strength of her love, mimicking all those licentious old doctors in seventeenth-century Dutch painting who diagnose lovesickness from a quickened pulse. A smaller amorino assists Doctor Love and interprets his ministrations by simultaneously touching the statue near her left breast and pointing to her heart. From her perch on a cloud, Venus lays her hand on the statue's head, both prolonging the animating caress and seeming to bless the event. As Cupid, Venus, and the amorino perform their miracle, two other putti remind us of Pygmalion's wooing: one opens a chest of jewels and another carries a basket of flowers. Crowning the entire tableau are two kissing turtle doves, a sign of what is to come between the sculptor and his work.

In contrast to Raoux's god of love, Lemoyne's Cupid comes to do his job with a decidedly smaller entourage, although he brings an artist to record the event. Flying into the scene, this vigorous Amor carries the animating fire in his left hand and touches the statue with his right, while Pygmalion looks on in wonder. Lemoyne, too, suggests animation through color change, and like Raoux he also uses color symbolically. Pygmalion is cloaked in the red of fiery passion, which also seems to surround Galatea, whom he places against a drapery backdrop. Adding to the sense of excited animation, Lemoyne activates the draperies, which turn and twist around Pygmalion and his statue in a complicated movement. But despite the signs of wonder, passion, and animation that pervade the scene, we are denied the pleasure of seeing Pygmalion caress his beloved, as we are in Raoux's painting. And in neither of these works do we see eye contact.

Lemoyne's Galatea turns away from her creator, her eyes fixed on some unseen realm, and in Raoux's work she gives her attention to Venus. The orienting of looks within these images thus emphasizes not the loving exchange between Pygmalion and Galatea, but the miracle of animation in which the statue takes center stage and the sculptor looks on as privileged beholder. Yet if the statue attracts our eye, the sculptor also begs for his share of attention. Indeed, both Raoux and Lemoyne insure that Pygmalion will also draw the viewer's gaze for these artists represent his response through theatricalized gesture and expression. Raoux's Pygmalion crouches down on one knee before his vision, whose awe-inspiring power is suggested in both his pose and the tilt of his body, which seems nearly bowled over. His mouth is agape, his arms are extended, his hands raised in a conventional gesture of surprise.

The movements are suitably large, the pose somewhat exaggerated, the expressions clearly theatrical.

If Raoux's Pygmalion is thrown back by his vision, the spectacle seems to bring Lemoyne's Pygmalion forward, approaching the object of his passion. With heels lifted, he is caught as if about to rise up and project himself toward the stone virgin he loves. He gazes with hope at his Galatea and spreads his arms wide in a grand operatic gesture. And like Raoux's Pygmalion, Lemoyne's protagonist seems frozen in a moment, caught in a pose; indeed, both painters metamorphose their sculptors into statues by placing them in a studied attitude that seems to suspend their movement. In Raoux's work, the position of Pygmalion's right hand—palm open and fingers splayed—even mimics that of his statue. Although both sculptor and sculpture are frozen in their postures, we anticipate the next movement of each, of the sculptor momentarily immobilized by his astonishment, of the statue newly endowed with mobility. The trick for the painter, of course, is to show these borderline states and to catch the statue as she is changing from lifeless matter to palpating flesh. Suspending Pygmalion's movement is appropriate for expressing his astonishment, a passion Descartes claimed "makes the entire body remain immobile like a statue."[4] Honoré Balzac would still use this image in his 1831 "Le Chef d'oeuvre inconnu," describing the artist-spectators transfixed before Frenhofer's masterpiece as "pétrifiés d'admiration."[5]

I shall relegate to a footnote the Freudian analysis that petrification begs, and suggest instead that in the hands of Raoux and Lemoyne, the Pygmalion theme mimics the ideal spectator's response before the work of art.[6] That response would be a reaction to the strong illusionary qualities of painting or sculpture, a supposed confusion between art and life. Such confusions, as we know, engaged eighteenth-century audience. Diderot and other critics feigned them in Salon reviews.

Although the sculptor acts as ideal spectator in both Raoux's and Lemoyne's *Pygmalion,* each painter also presents him as a gifted artist. Setting his scene in a sculptor's studio, Raoux shows the signs of art strewn in the foreground. On the floor beneath the statue we see a sketchbook and a bas-relief; another sculpted work stands to the left. Scattered on the ground are the sculptor's chisel and mallet amid other still life objects—flowers, shells, sketchbook, jewels, and so forth. These, too, have multiple roles to play. The flowers, shells, and jewels recall Pygmalion's mad infatuation with his sculpture, for these are the gifts he brings his statue in Ovid's text. The tools and examples of sculpture function as emblems of art. All together participate in the *beau désordre* that traditionally signaled visual delight, especially in images designed for erotic appeal. To stress that Pygmalion constitutes an allegory of sculpture, Raoux also includes in the background a studio scene of two apprentices copying a small modello set on a stool. Seen from the back, this modello appears to represent a nude woman, and hence this activity is compared with Pygmalion's earlier work in forming the statue.

In another sense, however, Raoux's work highlights the traditions of painting, his own art. The most obvious allusions to painting and its ideal types are the figures of Galatea and her look-alike, Venus. The similarities between these two are remarkable: they share the same blond tonality, the same delicate physiognomy, the same body type, the same hairstyle. So strong is the resemblance that Pygmalion's statue seems the embodiment of ideal beauty—the goddess of pleasure herself. Where other artists would use recognizable sculptures or at least sculptural types to represent Pygmalion's statue, Raoux's Galatea refers us to the Venetian painting tradition with its recognizable blond beauties.[7]

Like Raoux, Lemoyne also places his Pygmalion in a sculptor's studio, but one that looks like a grand antique building befitting a sculptor-king. Attributes and instruments of the sculptor's art are everywhere: a mallet lies at Pygmalion's feet, a classical bust sits on a stool behind the statue, and two heads are just visible in the left-hand corner. Drawing is represented in the putto artist who records the event, and he suggests the artist making a preliminary sketch for the very image we see. Lemoyne, moreover, signs and dates the painting by imitating chiseling on the floor, and he makes his mark just below the figure of Pygmalion to force an association between himself as the actual painter and the mythic sculptor whose story he depicts.

The Play of Self-Reference

Lemoyne was hardly unique in creating a self-referential Pygmalion, nor were painters the only ones to exemplify their own practices through the familiar story. Eighteenth-century writers, composers, and philosophers either used Pygmalion as a point of self-reference or appropriated his story toward their own ends.[8] Rousseau, for example, used Pygmalion to advance his theories of music and drama in a *scène lyrique* written in 1762–63. His *Pygmalion* was first performed in Lyon seven years later, its presentation a collaborative effort between Rousseau and Henri Coignet, an amateur who composed the music. Reviews of the Lyon performance in the Parisian press increased the work's fame, and in 1775 the Comédie Française performed the play in Paris. It remained in the company's repertoire into the nineteenth century.

Working with Coignet, Rousseau used *Pygmalion* to inaugurate a new genre called monodrama, which joined a literary text to instrumental music. The music, however, is not an independent work; it interrupts the declamations without coinciding with them and accompanies the mute actions of figures. As Van der Veen has pointed out, music provides the drama's emotional key by interpreting words after they have been spoken, preparing the audience for a line to come, and accenting the pantomime.[9] With orchestral sound replacing vocal music, *Pygmalion* also exemplifies Rousseau's musical theories. The French language, he believed, had lost its natural musicality and could not be combined harmoniously with an expressive musical score. At the moments in *Pygmalion* when passion reaches a high intensity, declamation breaks off and emotion is expressed through pantomime and music.[10] Rousseau justifies this practice in the *Dictionnaire de musique,* under "Récitatif obligé": "The actor, when he is agitated and transported by a passion that leaves him speechless, interrupts himself, stops himself, purposefully breaks up his speech. During these pauses the orchestra speaks for him. Thus filled, these silences affect the listener infinitely more than if the actor himself said all that the music makes understood."[11]

Where Rousseau drew on the Pygmalion myth to introduce a new genre, Boureau-Deslandes co-opted the sculptor's story to tell a materialist tale. His *Pigmalion; ou, La statue animée* attributes Galatea's animation neither to the gods nor to Pygmalion's lovemaking, but to the inherent sensibility of matter.[12] The work's loyalties are announced in the preface, which poses these questions: "What is matter? What is its essence?"[13] In this *Pigmalion,* there is no instantaneous transformation; the statue changes imperceptibly day by day, its metamorphosis from stone to living being attributed to matter's internal properties. Change is not quick but by degrees, nuances, and insensible movements that provoke an infinite *éloignement* from one state to another. "As movement is the condition through which matter must pass from the nonthinking state into the thinking state, the statue acquired by degrees all the movements to which a body is susceptible."[14] And in relation to movement, we can note parenthetically that in many eighteenth-century representations, it is Galatea's movement as much as the softening of her flesh that writers and artists represented. Boureau-Deslandes's tract, however, obscures the dividing lines between scientific process, divine intervention, and sheer desire. It is Venus who inspires Pygmalion to make his sculpture and promises to guide his hand: "Take your chisel; I will lead your hand, I will ignite your imagination. A masterpiece of art will be born."[15] And later we are never completely certain that Pygmalion's love has not helped to move the statue.

Falconet's Pygmalion[16]

When the sculptor Étienne Falconet exhibited his *Pygmalion* at the Salon of 1763, Ovid's story was already well known to the Parisian public, and artists had adopted the sculptor-king as a privileged forefather. Pygmalion, we might say, was approaching the height of his popularity, which surely had something to do with the success of Falconet's work. Described in the *livret* as representing "Pygmalion aux pieds de sa statue qui s'anime" (fig. 43), the sculptural group pleased critics and public alike. So celebrated was this marble that Falconet became known as "author of the Pygmalion." His prodigious success explains why collectors vied ardently for both the terra-cotta model and the finished piece, which today exists in two different versions (Paris: Musée du Louvre and Baltimore: Walters Art Gallery).[17] The work was widely disseminated through replicas in marble and *biscuit de Sèvres,* as well as in arrangements for clocks and other decorative objects. Such reproductions only increased the aura that surrounded the Pygmalion myth and magnified the fame of Falconet's small-scale masterpiece.

In some ways, Falconet's sculptural group repeats conventional formulae. The adoring sculptor kneels before his Galatea; his jaw drops in wonder, his eyes are riveted on the miracle he sees. Yet when rendered in stone, the Pygmalion theme posed special challenges for a sculptor called upon to represent the animation of a statue. Falconet's *Pygmalion* is marked off as "sculpture" by the pedestal on which it is framed, but Galatea is also represented as sculpture because she is placed on a round base set on a shaped block of stone. Still, we see that little by little she is coming to life, transformed from statue to woman. Falconet achieves this effect cleverly, using pose to suggest what painters showed through color when they rendered the legs marble and the upper body living flesh. He places Galatea's lower limbs in a conventional contrapposto that copies ancient types and orients them so a viewer facing the group sees them straight on. In positioning the arms and upper body, however, Falconet avoids any resemblance to an antique model. This deviation marks a "movement" in the sculpture as we imagine it breaking free of the frozen classical pose the legs still hold. From this same vantage, moreover, we see that he arranges the upper body at an oblique angle so that it registers both a change of position and a change of state as Galatea is transformed from an immobile statue to a pliant woman who turns and bends. Her inclined head and the faint smile playing over her lips further signal a change in Galatea's animation, as do her half-parted lids, which suggest a first tentative look at an astonished lover. In coming to life, however, Galatea remains Ovid's chaste and modest virgin,

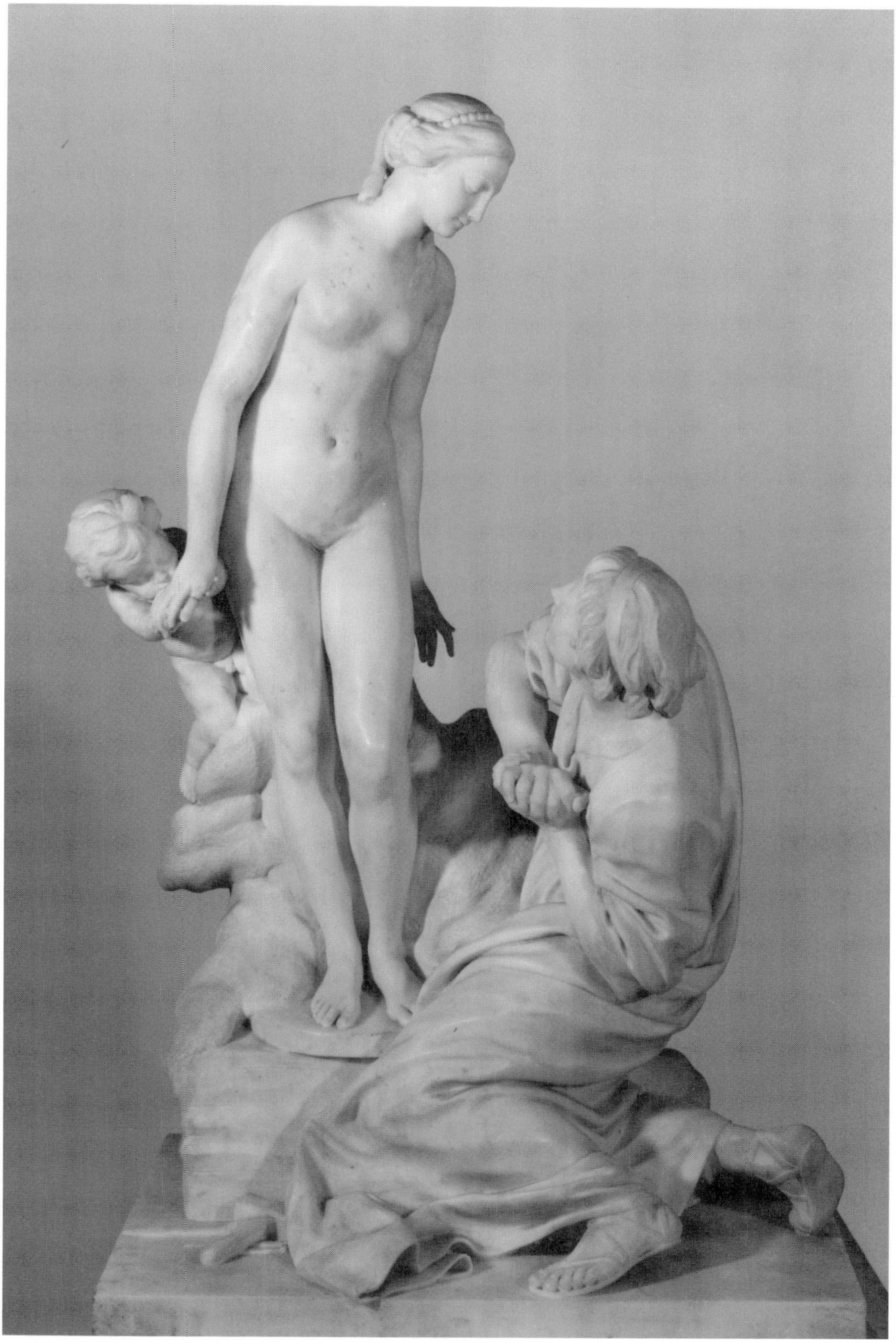

FIGURE 43. Étienne Falconet (French, 1716–91), *Pygmalion*, 1761. Marble 83 × 54 × 41.7 cm. Paris: Musée du Louvre. Photograph © Réunion des Musées Nationaux/Art Resource, NY.

the girl whom "you would think desirous of being moved, if modesty did not prevent."[18] With their lowered lids, her eyes can be read both as just beginning to open and as downcast in a traditional expression of feminine modesty. Thus even as Pygmalion kneels before Galatea, she shows deference to her creator.

As Diderot describes Galatea in his commentary on Falconet's sculpture, her psychology is uncomplicated by subtle emotions. Her primary characteristic is that she is newly born: "What innocence she has!" Diderot exclaims. He imagines that "she is having her first thought. Her heart begins to beat, but it will not be long before it throbs wildly."[19] The critic anticipates her physical response to Pygmalion's desire, but of her thoughts he says no more. Galatea seems the personification of love awakening, and she resembles the innocent young girls Diderot adored in Greuze's paintings, adolescents in whom sexuality stirs before they understand their longings. In the case of Galatea, Diderot imagines touching her marble/flesh and asks the viewer to do the same: "What softness in the flesh! No, it is not marble. Press it with your finger, and the material that has lost its hardness will yield to the pressure."[20] The invitation acknowledges Falconet as a new Pygmalion who can transform marble into flesh, a flesh the viewer might wish to touch. That touch is both erotic and diagnostic; Diderot exclaims over the body's softness even as he tests its physical properties.

Unlike Galatea on her pedestal, Falconet's Pygmalion is not coded as "sculpture," and his pose resembles no classical types for that art. Wide-eyed and gaping with astonishment, he signals naturalness in the feigned awkward expression and pose. His garment falls away at the neck, his elbow protrudes sharply, and his sandaled feet are placed to suggest the effort of keeping his balance. Here we have a virtuoso display of force and counterforce: Pygmalion's pose seems at once a movement arrested and a permanently unbalanced state. In a similar way, his physiognomy hovers between a momentary expression—a pause in the play of facial muscles—and a grimace fixed when the sense organs focus on a single object. Representing Pygmalion as a living sculptor metaphorically transformed into a statue would be particularly difficult to render in stone. It was perhaps Falconet's virtuosity in capturing this state, combined with the complexity of emotional expression he achieves, that led many contemporary viewers to focus their attention on the mythical sculptor. Indeed, Diderot reserves the most powerful evocation of "life" in Falconet's work for Pygmalion's expression: "O Falconet! how have you put in a piece of white stone surprise, joy, and love blended together? Emulator of the gods, if they have animated the statue you have renewed the miracle by animating the sculptor."[21]

If Diderot lauds Falconet's achievement, the critic's flattering praise takes an ironic edge as he sees both Falconet's skill and his hubris. Calling him "Emulator of the gods," Diderot warns the sculptor of the consequences—"guilty of Prometheus's crime, fear that an eagle also waits for you."[22] Here Diderot brings into play the other mythical "sculptor" who in eighteenth-century versions of his story both creates woman and incurs the god's wrath by stealing the divine fire that will animate her. For example, in Voltaire's *Pandore, opéra en cinq actes* (1740; originally titled *Prometheus*), Prometheus is a sculptor in love with his statue of Pandora.[23] Unlike Pygmalion, Prometheus cannot persuade the gods to animate his beloved, and he believes Jupiter jealous of his art. Desperate with love, Prometheus climbs to the sky and steals not the thunder god's fire, but Cupid's torch, since Prometheus reasons that Love reigns over all divinities. Prometheus animates his sculpture with torch in hand, boasting: "I stole it from the gods, I carried it to earth, this sacred fire of tender Love, a thousand times more powerful than that of the thunder god."[24] It is the same fire, the fire of Love, that brings Pygmalion's statue to life, and eliding these two stories of art's power again suggests how the desiring artist—more than the reasoning one—was fundamental to the Enlightenment's image of art making.

In his commentary on Falconet, however, Diderot recalls an aspect of the Prometheus myth not ordinarily associated with Pygmalion. As a punishment for stealing the fire, Jupiter orders Prometheus chained to a rock, and sends a vulture to devour his liver, which miraculously grows back every night. Reading further in Diderot's commentary, it becomes evident that the critic himself is this vulture, and he does, indeed, peck at Falconet's entrails. Referring again to the *Pygmalion,* Diderot qualifies his appreciation: "This piece of sculpture is very perfect. However, at first glance the neck of the statue seems a little strong or her head a little weak."[25] Pushing his talons deep into the sculptor's vanity, Diderot assures him that the *gens d'art* have confirmed his judgment, and cries in false lament: "Oh, how unhappy is the condition of the artist! How cruel and petty are the critics!"[26]

If the critics are cruel, Diderot is meanest of all, for he is out to steal Falconet's thunder by imagining another—better—composition. First he suggests reversing the direction of its action, placing Pygmalion to the left, the cupid, to the right of Galatea. Then finding that Pygmalion needs some adjustment, Diderot imagines a sequence of movements that lead to a final pose different than the one Falconet designed.[27] Diderot animates that pose by writing it as a series of movements: Pygmalion is sitting back on his heels when he notices the first signs of life in his statue. He scarcely believes his perceptions and lifts himself up slowly until he is level with the statue's heart. Placing the back of his left hand lightly on Galatea's breast, Pygmalion searches for her heartbeat while his eyes remain fixed on hers, waiting for them to open slightly. These changes Diderot justifies by the particular blend of passions he wants to see in Pygmalion: "I say that Pygmalion raises himself lightly; if the movements of surprise are prompt and rapid, they are here controlled and tempered by the fear either of being fooled or of the thousand accidents that could make the miracle fall short."[28]

In conceiving Pygmalion's emotional state, Diderot steals an image from Ovid: "The lover stands amazed, rejoices still in doubt, fears he is mistaken."[29] Diderot's Pygmalion seems to touch his Galatea as both scientist and lover, testing his own perceptions of movement. He touches her breast with the back of his hand, not simply for the pleasure of feeling soft flesh, but to ascertain if her heart moves. Falconet's sculptor, in contrast, shows no fear, and displays a closer range of mixed emotions—surprise, joy, and love. But without actually having to make the piece, Diderot is free to suggest an even more complicated expression. The critic pecks again at Falconet's liver: "It seems that my thought is newer, rarer, more energetic than that of Falconet. My figures would also be better grouped than his; they would be touching one another."[30]

In this commentary, Diderot puts himself in competition with Falconet, posing his textual sculpture as superior to Falconet's marble one. He is the better Pygmalion. In the coming years, the two would debate the relative merits of the visual and literary arts in their long correspondence. But in terms of *Pygmalion,* Diderot might also be responding to the degree of self-reference that makes Falconet's group a display of *amour propre.* It seems quite obvious that in choosing Galatea's animation as a subject, Falconet creates an allegory of sculpture. What might not be so obvious is the extent to which this work is an allegory of Falconet's sculpture in particular, that is, the extent to which he presents his *Pygmalion* as emblematic of sculpture. This aspect of Falconet's *Pygmalion* is most evidently signaled by the sculptor's reliance on his *Bather* (1757; fig. 44) for the figure of Galatea.[31]

Falconet's *Bather* had appeared at the Salon of 1757, where she enjoyed great success, and by 1763 the work had been reproduced countless times. When reconfigured within the *Pygmalion,* Falconet's *Bather* not only augments the other conventions that situate Galatea as representing a piece of sculpture, she also verifies Falconet's art as Sculpture and Falconet as a new Pygmalion. It was not amiss for painters or engravers to show Pygmalion's sculpture as a known piece of ancient art, but for a sculptor to use one of his own works as the model for Pygmalion's Galatea—well, that was sheer narcissism. Especially since like so many

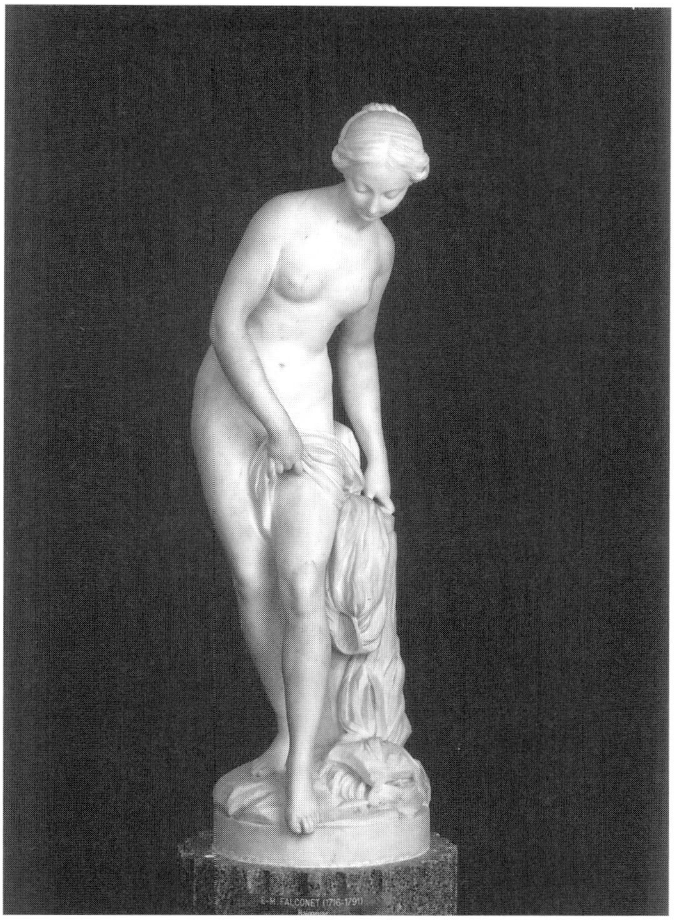

FIGURE 44. Étienne Falconet (French, 1716–91), *Bather,* 1757. Marble. 80.5 × 25.7 × 29 cm. Paris: Musée du Louvre. Photograph © Réunion des Musées Nationaux/Art Resource, NY.

other Pygmalions, Falconet's sculptor acts out both the artist's wonder before his own creation and the spectator's transport before the work of art.

If making Galatea his own *Bather* is Falconet's most spectacular moment of self-reference, Diderot seems to detect another when he looks at the cupid: "How much mischief in the head of that cupid! Sneaky little one, I recognize you; for my happiness, would that I not cross your path."[32] That Diderot recognizes this cupid is suggestive. Another of Falconet's best known works was his *Menacing Cupid,* which Jeanne Antoinette Poisson, marquise du Pompadour (1721–64) commissioned for the Hôtel d'Evreux in Paris and which appeared as a finished marble at the Salon of 1757 (fig. 45). In body type, facial features, and hairstyle, Falconet's *Menacing Cupid* resembles the unwinged amour who devours Galatea. It is not a question of quoting his previous work, however, but of a more subtle reference that avoids duplication.

Commissioned for a garden setting, the *Menacing Cupid* is executed on a larger scale and shows a seated cupid, a mischievous winged

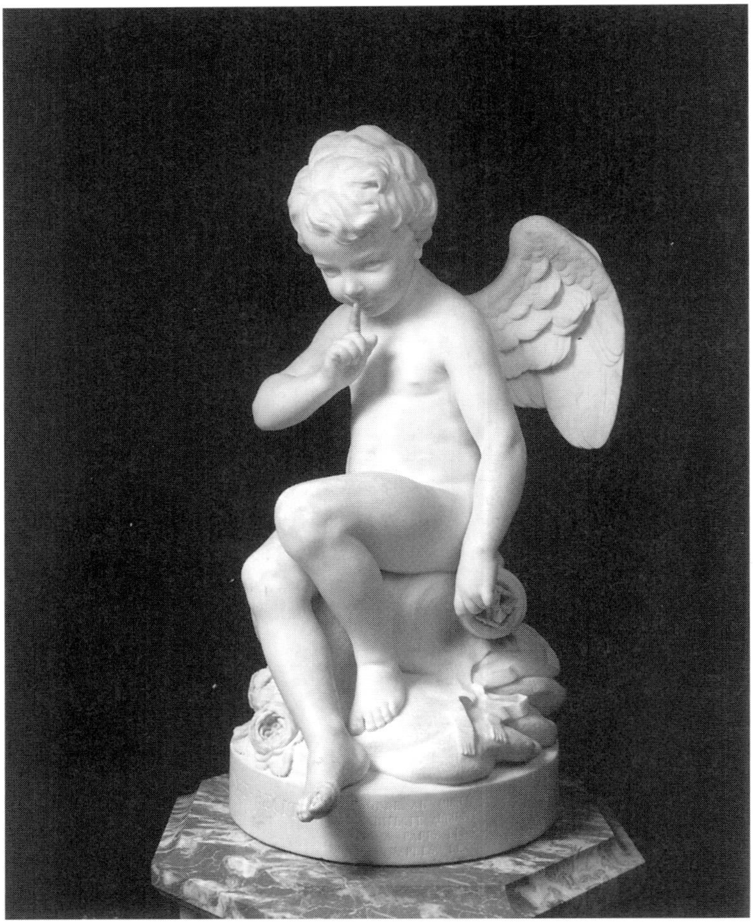

FIGURE 45. Étienne Falconet (French, 1716–91), *Menacing Cupid*, 1757. Marble, 91 × 50 × 62 cm. Paris, Musée du Louvre. Photograph © Réunion des Musées Nationaux/Art Resource, NY.

boy holding his right index finger to closed lips. We presume this gesture asks the viewer to keep some secret, to be discrete, for Cupid's other hand furtively draws an arrow from his quiver, threatening an attack on some unsuspecting victim.[33] This work, too, was a spectacular success, reproduced many times in marble, bronze, and biscuit, and spawning imitations and replicas, including a tabletop edition from Sèvres. So well loved was this *Menacing Cupid* that he not only decorated vases and snuffboxes but also appeared as a character in numerous engravings and paintings, including Fragonard's well-known work, *The Swing* (1767; London: Wallace Collection). Critics received Falconet's *Menacing Cupid* with fervent praise, admiring the lifelike quality of its execution.

The sculpture also has a special relation to the Pygmalion theme, for it was designed to transgress (if only imaginatively) the boundary between the animate and the inanimate. Falconet's stone imp communicates with real viewers, inviting spectators to keep a secret or warning them to beware the arrow that might come their way.[34] And he is, as Diderot put it, a sneaky one, a Cupid whose arrow one might well fear. The cupid Falconet includes in his *Pygmalion* also reminds Diderot that the sculptor both thematized animation and sought the semblance of life in his most successful and recognizable works.

Pygmalion, Self-reference, and a Theory of Sculpture

In his works, Falconet creates figures whose sentiments the viewer can imagine. His *Pygmalion* shows us both the sculptor and his statue moved by love. Falconet's interest in expression is closely tied to his theory of sculpture, as his writing makes clear:

> Although it seems within reach of all artists, [representing] *feeling* is an essential and rare talent. It must be inseparable from all their productions; it is that which gives them life. If the other studies are the basis of the art [of sculpture], feeling alone is its soul. . . . To express the forms of the body without joining feeling to them is to fulfill one's goal only halfway.[135]

In his *Reflections on Sculpture* published in the *Encyclopédie* (1761), Falconet points to animation as a key characteristic of all sculpture and cautions his readers against a cold imitation of the human body that showed "man before the vivifying breath that animated him."[36] A precise exactitude might make a work well rendered, but it cannot excite passion in the spectator: "It is living, animated, impassioned nature that the sculptor must express in marble, bronze, stone, and so forth."[37]

Falconet argues further that the moderns surpass the ancients at capturing a sense of animation. Modern sculptors have both perfected the depiction of expression and made themselves more adept at simulating living flesh.

> I must not forget here an important observation on the subject of the ancients. It is essential in relation to the manner in which their sculptors treated flesh. They were so little concerned with details that often they neglected the wrinkles and movements of the skin in the places where it stretches and folds over according to the movement of the limbs. This aspect of sculpture has perhaps been carried to a higher degree of perfection in our time.[38]

This perfection is evident in Falconet's *Pygmalion.* Look, for example, at Galatea's back. As she turns, her "skin" seems to stretch over her right shoulder blade and fold along the side of her left. Falconet is similarly careful to show the crinkles and creases in bending fingers and toes. It seems fitting, then, that Falconet should quote his own *Bather* to represent Pygmalion's masterpiece.

There is a clear correspondence between Falconet's theory and his *Pygmalion,* even if that sculpture was never intended as an exemplification. His theory, after all, may have been a retrospective description of practice mixed with conventional ideas. If *Pygmalion* demonstrates Falconet's ideas on animation and expression, it also exploits the potentiality of sculpture as a three-dimensional object occupying space. This potentiality Falconet also stressed in his *Reflections on Sculpture,* writing that if a sculptor "has composed and rendered one view well, he has satisfied only one part of his operation since the work has as many points of view as there are points in the space that surrounds it."[39] Indeed, *Pygmalion* offers the spectator many satisfying views. From the front one can enjoy Galatea's facial expression while catching a mere glimpse of Pygmalion's emotion. From behind, one barely sees Galatea's profile, but Pygmalion's open mouth and wide eyes are clearly in view. At the same time, the shaped cloud/stone has a dynamic form that makes the back view satisfying. Other views also have their pleasures, especially since Falconet's composition seems effortless as one form flows into or emerges out of another. Sculpture, as Falconet wrote, "is above all the enemy of forced attitudes that nature disavows."[40]

When we enjoy the back and side views, we find that the cloud, barely visible from the front, is a major part of the work. The back view also provides a different sense of metamorphosis, not from stone to flesh but from stone to sculpture. The "cloud" on which the putto rests is rendered as a shaped mass, which nevertheless resembles eroded stone. This mass contrasts with the back view of Galatea, who seems to rise from it as both apparition and finished work. Her articulated back, smooth skin, and soft fleshy buttocks contrast dramatically with the roughly shaped stone, as does the delicate cupid's body with its toes nestling in the cloud. By suggesting the material from which the sculptor wrests the appearance of life, the cloud refers to the process of sculpture. It is like the stone block that supports Galatea's base, an actual piece of stone shaped to look like (and to play the part of) a piece of stone, complete with a chink that seems "accidentally" hacked out of it. The chink is the detail that shows this stone has been deliberately shaped to resemble the sculptor's raw material it both is and represents. This confusion between art and life, between the fictive and the real, lies at the heart of Pygmalion's story.

Pygmalion's Enthusiasm

> It is not the art of poets and writers of prose alone that is inspired when divine power from the gods falls on their tongues, nay, the hands of sculptors also, when they are seized by the gift of a more divine inspiration, give utterance to creations that are possessed and full of madness.
>
> Callistratus, *Descriptions*

> Painting is still pleasing even when it is without the enthusiasm and genius that characterize it; but without the support of these two foundations, the productions of sculpture are insipid.
>
> Falconet, *Essay on Sculpture*

Enthusiasm was the life-giving force, albeit a metaphoric one, through which sculptors in eighteenth-century France animated their works. Falconet's *Pygmalion* strongly implies that the sculptor's enthusiasm, his passion, has brought his work to life and imparted to it the semblance of emotions. The only other potential enlivening force is Cupid, but this Love does not bring his torch to the scene. Nevertheless, some reviewers would insist on giving the animating power to this divinity, whom they see not simply as kissing Galatea's hand but as blowing into it the breath of life. Others would contend that Cupid merely enhanced the display of avid desire. In ravishing Galatea's hand with kisses, Falconet's Cupid does seem a substitute Pygmalion, reminding us of the affection the sculptor lavished on his work and suggesting that his desire has brought her to life. In so wonderfully exposing passion, Cupid also brings us back to the new Pygmalion, to Falconet, whose creative passion viewers also saw in the work. When Diderot writes: "A little cupid has seized one of the statue's hands; he does not kiss it, he devours it. What liveliness! What ardor!" his exclamations refer not only to Cupid's passion as the statue's animating force but also to Falconet's uncanny ability to endow stone with emotion.[41]

The review appearing in the *Mercure de France* confirms that contemporaries could also interpret Falconet's work as portraying Pygmalion's emotion—his passion for both his art and his sculpture—as the animating force. The *Mercure's* critic at first allies the piece with more traditional depictions: "A little Cupid, who has his mouth on one of the statue's arms, seems to be the source and the creator of the fire that gives her a soul."[42] Turning to Pygmalion, however, he has second thoughts: "Joy, surprise, and love are expressed with such an enthusiasm in this

Pygmalion that one wonders if the statue is not animated more by his looking than by the supernatural power of the gods he invokes."[43] The conclusion again suggests two linked readings: Pygmalion's love rather than Cupid's kiss has brought Galatea to life, and Falconet's enthusiasm has animated the entire scene.

Most flattering of all, however, were the panegyrics *Pygmalion* elicited. Consider, for example, "Sur son group de Pygmalion exposé au Salon du Louvre" offered by a M. Guichard. The poem opens by calling Falconet the "emulator of Pygmalion," and goes on to show how the modern sculptor was more gifted than his ancient model since he had no need of Venus:

> Beneath your fingers, without Venus, the marble is animated.
> It breathes, it moves, it seems inflamed.
> From an uncommon talent above human power!
> In studying your statue, one cries out: But is it one?[44]

The final line assures us that Falconet's animating power is metaphoric, playing on the confusion between art and nature that *Pygmalion* represents. Yet this sort of animating power is superior to that of old since it resides in the sculptor himself.

Falconet again is cast as greater than his rival Pygmalion in "Vers à M. Falconet sur la statue de Pygmalion" by Romilly fils:

> Greater than your rival, more certain of success
> Falconet you are assured an immortal hommage.
> You yourself animate your work.
> The fire of heaven is in your hands.[45]

The reasoning here is similar to other panegyrics—Falconet is greater than Pygmalion because he himself has animated the work. In the panegyric, "animation" has a metaphoric value, and so does "the fire of heaven"—that fire is the animating force that Prometheus snatched away and the divine flame of enthusiasm. It here stands for Falconet's inspired passion.

The Paternal Chisel

Creative fire was a common image of enthusiasm, as we have seen. Also widespread was the association of enthusiasm with sexual performance, which has a particular bearing on the Pygmalion story when the sculptor is conceived as "fathering" his statue. Diderot connected enthusiasm to sexual arousal in his commentary on the sketch.[46] A similar linking of enthusiasm with male sexual potency, even ejaculation, comes in Diderot's 1757 *Second entretien sur le fils naturel:* "The poet senses the moment of enthusiasm . . . He becomes aware of it as a trembling that begins in his chest and passes in an exquisite (*délicieuse*) and rapid way to the extremities of his body. Soon it is no longer a trembling. It is a strong and permanent heat which embraces him, makes him gasp, consumes him, kills him, but gives spirit and life to all that he touches."[47] In defining enthusiasm, Diderot characterizes it as a life-giving force contained in the artist's touch, an image that parallels that of the artist dispensing the fire of heaven through his hands. Yet Diderot's passage combines the metaphoric value of giving life with a description of physical symptoms that has been read for its implied association with sexual excitement, even orgasm. The poet pants and trembles before conferring life on a new creation.

The association of enthusiasm with male sexuality is most direct when semen is held as a "life-giving" or shaping force, and the sculptor makes his way into discussions of human reproduction. In Dubuisson's *Tableau de l'amour conjugal* of 1812, for example, semen's role in producing a child is likened to the sculptor's work in shaping his marble: "The semen is to generation what the sculptor is to marble; the male semen is the sculptor who gives shape, the female liquor is the marble or matter, and the sculpture is the fetus or the product of generation."[48] Dubuisson here follows an earlier tradition, and in his 1731 *Les principes de la nature ou de la génération des choses,* François-Marie-Pompée Colonna also used an artistic metaphor, this time making semen the instrument of reproduction guided now by the divine plan of an invisible workman. Semen is likened to the mallet and chisel:

> It is true that the semen is the visible agent, but one can say that like the Painter, the Sculptor, and other Artisans who use certain instruments to shape the matter they use to render their desired form, similarly, this invisible workman uses the male's seminal matter as the instrument to make the female matter able to generate an animal successfully.[49]

As an instrument of the divine artist, semen also contains an "esprit de feu céleste," which this text characterizes as a visible agent and the shaping force of matter. Although related to the Christian God, this heavenly fire harkens back to the fire of Prometheus and to other conceptions of the animating flame, the spark of life.[50]

Eventually this seminal fire migrates back to art, back to Pygmalion. In Barnabé-Firman de Rosoi's play or *drame lyrique* of 1780, *Pygmalion,* the sculptor addresses his statue, wondering why she does not live: "O you! Who can neither see me nor hear me; you who repel my touch, how is it possible that you are my work and that you cannot recognize your creator? Have not my burning hands, in modeling your contours, impregnated the marble become so docile, with this flammable substance, burning in my heart?"[51] The use of sexual metaphors both points to the imbrication of creativity and sexuality and suggests Pygmalion's caressing—even violating—of his statue. While the heart may have been the foyer of celestial fire, the hands and penis seem to be its exit points.

When the art of creating a sculpture, of shaping and cutting matter, is likened to semen's part in reproduction, it follows that the sculptor is the father of his work. This logic is borne out in eighteenth-century discussions of several related issues, for example, in comparing the individual who lives on through his progeny to the artist who insures his immortality with works that endure. Diderot, in fact, pressed the issue of paternity in his debate with Falconet over whether the artist should work for immortality or for the accolades of contemporary viewers, and Falconet's *Pygmalion* is a central example for Diderot in making his case. Diderot argued strongly for immortality, trying to convert the sculptor to his position. In a letter to Falconet from January 1766, Diderot asked if the sculptor could honestly say he would not give a louis to make his *Pygmalion* and several other works "forever invulnerable to the hand of time." Goading him further, Diderot asks: "you would not give as much, you who are their father?"[52]

The likening of artistic creativity to biological paternity had a long history in France, and throughout his correspondence Diderot quotes Michel de Montaigne (1533–92), the writer who perhaps most forcefully put forward this comparison. In his essay "Of the Affection of Fathers for Their Children" (1578–80), Montaigne compares two kinds of fatherhood—one that produces a child of the body and another that produces a child of the brain: "And I do not know whether I would not like much better to have produced one perfectly formed child by intercourse with the muses than by intercourse with my wife."[53] Intercourse with the Muses, however, results in a peculiar sort of insemination, a self-insemination in which the Muses play no part. Concerning children of the mind, Montaigne says to those with paternal claim: "We are father and mother both in this generation."[54] It is not coincidental that Montaigne concludes his essay by quoting Ovid's *Pygmalion*: "Its hardness gone, the ivory softens, yields/ Beneath his fingers."[55]

The idea that the artist not only fathers but also mothers—gives birth to—the work of art is evident throughout the eighteenth century, especially since terms like "naître à" could be used figuratively in referring to artistic creation. Voltaire, for example, used this language in his opera *Pandore* in which Prometheus is cast as having given birth to his sculpture/lover. As the play opens, Prometheus, the sculptor, proclaims before the statue he has made: "Miracle of my hands, charms that I have brought into being [fiat naître], I call you in vain, you do not hear me." Later, he avows that "to this object I have given birth [donné la naissance]."[56] Where some might simply pass over such language as mere turn of phrase, other examples make the convention more pointed.

By the eighteenth century, male pregnancy, which brought forth cultural production, Voltaire deemed superior and more difficult to woman's natural reproduction. Consider his well-known story of Gabrielle Émilie Le Tonnelier de Breteuil, marquise du Châtelet (1706–49) giving birth, various versions of which he recounted in 1749.[57] In writing to the comte d'Argental, he used Mme du Châtelet's maternity to introduce his own creativity, and claimed, "I will deliver my *Catelina* with much more difficulty."[58] To the abbé de Voisenon he noted, "I give birth in eight days to *Catelina*," and pointed out that although he does not know if Mme du Châtelet will be pregnant again, he is already carrying his *Electre*.[59] To the marquis d'Argenson he embellishes further: Mme du Châtelet has given birth to an infant who cannot speak, but he has made his characters articulate their thoughts. "It is more difficult," he writes, "to make those characters speak than to make babies."[60] Marie-Hélène Huet has examined this male maternity in terms of "monstrosity" and demonstrates its centrality as a trope for Romantic writers.[61]

Although Diderot seems to take a standard line on artistic paternity, Falconet has a somewhat more complicated position. On the one hand, he reduces to an absurdity the comparison between children of the flesh and those of marble. Writing to Diderot on 10 February 1766, Falconet attacks:

> I don't understand why this comparison is always made; look at the difference between the two families. Every day we destroy those of our works that displease us, and if we make better ones, we are applauded. Consequently, my friend, one day when you are not happy with your amiable daughter, break only an arm, nothing but an arm, with the good intention of producing a better creature, and then look for praise.[62]

This said, Falconet nevertheless embraces the idea of artistic paternity; indeed, he warms to it and provides his own conception, contrasting the artist's fertile "genius" to sexual impotence. Simply wanting to reproduce is not enough to insure either artistic production or sexual procreation. Without genius, the artist cannot make great works, and without an

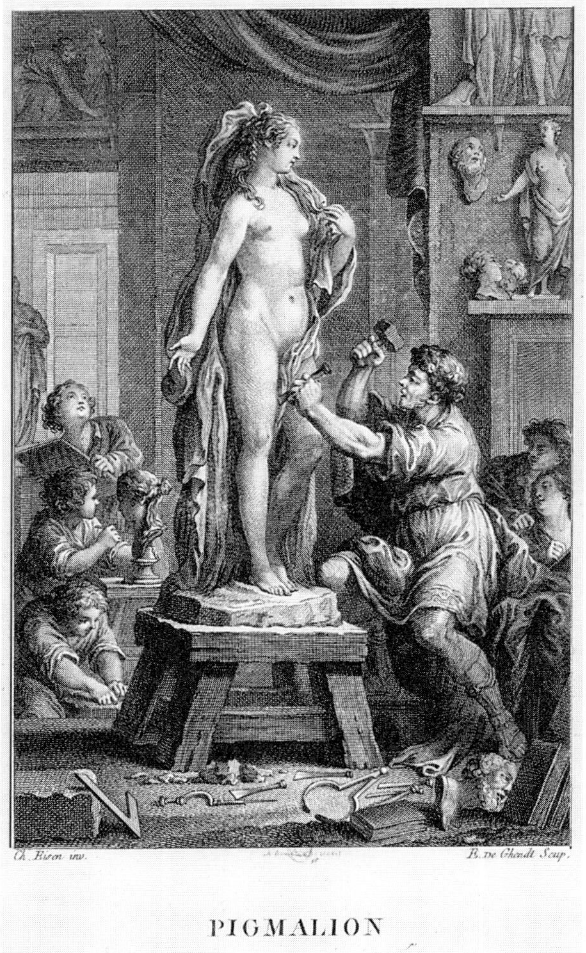

FIGURE 46. Emmanuel-Jean Nepomucene de Ghendt (1735–1815) after Charles Eisen (French, 1720–78), *Pygmalion; ou, La statue animée*, engraving. Photograph © Bibliothèque Nationale de France.

erection, the impotent man cannot inseminate. After proclaiming genius a pure gift of nature and unique cause of great works, Falconet continues: "[T]he greatest desire to have a good lineage, the strongest imagining of a pretty half-dozen children caressing their dear papa have never rendered an impotent man able to procreate."[63]

That Pygmalion fathers his work of art obviously complicates the tale of artistic creativity, shadowing it with the color of incest. In creating Galatea, Pygmalion is her father; in penetrating her, he becomes her husband/ lover. That complication is pictured, if only inadvertently, in those works that show Pygmalion's chisel poised on what looks to be a completed statue. An illustration for Boureau-Deslandes's *Pigmalion; ou, La statue animée* drawn by Charles Eisen and engraved by Emmanuel-Jean Nepomucene de Ghendt (1735–1815) shows us exactly this scene (fig. 46). There we see Pygmalion's chisel touching the body of what appears to be a fully finished (and even animated) work. With raised mallet, he is about to shape the statue, aiming his tool at a point suggestively located on her inner thigh. Because the work is so close to completion, it is difficult to discern if the chisel is an instrument that nuances the shape or an organ that sexually penetrates a female body, or rather the female body's simulacrum. Sometimes a chisel is not just a chisel.

Diderot suggests the dual potential of the chisel to signify a tool of both sculpture and procreation in his rewriting of Falconet's sculpture. We have already noted how the critic changed Pygmalion's pose; he lifts himself toward Galatea, placing his left hand lightly on her breast to find a heartbeat. But what is his right hand doing? It is busy grasping his chisel: "Pygmalion would hold [tiendrait] his chisel in his right hand and would grasp [serrerait] it forcefully; admiration embraces and grasps [serre] without reflection either the thing that it admires or that which it holds [tenir]."[64] Here Diderot suggests that Pygmalion's grasp of his chisel is not just a holding, it is also an admiring, a wonder that is free of reflection. And in holding his chisel, Pygmalion is grasped with wonder. For the left hand, Diderot mixes Pygmalion's surprise at seeing his work come to life with his fear that the miracle will fall short, but for the right hand holding the chisel, his emotion is pure and simple admiration. For Diderot, however, the chisel is more than either a mere symbol of the sculptor's craft or a simplistic representation of his sex.

In writing about sculpture, Diderot posed the chisel as that which allowed the sculpture to live, to be formed from, even born out of, raw material. In discussing the art in his "Salon of 1765," Diderot contrasted how painters and sculptors made lifelike illusions: "There's the block of marble, the figure is within it, it must be extracted . . . if it is modeled, it must live through its modeling, without any help from the resources of the palette [e.g., color] that give life to the work."[65] The notion that the chisel gave life to the work was not unique to Diderot, as evident in Romilly's panegyric to Falconet's *Pygmalion:* "The marble softens under your happy efforts: Your chisel gives it life."[66]

Rousseau's Pygmalion

No other eighteenth-century Pygmalion explored enthusiasm more fully than Jean-Jacques Rousseau in his *scène lyrique.* Among those contemporaries who understood Rousseau's *Pygmalion* as a meditation on problems of artistic inspiration was Frédéric Melchior Grimm. He wrote that what he saw in Rousseau's "sublime and original piece" was "a moving tableau of the transports, of the enthusiasm, of the delirium that can excite in a sensitive and impassioned soul a love of the arts and beauty."[67] It was supposedly the enthusiasm evident in this *Pygmalion* that insured its performance in Paris. The *Oeuvres complètes de J.-J.*

Rousseau, published in 1792, tells how the actor La Rive, who eventually played the part of Pygmalion at the Comédie Française, asked Rousseau for permission to perform the work after reading it and "found himself inflamed by the enthusiasm that emanated from the work."[68] Throughout the play, Rousseau makes certain assumptions about the relationship between aesthetic and erotic impulses, implying an easy correspondence between male arousal and enthusiasm when he renders Pygmalion enflamed at the same moment with the fires of love and genius.[69]

The action begins with the artist confronting his works strewn about him in the studio. Pygmalion is paralyzed by his own creations and mourns his loss of enthusiasm: "There is no soul, no life at all. It is only stone. . . . Oh my genius, where are you? What has become of my talent? All my fire is extinguished. My imagination has turned to ice. The marble emerges cold from my hands."[70] Here loss of enthusiasm merges the lovesick Pygmalion with the melancholic artist. Pygmalion is obsessed by a single thought that does not spur him to work, but paralyzes his creativity. Although Pygmalion has apparently lost his inspiration, he still feels himself consumed by an unknown ardor that sets him ablaze. The nature of that fire is revealed when Pygmalion approaches his statue of Galatea, which stands veiled in a corner of the studio. Lifting the veil, Pygmalion falls prostrate: "Oh, Galatea, receive my homage. Yes! I fooled myself; I intended to make you a nymph, and I made you a goddess."[71] Amid his contemplation of such perfection, however, Pygmalion notices what cannot be tolerated—he sees a flaw. His materialized statue-woman does not adequately match his interior ideal. He has not cut away enough of her drapery, he cannot see enough of her body. He "sees" the body in the stone as an imagined ideal, but he sees it as if a body actually existed under the sculpted marble veil.[72] Thus Pygmalion must gouge into the very substance of his Galatea to remove the stone garment that cloaks his vision.[73]

To correct the flaw, Pygmalion takes up hammer and chisel, intent on sculpting Galatea to greater advantage. Only by revisualizing his ideal vision, only when his vision returns to him, can Pygmalion be inspired to work again. Only then can Galatea come to life. He slowly advances toward his beloved statue and raises his chisel, but uncertainty stops the action short: "What trembling! . . . What disquiet! I hold the chisel with an uncertain hand . . . I cannot . . . I dare not . . . I'll spoil everything."[74] Screwing up his courage, Pygmalion again positions his chisel, and this time he strikes the statue. The effect is dramatic: Pygmalion drops his tool crying in terror: "Gods! I felt the palpitating flesh repel the chisel."[75] At first, the sculptor imagines he has hallucinated her movement, and we are left to wonder if it was his own trembling that Pygmalion felt when he struck the statue. Indeed, we are left to wonder if Pygmalion might not have sensed his own enthusiasm manifested as tremor.

It is movement and not softening, sight and not touch, that ultimately convinces Rousseau's Pygmalion that Galatea lives. Finding the courage to look at his statue again, Pygmalion sees it move and turns aside in fright, proclaiming himself mad. Finally, his doubts are dispelled: Galatea moves again. Amazed and entranced, Pygmalion watches as his statue comes alive, as his nude descends the staircase. She comes down from the pedestal, touches herself once and utters her first word: "Moi." She touches herself again and says, "C'est moi," then touches a marble, and responds to the new sensation: "Ce n'est plus moi." Her final words escape when she touches Pygmalion: "Ah! encore moi."[76]

Rousseau's Galatea comes to life miraculously, and she is apparently born with her perceptual and cognitive processes well advanced. She can already say "moi"; indeed, she knows the concept when she touches herself for the first time, even before she distinguishes herself from inanimate stone through touch. In Condillac's *Treatise on the Sensations,* touch is that sense by which we know there are bodies other than ourselves. It is precisely touch that enables his statue-man both to know its own boundaries and to distinguish itself as a subject, as a "moi" separated from other objects. If the statue "touches a foreign body, the 'I' that feels itself modified in the hand, does not feel itself modified in the foreign body. If the hand says 'I,' it does not receive the same response. The statue, therefore, judges these modes to be entirely outside of it."[77] Condillac argues that touch teaches the other senses to judge external objects; and without this sense, the statue-man imagines all its sensations to be modifications of itself.

Rousseau, however, is not content simply to invoke Condillac's theory of the sensations. In his *Pygmalion,* touch allows both differentiation and identification. His Galatea proclaims that she is the same as Pygmalion, her creator, even as she distinguishes herself from stone objects. The play obviously separates the animate from the inanimate, but at the same time Galatea's touch assures her that she is Pygmalion. Indeed, through the entire monodrama, Galatea is the mirror of Pygmalion's desire as she is when the sculptor cannot determine if he felt the statue's trembling or his own response.

Pygmalion and Narcissus

Rousseau's dialogue brings out Pygmalion's narcissism more clearly than do other eighteenth-century versions of the story. Alone in his studio Pygmalion confesses: "Vanity, human frailty! I cannot allow myself to admire my own work; I am intoxicated with self-love."[78] Even as he begs Venus to animate his work, Pygmalion exalts his own power: "Goddess of beauty, spare nature this affront: that so perfect a model must be an image of that which does not exist."[79] Although the sculptor tries to believe himself in love with a living being who resembles his statue, he finally admits that he adores his own work: "What darts of flame seem to fly from this object to fire my senses and to return with my soul to their source?"[80] Pygmalion's narcissism is manifested not only as excessive *amour-propre* but also as a libidinal investment in his own ideas embodied in a work of art. Pygmalion wants to make Galatea his double, or as he puts it, to "give her my life," to "animate her with my own soul."[81] It seems entirely within the logic of the drama, then, when a newly animated Galatea touches Pygmalion and says "moi." Pygmalion's love for Galatea is a love of his own imaginings; enthusiasm in Rousseau's hands has decidedly autoerotic dimensions.

It was not uncommon, however, for artists to think of their works as a part of themselves, as their mental image instantiated. At the same time that they embraced the idea of artistic paternity, both Diderot and Falconet also held that the work of art "is" the artist. Throughout their debate over the artist's immortality, Diderot time and again tries to force Falconet to admit that he cares about the future fate of his works. In an effort to convince him, Diderot argues: "The thought that I write, it is me; the marble that you animate, it's you; it's the best part of you, it is you at the finest moments of your life; it is what you make and another cannot."[82] And Falconet answers, "The marble that I work is undoubtedly myself."[83] But he goes on to deflate Diderot's arguments for immortality by pointing out how he cares little for the fate of his marbles after they leave his studio, comparing himself to the pear tree that produces pears: "The pear that this pear tree produces, it is the pear tree. Is it ripe? It falls without the tree into a pastry."[84] Although in this amusing example Falconet deflates Diderot's claim, in his own *Pygmalion* the sculptor did not make light of an artist's identification with his work. Indeed, Falconet's marble implicitly claims that he is Pygmalion, that Pygmalion is his double, that Pygmalion's statue is his own *Bather*. His statue makes this claim whether it is aimed at his contemporaries (as Falconet preferred) or at posterity (as Diderot wanted), and whether or not he consciously intended to do so.

Falconet chooses to show us a Pygmalion who does not grasp his paternal chisel but who rather presses his palms together, touching one to the other in a gesture that is neither the conventional one for "surprise" nor the standard one for prayer. It is a very unusual gesture, this clasping together of hands. No other Pygmalion before or after (save, of course, direct copies) makes it. The gesture is important for internalizing the drama within Pygmalion, and so the event becomes more and more the sculptor's vision. And because what he sees is not a vision sent from any god but Falconet's own *Bather*, that vision smacks of narcissism. Excessive vanity is suggested in the choice of his *Bather*, and erotic self-love in Pygmalion's response to a work that, as Falconet admits, is himself. Thus it seems appropriate that Falconet's Pygmalion directs his energy inward; he touches himself as one hand makes contact with the other. He takes himself as both the subject and object of his touching.

Among those who have interpreted and reconceived Ovid's *Pygmalion*, many have noticed echoes of Narcissus in the sculptor's passionate devotion to the ideal woman he created.[85] This association appears in French literature as early as the thirteenth-century *Romance of the Rose* and echoes in many eighteenth-century Pygmalion plays. Narcissus, like Pygmalion, had long been a double for the visual artist, his reflection suggesting the play of reality and illusion implied in Western conceptions of mimesis.[86] But the case of Pygmalion implies more when Galatea is presented as the mirror of his desire, for as Luce Irigaray has argued, woman as conceived in Western philosophy is never more than such a mirror.[87]

Venus among the Heroes

In presenting the story of Pygmalion as an allegory of art, eighteenth-century representations typically shaped two fantasies: one of making a work so lifelike, so apparently "sensible," that it would be confused with the real, and one of possessing the ideal sexual object, a modest and faithful Venus who mirrored her creator's passions. At the same time, Pygmalion's art making gave the lie to some common ideas circulating in the mid-eighteenth century. Not only did the sculptor's passions and desires allot little place to reason in the creative process, but also his confusion of fiction and reality suggested an uncontrolled imagination.

Equally problematic was that Pygmalion did not produce works for public edification or for the nation's glory but to arouse and satisfy sexual appetites. Although it might have been a common fantasy, creating an ideal love object was not advanced as a justification for art in an era when both official institutions and critical commentary more and more demanded that the arts have an ethical purpose. We might even imagine that Pygmalion belatedly pays for this betrayal when an incestuous lust grabs hold of Myrrha. The sculptor is more directly rebuked in those versions of his story that endow the animated statue with all the vices of real women.[88] Just as the gods sent Pandora to avenge Prometheus's theft, perhaps they animated Galatea to punish Pygmalion for making woman the privileged object of art. This, to be sure, is a perverse reading of the myth. But no matter how idiosyncratic, it raises a significant question: How appropriate was Pygmalion's story for expressing the goals of art in the mid-eighteenth century?

If some aspects of the tale encapsulated the aims of mimetic and expressive art, others did not accord well even with the purposes of sculpture as stated, for example, in *Iconologie par figures* (1791) begun by Hubert Gravelot (1699–1773) and completed by Charles-Nicolas Cochin, fils (1715–90), and Charles-Étienne Gaucher (1741–1804). There Sculpture is represented as a female figure using her chisel and mallet to sculpt a bust—not any bust, but one that announces sculpture as an art "particularly destined to perpetuate the memory of great men and, above all, the benefactors of humanity" (fig. 47).[89] Pictured as a woman, Sculpture here meets its goals better than when the art is instantiated in Pygmalion, who fashions a voluptuous statue he adores.

Given that Falconet became known as "author of the Pygmalion," it is perhaps surprising to find that he casts the depiction of sexual fantasies as an undesirable use of sculpture. One of his first reflections on sculpture, however, makes this point:

> Sculpture, after history, is the most durable repository of men's virtues and weaknesses. If we have in the statue of Venus the object of a stupid and dissolute cult, we have in that of Marcus Aurelius a celebrated monument to the tributes rendered to a benefactor of humanity. In showing us vice deified, this art renders much more striking the horrors that history has transmitted to us. On the other hand, the precious traits that remain to us of those rare men, who should have lived as long as their statues, revive in us the sentiment of a noble emulation, which elevates the soul to the virtues that they have prevented mankind from forgetting.[90]

Falconet here sets up a direct contrast between images of vice and virtue, but unlike Hercules choosing between Venus and Athena, the sculptor is poised between a female figure of vice and a male figure of virtue. And the image of vice has a suggestive relation to the Pygmalion theme.

It was, after all, a statue of Venus that impassioned the first Pygmalion, king of Cyprus, and this statue had deeply rooted associations with idolatry, deviant sexuality, and pagan cults. Such a statue could very well be taken to encode mankind's weakness and deify vice, especially if one also believed that Venus was not a goddess but, rather, a woman who instituted prostitution on the island of Cyprus. Not only did the cult statue of Venus recall the old Pygmalion's mad

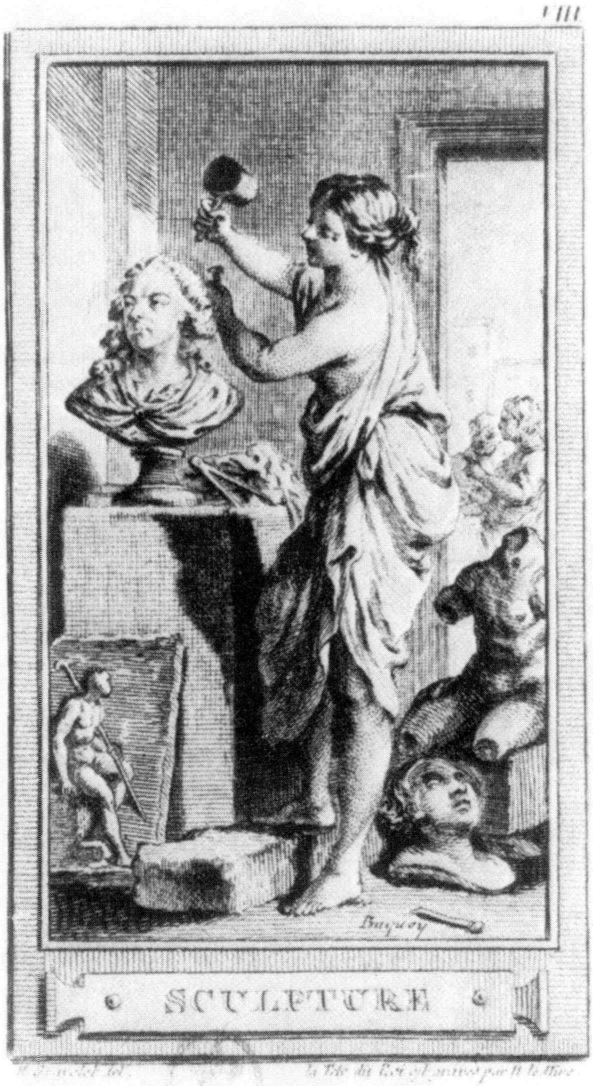

FIGURE 47. *Sculpture* from *Iconologie par figures*, Paris: 1791. Begun by Hubert François Bourguignon, called Gravelot (French, 1699–1773) and completed by Charles-Nicolas Cochin, fils (French, 1715–90) and Charles-Étienne Gaucher (French, 1741–1804). Photograph courtesy University of North Carolina Photographic Services.

lust, but many different versions of Ovid's *Pygmalion* equated Galatea and Venus. The likeness is visualized in Raoux's painting and verbalized in Rousseau's *scène lyrique* when the sculptor claims he has made a goddess. In Boureau-Deslandes's treatise one reads that Pygmalion formed his statue after a vision of Venus, making her a double of the goddess. But even if Falconet intended no reference to the specific statue that Pygmalion craved, it is suggestive enough that a statue of Venus, goddess of sexual desire, should exemplify the deification of vice.

Where Falconet connects the statue of Venus to a "stupid and dissolute" idolatry, the deification of vice, and human weakness, the statue of

Marcus Aurelius he associates with paying tribute to a human benefactor, noble emulation, and lasting virtue. Continuing this line of reasoning, Falconet presents as the ideal relation of spectator to work of art not Pygmalion before his Venus, but Caesar weeping as he sees the statue of Alexander the Great.[91] What Falconet proposes in theory (but does not always carry out in practice) would become state policy during the comte d'Angiviller's directorship of the French Academy, which began in 1775. In an address to the Academy delivered that same year, d'Angiviller outlined his ideas on a more virtuous art. He instituted a plan for sculpture by commissioning four marble figures each "representing some man celebrated by the nation for his virtues, talents, or genius."[92] The Salon of 1777 showed the first results of d'Angiviller's efforts, for example, in Étienne Gois's *Statue of the Chancellor of the l'Hôpital* (Versailles: Musée du Château), and d'Angiviller planned to order four new statues every two years. It was not only official patronage, however, that moved in this direction. In 1770, the "Republic of Letters" commissioned a public monument paid for by public subscription, choosing as its subject the image of Voltaire.[93]

The use of sculpture to revivify great men was part of a larger political shift toward a more moral art, and not only the artist's productions, but also public enthusiasm, could be harnessed toward this desired end. Enthusiasm for great works was a healthy contagion, and far from spreading disease to the next generation, it transmitted to them their national "gloire." In his *Encyclopédie* entry on enthusiasm, Cahusac put it this way: "The names of the Corneilles, the Molières, the Quinaults, the Lullys, the Lebruns, the Bossuets, the Perraults, the Le Notres go from mouth to mouth, and all of Europe repeats them and admires them; they are henceforth the immutable monuments to the glory of the nation and humanity."[94] And later in his essay he explained that "[i]t is in the nature of enthusiasm to communicate itself and to reproduce itself; it is a lively flame that spreads from one to the other, that nourishes itself from its own fire, and that far from weakening itself in spreading, takes on new force to the extent that it spreads itself and communicates itself."[95] Enthusiasm is predictably cast as enthusiasm for the timeless achievements of great men, the national *patrimoine*.[96]

Given the pressure to praise great men, it is indeed interesting that the Pygmalion theme not only endured throughout the eighteenth century but also gained new articulation in the nineteenth. Contradictions such as that between Falconet's "theory" and "practice" were common enough in the discourse of art making as well as within the *oeuvre* of an individual artist or writer.[97] The contradictions insured that theories of art making and viewing remained unstable. In the case of Falconet, however, we can question the extent to which his comments on vice and virtue in sculpture represent his personal beliefs, since they mirror so closely the views of the Academy to which he addressed his *Reflections*, and the Encyclopedists in whose publication he disseminated them. Indeed, Diderot likewise contrasted an image of Venus to those of great men in his "Salon of 1767."

As we have seen in chapter 2, Diderot laments that *Venus with the Beautiful Buttocks* brought debauchery into the gardens of Versailles, incorporating and encouraging vice. And in his remarks, Venus is at once the idol of vice and its target ("so many dissolute acts avowed in these inscriptions, so many insults made by debauchery even against its own idols").[98] Diderot further complains that such a work replaces the busts of great men that ought to adorn a king's estate: "Don't you think that busts of those who have served the country well, whether in arms, in the halls of justice, in the sovereign's council chamber, or in pursuing a career in letters or the fine arts, would give a better lesson?"[99] These comments, moreover, unveil an attitude toward female sexuality not unlike that found in the various Pygmalion stories in which Galatea, the Propoetides, and Myrrha are represented. Female sexuality is perceived as dangerous, set up as a venerated idol, and subjected to insults and defilement. Yet the part of Galatea could be turned to woman's advantage even if it required that women cast themselves as the created of art, as art's preferred object. In the same way that women inhabited allegorical figures not intended to glorify their virtues, so they could use the position of the statue to claim some parity with Pygmalion.

PART II: PLAYING GALATEA

One woman who astutely perceived the potential in playing Galatea was the dancer Marie Sallé (1707–56; fig. 48) of the Opéra Comique. Her 1734 *Pigmalion* enjoyed enthusiastic audiences and rave reviews when it opened in London. Called "an entirely original creation," *Pigmalion* played for two months straight.[100] We know about her performance from contemporary notices and, especially, from a letter published in the *Mercure de France*. This letter describes how Sallé won a double success, applauded as a dancer and as a poet in playing ballet-pantomimes of her own invention. Sallé not only danced the part of Galatea, but invented the entire ballet—from choreography to costume. Thus well before Rousseau or Falconet retold the story to exemplify their own art making, Sallé appropriated the theme and in her work revolutionized dance costume and advanced her dance-pantomime.[101]

In defiance of conventional stage costume, Sallé performed the role of Galatea not in *paniers* but in what looked to her audience like antique garb. The *Mercure de France* reported that she "dared" appear without

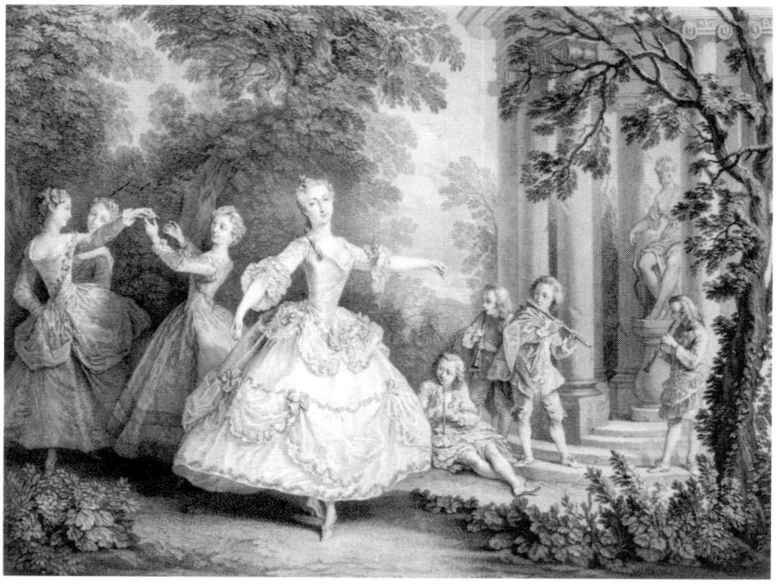

FIGURE 48. Gilles-Edme Petit (French, c. 1694–1760) after a portrait by Fenouil, *Portrait of Mlle Sallé. The French Terpsicore*, engraving. Photograph © Bibliothèque Nationale de France.

the traditional elements of costume, dressing herself in a simple drapery adjusted to look like that of a Greek statue.[102] In this costuming, Sallé anticipated the actor La Rive's innovative donning of antique dress when he played Rousseau's Pygmalion nearly a half-century later. It is more significant, however, that through *Pigmalion* Sallé transformed conventional dancing into expressive pantomime, giving it a dramatic charge and emotional resonance.[103]

At this time, the ballet was separate from an opera's drama. While the characters sang the story, the dancers created a mood—of sobriety, joy, magnificence—through their movements. Dancers, moreover, danced not for the sake of the story but for the sake of elaborate and virtuoso movements based on intricate patterns and steps. In her works—and specifically in *Pigmalion*—Sallé changed the course of dance history by combining opera-ballet with pantomime, using dance to tell a moving story. Dance historian and choreographer Susan Foster has pointed out that "Sallé's choreography for Galatea . . . embraced two distinct aesthetic traditions—the baroque opera-ballet and the parodic pantomime—and from them bodied forth a third, the action or story ballet (*ballet d'action*). In doing so, Sallé forecast the dissolution of the opera-ballet."[104]

Judging from the description of her *Pigmalion* published in the *Mercure,* Sallé did not feel the need to change Ovid's basic story, although the dance included no reference to Pygmalion's disgust for real women or to the Propoetides's wanton behavior. Rather, the performance opened with the sculptor, mallet and chisel in hand, dancing into the studio with his apprentices. They entered an atelier peopled with statues, and one among them drew everyone's admiration. That statue, of course, was Galatea impersonated by Mlle Sallé. The next sequence underscored Pygmalion's growing lovesickness. Looking at the "sculpture," which he has decorated with precious bracelets and an elegant necklace, Pygmalion sighs and kisses her hands. "He finally becomes impassioned; he expresses his anxieties, from there he falls into a reverie, after which he throws himself at the feet of Venus, whom he implores to animate his marble."[105] By emphasizing the emotions depicted, the description highlights those aspects of the dance pantomime that would bring its creator fame.

The correspondent again focuses on the emotions portrayed in picturing the scene of animation, but he also comments on the elegant attitudes and the growing complexity of the dance steps:

> Venus responds to his prayer; three rays of light appear and with appropriate music the statue begins to come out of her inanimate state by degrees, to the surprise of Pygmalion and his followers. She expresses her astonishment at her new state and at all the objects that surround her. Pygmalion, full of astonishment and transport, takes her hand to lead her out of her position. She taps, so to speak, the earth and forms some steps little by little, in the most elegant attitudes that sculpture could desire. Pygmalion dances before her as if to show her how to move, and she repeats his movements from the most simple to the more composed, to the most difficult. He tries to inspire the tenderness that fills him.[106]

As Sarah Cohen has pointed out, there is an obvious irony in the way Sallé has conceptualized the ballet's action.[107] This irony, however, remains unremarked upon in reports of the ballet, even as they comment on Sallé's role as both dancer and choreographer.

As Galatea, Sallé imitated Pygmalion in making her steps; as choreographer, she invented this Pygmalion and determined his movement. It was she who taught Pygmalion to dance. Sallé puts herself in the role of art maker, not by portraying a female artist who creates a simulacrum that she brings to life but by fully inhabiting the part of Galatea, by truly giving it life. Moreover, in performing the same steps as Pygmalion, Sallé upheld the technical equality of men and women dancers, a point that Cohen makes in reference to Sallé's choreography in general.[108]

Sallé's innovations earned her a place in eighteenth-century dance history, where by 1754 her work was absorbed into the category of *danse en action,* a term now associated with the dancer and *maître de ballet,* Jean-Georges Noverre.[109] Cahusac, however, applied this designation to Mlle Sallé's art in his treatise on dance, in which he draws this distinction between the "danse en action" and the "danse simple":

> The *Danse en action* is superior to the *Danse simple* in the way a fine history painting is superior to cut-out floral arrangements. The merit of the latter is entirely in mechanical arrangement. Genius orders, distributes, composes the former. Everyone knows how to make cut-outs, there is no merit in making them even if one does so excellently. One marches in the difficult path that leads to the temple of memory alongside Montesquieu when one paints like Van Loo.[110]

Like the history painting, the *dance en action* required more than simple imitation: it demanded invention. In addition, it called on the dancer to be a painter of human emotions, a quality that Cahusac valued highly. In this regard, he compares Sallé not with her contemporaries but with the ancient Roman dancer Tymele who rendered theatrical action in an exceptional way and who sometimes brought her spectators almost to the point of ecstasy.

> There is no theatrical action that she [i.e., Tymele] did not render with all possible force, vivacity, and energy. She was, above all, superior in renderings of gallantry. Never did anyone paint with so much fire, with colors at once so sweet and so vivid. She sometimes plunged the spectators into a kind of exaltation [ravissement] that approached ecstasy [extase]. Women in these moments were transported outside of themselves, they lost their heads, they cried out in pleasure. Mlle Sallé would have created the same impression if she had performed in a century when the theatrical dance had been better known.[111]

In another sense, the *danse en action* requires enthusiasm. Continuing the comparison with painting, Cahusac likens the *danse simple* to what the painter achieves as he masters the art of drawing and progresses in his studies until he can draw an entire figure. The *danse en action,* however, is conceived not in terms of technique but in terms of genius and enthusiasm. The dancer's imagination is like that of the painter warmed by the masterpieces of art. As a result, great men are reborn, memorable events are revived, colors speak, and the canvas breathes.[112] The Pygmalion theme is implied in this regard as the work of art comes to life, and by performing the *danse en action,* Sallé is like Pygmalion, for she reanimates the part she plays.

In his discussion of Mlle Sallé, Cahusac admires her talents as a "history painter," in particular, the ability to invent a composition and to render human emotions. And he claims that she "reasoned" all that she did. Focusing not on Sallé's *Pigmalion* but on her performance in the *passacaille* of *L'Europe galante,* Cahusac calls it a "tableau" full of art and passion, all the more estimable since it was entirely the invention of the dancer: "She had embellished the design of the poet and so she raised herself above the rank of the simple artist to elevate herself to the rare class of creative talents."[113]

Although it may seem odd that a writer who elsewhere appears so bent on masculinizing the arts would laud a woman's talent and reasoned invention, such a contradiction was by no means unusual. Recall, for example, that Diderot makes Mlle Clairon the prime example of the actor's art in a treatise that proclaims women far below men in this ability. Moreover, like Sallé, Clairon not only excelled in emotional expression, but she also played her part dispassionately and planned it in every detail, as Diderot described in his *Paradoxe sur le comédien.* In her *Réflexions sur la déclamation théatrale,* Clairon even portrays herself as a history painter, pointing out that a knowledge of history and geography are indispensable for the actor so that she can know the proper character, costume, and movement for each part.[114]

Given the general attitudes about woman's creativity, Cahusac's absorption of Mlle Sallé into the *danse en action* is telling. Despite the similarities, there were significant differences between Sallé's *danse pantomime* and Noverre's *danse en action.* As Cohen has pointed out, the latter distinguished male and female actions and movements and established a firm division of genders: "[I]n the narrative arena of the *ballet d'action,* distinguishing male from female movement was integral to nature's drama."[115] Noverre even built entire ballets, his *Misogyne,* for example, around sexual difference. Although Sallé generally danced parts that were "feminine" in their emotions and circumstances, her virtuoso movements impinged on the terrain reserved in the *danse noble* for men.[116] In *Pigmalion,* not only did Sallé invent and choreograph the work, but as Galatea she also danced the same steps as the sculptor, showing herself equally adept at the techniques of the art.

The singling out of Clairon and Sallé suggests the logic of the exception. This logic allowed a few women their talents, while denying them to the vast majority. Thus if specific women found a way to turn Pygmalion to their own ends, their performance did little to change attitudes toward women's cultural production in general. Moreover, the unstable gendering of Pygmalion, in specific, and the artist, in general, made it imperative that woman's lack of ability be continuously reinforced to deflect the danger of one slipping into the other—the woman into the artist, and concomitantly, the man-artist into the woman.

During the eighteenth century, positive accounts of artistic enthusiasm were written only for the male artist and aimed, in one way or another, at reaffirming his masculinity. That this affirmation could never be definitive actually weakened women's claim on the position of artist. As a general rule, women artists were not able to (re)appropriate for themselves the feminine aspects of the male creator. Attributing "feminine" properties to the male artist made it imperative that woman's incapacity for making (great) art be constantly reaffirmed. Even though women could never be neatly separated from the feminine properties positively associated with art making, in theory they could be held apart from them if the capacity to produce art was put firmly out of their reach.

Some versions of Pygmalion, notably Michel de Cubières-Palmézeaux's *Galatée* (1777), worked to foreclose any attempts at role reversal. There the play revolves around Pygmalion's elaborate plot to test Galatea's faithfulness, for the action takes place following her animation and their marriage. Pygmalion pretends that he needs to take up a sculpture commission in a distant land, but leaves her a statue—a perfect likeness of himself—to keep her company during his absence. He warns her, however, that this statue is not Pygmalion and any falling in love with it, any attempt to animate it as a lover, he will take as disloyalty. Pygmalion then contrives to take the place of the statue, to see for himself if Galatea will heed his warning. Galatea does try to work magic on the statue, and her attempt is played for laughs. Her astonishment at his movement is a joke on her, for it is the living Pygmalion and not a statue who moves. All ends happily, however, for after she believes the statue has come to life, Galatea does not make love to it, proclaiming herself a faithful wife.[117] A faithful wife she may be, but a creative animator Galatea is not.

The second woman whom we know played Pygmalion's beloved was Mlle Raucourt (Josèphe-Françoise Saucelle, 1753–1815; fig. 49), who enacted Galatea in Rousseau's *scène lyrique* when it opened at the Comédie Française in 1775.[118] The part came at a particularly important moment. By 1775, rumors about a dissolute life had had a negative effect on the actress's career, and for a time she recouped her losses while playing Galatea. And those losses were substantial. The young Raucourt (she was only seventeen at the time) had made her Paris debut in 1772 as Dido, taking the capital by storm. Calling her a phenomenon, the *Correspondance littéraire* reported that she had played her role "with a success and applause impossible to imagine if one has never seen the intoxication and enthusiasm of Paris."[119] The review continued, "The enthusiasm of

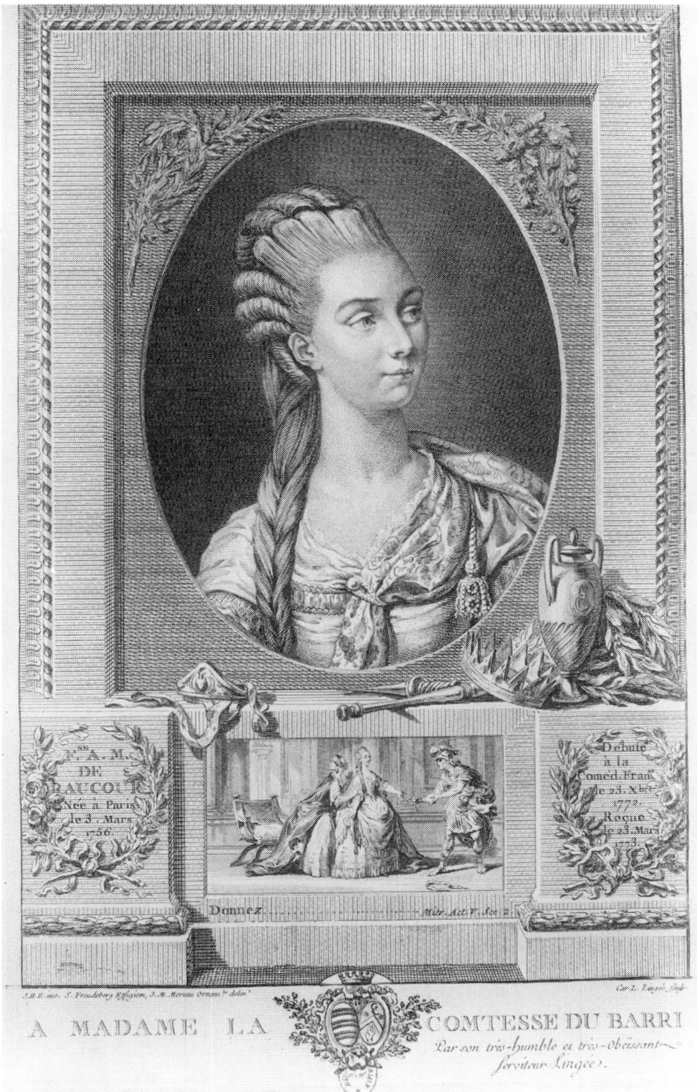

FIGURE 49. Charles Louis Lingée (French, 1748–1819) after a portrait by Sigmund Freudenberger (French, 1745–1801), *Portrait of Mlle Raucourt*, engraving. Photograph © Bibliothèque Nationale de France.

the public knew no limits. There were cries of admiration and acclaim; people became heated up without realizing it; everyone was perfectly drunk. After the play, this same enthusiasm spread in the private residences. Those who had seen *Dido* dispersed themselves to different quarters, arriving like madmen speaking with transport of the debut, communicating their enthusiasm to those who had not seen her."[120] Grimm even commented on the staying power of this enthusiasm: "For nearly a month these transports have continued in all their fire; it is one of the strongest and, above all, one of the longest relapses into enthusiasm that I have seen in Paris."[121] Undoubtedly her age, her newness, and her apparently unassailable virtue raised the dramatic effect she produced. Reading on in the six-page account, we find that "[i]t is said that this charming creature, so imposing in the theater, is very simple off stage, that she has all the candor and innocence appropriate to her age."[122]

In 1774, however, it was evident that the young actress was not so virtuous as she first appeared, and in July of that year the charge of tribadism was added to the list of her sexual and financial vices. The *Mémoires secrets* spread the slander about her and other actresses, reporting that "the vice of tribadism is very fashionable among our ladies of the opera," and singling out Françoise Raucourt and Sophie Arnoud as guilty of such immorality.[123] And in the next year, the *Correspondance littéraire* would note that Raucourt had been accused of joining to the tastes of her sex, all the vices of men.[124] Despite her brief return to favor as Galatea, it would be only a slight exaggeration to claim that writers for the *Mémoires secrets* were obsessed with Raucourt as the leader of tribades, the chief "lesbienne," and so forth.[125] True or not, such publicity had its effect on the public's perception of her acting, at least as reported in the press. By the end of 1774, the parterre hissed Raucourt and publicly embarrassed her at the theater.

It seems to me wonderfully ironic and poignantly telling that Raucourt should make her comeback playing Rousseau's Galatea. First, the part has only three very short lines, as the reviewers noted, and it mostly required that she stand in a beautiful pose. Given all that was written about her in the *Mémoires secrets,* it seems that their reviewer is sarcastic when he writes of her acting: "Mademoiselle Raucourt has represented the statue and was truly beautiful in this pose. People said it was her best role yet."[126] The review in the *Correspondence littéraire* was a bit less laudatory, noting that "Mademoiselle Raucourt's beautiful head has contributed more than a little to the success of Galatea, but as superb as she appeared as a statue, we would have found her more sublime if her hair had been more picturesque, her rouge less dark, her arms a little shorter and her feet a little smaller."[127] At the same time, the critic found her acting less than perfect: "We would have been better satisfied with her performance if, when she came to life, she put more gradation in her first movements, if her art came alive before her head, in a word, if she had less coquetry and more truth."[128]

Despite these criticisms, it seems that audiences found Raucourt superb as a statue, and this assessment appears to have been widespread. Another critic, for example, noted that "it is impossible to imagine a view more seducing than that of this actress posed on the pedestal at the moment when the veil that covers her is drawn off. Her head was that of Venus, her leg half uncovered, that of Diana."[129] And indeed, the part does seem ideal for someone like Raucourt, who apparently had a remarkable physical presence on the stage. Contemporary descriptions suggest she was a powerful woman with force and energy, of an antique beauty rather than a feminine grace and charm. Unveiled as the statue of Galatea, Raucourt, I imagine, held center stage in much the same way that the statue draws all eyes in Sallé's ballet. But how would she seem in saying the lines Rousseau imagined, melting into Pygmalion's arms and sighing, "Moi, encore"? The *Correspondence littéraire* perhaps acknowledged the irony in November, 1775, in a comment on the "Loge de Lesbos," a society more mysterious—and certainly more debauched—than the Masons. "Our superb Galatea," the writer remarks, "has been said to be one of the high priestesses of that temple."[130]

I like to think it is Raucourt whom Moreau le jeune imagines as Galatea when he shows the statue turning her back on Pygmalion (fig. 50). Moreau le jeune's engraving of Pygmalion and Galatea, which illustrated Rousseau's collected works (Brussels, 1774–83) is quite singular and deviates from all earlier French versions of the story. The Galatea Moreau le jeune shows is scarcely the timorous, trembling creature Rousseau desires. Having stepped off her pedestal, this Galatea turns her back on Pygmalion. His gesture more or less adheres to the codes that signal surprise, but it could easily be interpreted as a plea because the outstretched hands slip into a sign of entreaty. Is Pygmalion surprised because Galatea has come to life or because she has turned her back on him? Does he plead with her to look at him or to get back on that pedestal?

Once Galatea has stepped off her pedestal, she strides toward a sculpture of a nude man. The scene is by no means specified in the stage directions that accompanied Rousseau's text. Although the script places the event in a sculptor's atelier strewn with "marble blocks, sculpture groups, sketches for statues," it tells us only that at a critical moment "Galatea takes a few steps and touches a marble."[131] But the marble Moreau le jeune chooses to represent is interesting, especially since the stony sculpture also shows an equivocal gesture. He seems about to lurch forward, but he could also be read as fending off Galatea's presumptuous advance. Is she trying to repeat Pygmalion's life giving touch on a figure she finds more pleasing than he? Most obvious in this version of the story is that Pygmalion no longer seems to control Galatea. It is difficult to imagine this Galatea, striding so confidently, almost enthusiastically, toward the marble sculpture, turning in the next moment to melt into Pygmalion's arms, saying, "Ah! moi, encore." Rousseau's Pygmalion may have thought he sculpted a goddess, but in Moreau le jeune's version he gets a nymph. Or maybe even a nymphomaniac. As soon as Galatea moves from art to nature, from sculpture to woman, as

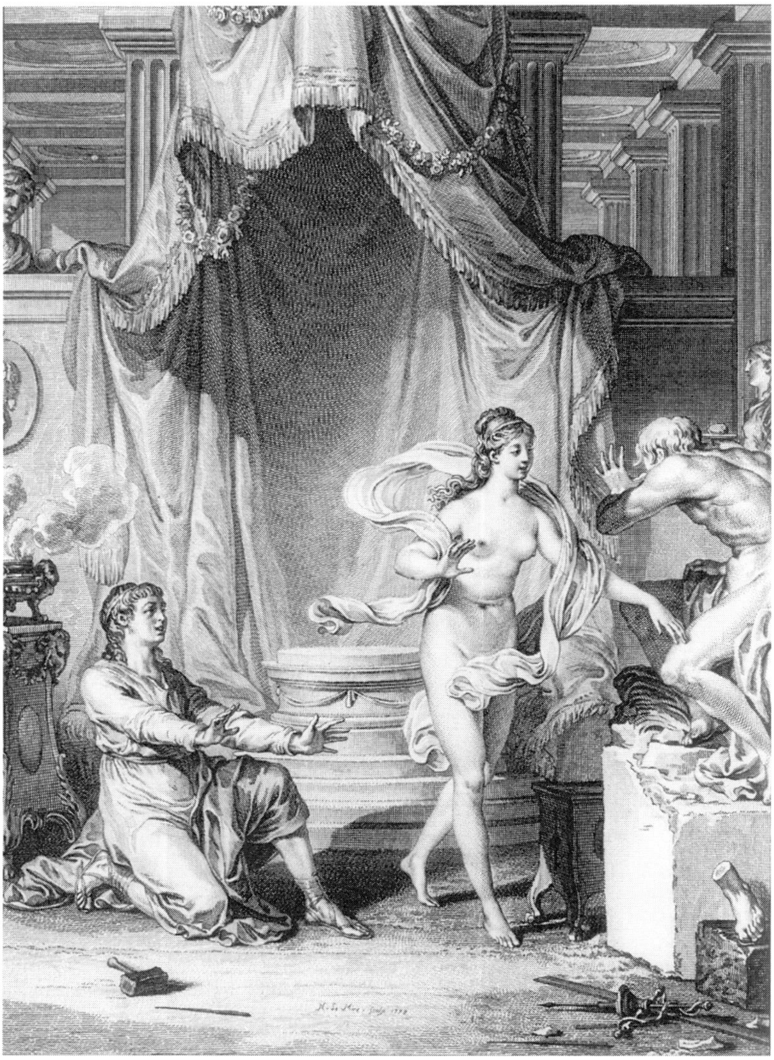

FIGURE 50. Noël Le Mire (French, 1724–1801) after Jean Michel Moreau (called Moreau le jeune; French, 1741–1814), *Pygmalion and Galatea*. Illustration for J. J. Rousseau's *Pygmalion* in the plates from *Collection complette des oeuvres de J. J. Rousseau* (Brussels: J. de Boubers, 1774–83). From the copy in the Rare Book Collection, The University of North Carolina at Chapel Hill. Photograph courtesy University of North Carolina Photographic Services.

soon as she steps off her pedestal, she is at risk. She could very well be the materialist Galatea who takes pleasure as her sovereign.[132]

The image of Raucourt as a cheeky Galatea underscores the irony of having a reputed tribade play Galatea as male creators—Ovid, Rousseau, and Falconet, to name only a few—wanted her to be. Could the part metamorphose her—if only momentarily and only in the public's imagination—from tribade back to the modest girl she once was? Or rather, did the notorious Raucourt taint the statue's innocence? Perhaps both. But to see the full implications of this question, we must return to the beginning of her career, when her virtue as well as her acting created such a stir.

A virtuous actress was an anomaly, and none would underscore the actress's vice more forcefully than *Pygmalion's* author. In his diatribe against them, Rousseau railed: "Is it even necessary to discuss the moral differences between the sexes to feel how unlikely it is that she who puts herself up for sale in a play would not soon do the same in person, and never let herself be tempted to satisfy the desires that she takes so much effort to excite?"[133] Rousseau not only casts the actress as a prostitute, he presents her as confusing her stage role with her real person. In this his actress resembles the many other women—novel readers, masturbators, mystics, and nymphomaniacs—who confused fantasy with real life and gave themselves over to their passion. Any actress who played Galatea would thus be other to the modest ivory virgin Pygmalion loved. Stepping off the pedestal, she would give herself to any taker.

Raucourt's return to popularity was short-lived, especially since her spending eventually brought her to bankruptcy. The press was ready to give voice to the complaints against her, attributing her fall once again to her immoderate luxury and taste for tribadism. The commentary in the *Correspondance Littéraire* of 3 June 1776 observed, "After all of Paris had taken great pleasure from Mlle Raucourt's debut and offered her its admiration, she has recently come to be booed on the stage and has scandalized even those persons in society least susceptible to it. Never was an idol admired [encensée] with more intoxication; never was an idol broken with more scorn."[134] Here Raucourt is transformed into a statue as she was on the stage, an idol raised and then brought down by the public. Once the venerated object of a stupid and dissolute cult, Raucourt becomes a target even for those who seem impervious to vice. Not unlike the statue of Venus that perverted the aims of sculpture, this Galatea remained the object of adulation and scorn.

I want to conclude with the woman who lusted after Pygmalion, or more precisely, after Falconet's *Pygmalion*: Catherine II, empress of Russia. So zealous was her pursuit of *Pygmalion* that she first obtained the terra-cotta model Falconet had given to his friend Collin, Mme de Pompadour's *chargé des maisons et affaires.* Although Falconet did not want to take a gift back from a friend, he asked Diderot to intervene. Diderot succeeded in the mission, and Catherine recompensed Collin by sending him medals. But Catherine wanted more; she wanted the marble, which belonged to the president of the *parlement*, Thiroux d'Arconville. In 1768, Diderot was again charged with obtaining it, but this time he failed.[135] Catherine's zeal for the subject continued, and when the king of Sweden asked the writer Jean-François Marmontel (1723–99) to find a gift for Catherine at Sèvres, Marmontel chose a Pygmalion and Prometheus pair. To accompany the pair, he wrote some verses in honor of the empress, and these were inscribed on enamel affixed to their bases. To Prometheus, Marmontel added:

> The one whose genius illuminates mankind
> And allows its exalted soul to take flight
> Can say: the scepter in my hands
> Is the torch of Prometheus.[136]

And to Pygmalion:

> Creator of morals, with the sublime gift
> Of making herself obeyed and loved
> She has only to wish for the marble to be animated
> And the marble will come to life.[137]

In these poems, Marmontel refers obliquely to Catherine's authorship of the Nakaz, her political and philosophical testament written for the legislative commission she organized in 1767 to draw up a new legal code. But her power to animate comes from her governance, from her ability to force others to obey. It is her scepter, symbol of rule, that Marmontel compares to Prometheus's torch, and she can effect change—turn marble into living flesh—simply because it is what she wishes. If neither love nor desire nor genius can metamorphose a woman into Pygmalion, imperial power can, and does, perform the miracle.

CHAPTER 6

Inspired by Heloise

Throughout the eighteenth century, Pygmalion stood as the model artist. His story tells of a creator moved by love and gifted with divine favor, a creator who transforms his desire into art and his art into life. Representations of Pygmalion, both visual and textual, condensed a remarkable number of ideas about art making in eighteenth-century France. Far from Cahusac's rational artist, Pygmalion showed signs of delusion, madness, and erotomania; imagination and passion drove his art. No mythical woman creator equaled Pygmalion in renown; none functioned so successfully as a paradigm for the artist.[1] One historical woman writer did, however, fire many imaginations. Although theory would not pose her as a model artist, professionals and amateurs alike emulated her writings for more than a century. Like Sappho, this deviant represented the enthusiasm of love and the passion of desire.

I am referring, of course, to Heloise, the twelfth-century abbess whose letters seduced the minds and hearts of many eighteenth-century readers, writers, and artists. From 1693 to 1800, French editions, versions, and variations of the correspondence between Heloise and Abelard issued without pause. These included at least three faithful translations of the letters and more than fifty different versions of them, as well as prose narratives, plays, almanacs, satires, and nine novels loosely based on the legend. The most famous of those novels was Jean-Jacques Rousseau's immensely popular *Julie, ou La nouvelle Héloïse,* published in 1761. Our own obsession with Rousseau's Julie, however, has nearly eclipsed the eighteenth-century fascination with Heloise, which brought special focus to the passionate letters of a twelfth-century nun—a woman who imagined voluptuous pleasure in the arms of a castrated man.[2]

This chapter revolves around a painting, *A Lady Reading the Letters of Heloise and Abelard* (fig. 51), that pictures a woman responding to

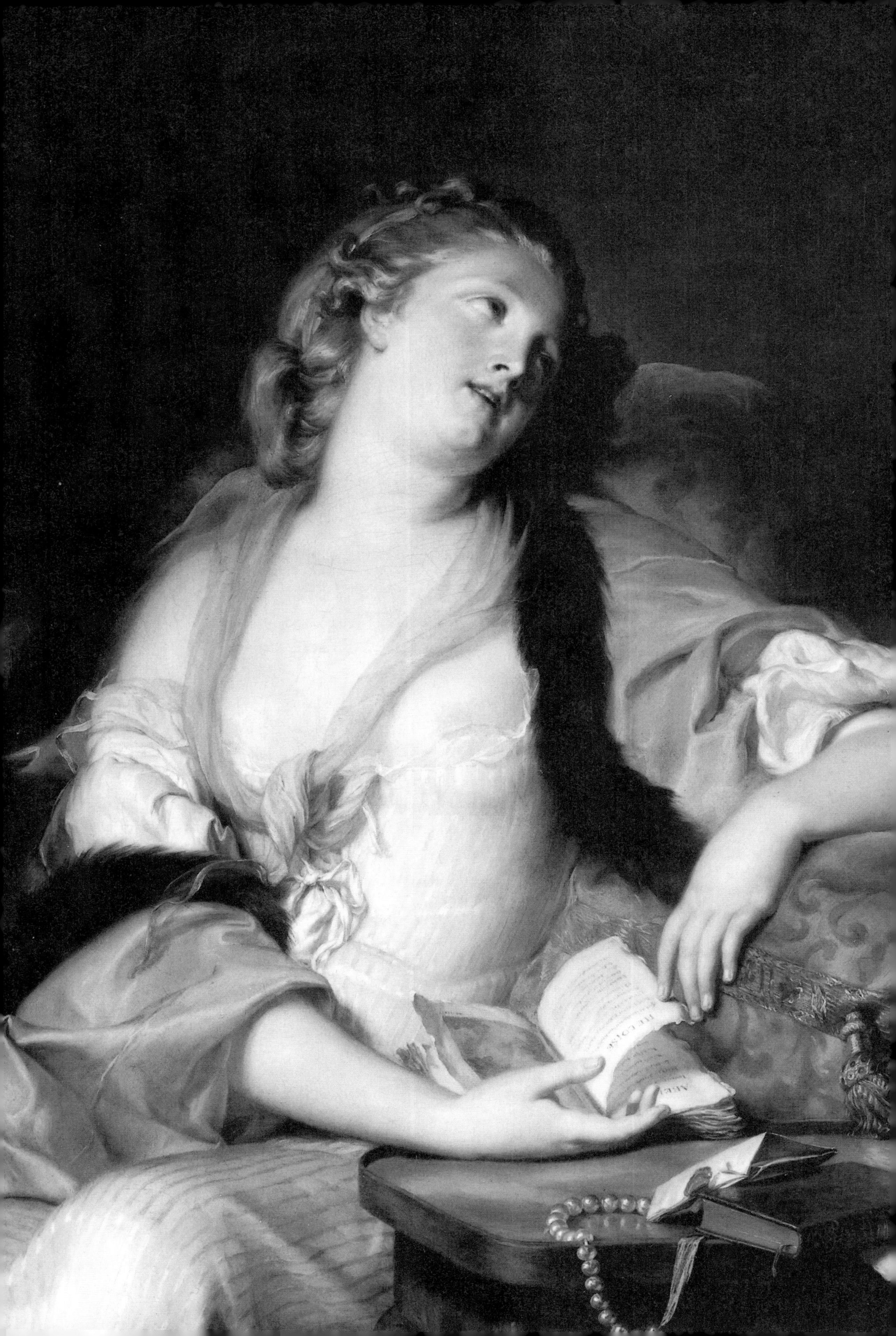

that famous correspondence. Or better said, responding to the letters of Heloise, for it was her writing that inspired both men and women in their passionate appeal to a lover grown cold through religion's embrace. My analysis of *A Lady Reading* works over many of the themes developed in earlier chapters and opens a discussion of Heloise as inspired writer, deviant woman, and model for emulation. Although some might dismiss this seductive painting as pandering to a male subject's desiring look, I argue that its inscription of Heloise and representation of enthusiasm together invite other readings.

Desiring Heloise

We see a woman inspired by the passionate abbess in *A Lady Reading the Letters of Heloise and Abelard,* now in the Art Institute of Chicago. When the painting emerged from a private collection in 1994, experts named its maker as Jean-Baptiste Greuze. The woman's ecstatic expression, the sensuously painted materials, and the suggestive *deshabillé* all recalled (and continue to recall) that artist. More recently, however, Pierre Rosenberg and Colin Bailey have named the painting's true author as Augustin Bernard d'Agesci (1756–1829). They found their evidence in Alexandre-Joseph Paillet's 1785 catalog for the posthumous sale of the marquis de Véri's collection, and cite the following entry:

> By M. Bernard, currently a student in Rome, another woman represented from the front, the breast uncovered and the head thrown back on a magenta cushion; she has leaned her left arm on another cushion and in her right hand holds a book entitled *Heloise*; in front of her is a table on which one sees another book, a letter, and a pearl necklace.[3]

Based on this record and the artist's chronology, Rosenberg and Bailey have dated the work to the late 1770s or early 1780s, the time when Véri was amassing his collection.

A Lady Reading pictures an elite woman, a fashionable lady, marked as such by her dress, her pearls, her music, her furnishings, her books. We catch her in a private moment, perhaps in her boudoir, and she appears in a suggestive *deshabillé,* her gown falling from her shoulders, her scarf scarcely covering her breast. She has been reading the popular letters, or some version of them, still so chic in polite society.[4] The image suggests that this reader identifies with the name of Heloise, which is one of the most prominent and legible elements on the painted surface. Notice how the fingers of both her hands point to that name, and how it is captured in the virtual circle of her arms. And given that the lady sits alongside

FIGURE 51. *(opposite)* Augustin Bernard d'Agesci (French, 1756–1829), *A Lady Reading the Letters of Heloise and Abelard,* c. 1780. Oil on canvas, 81.3 × 65.8 cm. Mrs. Harold T. Martin Fund; Lacy Armour Endowment; Charles H. and Mary F. S. Worcester Collection, 1994.430. The Art Institute of Chicago.

her own correspondence even as she holds that of Heloise (notice the letter in the foreground), the work veers toward the allegorical portrait, presenting the woman as an updated version of the impassioned abbess.

Looking at this new Heloise, we can see that her attention has left the pages of her book and is now focused inward. The upturned eyes, open mouth, and thrown back head suggest that reading has provoked a voluptuous rapture, and her ecstatic state recalls the paroxysms of bookish women like the one Baudouin shows us in *Reading* (fig. 20 above). Yet unlike that slitty-eyed coquette, Bernard d'Agesci's lady does not so clearly evoke the pose of Bernini's Saint Teresa (fig. 19 above). Although her head is thrown back, the woman reading Heloise sits more upright in her chair and rests against her pillow rather than collapsing into it. Her arms do not hang limply at her sides, but encircle the book her fingers touch. At the same time, however, Bernard d'Agesci's image points to a confounding of the sacred and profane similar to that produced when Baudouin recalls Saint Teresa in his masturbating reader.

In her expressive head and face, Bernard d'Agesci's lady descends from Charles Le Brun's diagram for *le ravissement* as pictured and explained in his *L'expression des passions* of 1678 (fig. 52).[5] Le Brun advises artists to depict this passion with the head bending to the left toward

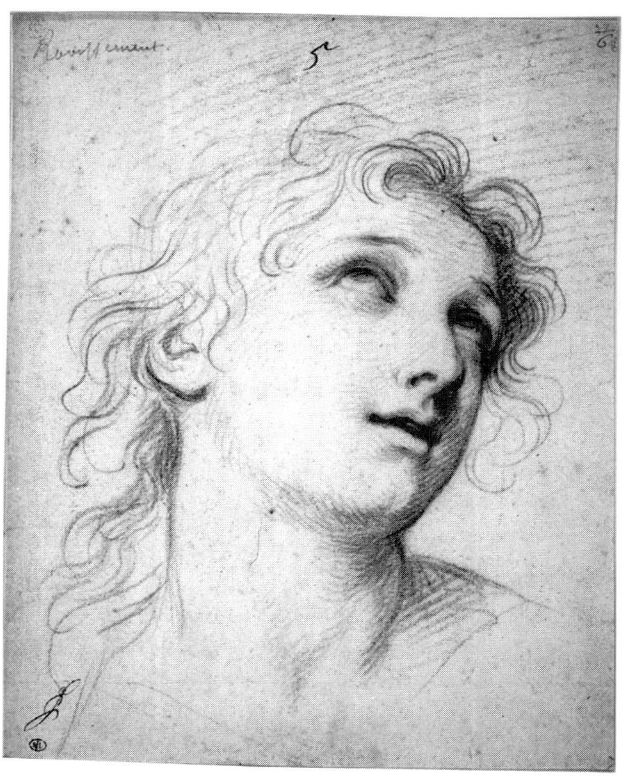

FIGURE 52. Charles Le Brun (1619–90), *Le ravissement.* Drawing for *L'expression des passions,* published in 1678. Charcoal on white paper, 24.5 × 20.3 cm. Paris: Musée du Louvre. Photograph © Réunion des Musées Nationaux/Art Resource, NY.

the heart and the eyes cast upward, seemingly directed toward heaven. The eyebrows and pupils should be raised and the mouth partly open, with the corners slightly elevated. Significant here is Le Brun's association of *le ravissement* with wonder (*l'admiration*), especially wonder caused by some object beyond the mind's powers of comprehension, for example, the power of God and His grandeur. Although Le Brun defined *le ravissement* as an elevating of the mind to God, the term had other meanings as well. It signified the action of carrying someone away by force, the state of being raised up to heaven, and the emotion experienced when transported by joy into a kind of ecstasy.[6] These different meanings insured that Le Brun's *le ravissement* appeared in a variety of contexts from religious paintings to erotic mythologies.

Carle Van Loo, for example, shows the emotion of a saint transported to heaven in his depiction of *Saint Stephen Martyr* (1760; Valenciennes), whereas Noël Nicholas Coypel paints *le ravissement* on the face of the young woman Zeus abducts in his *Rape of Europa* (1726–27; fig. 53). In these examples, the action of a subject—God or Zeus—provokes the passion displayed on the object of his attention. But the

FIGURE 53. Noël Nicholas Coypel (1690–1734), *Rape of Europa*, 1726–27. Oil on canvas, 127.6 × 194 cm. Philadelphia: Philadelphia Museum of Art, Gift of John Cadwalader. Photo by Graydon Wood, 1991.

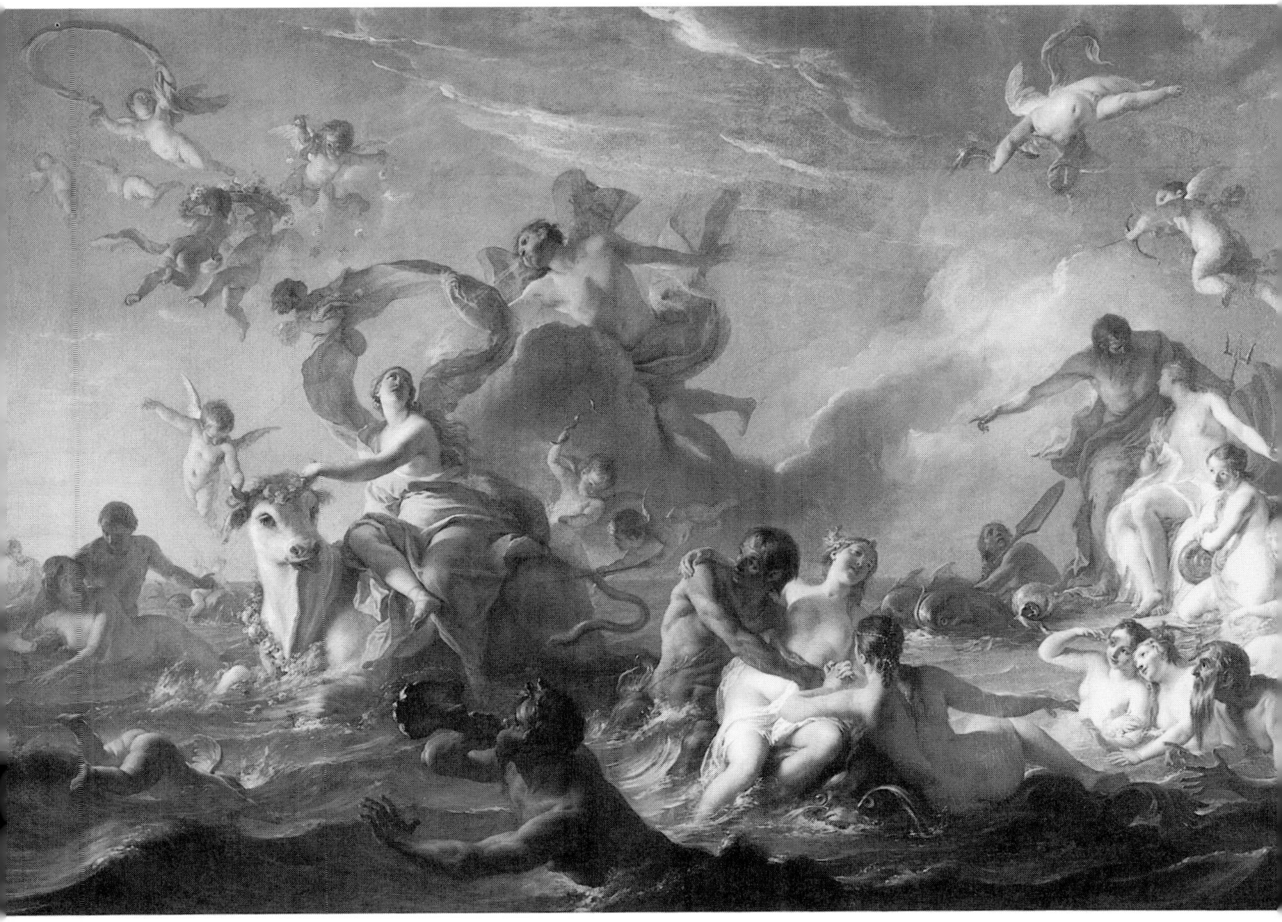

lady who reads Heloise takes pleasure in her own imaginings, and the joy of reading provokes her fantasy and passion. Looking again at *A Lady Reading,* we can now see the painting as a textbook example of Le Brun's formulaic expression. Bernard d'Agesci, moreover, used the expression in a variety of appropriate contexts in *The Rape of Europa* (c. 1785; Niort: Musée Bernard d'Agesci), *The Muse Erato* (1785–86; Niort: Musée Bernard d'Agesci), and *Young Girl Pausing While Reading a Novel* (c. 1780; current whereabouts unknown).[7]

While *A Lady Reading* calls on an established academic formula to represent ecstasy, it also appeals to an expressive figural type popularized by Greuze. We are perhaps most familiar with this type in the artist's late works that show overblown nymphets, for example, his *Souvenir of Fidelity* (c. 1789; London: Wallace Collection) or *The Dove Returned* (c. 1789; Moscow: Pushkin Museum).[8] Yet in earlier paintings, Greuze used a similar expression to characterize the emotions of both young girls (*Votive Offering to Cupid,* c. 1767; London: Wallace Collection) and mature women (*The Well-Beloved Mother,* 1769; fig. 57 below). And prints after these works increased the circulation of Greuze's ecstatic women. The artist likely put his stamp on this iconography in 1765, when he showed a group of paintings at the Salon that included several portraits of Mme Greuze and drawings for *The Well-Beloved Mother.* Although many of these have not been matched with extant works, contemporary descriptions suggested that their expression signaled an ecstatic state. For example, in referring to a portrait of Mme Greuze, Diderot asked his readers to "look at this fine fat fishwife with her head twisted backward and whose pale coloring, showy kerchief all mussed, and expression of pain mixed with pleasure depict a paroxysm that's sweeter to experience than it is decorous to paint."[9] "Head twisted backward," "pale coloring," "mussed" kerchief, and "expression of pain mixed with pleasure" are terms that might also describe the woman reading Heloise, and whether or not he intended to do so, Bernard d'Agesci profited from Greuze's popularity.

Like much of Greuze's work, Bernard d'Agesci's *A Lady Reading* also relies on pictorial effects to enhance sensual appeal and erotic allure. Although the woman's attention has wandered from the printed book, we see that she maintains a tactile relation with her reading material. Her fingers linger on gold-tipped pages that record the history of her touch in their bent and worn edges. The painting, moreover, arouses the viewer's tactile sensations not only through depicting touch but also through the synesthesia of optical effects. The look of soft fur, smooth pearls, and nacreous skin invites the hand, while the artist's suave and fluid touch encourages the eye to glide effortlessly over the glazed surface. Indeed, there is much about the painting that seduces the beholder, not the least of which is the captivating still life, a trompe l'oeil that entices us to ask what lies behind the painted image.

This effect is especially striking because prominently displayed in the foreground is a book bound in leather, marked with a ribbon, and inscribed with a title and author. The book is *L'art d'aimer* by Pierre-Joseph Bernard, called Gentil-Bernard, an eighteenth-century military officer turned fashionable librettist and poet. What makes this painted book so enticing is that its specificity is set against the illegibility of other painted objects. The sheet music curling over the book, its melody cannot be recognized, much less played. The open book shows its text, but the words dissolve into a blur of lines. We can see that the book is illustrated but not what the picture shows. In terms of the book's illustration, we are even teased by a signature that we cannot possibly decipher.

Contributing to the painting's seductive appeal is the letter that rests on *L'art d'aimer.* Prominent in the foreground, it functions as the legendary veil painted by Parrhasius. Just as Zeuxis wanted to lift that veil, the viewer wants to unfold the letter to see what might be written there. All she can know about the letter, however, is this: it is represented as if it had been sealed by someone, and then opened, even torn, and read—by someone. It could be initiating or breaking, anticipating or remembering a relation. It might be from a man, it could be from a woman, it might even be her own letter returned to her. But of course there is nothing beyond what we see, no message or sender save the one we imagine. And the opacity of the letter—the thick whiteness of its paper—is contrasted to the actual painted veil worn by the woman, a transparent veil that shows us what lies beneath it.

Together the letter and *L'art d'aimer* function as part of a still life that increases the visual coquetry of the work. Protruding over the table's edge, these painted objects offer the illusion that a viewer can cross the distance between herself and the painted woman lost in her fantasies. But the still life also functions to keep the viewer at bay, since it pushes the woman further back into the illusory space. And if the still life draws us toward and pushes us from our new Heloise, it also refers to her and resembles her. Notice, for example, how her pearls echo the color of her dress, whose striped fabric, in turn, captures some of their luminescence. The lavender thread on which they are strung repeats the color of the ribbon that winds through her hair and the border that edges her veil. As the pearl necklace falls off the table, it recalls the slipping veil that drops off her shoulders to frame her breasts.

Those pearls especially invite viewers to touch, to enhance their luster by rubbing them with our fingers.[10] But they also function as attributes, as part of the work's iconography. In presenting the reader

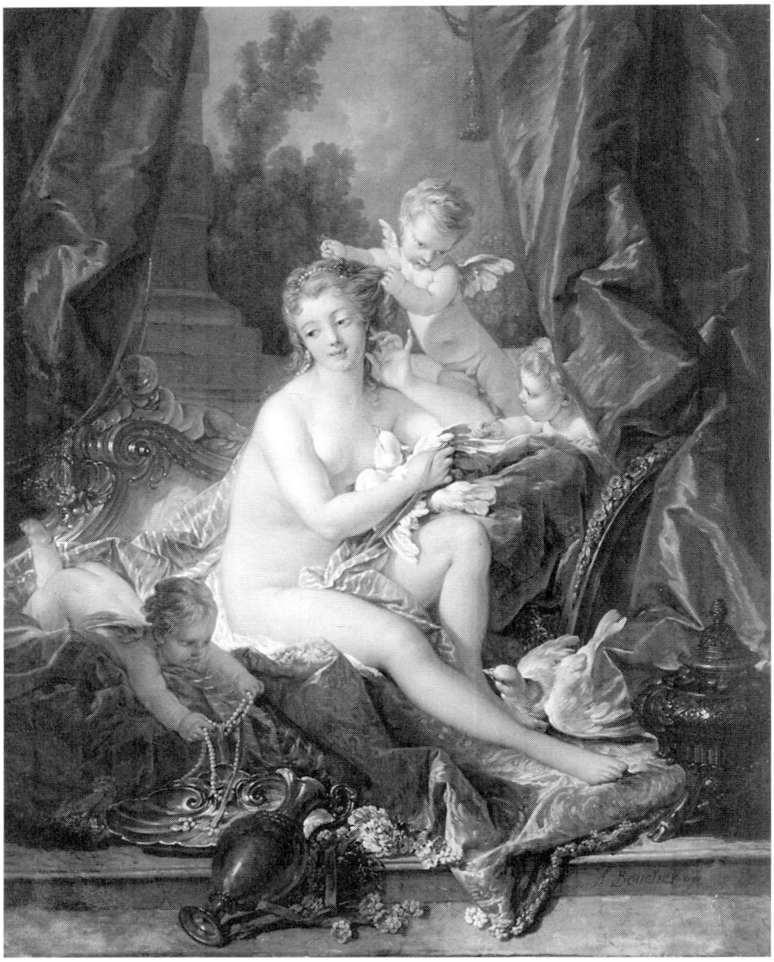

FIGURE 54. François Boucher (1703–70), *Toilet of Venus*, 1751. Oil on canvas, 108.3 × 85.1 cm. New York: Metropolitan Museum of Art, Bequest of William K. Vanderbilt, 1920 [20.155.9]. Photograph: Photographic Services, The Metropolitan Museum of Art, New York, NY.

as a woman who wears pearls, the image suggests she is a goddess of love, as in François Boucher's *Toilet of Venus* (1751; fig. 54), or an arrogant Cleopatra, as in Giovanni Battista Tiepolo's Palazzo Labia fresco (Venice, 1746–47).[11] She herself is a "perle," a valued person, a treasure, and she is *perlée,* executed with care. The artist's careful, nearly caressing touch makes her an art of love, as does her coloristic rhyming with Gentil-Bernard's *L'art d'aimer.* Her mantle repeats the red and brown of the book, but in reverse; where her red wrap is edged with brown fur, the brown leather of the closed book wraps around its red edges. But inside and outside are reversed, and where the book is closed to our prying eyes, she seems resolutely open to our gaze.

Open to the Gaze

If in its visual qualities the painting seduces everyone's eyes, whom does the painted woman solicit? Some feminist interpreters have already suggested that the work invites the desiring look of a male subject, a reading that obviously privileges heterosexual desire.[12] Although this interpretation can certainly account for Véri's interest in the painting, it does not exhaust the possibilities the image itself offers nor does it account for the responses of other viewers, be they eighteenth-century connoisseurs or twenty-first-century scholars. Moreover, those who have claimed the painting attracts the "male gaze" demonstrate that today the image also solicits that of the feminist interpreter. Indeed, the painting is a lure for anyone attracted to women, and I imagine *A Lady Reading the Letters of Heloise* trapped all sorts of desires with her seductive charms. I can see a desiring woman drawn to this picture of a woman's solitary and blissful pleasure. And eighteenth-century libertines, be they men or women, *femmes-philosophes* or freethinking materialists, I can envision Bernard d'Agesci's work courting their gaze. But I also imagine it as inviting a medical gaze, that of Tissot or Bienville, who would delight in looking askance at this woman's arousal. There are, in fact, good historical grounds for questioning the lady's appeal to every man's gaze, and even sounder ones for exploring how she solicits a woman's look.

We have already seen that the spectacle of solitary female pleasure was not always satisfying to a certain sort of male gaze that we might call patriarchal. Such a gaze could be assumed by men or women, although much of our evidence for it comes from male writers. As I have argued, this gaze emerged in medical, philosophical, and moral texts about women. It saw that women had sensitive nervous systems; their imaginations carried them off. They were susceptible to thinking themselves the heroines they read about in novels or viewed in paintings. And this kind of woman is indeed what *A Lady Reading* shows as she identifies with the name of Heloise.

Reading or looking at an illustrated book, especially an erotic tale or even a love story, moralists pictured as an antisocial activity. For medical men like Bienville, it led not only to solitary pleasures but also to nymphomania, a disease whose ultimate source lay in the female imagination run amuck. Doctors also warned that female emotion was easily transmitted from woman to woman and that nymphomania had reached epidemic proportions in Paris, spreading like wildfire as women led one another to indecent practices. Such women were decidedly not objects of pleasure for a certain kind of male gaze.

There are other ways *A Lady Reading* both raises and deviates from patriarchal assumptions. Notice, for example, the broken red seal so prominently displayed on the letter. In Western (and Christian) symbolism, the broken seal figured the loss of virginity, and for eighteenth-century French viewers, the painter most preoccupied with that theme was Jean-Baptiste Greuze. In images such as *The Broken Eggs* (1756;

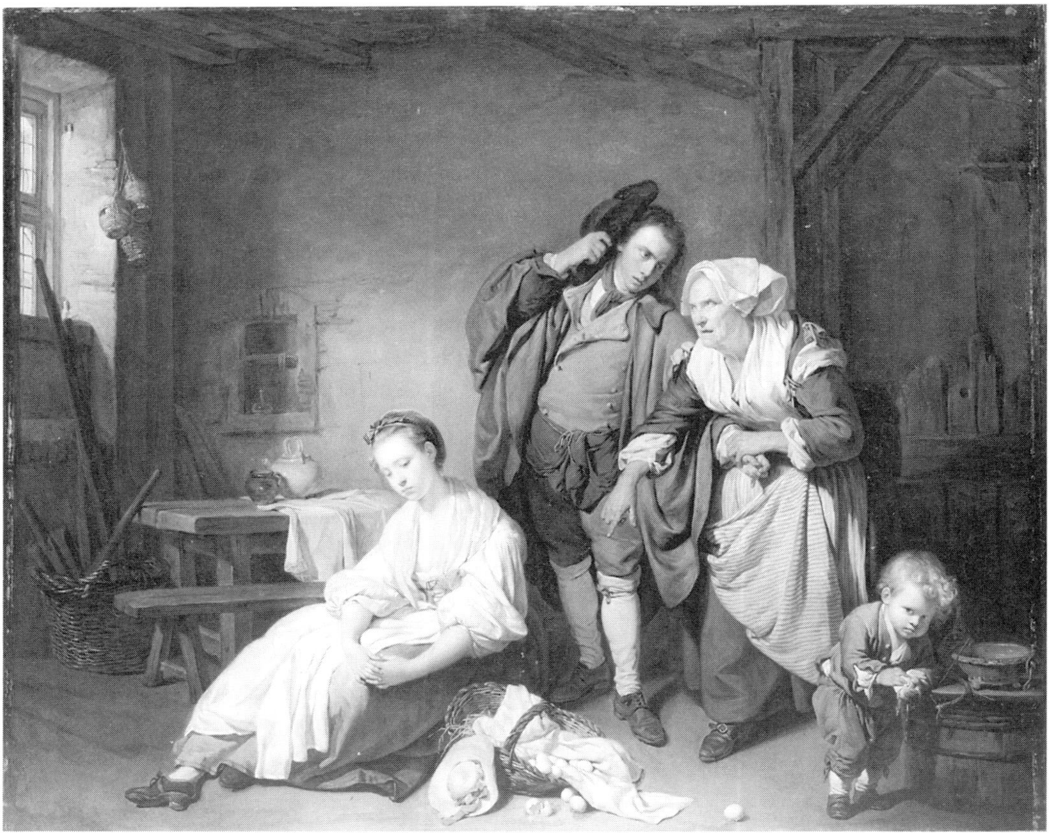

FIGURE 55. Jean-Baptiste Greuze (French, 1725–1805), *The Broken Eggs*, 1756. Oil on canvas, 73 × 94 cm. New York: Metropolitan Museum of Art, Bequest of William K. Vanderbilt, 1920 [20.155.8]. Photograph: Photographic Services, the Metropolitan Museum of Art, New York, NY.

fig. 55), the deflowered virgin is a figure of regret, of the regret associated with the loss of the girl's capital on the marriage market. Woman's chastity secured a social order in which fathers transferred their wealth and power to sons, whom they wanted to know were their own, but passed their daughters to other men with the assurance that someone else had not already impregnated them. Such images might be read as a warning for the female viewer, but many provided an erotic stimulus as well.

Consider Diderot's famous response to Greuze's *Young Girl Mourning Her Dead Bird* (fig. 56), shown at the Salon of 1765: "A delicious painting, the most attractive and perhaps the most interesting of the Salon."[13] He mixes exclamations about the beauty of the painting and praise for that of the girl with comments about her emotions: "Her pain is profound, she feels her misfortune fully, she is entirely absorbed by it."[14] Her grief moves the critic to imagine he can console the nubile and seductive young woman as he slips (and this slip is no accident) from recognizing her as image to mistaking her for the real: "When one first perceives this painting, one says, 'Delicious!' If one stops in front of it or returns to it, one cries out, 'Delicious! Delicious!' Soon one is surprised to find oneself talking with this child and consoling her."[15]

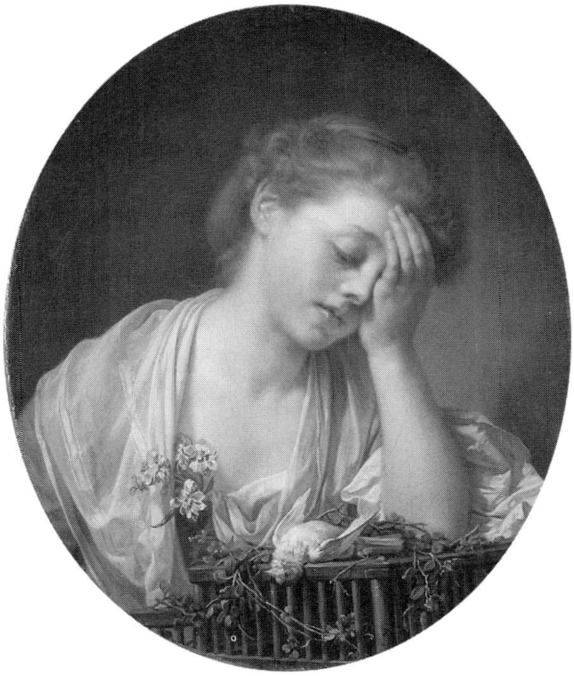

FIGURE 56. Jean-Baptiste Greuze (French, 1725–1805), *Young Girl Mourning Her Dead Bird,* Salon of 1765. Oil on canvas, 52 × 45.6 cm. Edinburgh: National Gallery, Scotland. Photograph courtesy National Gallery of Scotland.

In Diderot's narrative, the sight of distressed femininity gives rise to an erotic involvement with the image and a supposed confusion of the fictive and the real. Here sympathy slides into seduction. But the woman reading the letters of Heloise is neither a fallen girl nor a grieving lady, nor is she in need of anyone's consolation. Like Freud's narcissistic woman, this reader seems sufficient unto herself. If her expression registers that seductive mix of pain and pleasure, it is not one provoked by lamenting her broken hymen. Even if we insist on reading the broken seal as a sign of virginity's loss, there is reason to believe it is a loss the woman contemplates with renewed pleasure.

In associating the reader with Heloise, Bernard d'Agesci's painting implicitly connects her with a deviant woman who disregarded patriarchal norms: Heloise in her letters never regrets her loss of virginity. As Peggy Kamuf has pointed out, Heloise is pleased by Abelard's seduction but resists his proposal of marriage in contradictory ways.[16] On the one hand, she repeats what Abelard has told her: that the philosopher shuns all lower entanglements, like marriage, in favor of his vocation. On the other, she still presses for a sexual relation, protesting that "[t]he name of wife may seem more sacred or more binding, but sweeter for me will always be the word mistress, or if you will permit me, that of concubine or whore."[17] This statement was perhaps the most famous of all quotations from the letters of Heloise, and even before seventeenth-century translations first made those letters available to elite culture, readers found this passage cited elsewhere, for example, in the *Romance of the Rose.* Nearly every eighteenth-century version of the legend included it as well. In preferring the name of whore, Heloise both strains the limits of Abelard's thinking and defies the conventional logic that orders society.

Questions of sexuality and transgression insistently adhered to the name of Heloise, and her passion could make reading the letters or hearing the story risky business. Jean-Baptiste Guys noted in the preface to his 1752 play *Abailard et Héloïse* that as a theater piece the story would be dangerous if its subject were not "sweetened." The love story of a young woman seduced by her teacher, the tale of mutual passion founded on a crime, could leave "dangerous impressions in the hearts of its viewers."[18] In other words, good girls shouldn't read Heloise.

Abelard's Gaze

If Bernard d'Agesci's painting has the potential to attract a disapproving male gaze, it is certainly capable of soliciting a lascivious one, that of a suitor who imagines himself this woman's lover and fancies that his love note has played its part in arousing her desire.[19] This scenario would displace Heloise's writing as what has provoked the woman's enthusiasm and situate the assumed lover as the actual object of this reader's passion, casting him as Abelard to her Heloise.

There is surely a note of wistful envy when Diderot writes to Sophie Volland about Heloise's devotion: "Oh, how that man was loved."[20] Yet if he considered the context, what man would want to be a new Abelard, since for the eighteenth century he was less the gallant lover and more the *hero mutilé*? Recall that Heloise's guardian, Fulbert, sent his henchmen to castrate Abelard in revenge for violating his—that is, the guardian's—authority. This part of the story appealed to "sensitive" souls of both sexes who could shiver at the horrible spectacle and, like the Parisian women in Abelard's day, shed tears at the loss.[21] The mutilation of Abelard, moreover, was often the central moment in eighteenth-century retellings of the story, be they dramatic or poetic.[22]

No matter how he was loved, many eighteenth-century texts presented the castrated Abelard as monstrous. In Claude Joseph Dorat's imagined "Épître d'Abelard à Héloïse" (1760), Abelard describes his state as contradictory, as a man in whom maleness has been destroyed. "The man," he writes, "is annihilated in the man who breathes."[23] Although Abelard retains the outward appearance of a living man, he is reduced to a mere facsimile, for a man must have a working set of reproductive organs able to penetrate and inseminate. In a similar vein, the playwright Jean-Baptiste Guys (*Abailard et Héloïse*, 1752) casts Abelard as the living dead, giving these words to the character who reports his fate: "One has destroyed the man in him without destroying him . . . He is dead without dying; he is living without being alive . . . Abailard is no longer Abailard."[24] And in Jean-Henrí Marchand's play, *Abaillard et Héloïse* (1768), Heloise responds to the terrible news by declaring her lover a nothing: "A sacrilegious hand has reduced to a nothing [néant] the dearest spouse, the most faithful lover."[25] Abelard later describes himself as a sterile plant, a torch without light that must be cast out of society.[26] With these characterizations of Abelard in mind, we can turn again to the letter's red seal prominent in Bernard d'Agesci's painting. If it is possible to see this broken seal as a sign of virginity's loss, it is also possible to see it as recalling the wound of castration, especially in view of the story read.[27]

A Freudian Look?

Given that signs of the castrated Abelard are combined with the image of woman, Bernard d'Agesci's painting today easily solicits a psychoanalytic gaze, a Freudian look. Here is the image of woman as that which man desires and fears, as the promise of pleasure and the threat of castration. Encapsulated here is the story of a man who violates the father's law and is appropriately punished. In his castrated state, Abelard resembles woman, at least as Freud's little boy imagines her. How tempting it is to assume the Freudian gaze, and with it to go even farther. In the correspondence between Heloise and Abelard, Abelard disavows his sexual desire. The correspondence thus presents him as the object of Heloise's desire, not as the subject of his own. Becoming such an object relegates him to a "feminine" role. But here we actually don't need Freud's gaze, since the dominant eighteenth-century view of sexual relations defined the man as the pursuer and the woman as his object.

Perhaps it was to avoid this further taint of effeminacy that Dorat, against the evidence of the actual letters, constructs a hero who still desires, who still burns, despite his castrated state. Dorat imagines Abelard responding to Heloise's desire by proclaiming his own: "In a body that has turned to ice, I have a heart of flames. And I unite in myself, by a frightening contrast, life and nothingness, cold and fire."[28] Similarly, in Charles-Pierre Colardeau's "Lettre d'Abeilard à Héloïse" (1759), Abelard writes to his "trop sensible" Heloise: "I tell you that I am not able to read a single one of your thoughts without putting my lips to them, still burning with the same desires, the same fires that consumed my heart in our secret meetings."[29] Yet this letter also moves toward the historical Abelard's actual response to Heloise's passion, asking Heloise to banish sinful thoughts from her mind forever. At the same time that he proclaims an ongoing passion, Abelard calls the pleasurable union of man and woman a path to corruption. Hell, he now believes, inspired the insinuating eloquence with which he first seduced his beloved. He rejects his former sexual desire, characterizing it as an "excessive passion that enslaved him shamefully" and prays that God will efface even its memory.[30]

Although the eighteenth-century Abelard may admit that he still loves, he ultimately joins his predecessors in rewriting the meaning of his castration. As Kamuf points out in her reading of the actual correspondence, castration affords Abelard a way to break with Heloise's passion and to enter the stable order of divine law.[31] In other words, through castration he resolves his deviance as he rejects a desiring woman. Abelard figures castration not as a fragmentation but as a cutting out of impurity, the removal of a dangerous growth that itself threatened his integrity: "So when divine grace cleansed rather than deprived me of those vile members which from the practice of utmost decency are called 'the parts of shame' and have no proper name of their own, what else did it do but remove a foul imperfection in order to preserve perfect purity."[32]

Castration allows Abelard to take a position from which he can imagine himself as whole, as purely perfect. Kamuf implies that such a rewriting of castration allows Abelard to maintain the privileges defined as masculine in the Lacanian Symbolic.[33] Among those privileges are the rights to reason, subjectivity, the making of culture, and the enforcing of law. To position oneself as a "man" in the Symbolic is to *imagine* oneself as perfectly whole, specifically in relation to the woman, who is perceived as already castrated. But Abelard achieves the same end—separating himself from a woman—with a different logic. For him, Heloise is imperfect not because something is missing but because he can see her desire.

In Abelard's case, castration is a reality rather than an imagined threat. Yet his actual mutilation functions in a way parallel to the threat of castration in psychoanalytic theory in the sense that both ultimately prove a blessing. It is precisely the threat of castration that allows the little boy to separate from the mother and identify with the father, a process that insures the little boy's access to the masculine position of speaking subject. Abelard theorizes his misfortune into a good that allows him to disidentify with lustful passion and to separate himself from Heloise. Through his castration, Abelard identifies with the father's law and assumes a position as its representative. Even in his castrated state, Abelard imagines that he has the phallus—the privileged signifier of signification—-and the social power it confers.

The castrated Abelard, we might say, is even more phallic than the libidinous tutor he once was, mouthing again and again the dictates of proper authority and trying to force Heloise to accept them. Eighteenth-century writers, moreover, picture him as separating not only the proper from the sexual but also the reasonable from the passionate. In describing the effects of amorous passion on his reason, Colardeau's letter imagines these words for Abelard: "The love with which I burned for you was so ardent and [it] so obscured all the light of my reason, that I no longer knew what was appropriate or salutary."[34] This Abelard would stand alongside Tissot and Bienville in casting a judgmental eye on the woman reading the letters of Heloise. The painting might appeal to his gaze, but he would be ready to condemn its erotic effects.

Looking Like Heloise

The tragic nature of Heloise's story might very well raise the question of why any woman—the one pictured by Bernard d'Agesci, the one standing before Bernard d'Agesci's picture—might identify with Heloise or feel pleasure when reading her letters. Or why these letters would set off anyone's erotic fantasy or inspire her own writing. Certainly the story offered the delicious pleasure of shedding tears, yet that is not the state in which we find the woman depicted by Bernard d'Agesci.

In the exchange of letters, both in the actual letters and in the eighteenth-century versions of them, Heloise sometimes disregards Abelard's castration. As far as her desire goes, it is intact, as is her ability to experience ecstatic pleasures. An imaginary or remembered Abelard—or an Abelard augmented by imagination—will set off her fantasies. In Colardeau's popular 1758 version of Heloise's letter, her aroused state might easily match the one Bernard d'Agesci's lady seems to experience:

> Come, we can still know pleasure,
> Search it in our eyes, find it in our souls.
> I burn . . . I feel all the flames of love.
> Let me lean on your loving breast.
> Find ecstasy on your mouth, breathe there our fires.
> What moments, Abelard, sense what joy!
> Oh Sweet Voluptuousness . . . Pleasures . . . I drown myself in them.
> Take me in your arms, press me to your heart.
> We fool ourselves, but what sweet deception.
> I no longer recall your horrible destiny,
> Cover me with kisses . . . I will dream the rest.[35]

In this text Heloise calls herself and the reader to dream, and Bernard d'Agesci's painting invites its viewers to do the same. In both cases the invitation is proffered as something not shown or said, something marked in the text by ellipses, marked in the painting by the illegible open book and hidden letter. As in the case of Abelard, the imagination must supply what is missing.

What can the Freudian gaze make of Bernard d'Agesci's new Heloise with her active imagination and desire? Or of a desiring woman standing before the spectacle of this woman's pleasure? A masculine woman? A "deviant" woman? Or can it make of her a *néant,* a nothing, since Freud, as we well know, could not account for female sexuality. If Bernard d'Agesci's painting solicits the Freudian gaze, it leads that gaze onto uncertain terrain. The painting entices me to imagine what a woman wants, which was for Freud, "the great question that has never been answered, and which I have not been able to answer, despite my thirty years of research into the feminine soul."[36]

With nearly as many years of research into the psychoanalytic soul, Shoshana Felman has pointed out that for any woman to ask the question of what a woman wants is to displace the question radically. It then becomes a question of a woman's desire to interpret—in this case, my desire to interpret. Felman defines an interpretive practice that attends to those aspects of the text that resist dominant cultural assumptions, and throughout these chapters I have tried to extend that attention to the visual image. These points of resistance constitute the pictorial or textual dynamic as what Felman calls a "field of clashing and heterogeneous forces" characterized by a "never quite predictable element of surprise."[37] Once located, resistance and transgression can be amplified by the desire, by the intervention of a particular interpreter. This intervention opens up the field of interpretation, taken as both a unique encounter with the painted image and a pragmatic act, a particular reworking of collective or individual expectations.

What the Women Want

Although crisscrossing Bernard d'Agesci's *A Lady Reading* with various female desires might seem an obvious interpretive move, art historical discussions of the painting have excised those of women viewers. Not only have some ceded the painting to a theoretical male gaze, but others have occluded aspects of eighteenth-century criticism that draw our attention to women viewing images of female rapture. Take, for example, Martha Wolff's 1996 essay published in *Burlington Magazine,* which marked the painting's entry into the scholarly literature.[38] Wolff was among those scholars who attributed the painting to Greuze, and she tied *A Lady Reading* to the works Greuze exhibited at the Salon of

1765. These conclusions led her to pinpoint an important eighteenth-century analysis of how spectators responded to pictures of a woman's *ravissement.* That analysis appeared in Diderot's "Salon of 1765" as part of his article on Greuze.

In summarizing this article, Wolff argued that "the burden of Diderot's commentary is to point to the equivocal nature of an image that can raise blushes in viewers of an isolated head study, but becomes decent in the moralizing context of the rapturous mother."[39] Referring only to "viewers," however, cuts out the sexual differentiation of spectators central to Diderot's analysis. Indeed, Diderot's Salon comments turn on the difference between the way women and men react to the display of *ravissement* in Greuze's female figures. It is the only art critical text I know that takes up the question of men's and women's responses to the painted expression of female pleasure. Diderot's conclusions only confirm the attitudes toward women and spectatorship that we have explored throughout these chapters.

In the "Salon of 1765," Diderot opens the issue of the spectator's response by praising painting number 114, a portrait of Mme Greuze: "Here, my friend, is something to show how much remains equivocal in the best picture."[40] In his remarks, Diderot may have been inspired by other Salon critics, or even by actual events, since commentators reporting on this work remark that "several persons have seemed anxious to know in what situation she is represented. One sees her head inclined, the eyes half closed, the mouth open, and the teeth clenched."[41] Diderot, however, complicates the issue, asking, "How does it happen that in one place a character is decent, and in another it ceases to be so? Are accessories and circumstances necessary to judge physiognomy accurately?"[42] Turning to the drawing of a head, a sketch for the mother in Greuze's *The Well-Beloved Mother,* Diderot remarks that "[t]his partly opened mouth, these swimming eyes, this unstable posture, this swollen neck, that voluptuous fusion of pain and pleasure in this place make all respectable women lower their eyes and blush."[43] Thus it is not any viewer, but the respectable woman, who blushes at the expression, and the "respectable woman" is here implicitly contrasted to the painted one, who in putting her pleasure on display displays a different character.

Diderot continues his investigation of woman's response, noting that although women blush at the expression when they are left to imagine the context, they don't even see it when it is apparent in another work shown at the same Salon—Greuze's compositional sketch for the same painting: "We have the same neck, the same mixture of passions, and none of them even notices." Men, on the other hand, stop to enjoy the view:

> Furthermore, while women pass by this work quickly, men linger in front of it, I mean those who are connoisseurs, and those who under the pretext of being connoisseurs remain to enjoy a powerful display of voluptuousness, and those like myself to whom both descriptions apply.[44]

Diderot plays on the meaning of voluptuousness, which moves between erotic and aesthetic poles. The voluptuous display is enjoyed here by a certain type of male gaze, a lascivious one that can appear under the cover of erudition or connoisseurship. By qualifying which men linger to enjoy the work ("I mean those . . ."), Diderot suggests that not all male viewers share the same gaze. He does not in any way censor the man's desiring look or his taking pleasure from a painted woman. On the contrary, he seems to relish it, counting himself among those who appreciate both the art and its eroticism. The commentary implies that men do not have to mask their desiring gazes since they are free to gawk at the painting.

Although the responses Diderot describes are not necessarily those of any real viewer, we are encouraged to imagine them as real not only by the coherence of his narrative context but also because they well accord with contemporaneous attitudes toward man's and woman's erotic imagination. He pictures the response of the *respectable* woman, whose lowered eyes and blushing cheeks were both signs of modesty, the quintessential female virtue most useful to society. But his comment also points to the place of viewing, the public space of the Salon in which woman's response must appear modest. Diderot's respectable women, however, are neither as innocent nor as moral as their blushes might suggest. The response of even the modest woman depends on her identification of the expression as that of female orgasm, even (or especially) when there is no context to guide her in making this assessment. Rather than reading this contextless expression in some other way, Diderot's women immediately jump to the happy prospect that it expresses orgasm, which suggests something about the bent of woman's imagination, at least as the critic sees it.

The situation changes when Diderot suggests that women who blush at the expression when they are left to imagine the context, don't even see it when it is apparent in Greuze's sketch for *The Well-Beloved Mother* (fig. 57). Does his comment imply that with context to control the female imagination women actually don't notice anything immodest about the expression? Or is it that blissful women are decent when their pleasure comes from bearing children rather than reaching climax? Or does their failure to see the similarity justify woman's exclusion from the category of connoisseur? Or is it that the sketch, despite the title of

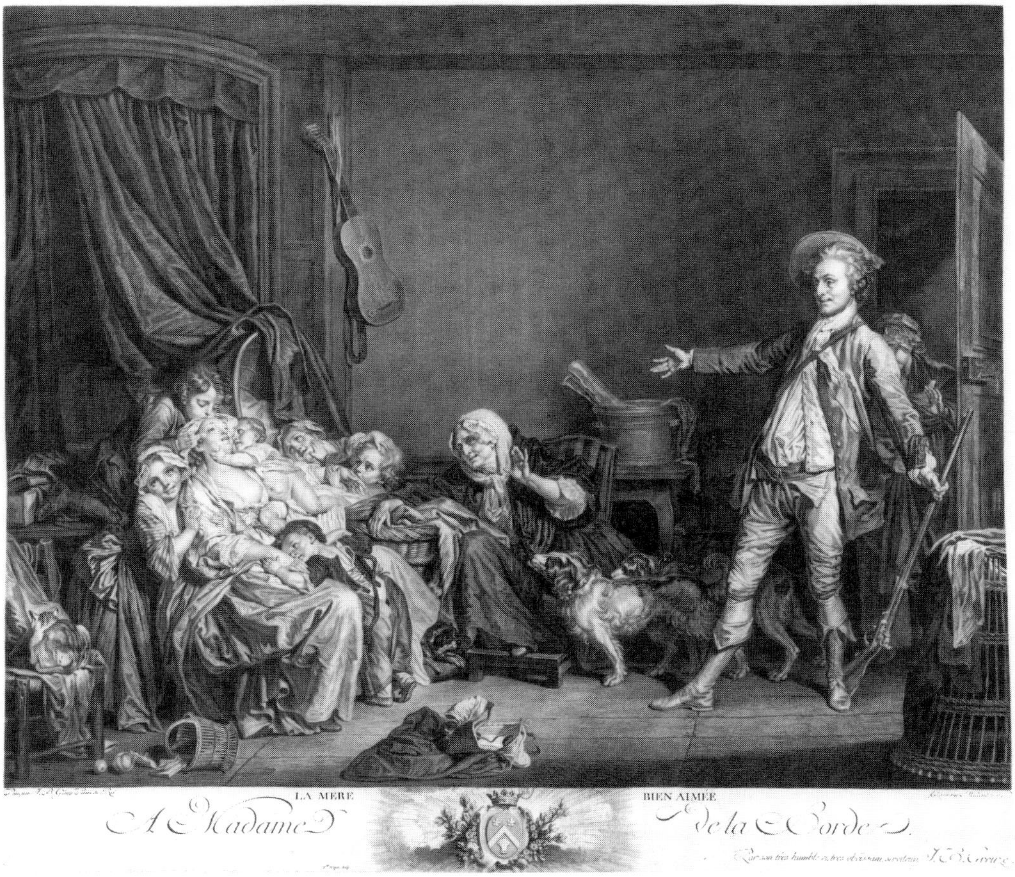

FIGURE 57. Jean Massard (French, 1740–1820) after the 1765–69 painting by Jean-Baptiste Greuze (French, 1725–1805), *The Well-Beloved Mother,* 1776. Engraving. Photograph © Bibliothèque Nationale de France.

The Well-Beloved Mother, is not about their pleasure? This compositional sketch is the only work among the group of images that includes any male figure, in this case, the father, who witnesses the touching scene.

Once a man enters the picture, he becomes the main interest, and his point of view dominates. When Diderot treats this image, his text points to the father who is "so gay, so happy to be this woman's husband and so vain about being the father of so many children." According to Diderot, Greuze makes the father say, "I'm the one who did that!" and describes him as "a big young fellow who carries himself well and in whose satisfaction one discerns his vanity at having produced this pretty swarm of brats."[45] Diderot's account seems here to reserve woman's voluptuousness for the male viewer, who enjoys its display in the same way as the father in *The Well-Beloved Mother.* And this father is no castrated Abelard; as the swarm of children and his upright gun together suggest, his manhood is fully intact.[46]

When worn by a woman depicted in relation to a man (specifically when worn by the wife in *The Well-Beloved Mother*), her expression easily becomes a measure of his virility and pleasure. Women viewers walk on by without noticing or enjoying the woman's lascivious expression; by this I do not mean to suggest that women viewers do not generally find pleasure in eroticized representations of motherhood, but only that this particular representation focuses more prominently on the proud papa and his position as privileged beholder of what he has wrought. Where a woman is shown alone, as in the sketch for the mother's head, the representation of female pleasure seems more accessible to the woman viewer, even if she has to dissimulate her interest in it. What I am arguing here was not, I believe, Diderot's point, but it is mine, and it is important for my interpretation of *A Lady Reading the Letters of Heloise.* This painting focuses on a solitary woman's passionate response to another woman's published letters and stresses her identification with the writer's passion.

Diderot's "Salon" further suggests that the context of viewing also determines the response to painted expressions. Insofar as viewers have social constraints, their reactions change depending on the place and company in which a painting is seen. Actual women might have been able to enjoy Bernard d'Agesci's painting without pretense since it was housed in a private collection and never displayed in the public space of the Salon. We know that in the eighteenth century women patrons did order titillating works. One of these patrons, Jeanne d'Albert de Luynes, comtesse de Verrue (1670–1736), was even called La Dame de Volupté. In this context, it is perhaps suggestive that Jean Bécu, comtesse du Barry (1743–93) owned a sketch for an expressive head by Greuze called *The Dreamer* (c. 1760; fig. 58), which shows a sensuality also evident in the works that have concerned us here. Although the expression is not identical, Greuze's dreamer, like Bernard d'Agesci's reader, appears in *deshabillé.* Her chemise is brought down below her left nipple, and a thin veil covers her head and shoulders. Her head is inclined back, her eyes have a swimming, unfocused look. Yet we do not know what has provoked her dreams, and the two paintings differ most in this regard. Greuze's dreamer is free of iconographic detail, free of context, but this is hardly the case for the woman reading Heloise.

Reading Heloise: Impassioned Transport

Heloise's letters as interpreted in the eighteenth century provide the most significant context for viewing Bernard d'Agesci's reader. This context will release rather than constrain my imagination as I explore further how we might understand this painting. Throughout the eighteenth century, many examples of both the letters and the legend appeared in France, although the latter were greater in number and

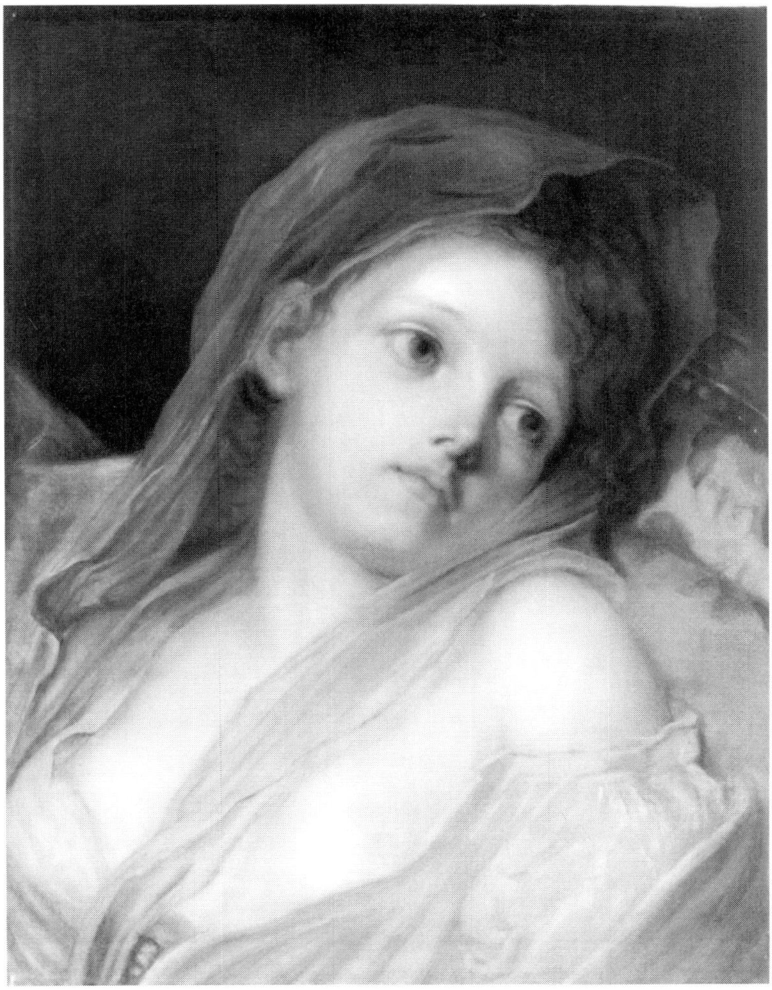

FIGURE 58. Jean-Baptiste Greuze (French, 1725–1805), Copy after? *The Dreamer,* c. 1760. Philadelphia: Philadelphia Museum of Art.

circulated more widely. When I say legend, I am using Charlotte Charrier's term to describe those versions of the letters that deliberately altered the original documents in some substantial way, usually to fit the operative conventions of lovemaking. Nonetheless, all were dependent on the artistry of Heloise and ultimately inspired by her writing, even if some were once or twice removed from it.

Had Bernard d'Agesci wanted to refer to one particular version of the Heloise letters, he certainly could have done so. After all, he made specific his reference to Gentil-Bernard's *L'art d'aimer,* which lies unopened on the woman's writing table. In contrast, the artist inscribes the name Heloise and the partial name Abe(lard) in the place where viewers would expect to find a book's title. Yet these words do not easily function as one. They do not tell us if the lady reads, for example, "Lettre d'Héloïse à Abailard," or "Les lettres d'Héloïse et d'Abailard, mises en vers françois," or "Épître d'Héloïse à Abailard," or "Les véritables lettres

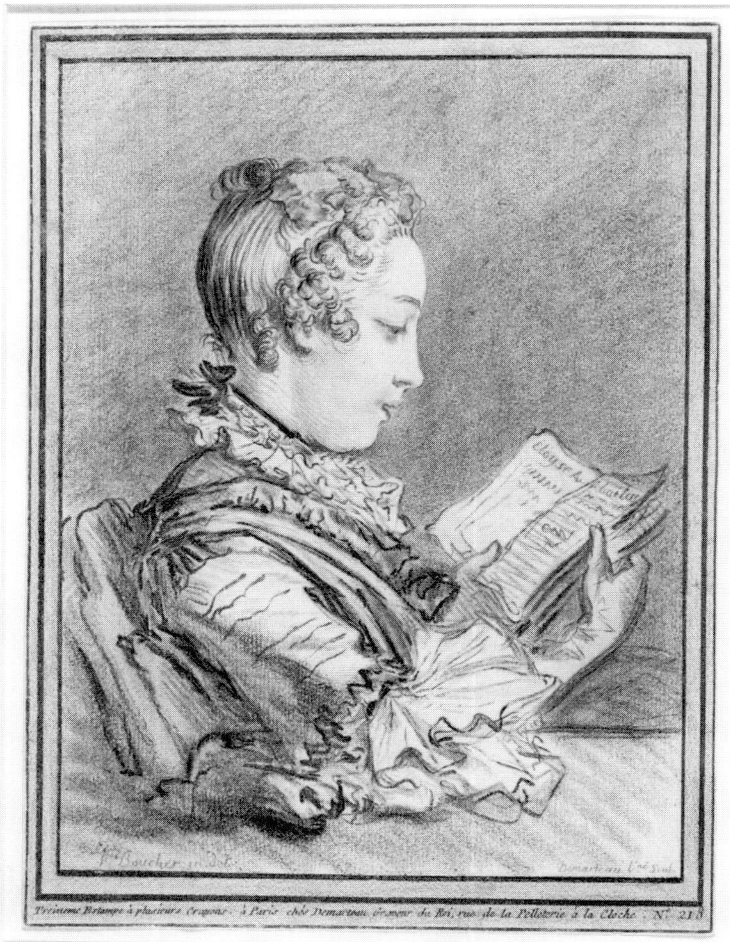

FIGURE 59. Gilles Demarteau (French, 1729–76) after François Boucher (French, 1703–70), *Young Girl Reading the Letters of Heloise,* c. 1770. Crayon manner engraving in black, blue, and red on laid paper, sheet trimmed within plate mark, 8 11/16 × 6 5/8 in. Washington, DC: National Gallery of Art, Katharine Shepard Fund. Photograph ©2002 Board of Trustees, National Gallery of Art, Washington.

d'Abeillard et d'Héloïse." Since it is the reader's identification with the name Heloise that seems paramount in the painting, perhaps the artist was not concerned with exactly which version of the letters his reader enjoyed. The same might be said for Boucher, whose drawing of a woman reading Heloise we know from Gilles Demarteau's engraving (fig. 59).

Although nothing about Boucher's image suggests that this young woman experiences the transport that delights Bernard d'Agesci's lady, she is fully absorbed in her reading. What she looks at, moreover, is no more legible than the text in Bernard d'Agesci's painting, although we can decipher on top of the left page the word "Eloyse" and perhaps also "A" or "&." With a bit more difficulty we can see (or perhaps imagine) the word "Abailard" emerge from the scrawl of lines on the right page. What Boucher's reader could have before her is a letter from Heloise to Abelard. Heloise's name appears in its entirety on the book's topmost left page—the "from" page. What she has begun to read may even be Heloise's second (and final) love letter—or some version thereof—since the image also suggests that she has just completed a letter from Abelard, whose truncated name is evident on the "from" page—the left hand page—of the underlying sheet.

It is worth noting that Heloise's second letter is the most passionate of the correspondence. In it she confesses her erotic desire and allows that she can never escape it, not even when she is asleep, not even during religious rituals.

> In my case, the pleasures of lovers which we shared have been too sweet—they can never displease me, and can scarcely be banished from my thoughts. Wherever I turn they are always there before my eyes, bringing with them awakened longings and fantasies which will not let me sleep. Even during the celebration of the Mass, when our prayers should be purer, lewd visions of those pleasures take such a hold upon my unhappy soul that my thoughts are on their wantonness instead of on prayers.[47]

Eighteenth-century versions of the letters privileged this passionate Heloise. Colardeau's heroine tells us she burns from sunrise until sunset; she burns in the coolness of the nights, always she burns. Scarcely does she close her eyes then she dreams her love and desire.[48] Colardeau's Heloise is never free of her passion, nor is the Heloise depicted by the duchesse d'Aiguillon in 1758. This Heloise calls her passion a "blind transport" and herself a "mad lover" whose sin still lights a "guilty flame" in her breast. It would, she says, take a superhuman effort to "stifle the passion in a heart as tender, as passionate, as agitated as mine."[49] And she offers perhaps the most vivid of all figures for her emotional state: "My soul, plunged into an ocean of fire, is lost."[50] This Heloise repeatedly admits that although she knows her pleasures are impure, she cannot—or will not—give them up.

Perhaps what made Heloise so fascinating to eighteenth-century readers was precisely that after taking the veil she clung to her sexual desires. At this time, the nun in love was of ongoing interest, whether she be represented in the writings of Heloise and the *Lettres portugaises* (which appeared in France in 1669), in pornographic brochures like the anonymous *Vénus dans le cloître; ou, La religieuse en chemise,* or in racy pseudomemoirs, such as Diderot's *La religieuse* (written about 1760, but not published). Heloise implies in her second letter that although her nun's habit suggests a holy woman devoted to God, it actually veils a passionate one who burns for her Abelard.[51] She particularly stresses that despite all appearances she has not repented her sins:

> How can it be called repentance for sins, however great the mortification of the flesh, if the mind still retains the will to sin and is

> on fire with its old desires? It is easy enough for anyone to confess his sins, to accuse himself, or even to mortify his body in outward show of penance, but it is very difficult to tear the heart away from hankering after its dearest pleasures.[52]

It is as the unrepentant Magdalene that Eisen depicted Heloise in the only full-page engraving that illustrated the 1766 edition of Colardeau's poem (fig. 60). In this image Heloise appears in a garb reminiscent of a

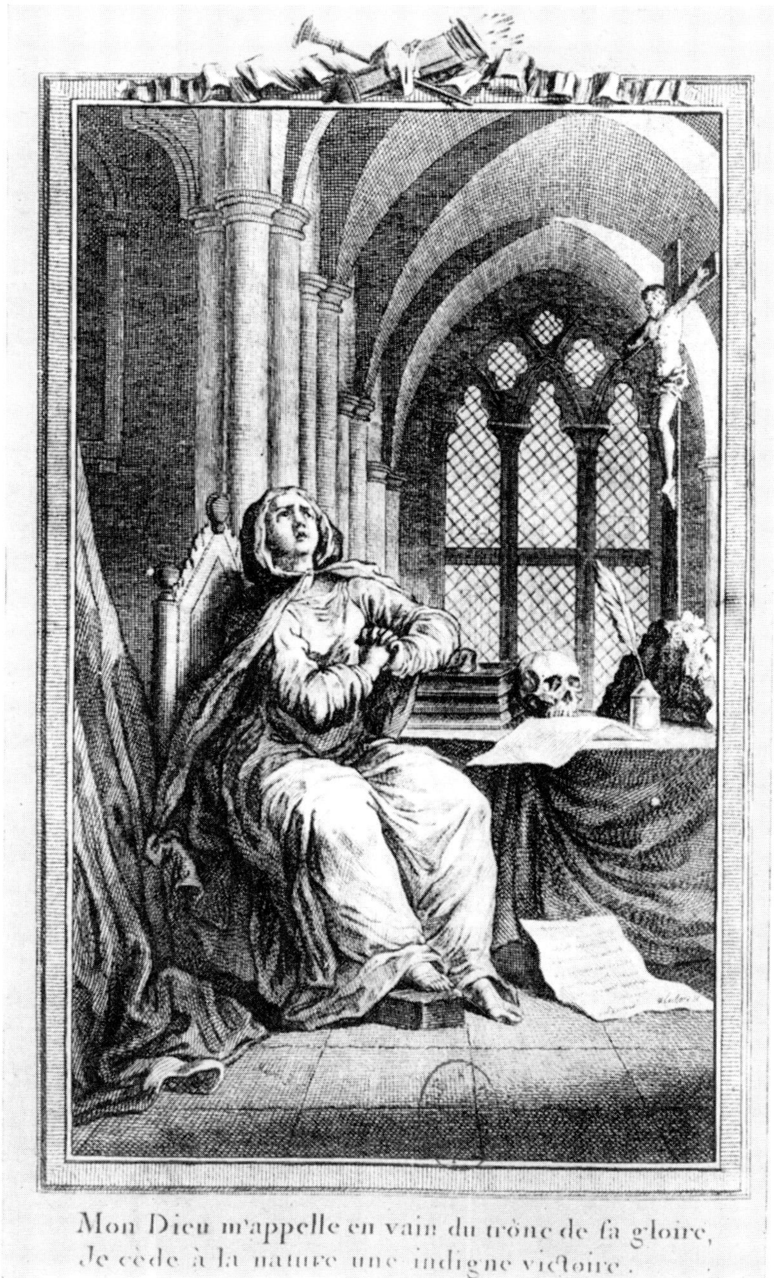

figure 60. Jean Massard (French, 1740–1820) after Charles Eisen (1720–78), *Heloise in Her Cell*, for Charles-Pierre Colardeau, *Lettre amoureuse d'Héloïse à Abailard* (Paris, 1766). Engraving. Photograph courtesy University of North Carolina Photographic Services.

nun's habit, but her costume lacks both specificity and markers of the religious life (e.g., a rosary on the belt, a cross on the chest). The hooded and lined cape she wears might as easily be the traveling garment of an eighteenth-century lady as the habit of a twelfth-century abbess. We see this Heloise seated in a space that resembles a chapel in some Gothic cathedral, with arched vaults, tracery window, and clusters of engaged columns. Yet the furnishings suggest we encounter Heloise in her cell; she is seated before a draped table, her foot resting on a cushioned stool. Some of the prominent objects surrounding her—specifically, the crucifix set into a rock base, the skull, and the pile of books—associate Heloise with visual depictions of Mary Magdalene, who is often shown at the crucifixion or alone in contemplation. Heloise's gesture and position reinforce this association; seated before the crucifix, she imitates the Magdalene's gesture at the foot of the cross, vigorously clasping her hands together in gesture of entreaty.[53]

Comparing Heloise with Mary Magdalene had a long history in France. In Jacques Alluis's *Histoire des amours d'Abailard et d'Héloïse* (1675), Abelard himself makes the association in urging Heloise to break her attachments to things of the flesh. Explaining that to combat sexual desire she must have confidence in God, Abelard likens Heloise to the Magdalene, who wept when she believed God had abandoned her. He likens himself implicitly to Martha, who tells the penitent that Jesus will always be with her if she is attentive to her duties.[54] Many earlier translators worked hard to avoid the suggestion that Heloise was a sinning hypocrite, and they also compared Heloise with the Magdalene. F. de Grenaille, for example, rewrote her letters in his *Nouveau recueil des lettres des dames tant anciennes que modernes* (Paris, 1642), noting that "[l]adies do not take offense at my having read them letters of this French Magdalene, given that I do not present her as debauched, but only as penitent."[55] Here Grenaille brings Heloise back to God, as other seventeenth-century writers would. Some versions of the correspondence, such as *Le philosophe amoureux* of 1697, invent a third personal letter to Abelard. In this case, the letter announces that a grave illness has transformed Heloise. Telling Abelard that he has lost her, Heloise confesses that a rival has "ravi mon coeur." Of course, the rival who has carried off her love is none other than God Himself. Having accepted God, she submits to Abelard's pastoral authority as her spiritual advisor: "Forget the names of Lover and Husband, but preserve always that of Father."[56]

Eisen's Heloise may recall the Magdalene in pose and attributes, but she neither repents nor regrets her past desires. His illustration does not leave us to guess her thoughts, since it is captioned with a line from Colardeau's poem: "My God calls me in vain to the throne of his glory. I cede to nature a scandalous victory."[57] Rather than heed the voice of

God, Heloise listens to her natural urges. The choice of caption would appear to stress the hypocritical nature of Heloise's condition—a nun who seeks not divine love but earthly pleasure. Yet I doubt this is the case. The lines of the poem following those included as the engraving's caption suggest the impossibility of extinguishing her ardor with religious rites: "Penitential robes, irons, prayers, vows/All are in vain, and my tears cannot extinguish my fires."[58] Many Enlightenment writers characterized the nunnery and the celibacy it demanded in a decidedly negative light as unnatural and perversely stifling human sexuality. The convent was a place women were sent against their will (as Heloise says she was), a place that would drive them toward illicit sex, lesbianism, or solitary acts. A place where they could commit a crime or go mad. Such an argument emerges in works like *La religieuse en chemise, Thérèse Philosophe,* and Diderot's *La religieuse.*

Shut up in the convent, Heloise verges toward love madness, and writers in the seventeenth and eighteenth centuries characterized her passion as pathological—or nearly so. We have already noted how Colardeau and the duchesse d'Aiguillon figure her obsessive emotion in rewriting her letters. Others would be more direct about her state of mind. Pierre Bayle, for example, described Heloise as the *amoureuse furieuse* in his *Dictionnaire historique et critique* (1697): "She had conceived a love so burning, so excessive, that it stifled in her soul all feelings of honor, and it was so deeply rooted and so disconcerting that she was never freed from it. Although the poor Abelard had been mutilated and she had taken the veil, a part of this madness remained always."[59] This Heloise was by no means forgotten, and the psychiatrist Étienne Esquirol (1772–1840), writing in the early nineteenth century, chose the medieval lovers to show the intersection of theomania and erotomania. He describes *monomanie érotique* as an *affection mentale* "in which the ideas of love are fixed and dominant as the ideas of religion are fixed and dominant in theomania. In the work of Heloise and Abelard, erotomania is associated with religious ideas that dominated the epoch in which they lived."[60]

Both her obsessive passion and her mixing of sexuality and devotion led writers to consider Heloise as suffering from a mental disease brought on by unrequited love. In thinking about her plight, one might recall the discourse of nymphomania, not only the claim that any woman could be struck with the disease, but also the more frightening prospect of the dissimulating woman who hid her filthy impulses under a modest exterior. As portrayed in eighteenth-century texts, Heloise is dangerously close to nymphomania. She loves without hope of return, she burns constantly, she is obsessed with sexual thoughts. Yet she never takes the step into madness, and in the many poetic versions of her letters that circulated in eighteenth-century France, readers are asked more to sympathize with her plight than to condemn her duplicity.

Perhaps like the Portuguese nun, Heloise saves herself through her writing.[61] And it is here that Eisen's Heloise differs significantly from the Mary Magdalene she mimics. Unlike the Magdalene, this Heloise writes. We see on her table a pen in its inkwell and a sheet of letter paper with writing on it. It is not clear if the paper holds a missive she is composing or part of a letter she has received. On the floor lies another letter, and although its contents are illegible, Eisen shows us that Abelard has signed it. Is Heloise here responding to the letter? Is she thinking about, indeed nearly enacting, the substance of her response, a response that will graphically depict her unrequited passion and desire? This abbess will achieve immortality through her letters rather than through her prayers. The duchesse d'Aiguillon imagines Heloise predicting her fate and writes that the names of Abelard and Heloise will be united in death; her love will pass to posterity and will be as immortal as his glory.[62] Her love, of course, would pass to posterity only through her writings.

Bernard d'Agesci in Context, or The Art of Love

It is the passionate Heloise that Bernard d'Agesci's lady seems to enjoy, and the artist goes so far as to suggest she indulges in that "dangerous supplement" to reading. Not only does her expression signal *le ravissement,* but we can see other bodily symptoms that suggest passion has led to pleasure of a physical sort. Her skin tones are pale, and a flush appears on her chest, neck, and cheeks, underscored by the red—symbolic of fire and passion—that surrounds her in the mantle and pillow. The painting also shows her nipples as a site of erotic stimulation, although the artist has not heated them up by intensifying their red color. Rather the painting suggests more subtly their titillation, showing them touched by the folds of her dressing gown. An excitation in this part of a woman's body, moreover, migrated to other, even more sensitive areas. In relation to woman's pleasure, the association between nipple and clitoris was longstanding, and the doctor Amboise Paré posited their connection as early as the sixteenth century.[63] The work invites viewers—and especially female viewers—to imagine themselves in the state of active imagining and self-stimulation provoked by reading the letters of another woman.

Does this woman's passionate response, however, preclude that she is learning other lessons from Heloise's correspondence? In considering this question, Gentil-Bernard's *L'art d'aimer* broadens and refines our viewing context. The title has a particular import since it refers back to

Ovid's text of the same name, which taught both men and women the arts of seduction. In repeating this title, Gentil-Bernard figures himself as the new Ovid, as inheritor of the classical tradition. However coincidental, the reference to Ovid seems especially apt since Heloise mentions *The Art of Love* in a letter to Abelard, calling Ovid that "master of sensuality and shame," an epithet that could easily be applied to painters like Greuze and Bernard d'Agesci. And Bernard d'Agesci even seems to place himself in an Ovidian tradition, for the name Berna[rd] he inscribes on the *L'art d'aimer* identifies the authors of both poem and painting.[64]

A Lady Reading the Letters of Heloise is not the first instance of a book entitled *L'art d'aimer* appearing in a visual image. Charles Coypel shows a volume with that name in several works that take as their theme the love lesson. One of those works is known as *L'amour précepteur,* and the image circulated in Bernard Lépécie's engraving of it (1730; fig. 61).[65] There Cupid masquerades as an abbé instructing his four young charges. It is not difficult to see through the disguise, for not only is Cupid seated on a chair obviously too large for his small size, but also his wings are visible beneath his cape, as is his quiver of arrows behind his back. Dressing Cupid as a cleric may have had a particular relation to contemporary life since abbés often tutored the privileged young ladies of elite families.

Coypel's cupid-abbé feigns a pedantic look and mimics a rhetorical gesture to show he is instructing a young beauty who kneels at his feet. He holds open a book for her edification, and although she touches that book gently, her eyes are not cast upon it. Rather, she looks up at Cupid, apparently enraptured more by the master than the lesson. Behind her a second girl watches the instruction, while two others, head to head, read what might be another version of the textbook or—judging from its size—a novel or romance. Although we cannot see what engrosses these two young pupils, we do know that Cupid holds a classic, for clearly written across the left hand page is the title "L'art d'aimer."

Tutoring by an amorous cleric also has a special relation to the theme of Abelard and Heloise. Even when he first became Heloise's teacher, Abelard already had affiliations with a religious order. Moreover, like the eighteenth-century abbés who provided private instruction for young ladies, Abelard tutors Heloise because as a woman she cannot attend public instruction. Yet unlike the young women Coypel represents who study no weighty tomes, Heloise learned more than the art of love even as she welcomed Abelard's seductions.

In the letters she writes to Abelard, Heloise shows mastery of rhetoric, debate, philosophy—of the very cultural discourses Abelard controlled. These she turns against the master, making evident their contradictions and pushing their logic beyond its limits.[66] In Heloise's love letters,

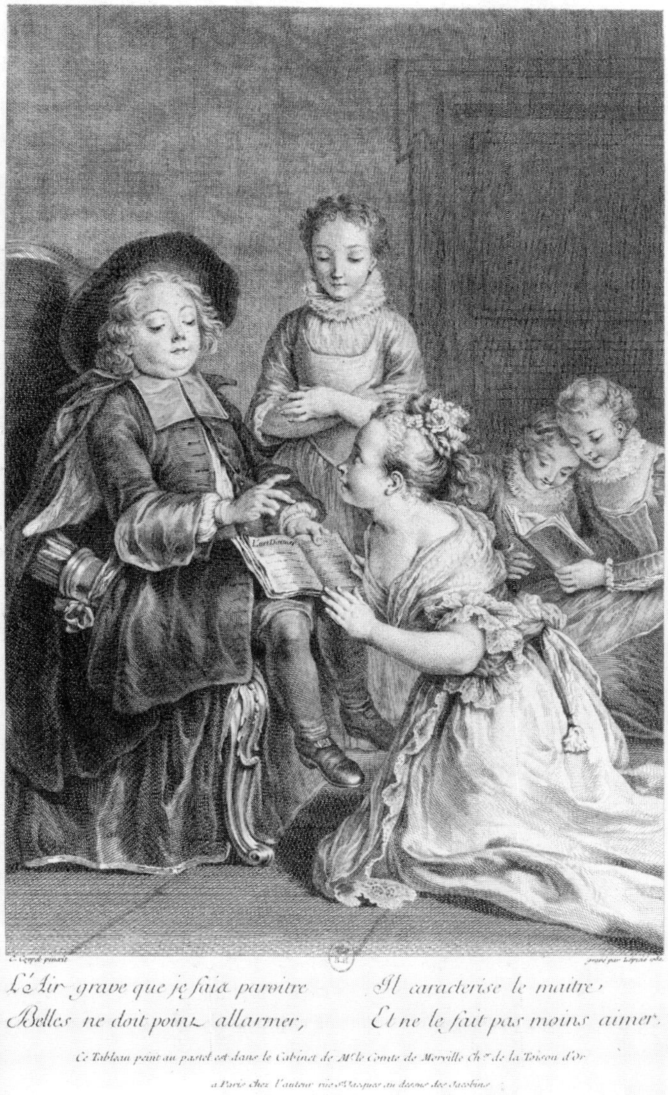

FIGURE 61. Bernard Lépicié (French, 1698–1755) after the c. 1730 painting by Charles Coypel (French, 1694–1752), *L'amour précepteur*, 1730. Engraving. Photograph © Bibliothèque Nationale de France.

passion and learning go hand in hand as she deploys a whole arsenal of rhetorical strategies and cites an impressive number of learned writers to make the case for her passion. She is both an emotional and a learned woman, whom eighteenth-century biographers described as famous for her profound erudition in Greek and Hebrew and known in the four corners of the world for her beauty, wit, and profound knowledge.[67] In her summary of their lives, the duchesse d'Aiguillon notes that the letters of Heloise and the writings of Abelard will attest eternally to their "taste, erudition, and love."[68]

It was perhaps this combination of sexuality and seduction, knowledge and philosophy, that also interested eighteenth-century readers captivated by the confusion of religious devotion and carnal desire. As we have seen, eighteenth-century (materialist) attitudes marked a change from those proffered in Molière's *Les femmes savantes* (1672), a work that made woman's knowledge shameful by ridiculing women who scorned the legitimate pleasures of marriage for the delights of learning. Molière's Armande, however, is no Heloise; she would never have advised Abelard to revel in the pleasures of physical love.

Sexuality and knowledge were tied together in both positive and negative ways throughout the eighteenth century, especially when it was a question of women's knowledge. For many, woman's learning put her in moral danger precisely because it made her more susceptible to sexual seduction, and this notion emerges in recreations of the Heloise story. In Marchand's 1768 play *Aballiard et Héloïse,* for example, Heloise's uncle and guardian Fulbert offers this response to Abelard's claim that through her genius Heloise has penetrated the secrets of philosophy and religion: "The mind [l'esprit] often loses itself in sublime ideas, and the excess of heat carries it to the greatest errors. Enthusiasm rattles you and you don't perceive it. A precipice opens and you plunge into it."[69]

Fulbert's speech suggests a confusion between the heat of sexual passion and the desire to be carried away by the secrets of knowledge, the "chaleur" of knowing. Like the woman poised on the brink of nymphomania, the woman who warms herself with sublime theses, the enthusiastic woman, puts herself on the edge of a precipice. Although some would denounce women's knowledge as sexual transgression, others would endorse such deviance. In *Thérèse Philosophe,* women who think critically combine sexuality with philosophy; Baudouin's *Reader* enjoys both heavy reading and novels she can hold with one hand; Boureau-Deslandes's Galatea takes her sensual pleasures right alongside her intellectual training.

It is admittedly difficult to see a learned or even a literary woman in Bernard d'Agesci's image. Yet consider further how *L'art d'aimer* adds to its context. Gentil-Bernard's poem brought its author much success, and for many years he declaimed parts of it in social and intellectual salons, including that of Mme du Châtelet.[70] It is as emulator of Ovid and private tutor that La Mettrie characterizes Gentil-Bernard in his "L'école da la volupté" (1746). La Mettrie calls him the apostle and rival of Ovid, and asks when he will give the public his lessons in *l'art d'aimer.*[71] But Gentil-Bernard's poem contains more than lessons of love. It is a disquisition on the glories of woman figured in the most conventional way, an exaltation of the ecstasies and fires of love, and a compilation of arcane references to literature, mythology, and ancient texts, with a dash of materialist philosophy. It mixes the erotic and the erudite in a way that might have satisfied Heloise's taste for impure bodies.

Heloise's Enthusiasm

Heloise was not only a learned and impassioned woman, she was also a passionate writer who could put before the eyes of her readers that which she saw in her imagination. Her position in the eighteenth century was like that afforded Sappho in the French tradition, a woman who not only suffered from lovesickness, but who also represented it with clarity and enthusiasm. In her letters, Heloise vividly evokes past scenes that she now imagines, by which I mean that she sees again through that internal eye called imagination. And because she sees them so vividly, she is moved to portray her emotional state in a way that allows the spectator to experience it as well. This interplay between the artist's imagination and the spectator's emotional response characterized the eighteenth-century notion of creative enthusiasm. Bernard d'Agesci's reading woman celebrates Heloise as an inspired writer, as one who can bring the spectator to experience vicariously the emotions depicted and project herself into the scenes described. But even if—or perhaps, especially if—we imagine Bernard d'Agesci's lady is reading an eighteenth-century version of the letters, Heloise's art still remains the inspiration.

Despite all the changes and versions of the Heloise legend, the emulation of her writing sustained over several centuries suggests that she moved not only readers but also writers and creative artists as well. Her letters both inspired passion and ignited the fires needed to create art. Like Sappho, Heloise made evident the connection between erotic and poetic enthusiasm. Although treatises do not acknowledge her as they did the ancient poet, practice bears out Heloise's position as a model for emulation. From Boileau's 1674 translation of Longinus's *On the Sublime*, French theory pictured both enthusiasm and emulation as a kind of possession, a possession by the voice, passion, and style of the writer or artist emulated. It is through inspiring others to emulation that the artist achieves immortality. Although in making his painting Bernard d'Agesci may emulate Greuze and Le Brun, the image suggests that Heloise's letters have put another woman into an enthused state. We can easily imagine that the woman who reads the passionate abbess is inspired to emulate Heloise, that she is preparing to write her own text, to represent her emotions in reply to the letter lying on the table beside her.[72]

Possessed by Heloise?

If we consider the case of Heloise within the discourse of enthusiasm that circulated in eighteenth-century France, we find that to rewrite the letters of Heloise or even to paint a woman inspired by reading those letters, an artist had, in theory, to become Heloise or a woman moved by her. He had to project himself into the scene of a woman's writing or reading. Considered in this way, emulation suspends the boundary between the artist and the desiring woman, between the genius and the potential nymphomaniac. It was perhaps to preserve these boundaries that the author of *Julie, ou La nouvelle Héloïse* declared women unable to express passion effectively.

In his *Lettre à M. d'Alembert sur les spectacles* of 1758, Rousseau includes this note:

> Women, in general, do not like any art, know nothing about any, and have no genius. They can succeed in little works that require only facility, taste, grace, and sometimes even some philosophy and reasoning. But women's writing will always lack that celestial flame which warms and sets fire to the soul, that genius which consumes and devours, that burning eloquence, those sublime transports which carry their raptures to the depths of hearts—all their works are as cold and pretty as they are. They can have as much wit as you please, but never a soul; they are a hundred times more reasonable [sensé] than passionate. They do not know how to describe or even to feel love. Sappho alone, as far as I know, and one other woman, deserve to be excepted. I would bet anything that the *Lettres portugaises* were written by a man.[73]

Here Rousseau invokes enthusiasm, historically tied to, if not elided with, genius. Long figured in metaphors of fire, enthusiasm is the celestial flame that sets the soul ablaze. Terms like "burning eloquence" and "sublime transport" also invoke the inspired artist carried off by enthusiasm. Women, according to Rousseau, cannot feel this artistic passion, this overwhelming desire to make art; they are cold, lifeless, without genius. Anything they produce comes from hard work rather than from insight. Rousseau gives to women qualities that we have seen quite universally attributed to them: quick wit, taste, grace. His contrast between the reasonable and the passionate, however, is unexpected in view of the prevailing notion that passions dominated women. In this context, however, passion is the passion, the enthusiasm, needed to create great works, in other words, an emotion generally denied to the sex.

Rousseau must know that to seem credible, he must acknowledge the passion of at least one woman and exempt her from his generalization. That woman is the one Longinus praised in his treatise on the sublime: the sublime and passionate Sappho. But who is the "one other" deserving of exception, and why isn't she named? His "one other" might refer to the anonymous writer of the *Lettres portugaises,* but his syntax does not make this clear. The line, "I would bet anything that the *Lettres portugaises* were written by a man," underscores his overall logic, but it is curiously unconnected with the sentence it follows. His contention that a man wrote the *Lettres portugaises* is not phrased to cancel out the claim that there is "one other" woman deserving of exemption. Indeed, one can more easily read "one other" as *not* referring to the supposed Portuguese nun. This lack of specificity allows that two women could express passion and opens the possibility that it is Heloise who remains unnamed. Rousseau was, after all, writing the *Lettre à M. d'Alembert* at about the same time he was finishing *La nouvelle Heloïse,* and their dates coincide with the period of greatest interest in Heloise's passion.[74] But if Heloise can be taken as that "one other," does attributing the *Lettres portugaises* to a man cast doubt on her passion as well, if only by association? Readers would likely have connected the letters of Heloise and those of the Portuguese nun not only because of their obvious thematic similarity (the religious woman in passionate love), but also because they were sometimes published together in the same volume. Does attributing the *Lettres portugaises* to a man deflect our attention from, or draw it to, the writer Rousseau invokes in titling his story of ill-fated love? And does that story tell us anything about Heloise's passion or Rousseau's use of it?

In a letter to Julie, her tutor and lover Saint-Preux expresses his pity for Heloise and his disdain for Abelard:

> When the letters of Heloise and Abelard fell into your hands, you remember what I told you about reading them and about the Theologian's conduct. I have always pitied Heloise; she had a heart made for love: but Abelard has never seemed to me anything but a wretch deserving of his fate, and as little acquainted with love as with virtue. Having judged him, must I imitate him? Woe to whoever preaches a moral he is unwilling to practice! Love is deprived of its greatest charm when honesty abandons it. To appreciate its full value, the heart must delight in it and raise us by raising up the loved one. Take away the idea of perfection and you take away enthusiasm.[75]

This quotation is the first of only two instances in the entire novel in which Rousseau specifically mentions Heloise and Abelard. Given the title of the book and the implied relation to the medieval lovers, it is thus a significant moment. Saint-Preux claims to be imitating Abelard, and does so in seducing his student Julie. However, it is more Heloise whom he emulates, at least in the tone of his letters. Here Saint-Preux speaks of enthusiasm and its idealizing effects—how enthusiasm gives the glow of perfection to the loved one. The passage echoes another in Rousseau's *Preface to the New Heloise, or Conversation on Novels between the Editor and a Man of Letters.* This statement comes from the character designated "R," who emerges in the course of the dialogue as representing Rousseau's position:

> Enthusiasm is the final degree of passion. When passion is at the full, it perceives its object as perfect; makes it into its idol; places it in Heaven; and just as the enthusiasm of devoutness borrows the language of love, so does the enthusiasm of love borrow the language of devoutness. It can see nothing but Paradise, Angels, the virtues of Saints, the delights of the celestial abode. In these transports, in the midst of such lofty images, will love evoke them in pedestrian terms? Will it bring itself to lower, to sully its ideas with vulgar phrases? Will it not elevate its style? Give it nobility, dignity? How can you speak of Letters, of epistolary style? When writing to one's beloved, who cares about that! It is no longer Letters one writes, but hymns.[76]

Now this is an interesting passage indeed, tying together three forms of enthusiasm—the religious, the erotic, and the poetic. But here the passage implies something quite different from what Rousseau notes about women writers in the *Lettre à M. d'Alembert.* By locating the language of love in mystical writing, Rousseau—at least for most of his readers—locates it in a feminine domain, in the realm of woman's passion. If Rousseau's preface is intended as a dialogue with Diderot, as many have argued it is, the comment is especially suggestive since in his *Sur les femmes,* Diderot flatly states that only women could achieve the state of exaltation that Rousseau describes, only women could sense the god.[77] Rousseau's comments here seem to contradict his contention that women know nothing about passion and cannot write it well, since he suggests that the very language of love is taken from the mystics.

Interpreters have associated the passion of Bernard d'Agesci's image with the overheated language of Rousseau's novel, and some have tried to link the painting with it directly.[78] Appealing to Rousseau when the name Heloise appears prominently in the painting, when there has been an enduring passion for her letters, seems to me another way of erasing a woman's influence, intentionally or not. Had Bernard d'Agesci wanted to invoke Rousseau, he could have done so explicitly, as did the painter Febvre when he made the image that Herbert engraved in 1765 as *La nouvelle Heloyse* (fig. 62). With its curious mix of elements—the costume *espagnole,* the menacing cupid, the antique setting—this engraving deserves more attention than I will give it here. I mention the image only to make this observation: in contrast to *A Lady Reading,* this engraving includes two direct references to Rousseau's novel. The first is its title, which presumably names the reading woman we see, and the

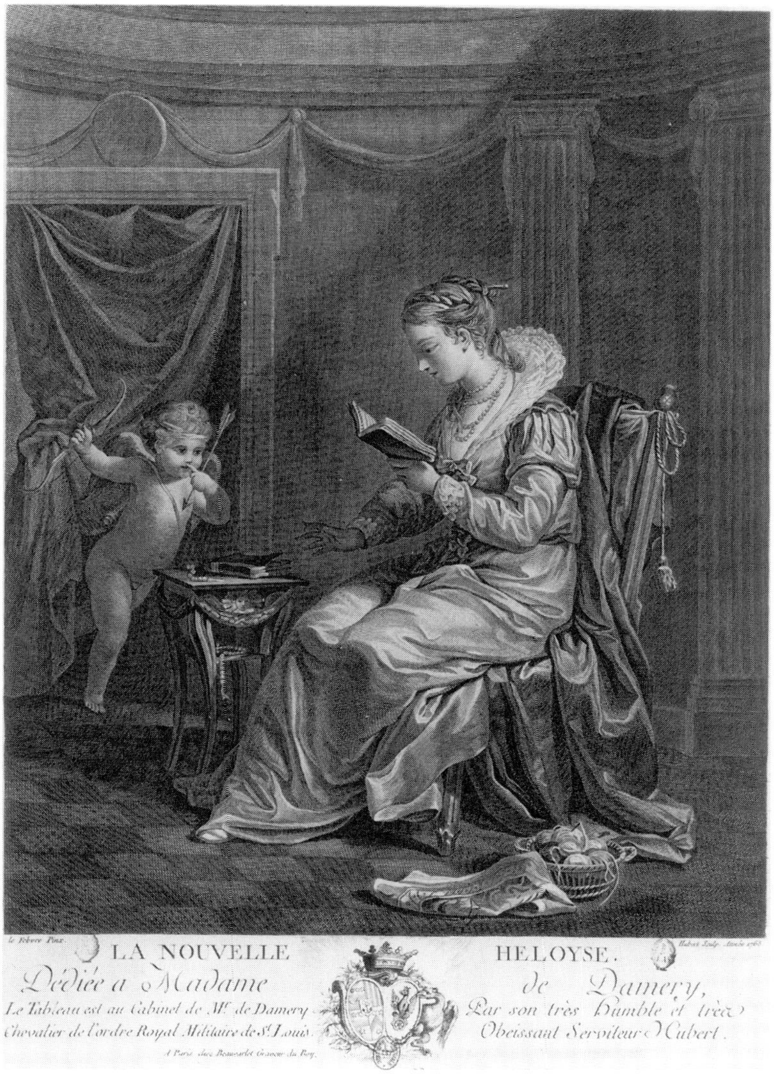

FIGURE 62. Herbert after Febvre, *La nouvelle Heloyse*, 1765. Engraving, Photograph © Bibliothèque Nationale de France.

second is its inscription of the words "La Nouvelle" on the top right-hand page of the book that absorbs her concentration. We might say she is *the* new Heloise, while Bernard d'Agesci shows us *a* new Heloise.

There is another way to pose the question of Rousseau's "influence" on *A Lady Reading Heloise* that appeals to neither some generalized *sensibilité* nor some specific reference. Is the woman Bernard d'Agesci represents a new Heloise in the manner of Julie? Kamuf has argued that unconverted sexual desire persisting in Heloise's discourse will have to be transformed before Heloise can be renovated as Julie. Before her marriage, Julie undergoes an "internal revolution" and, as Mme Wolmar, she converts the unconverted remains of Heloise's desire. She corrects the disorder of her feelings and reestablishes them according to laws of duty and nature.[79] In Kamuf's analysis, Rousseau's Julie rids herself of the unregulated sexual desire that clings to Heloise. Taking a different approach, Anne Vila reaches a related conclusion. She observes that Julie's plan for happiness depends on two assumptions. "First that to stay healthy and robust, the soul should enjoy only carefully metered doses of sensible pleasures, and second, that to stay virtuous, one must constantly subordinate one's desires and passions to the rule of reason."[80] Vila comments in passing that Julie's program for controlling her sensibility resembles Tissot's cure for masturbation. In fact, in her analysis of *La nouvelle Héloïse,* Vila shows Rousseau's dependence on Tissot. Unlike both the converted Julie and the Julie who sets out to regulate sensibility, Bernard d'Agesci's lady evokes unrestrained passion rather than control, and even revels in the self-stimulation reading can provoke.

Julie certainly disavows her earlier passion more than Heloise ever would, and the second mention of Heloise in Rousseau's novel (and the only direct comparison of Julie and Heloise) alludes to Julie's inner transformation. In a letter to Julie, her friend Claire warns her: "[D]o you not see that after arising again from a fall one must stand straight, and that to lean in the other direction from the fall, is the way to fall again? Cousin, you were a lover like Heloise, now you are devout like her; would to God it be with more success!"[81] In her letter, Claire hopes that Julie will not succumb to Heloise's fate, which was never to extinguish her desire. But her words are prescient—Julie does lean too far, she is on the verge, poised to fall again. But where Heloise lives even after her fall, Julie is destined to die from its possibility.

It is this Julie teetering on the edge who interests Elizabeth MacArthur. Her interpretation of the novel focuses on its conclusion and Julie's tragic death. MacArthur suggests that because Julie's uncontrolled desire for Saint-Preux upsets the social order, she must die rather than have her desire ignite again, as it threatens to do in her last letters.[82] MacArthur compares Julie's desire to a "mine beneath the Utopian community of Clarens," which might explode at any moment. Julie's desire thus becomes a destabilizing force in Rousseau's text, one that the author cannot control. MacArthur's reading of *Julie, ou La nouvelle Heloïse* takes as a good the subversive possibilities of woman's desire, just as her desire to interpret finds a reading that disrupts the vision of Julie as the perfect model of compliant, submissive womanhood. MacArthur offers the possibility that a woman's desire is always there waiting, waiting to explode into the male text and shatter its premises.

If *Julie, ou La nouvelle Heloïse* tried, perhaps in vain, to replace Heloise with a converted Julie, what about Bernard d'Agesci's painting? In this image, Heloise is evoked through her writing (or an imitation of her writing), which has replaced both Gentil-Bernard's poem and the unsealed letter as the object of the woman's attention. Everything about the painting suggests that this new Heloise revels in her pleasurable state; like the abbess whose work she reads, this new Heloise does not disavow sexual passion or desire. Well after Rousseau published *Julie,* Bernard d'Agesci kept Heloise in play, reminding the viewer of what moved his woman to *ravissement.*

True Confessions?

In *Les confessions* (1782–89), Rousseau ties his writing of *Julie, ou La nouvelle Heloïse* not to the popularity of the Heloise legend, nor to any possession by Heloise, but to a reverie fueled by picturing to himself his own amorous past.[83] While reveling in a dreamy indolence—a state eighteenth-century medicine would view as feminine—Rousseau remembers all the circumstances of meeting the women who ravished his heart. "I saw myself," he writes, "surrounded by a seraglio of *houris* whom I used to know, and the lively inclination I felt for them was not a new feeling to me. My blood caught fire, my head turned."[84] These memories bring on a sudden and extravagant intoxication that seizes his mind, and "the impossibility of attaining real beings" throws poor Jean-Jacques into the "regions of chimera." Sensitive as a woman, Rousseau pictures himself as having the classic symptoms of lovesickness or even a love madness induced by imagination. He is in a continual ecstasy, he passes his time lost in his thoughts, he loses all appetite for food. And like the nymphomaniac Bienville described, Rousseau becomes angry when anyone distracts him from his obsession: "When ready to depart for the enchanted world, I saw wretched mortals arrive who came to keep me on this earth, I could neither moderate nor hide my vexation."[85]

Increasingly Rousseau projects himself into his fantasy world, first picturing two women with all the charms of "the sex he adored" and then imagining himself as a lover: "Smitten with my two charming models, I identified myself with the lover and the friend as much as possible. But I made him young and amiable, giving him, in addition, the virtues and defects that I felt in myself."[86] So intensely present is this imaginative world that Rousseau claims he is moved to project it as art: "These fictions, by dint of repetition, at length gained more consistency, and fixed themselves in my brain in a determined form. It was then that the fantasy led me to express on paper some of the situations fancy offered me. And recalling all that I had felt in my youth, these fantasies thus, in some measure, gave an object to my desire to love, which I had never been able to satisfy, and by which I felt myself consumed."[87] Here the sensitive Jean-Jacques also claims that through making art he can satisfy desires he could never satiate in "real life." His first attempt produces a few incoherent letters unconnected to one another.

Although making art gives Rousseau a way to satisfy vicariously his passion, that passion abates when there is outdoor work to be done but returns when the weather turns inclement and he is relegated to a forced inactivity. Thus like the rural woman whose work protects her from the vapors, Rousseau is free from fantasy when he labors in the salubrious country air. Once confined to the house, his imagined female friends appear everywhere before his eyes. It is indeed striking how well these true confessions repeat the theoretical connections between creative fervor and mental illness (e.g., lovesickness, melancholia, even nymphomania) that circulated in eighteenth-century culture. Rousseau paints himself as the enthused, nearly mad artist, absorbed fully, even obsessed, by what his imagination creates: "I was no longer myself for a moment, my delirium no longer left me."[88] Rousseau repeats again and again that he conceives his work in a moment of delirium, a moment of enthusiasm, a moment of ecstasy. Yet he also transforms himself into an artist forced to make art, an artist who can both exorcise his phantoms and bring a reasoned order to his incoherent longings: "After many useless efforts to banish all these fictions from my mind, I was, in the end, entirely seduced by them, and I occupied myself only with trying to put them in some order and sequence, to make them some kind of novel."[89]

The impassioned artist-lover, however, reappears with the coming of spring—a cliché that seems remarkably contrived. Like the nesting birds and randy squirrels harkening to nature's call, Rousseau, too, is urged toward love: "The return of spring had increased my amorous delirium and in my erotic transports, I had composed for the last parts of *Julie* several letters in which one can sense the rapture in which I wrote them."[90] He also ascribes this rapture to his finally finding a real love in Mme de Houdentot, and again his response incorporates all the familiar symptoms of lovesickness: "As I have already said, it was love this time, and love in all its energy and madness. I will describe neither the agitations, nor the tremblings, palpitations, convulsive emotions, nor faintings of the heart that I continually experienced."[91] With this happy convergence of real and imagined love, art takes on the glow of truth. This glow, however, seems less bright to those who read these outpourings.

Rousseau reports that Diderot found his work "loaded with words and redundancies." But Diderot's criticism comes as no surprise to the canny Rousseau: "I myself had already noticed it; but it was the babbling of the fever: I have never been able to correct it."[92] And where in *Les confessions* he claims the rhetoric of *Julie, ou La nouvelle Héloïse* as a natural language of passion, in the preface to that novel he again justifies it by appealing to the real: "How can you speak of Letters, of epistolary style? When writing to one's beloved, who cares about that!"[93]

Far from presenting Rousseau as an emulator of Heloise, *Les confessions* figure him as a new Pygmalion. Like Pygmalion he turns from real women to those he imagines and justifies his initial fantasy of the two female friends: "[S]eeing that nothing that existed was worthy of my delirium, I nourished it in the ideal world, that my creative imagination soon peopled with beings after my own heart."[94] And later in the same account he makes the comparison explicit as he describes the precious materials he bought to craft his novel: the gilt paper, the azure and silver powder to dry the writing, and the blue narrow ribbon he secured to tack sheets together. Like the sculptor-king, Rousseau adores and adorns his creation: "I thought nothing sufficiently elegant and delicate for the two charming girls, whom I loved madly like another Pygmalion."[95] And this Rousseau-Pygmalion is like all the other manifestations of the sculptor-king, a man in whom the "feminine" qualities have been transformed and reclaimed for his artistry.

Unlike Rousseau's *Les confessions,* Bernard d'Agesci's image of *A Lady Reading the Letters of Heloise and Abelard* keeps Heloise in the picture. Her correspondence and its popularity provide a context for interpreting Bernard d'Agesci's work. More significantly, in recreating the emotional tenor of Heloise's letters in the woman those letters have set to dream, the painting suggests—however inadvertently—that its author has emulated both Greuze and Heloise, that he is possessed by the painting of a man and the writing of a woman.

Rousseau, in contrast, attributes the passionate tone of his *Julie, ou La nouvelle Héloïse* to his overheated imagination inspired by memories of past loves. In telling his life story, there is no acknowledgement that Heloise or her cult inspired his Julie in any way, and elsewhere Rousseau denies that women, as a group, can express or even feel passion. The artist he purports to emulate is Pygmalion, whom Rousseau put at the center of a *scène lyrique* that takes enthusiasm as a major theme. Intentionally or not, Bernard d'Agesci's painting brings our attention to the woman writer and the effects of her art, for the painting depicts a woman inspired by Heloise, a desirable and desiring woman passionately moved by love.

Taking one final look at this painting, I must admit that Diderot was right—the context of viewing does change how an image is read. Looking only at the female figure and the sensuous surfaces that adorn it, I see Bernard d'Agesci's reading lady in a state of *ravissement* that suggests her sexual passions and pleasures and arouses those of the viewer. If I consider only the painter whom Bernard d'Agesci emulates, I see one man inspired by another. But if I pay attention to the book the painted woman holds, I see that the image pictures her *ravissement* as a barometer of a woman's—that is, Heloise's—poetic enthusiasm. As art's motor force, as the passion that moved the artist to create, enthusiasm was never far from sexual desire. Bernard d'Agesci's inspired reader seduces me by offering both the spectacle of her passionate transgression and the intellectual pleasure of subversive reading.

I know that in reaching this conclusion I stand in the position Diderot reserves for himself and men of his ilk, those art experts who stop both to analyze the painting and enjoy its voluptuous spectacle. But elbowing my way into the scene, I bring to the visual arts a set of interpretative practices that depend on reading women—women like Shoshana Felman, who challenge us to interpose our own voices into the texts we read and the images we see. Taking up this challenge creates a viewing space different from the one Diderot imagined. In entering this scene women like myself do not lower their heads and walk on by. They stop to enjoy, to intellectualize, and to appropriate a powerful display of voluptuousness.

CONCLUSION

Closing the Circle, Opening the End

The piercing light of reason never severed the ties that bound the arts to imagination and passion in eighteenth-century France. Although some writers attributed art making to reason or to a reasonable enthusiasm, separating enthusiasm from passionate transport proved difficult to effect and impossible to maintain. Just as difficult was enforcing a firm boundary between the imaginative artist and the delusional woman or man. Only a proverbial line separated genius from madness, and that line never could keep them apart. To paraphrase Diderot's comments on the painter Doyen, artists were often but a step from the abyss. If their excited brains overheated, down they plunged into chaos and disorder.[1] Poised thus, the artist resembled a woman much more than a reasonable man. General belief endowed women with strong imagination and ready passion and also cast them as lacking in reason and restraint. Thus women were more apt to teeter at the brink, and without vigilant social control they would surely fall.

What often pushed women over the edge was love's passion. From Ferrand to Bienville, writers on lovesickness cast women as more susceptible to the diseases of love, which ranged from an innocent melancholia—a longing to be with the beloved—to a disgusting erotomania in which all modesty was cast aside. If more innocent, melancholia was not without its perils, for it could easily slip into a dangerous condition. Sharing a passionate woman's inclination, the artist was mad for love. Throughout the eighteenth century, love and desire remained mythical springs of art, embodied in Pygmalion, Apelles, and the Rousseau who confesses, but also in Sappho and Heloise. The artist's love story held different outcomes for men and women, but the discourses of art making opened places for both, even though the positive entwining of passion, imagination, and sexuality theoretically justified only male creativity.

Having come to the end of my analysis, I am now struck by how writers and artists explored both the mergers and boundaries of enthusiasm and art. For example, in Bernard d'Agesci's *A Lady Reading the Letters of Heloise and Abelard* (fig. 51 above), we find amatory, religious, and poetic enthusiasm mingled in a *ravissement,* a transport we might wish to share. It is the *ravissement* of a woman who, like Heloise herself, is pushed toward, but not beyond the limit. Heloise indulges her sexual imaginings even at Mass, but if desire drives the abbess to the edge of sanity, it is only for the moment. She returns to make art, to write her passionate letters, and to argue for her love. Turning to the painted lady who holds some version of those letters, we see that she imagines, clearly she imagines. Yet even as she is lost in her fantasies, the painting keeps her situated in the real. It stresses the physicality of the objects that surround and embellish her, and includes tokens—the unsealed letter, for example—that suggest some connection between what she lives and what she dreams. These tokens allow the viewer to infer that the lady reading identifies with Heloise because of some actual resemblance between them. I take this resemblance to lie not only in their heightened emotion but also in their potential to represent that emotion in artful writing. What we see, then, is both the passion of love and the fire of creative enthusiasm.

In his rendering of Pygmalion (fig. 43 above), Falconet shows a fantasy, a representation of the artist in which reason gives way to passion, imagination, and desire. The sculpture, however, depicts a reasonable miracle and tries to control the unruly forces it represents. Galatea's awakening is subtle rather than dramatic, and mythological trappings are kept to a minimum. The sculptor's awkward pose signals that he is a "real" man, while Galatea's positioning suggests she is a piece of art. Still, the edges are apparent, and reason's control, in doubt. The cupid devouring Galatea's hand visualizes the sculptor's desire, and the roiling, vaporous cloud makes it apparent that we are in the midst of a vision even as the other accoutrements—tools and block of marble—suggest the mundane studio.

The sculpture itself explores the boundaries of the real and the illusory, for if we see the idol becoming a woman, we also see the man becoming a statue. To live, to move, and to feel are elided in the figure of Galatea, who as an animated creature is endowed with emotion. Pygmalion, too, is nothing if not emotion, for his figure blends love, wonder, and astonishment. Yet overcome by his passions, the "real" man is petrified, frozen like the piece of stone he actually is. Pygmalion becomes the one conquered by his vision and held in his place. Unlike the artist

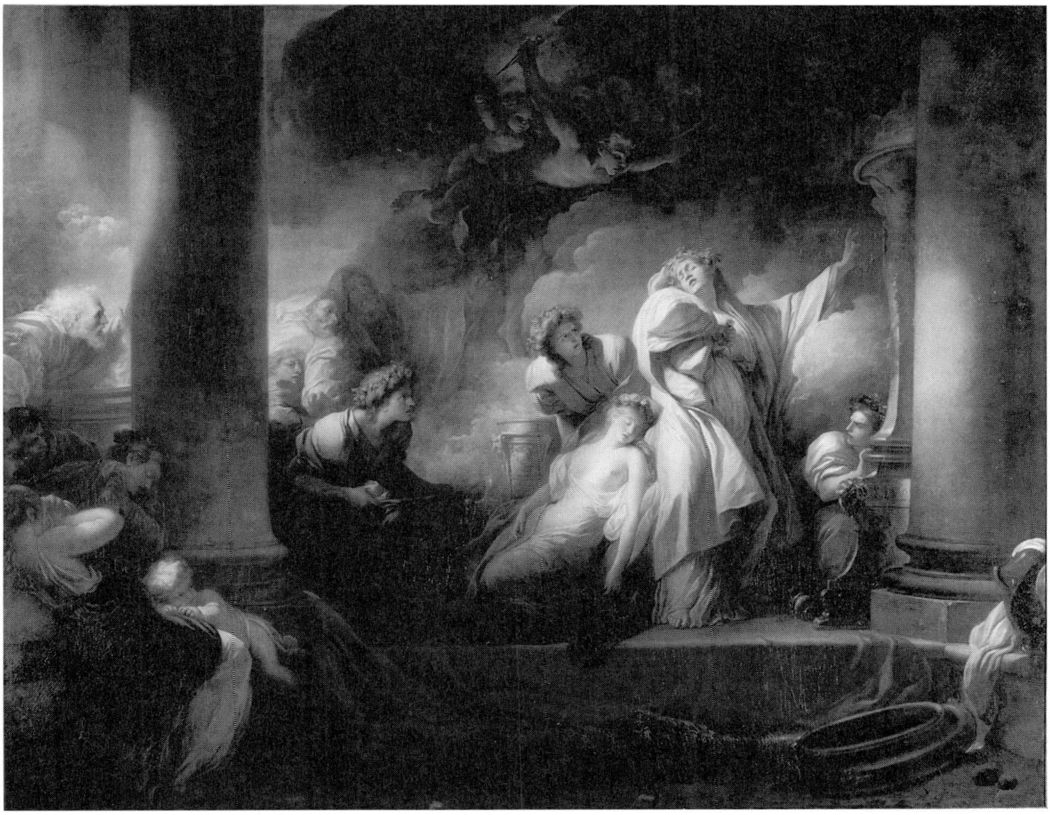

FIGURE 63. Jean-Honoré Fragonard (French, 1732–1806) *Coresus Sacrificing Himself to Save Callirhoe,* Salon of 1765. Oil on canvas, 300 × 400 cm. Paris: Musée du Louvre. Photograph © Réunion des Musées Nationaux/Art Resource, NY.

Falconet hails in his treatise on sculpture, Pygmalion is not in thrall to a great man; it is not the noble deed that moves him. Like the lascivious king of Cyprus, he is entranced by a statue of Venus, or a substitute Venus who looms over the sculptor subjugated by love. It might be this statue love as much as astonishment that has rendered Pygmalion in a thing-like state. As Galatea moves free, passion enslaves Pygmalion.

The fascination with mergers and boundaries that this analysis highlights also opens possibilities for interpreting works that I have not discussed in the preceding chapters. Take, for example, Fragonard's *Coresus Sacrificing Himself to Save Callirhoe* (fig. 63), exhibited in 1765, the same year the last textual volume of the *Encyclopédie* appeared.[2] Fragonard's painting has found no established place in our general histories of art, even though it was a key work at the Salon and hailed by Academy, critics, and public alike. The painting does not fit comfortably into the opposition of rococo versus neoclassicism that still governs much thinking about art production in eighteenth-century France. Nor does it fit well with our vision of enlightened rationality.

The story of Coresus and Callirhoe is filled with different sorts of enthusiasm, all of them represented in the painting. There is the passion of Coresus, a priest of Dionysus who suffers from unrequited love for Callirhoe. There is the uncontrolled sexual mania of his followers punished because Callirhoe has rebuked the priest's love. There is the ominous power of the oracle who controls the multitude and decrees that erotomania will cease only when Callirhoe dies or someone is sacrificed in her stead. There is the madness that finally drives Coresus to sacrifice himself instead of Callirhoe, which is the action Fragonard depicts.

The figure of Coresus disturbed many eighteenth-century spectators because he appeared to them "effeminate."[3] Although it might be difficult to know what struck them as feminine about his physical appearance, it is easier to say that the stance many would recognize as belonging to a woman. Coresus mimics in his standing pose the gestures and posture of Bernini's Saint Teresa swooning in ecstasy. Worn by the high priest, the pose mingles transport, orgasm, and death; although Coresus stabs himself, he appears as a woman penetrated and ravished by her God. His is a possessed body, an emotional body, a body that love's madness has convulsed. It is also a body that gives pleasure to spectators who wish to experience vicariously its painful and pleasurable transport or to expend their emotions in response to his mad act. We see in Fragonard's painting not only the high priest's suicide but also the responses of those who witness it. Their reactions present to real viewers different emotional possibilities and suggest how they might respond to the painted image as if present at the actual event. Fragonard's painting does not condemn the fanatical enthusiasm of the ancients but displays it in all its spectacular effects. *Coresus Sacrificing Himself to Save Callirhoe* acknowledges that art is powerful precisely because it moves our emotions. Fragonard not only exploits this truth, he offers it as a theme of his painting. This, I believe, is why *Coresus and Callirhoe* is a work central to understanding art making and viewing in Enlightenment France.

Although theorists debated the extent to which artists, rather than spectators, became emotionally involved in the scenes they portrayed, few doubted that imagination and passion were in some way essential to art production. This is the case even for Diderot's *Paradoxe sur le comédien,* a text that presents Mlle Clairon as the model for the creative genius as rational performer. Diderot praises Clairon's acting because she can imitate coldly "the roar of the brute," but this is not the whole story. Diderot also admits that to make the monster roar Clairon must first "imagine a mighty phantom." To imagine that phantom was to visualize its passions in all their intensity. Only through her powerful imagination could this woman without sensibility "become" the part she played.

Diderot argues, to be sure, that Clairon's stage performance is a re-creation, a re-creation enabled not by any propensity to experience real emotions but by an expertise at imitating all the passions. Although published in the *Correspondance littéraire,* Diderot's theories of acting were likely known only to a handful of his contemporaries. Yet even if these ideas had circulated widely, I wonder if there would have been any notable effect. As a model for the artist, Diderot's cold Clairon has little to capture the spectator's imagination. It is difficult to work up enthusiasm for a character whose defining feature is her lack of emotion. Others with more engaging stories surely grabbed the spectator's attention and won starring roles in the drama of art. Holding center stage were Sappho, Heloise, and Pygmalion—inspired artists moved by love.

NOTES

INTRODUCTION

1. On the issue of Staël's beauty, see Mary D. Sheriff, *The Exceptional Woman: Elisabeth Vigée-Lebrun and the Cultural Politics of Art* (Chicago: University of Chicago Press, 1996), 243–45.

2. Ibid., 259–61.

3. Ibid., chapters 7 and 8, especially pages 239–61.

4. Along with Benjamin Constant, Staël would try to recoup enthusiasm as a political concept. When Vigée-Lebrun made her portrait, it was not likely she knew anything of Staël's ideas on this aspect of enthusiasm. Indeed, it was not until the 1813 publication of her *De l'Allemagne* that Staël's ideas reached a more developed state. (See K. Steven Vincent, "Benjamin Constant, the French Revolution, and the Origins of French Romantic Liberalism," *French Historical Studies* 23 [fall 2000]: 607–37.) It is very likely, however, that both women were aware of the positive value of poetic enthusiasm, and as we shall see in chapter 1, poetic enthusiasm had long been valued in France.

5. Mary D. Sheriff, *J. H. Fragonard: Art and Eroticism* (Chicago: University of Chicago Press, 1990).

6. In using the phrase "of imagination born," I am reprising the words d'Alembert used in the *Discours préliminaire* to the *Encyclopédie* to describe the fine arts as a realm of knowledge. See below.

7. Michèle Le Doeuff, *The Philosophical Imaginary,* trans. Colin Gordon (Stanford: Stanford University Press, 1989), 7.

8. Joan DeJean, *Fictions of Sappho, 1546–1937* (Chicago: University of Chicago Press, 1989), *Tender Geographies: Women and the Origins of the Novel in France* (New York: Columbia University Press, 1991), and *Ancients against Moderns: Culture Wars and the Making of a Fin de Siècle* (Chicago: University of Chicago Press, 1997); Page duBois, *Sowing the Body: Psychoanalysis and Ancient Representations of Women* (Chicago: University of Chicago Press, 1988), and *Sappho Is Burning* (Chicago: University of Chicago Press, 1995).

9. Giulia Sissa, *Greek Virginity,* trans. Arthur Goldhammer (Cambridge, MA: Harvard University Press, 1990).

10. Peggy Kamuf, *Fictions of Feminine Desire: Disclosures of Heloise* (Lincoln: University of Nebraska Press, 1982); and Marie-Hélène Huet, *Monstrous Imagination* (Cambridge, MA: Harvard University Press, 1993).

11. See, for example, Armand Delatte, *Les conceptions de l'enthousiasme chez les philosophes présocratiques* (Paris: Société d'Édition Les Belles Lettres, 1934).

12. Anthony Ashley Cooper, third earl of Shaftesbury, *Characteristics of Men, Manners, Opinions and Times,* ed. Lawrence E. Klein (Cambridge: Cambridge University Press, 1999). The *Characteristics* were first published in 1711.

13. Between 1693 and 1796 the following were published in Paris: three accurate French translations of the letters, more than fifty different prose or poetic versions of the letters, four novelizations, two plays, and nine imitations or parodies, some with only a slight connection to the story. For the Heloise legend, see Charlotte Charrier, *Héloïse dans l'histoire et dans la légende* (Paris: Libraire Ancienne Honoré Champion, 1933).

CHAPTER 1

1. Jean Le Rond d'Alembert, *Discours préliminaire de l'Encyclopédie* (Paris: Éditions Gonthier, 1965), 57. Unless otherwise noted, all translations are my own.

2. Ibid., 155.

3. "Poetry" here does not refer to a specific art form, and d'Alembert claims the term should be understood in its "natural signification," as synonymous with invention and creation. Elsewhere in the *Discours préliminaire de l'Encyclopédie* the fine arts are called "Painting" because their productions are portrayals or imitations (68). A close examination of the chart suggests that the fine arts are not as well systematized as the other branches of knowledge. Indeed, the problem of ordering the arts, as Simowitz has argued, is evident even in the chart's typography. Amy Simowitz, *The Theory of Art in the Encyclopédie* (Ann Arbor: UMI Press, 1983), 5.

4. D'Alembert, *Discours préliminaire de l'Encyclopédie,* 68.

5. This was the position, for example, of Abbé Jean-Baptiste Du Bos (1670–1742), to whom both Diderot and d'Alembert owed a great debt in their thinking about the fine arts.

6. Abbé Étienne Bonnot de Condillac, *Essai sur l'origine des connaissances humaines,* in *Oeuvres complètes,* 16 vols. (Paris: Lecointe and Durey, 1821–22; reprint, Geneva: Slatkine, 1970), 1: 100.

7. Louis de Cahusac, "Enthousiasme," in Denis Diderot and Jean Le Rond d'Alembert, *Encyclopédie, ou Dictionnaire raisonné des sciences, des arts et des métiers, par une société des gens de lettres,* 17 vols. (microfiche facsimile of 1751–80 ed., Zug, Switzerland: InterDocumentation Co. Ag, 1967), 5: 720.

8. Jean François, marquis de Saint-Lambert, "Genie," in *Encyclopédie,* 7: 582.

9. D'Alembert, *Discours préliminaire de l'Encyclopédie,* 70.

10. For an inspired reading of d'Alembert that brings into focus the oscillation between the particular and the universal in the *Discours préliminaire,* see Claudia Moscovici, "Beyond the Particular and the Universal: D'Alembert's 'Discours préliminaire' to the *Encyclopédie,*" *Eighteenth-Century Studies* 33 (spring 2000): 383–400.

11. D'Alembert, *Discours préliminaire de l'Encyclopédie,* 70.

12. Ibid.

13. Ibid., 60.

14. Ibid., 123.

15. Cahusac, "Enthousiasme," in *Encyclopédie,* 5: 719.

16. Roger de Piles, *Cours de peinture par principes,* intro. Roger Puttfarken (Nîmes: Éditions Jacqueline Chambon, 1990), 74.

17. Plato, *Phaedrus,* trans. and with an intro. by W. C. Helmbold and W. G. Rabinowitz (Indianapolis: Bobbs-Merrill, 1956), 26.

18. Cahusac, "Enthousiasme," in *Encyclopédie,* 5: 719–20.

19. Abbé Charles Batteux, *Les beaux-arts réduits à une même principe* (Paris, 1747; reprint, New York: Johnson Reprint Corp., 1970), 32.

20. Ibid.

21. Cahusac, "Enthousiasme," in *Encyclopédie,* 5: 719.

22. De Piles, *Cours de peinture par principes,* 75.

23. Ibid., 74–75.

24. Longinus, *On the Sublime,* trans. and ed. W. Hamilton Fyfe, revised by Donald Russell (Cambridge, MA: Harvard University Press, 1995), 163–65.

25. For the relation between Boileau and Longinus, see Jules Brody, *Boileau and Longinus* (Geneva: Droz, 1958).

26. De Piles, *Cours de peinture par principes,* 74.

27. Cahusac, "Enthousiasme," in *Encyclopédie,* 5: 720.

28. Ibid.

29. Ibid.

30. Ibid., 720.

31. Ibid.

32. Condillac, *Essai sur l'origine des connaissances humaines,* in *Oeuvres complètes,* 1: 110.

33. René Descartes, *The Passions of the Soul,* trans. Stephen H. Voss (Indianapolis: Hackett Publishing Co., 1989), 56. For Descartes, wonder is physically caused by a sensory impression in the brain (an impression that represents the object as rare and worthy of consideration) that becomes immobilized when the animal spirits, which flow into the muscles, keep the sense organs fixed in the same position. For a comprehensive discussion of wonder, see Lorraine Daston and Katharine Park, *Wonders and the Order of Nature, 1150–1750* (New York: Zone Books, 1998). Especially pertinent to my discussion is chapter 8, "The Passion of Inquiry," 303–28.

34. "Passions," in *Encyclopédie,* 12: 144.

35. Ibid., 12: 146. The analysis of the passions depends on widespread notions found not only in Descartes but also in the writings of Nicolas Malebranche (1638–1715). See especially his work, *Recherche de la vérité* (first ed., 1674–75; final ed., 1715), which has an extensive discussion of imagination. There the passions act on the imagination, and imagination, in turn, combats reason by representing things falsely. The dangerous alliance of passion and imagination leads to madness, fantasy, illusion—and enthusiasm. In *The Search after Truth,* trans. and ed. Thomas Lennon and Paul Olscamp (Cambridge: Cambridge University Press, 1997), 87–190.

36. Descartes, *The Passions of the Soul,* 58–60. Daston and Park discuss the relation of astonishment to wonder in *Wonders and the Order of Nature,* 316–17.

37. De Piles, *Cours de peinture par principes,* 74.

38. Denis Diderot, "Salon de 1767," in *Oeuvres complètes,* 25 vols. (Paris: Hermann, 1990), 16: 211.

39. Ibid., 16: 211–12.

40. Cahusac, "Enthousiasme," in *Encyclopédie,* 5: 720.

41. Abbé Étienne Bonnot de Condillac, *Traité des sensations,* in *Oeuvres complètes,* 16 vols. (Paris, 1821–22; reprint, Geneva: Slatkine, 1970), 3: 45–46.

42. Ibid., 3: 47.

43. Descartes, for example, listed desire among the passions in his treatise. Desire there is a disposition of the soul that pushes it to will for the future things it represents to itself as suitable. It is, moreover, a passion that has no antithesis. *The Passions of the Soul,* 66–67.

44. Cahusac, "Enthousiasme," in *Encyclopédie,* 5: 720.

45. Ibid.

46. While affording reason an important role in the arts, Voltaire and Diderot both give animating power back to imagination and realign it with enthusiasm. See Voltaire, "Enthousiasme," in *Dictionnaire philosophique,* ed. Béatrice Didier (Paris: Imprimerie Nationale Éditions, 1994), 241. And Diderot in his "Essai sur la peinture" is close to Voltaire when he argues that expression is the realm of imagination and enthusiasm, but *ordonnance* demands the admixture of reason. The artist, moreover, must have a meticulous balance of enthusiasm and reason. See "Essai sur la peinture" in *Oeuvres complètes,* 14: 393–94.

47. Cahusac, "Enthousiasme," in *Encyclopédie,* 5: 719.

48. Ibid., 5: 720.

49. "Raison," in *Encyclopédie,* 13: 773.

50. Cahusac, "Enthousiasme," in *Encyclopédie,* 5: 721.

51. Chevalier Louis de Jaucourt (1704–80), "Femme (Morale)," in *Encyclopédie,* 6: 472.

52. For a consideration of the exception, see Sheriff, *The Exceptional Woman,* 1–2.

53. Condillac, *Essai sur l'origine des connaissances humaines,* in *Oeuvres complètes,* 1: 85.

54. Ibid., 1: 87–88n. 1.

55. Voltaire, "Imagination," in *Encyclopédie,* 8: 561.

56. Ibid., 8: 561.

57. Condillac, *Essai sur l'origine des connaissances humaines,* in *Oeuvres complètes,* 1: 97.

58. Ibid.

59. Descartes, *The Passions of the Soul,* 29.

60. Voltaire, "Imagination," in *Encyclopédie,* 8: 561.

61. *Imagination d'invention* approaches what in other venues is called genius; it is a gift that nature gives to only a select few and as such is not something that can simply be willed. To prove his point, Voltaire argues that if you ask a hundred persons to imagine a new machine, ninety-nine of them will imagine nothing despite their efforts.

62. Voltaire, "Imagination," in *Encyclopédie,* 8: 562–63.

63. Ibid., 8: 562.

64. Aristotle, *Poetics,* trans. and ed. Stephen Halliwell (Cambridge, MA: Harvard University Press, 1995), 89.

65. Batteux, *Les beaux-arts réduits à une même principe,* 35.

66. See infra, 88–89.

67. Batteux, *Les beaux-arts réduits à une même principe,* 34–35.

68. Abbé Jean-Baptiste Du Bos, *Réflexions critiques sur la poésie et sur la*

peinture, intro. by Dominique Désirat (Paris: École Nationale Supérieure des Beaux-Arts, 1993), 14.

69. Ibid., 141.

70. See David Marshall, *The Surprising Effects of Sympathy* (Chicago: University of Chicago Press, 1998), 105–34.

71. Denis Diderot, *Paradoxe sur le comédien* (Paris: Bordas, 1991), 89–90.

72. Ibid.

73. Denis Diderot, *Le neveu de Rameau,* in *Oeuvres complètes,* 12: 165.

74. Ibid.

75. De Piles, *Cours de peinture par principes,* 75.

76. Condillac, *Essai sur l'origine des connaissances humaines,* in *Oeuvres complètes,* 1: 96.

77. Diderot, "Salon de 1767," in *Oeuvres complètes,* 16: 273. On the relation of this quotation to the "Essai sur la peinture," see note 46.

78. Ibid.

79. Étienne Falconet, *Réflexions sur la sculpture,* in *Oeuvres complètes,* 3d ed., 3 vols. (Paris, 1808; reprint, Geneva: Slatkine, 1970), 3: 14. "Borromini" is the Italian architect Francesco Borromini (1599–1667) and "Meissonnier," the French designer and architect Juste Aurèle Meissonnier (c. 1693–1750).

80. Du Bos, *Réflexions critique sur la poésie et sur la peinture,* 175.

81. Ibid.

82. Raymond Klibansky, Erwin Panofsky, and Fritz Saxl, *Saturn and Melancholy: Studies in the History of Natural Philosophy, Religion, and Art* (London: Nelson, 1964), 17.

83. "Mélancholie," in *Encyclopédie,* 10: 308.

84. Philippe Pinel, *Nosographie Philosophique; ou, La méthode de l'analyse appliquée à la médecine,* 3 vols. (Paris: J. A. Brosson, 1813), 1: 97.

85. "Mélancholie," in *Encyclopédie,* 10: 308.

86. Pierre Pomme, *Traité des affections vaporeuses des deux sexes* (Paris: Desaint et Saillent, 1760), 14.

87. Ibid., 28–30.

88. Nicolas Chambon de Montaux, *Des maladies des femmes,* 2 vols. (Paris: Hotel Serpente, 1784), 2: 451–74.

89. Samuel-Auguste-David Tissot, *De la santé des gens de lettres et des valetudinaires,* in *Oeuvres complètes de Tissot* (Paris: Allent, 1809), 57.

90. Diderot, "Essai sur la peinture" in *Oeuvres complètes,* 14: 377.

91. Cahusac, "Enthousiasme," in *Encyclopédie,* 5: 720. Cahusac here assumes a widely accepted concept of memory as the process of saving and retrieving the signs for perceptions, and of imagination in its more primitive form as the faculty that draws the stored signs out from memory and conjures the perception or simple idea associated with them. Condillac, *Essai sur l'origine des connaissances humaines,* in *Oeuvres complètes,* 1: 27–39.

92. Cahusac, "Enthousiasme," in *Encyclopédie,* 5: 720.

93. Ibid.

94. Luce Irigaray, *Speculum of the Other Woman,* trans. Gillian Gill (Ithaca, NY: Cornell University Press, 1985), esp. 168–79; and Judith Butler, *Bodies That Matter* (New York: Routledge, 1993), 27–55.

95. For Irigaray and Butler, Plato marks the beginning of philosophy's disavowal of the feminine, its figuring of the feminine as unthematizeable

materiality. Butler reminds us that for Plato material objects are copies of Forms that exist only as instantiations of Forms. She explores where and how this instantiation occurs, focusing on the "receptacle" or the "receiving principle" in Plato's *Timaeus,* whose nature he likens to a mother, a nurse, and the "dynamic nature that receives all the bodies that there are" (40). While always the same, this receptacle has no form or shape and is not a body. Butler goes on to recapitulate Irigaray's argument that the figures of the nurse and mother cannot then be fully identified with the receptacle, for those are specular figures—not the feminine, but figures for the feminine. As such, they displace the feminine at the very moment they claim to represent it (41). Thus, rather than envisioning a femininity that contributes to reproduction, Plato posits a phallic Form that reproduces a version of itself through the feminine but without its participation or assistance.

96. See the discussion in Butler, *Bodies That Matter,* 41. When Irigaray turns to Plotinus's "The Impassivity of the Unembodied," she concentrates our attention on particular passages from Plotinus's attempt to read Plato's notion of the receptacle through the Aristotelian category of matter. Irigaray emphasizes here that matter, the All-Mother, is "sterile, not female to full effect, female in receptivity only, not in pregnancy," and presents us with an image of this teaching, an image of Hermes with "the generative organs always in active posture; this is to convey that the generator of things of sense is the Intellectual Reason-Principle" Irigaray, *Speculum of the Other Woman,* 179.

97. Cahusac, "Enthousiasme," in *Encyclopédie,* 7: 520. Those Cahusac names are the authors Pierre Corneille (1606–84), Jean Racine (1639–99), Molière (1622–73), and Philippe Quinault (1635–87); the composer Jean-Baptiste Lully (1632–87); the painter Charles Le Brun (1619–90); the theologian and bishop Jacques Bénigne Bossuet (1627–1704); and the landscape architect André Le Notre (1613–1700). Perrault is likely the architect and architectural theorist Claude Perrault (1613–88).

98. Indeed, Cahusac even represents the arts as masculine and offers this image in his treatise on the dance: "On croit voir alors plusieurs enfans d'un même père, heureusement nés, élevés avec soin, & chargés d'emplois différens. Chacun d'eux, avec des traits marqués qui le distinguent, en a cependant qui lui sont communs avec les autres. C'est un air de famille qui frappe & qui rappelle malgré soi, le souvenir du père & des frères." Given that the arts are usually represented by the sister muses and that painting and poetry are called the "sister arts," figuring them as a father with his sons is a notable change. Louis de Cahusac, *La danse ancienne et moderne; ou, Traité historique de la danse,* 3 vols. (1754; reprint, Geneva: Slatkine, 1971), 1: 5.

99. Cahusac, "Enthousiasme," in *Encyclopédie,* 5: 721.

CHAPTER 2

1. For a study of sensibility, medicine, and literature in France, see Anne Vila, *Enlightenment and Pathology: Sensibility in the Literature and Medicine of Eighteenth-Century France* (Baltimore: Johns Hopkins University Press, 1998). It is useful to note here that arguments about woman's more delicate fibers appeared much earlier and were based in other scientific or philosophical systems. These often presented a strikingly similar view of the "normal" woman. For example, Nicolas Malebranche tied the delicacy of woman's brain fibers to the action of her imagination in his *The Search after Truth,* 130–31. And although François Poulain de La Barre (1647–1723) drew different conclusions about woman, similar assumptions about her sensitivity emerge in his *De l'égalité des deux sexes* (1673). See François Poulain de La Barre, *The Woman as Good as the*

Man, or The Equality of Both Sexes, trans. A. L., with an intro. by Gerald M. MacLean (1677; reprint, Detroit: Wayne State University Press, 1988), 126–29.

2. "Sensibilité (Morale)," in *Encyclopédie*, 15: 52. The entry defines sensibility as a "tender and delicate disposition of the mind that renders it easily moved and touched."

3. In *Enlightenment and Pathology*, Vila very thoroughly recapitulates the related entries in the *Encyclopédie*. Although the entry on sensibility might popularize the medical theories it discusses, it is precisely this popularization—and the attempt to reach a broad audience—that makes the entry useful to me.

4. Henri Fouquet, "Sensibilité, Sentiment, (Médecine)," in *Encyclopédie*, 15: 38.

5. Ibid.

6. Charles Bonnet, *Essai analytique sur les facultés de l'âme* (Copenhagen, 1760; reprint, Hildesheim: Georg Olms Verlag, 1973), 155.

7. Fouquet, "Sensibilité, Sentiment (Médecine)," in *Encyclopédie*, 15: 47.

8. Edme de la Beauchêne, *De l'influence des affections de l'âme dans les maladies nerveuses* (Montpellier and Paris: Méquignon, 1781), 6–7.

9. Beauchêne, *De l'influence des affections de l'âme dans les maladies nerveuses des femmes*, 19–20.

10. Diderot, "Salon de 1767," in *Oeuvres complètes*, 16: 370–71.

11. Ibid., 16: 373.

12. Jaucourt, "Femme," in *Encyclopédie*, 6: 472.

13. Pierre Roussel, *Système physique et morale de la femme* (Paris: Vincent, 1775), 30–31. This notion appeared much earlier, and here Roussel verifies from his new physiology an old prejudice. Malebranche, for example, argues that their impressionability gives women great understanding of all that strikes the senses, rendering them able to set fashions, judge language, discern elegance, and recognize good manners. In a word, it gives them taste. At the same time, women are distracted by trifles and "normally" they are "incapable of penetrating to truths that are slightly difficult to discover. Everything abstract is incomprehensible to them" (Malebranche, *The Search after Truth*, 130). Because they cannot use their imaginations for working out complex and tangled questions, women consider only the surface of things; their interest is in "style" and not "reality."

14. Roussel, *Système physique et morale de la femme*, 35–36. This sort of equivocation, however, was not new to the medicine of sensibility. For example, we find a parallel argument in Malebranche. Delicacy of mind, he admits, is not found in every woman; some have the sort of "animal spirits" that generate minds stronger than those found in some men. There are learned women and courageous women just as there are men whose minds are soft, effeminate, and incapable of penetrating anything. This idea prepares the reader for a later consideration of the "effeminate mind," most often found in those who constantly seek amusements and pleasure: the nobility, courtiers, the rich, and the young. These activities are feminine and feminizing; the men who engage in them gradually acquire such delicacy and softness that their minds fall into an "effeminate state." Such minds become—like the normal female mind—sensitive about manners and style. And like women, their intelligence is suited only to what can be sensed and not to "things depending on reason." In Malebranche we find the double move: he separates generally, or in the "normal" case, the male from the female mind and presents categories—the exceptional woman and the effeminate mind—in which the two are confused.

Minds of similar habits attached to differently sexed bodies emerge as like one another. Malebranche, *The Search after Truth,* 130–33, 155–56.

15. Beauchêne, *De l'influence des affections de l'âme dans les maladies nerveuses,* 23.

16. For an excellent and detailed study of La Mettrie's thought and influence, see Kathleen Wellman, *La Mettrie: Medicine, Philosophy, and Enlightenment* (Durham, NC: Duke University Press, 1992). Wellman also points out that La Mettrie made imagination the basis for all thought processes and deemed it the most significant faculty (179).

17. Julien Offray de La Mettrie, *Machine Man,* in *Machine Man and Other Writings,* trans. and ed. Ann Thomson (New York: Cambridge University Press, 1996), 17.

18. Ibid., 17–18.

19. Ibid., 18.

20. Even when the medicine of sensibility was long established, women took issue with the picture of woman's mind that it constructed. For example, in *Les femmes comme il convient de les voir* (1785), Mme de Coicy argues: "L'Anatomie la plus exacte n'a pu encore remarquer aucune différence entre la tête de la femme et la tête de l'homme. Leur cerveau est entiérement semblable; ils voyent; ils entendent par des organes qui sont exactement les mêmes." She goes on to point out that men and women receive the same sense impressions and conserve them in the same way. All physical difference resides in the reproductive organs, which Coicy sees as having nothing to do with understanding. Differences in understanding, she argues, come from education and the manner in which society forces women to live. Mme de Coicy, *Les femmes comme il convient de les voir; ou, Aperçu de ce que les femmes ont été de ce qu'elles sont, et de ce qu'elles pourroient être,* 2 vols. (Paris and London: Bacot, 1785), 1: 8.

21. Beauchêne, *De l'influence des affections de l'âme dans les maladies nerveuses,* 17.

22. Roussel, *Système physique et morale de la femme,* 31. Roussel refers his readers directly to Thomas's work.

23. It is also worth pointing out that the section opens by explaining why Descartes valued the "esprit philosophique" of women. Thomas attributes Decartes's attitude not to his respect for woman's reason or ability but to the philosopher's vanity. Two princesses admired Descartes, while other men criticized and envied him. Thomas asks, could Descartes really find in the women, "cette raison froide qui marche sans se précipiter jamais, et mesure tous ses pas?" Antoine Léonard Thomas (1732–85), "Essai sur le caractère, les moeurs et l'esprit des femmes dans les differents siècles," in *Qu'est-ce qu'une femme?* with an intro. by Elisabeth Badinter (Paris: P.O.L., 1989), 108–9.

24. Thomas, "Essai sur le caractère, les moeurs et l'esprit des femmes dans les differents siècles," 109.

25. Ibid. Here Thomas seems to invoke the sort of phenomena that Edmund Burke defined as sublime in *A Philosophical Enquiry into the Origin of Our Ideas of the Sublime and Beautiful* (1757). There the sublime is gendered as masculine. See W. T. J. Mitchell, *Iconology: Image, Text, Ideology* (Chicago: University of Chicago Press, 1986), 116–50.

26. Batteux, *Les beaux-arts réduits,* 33.

27. Ibid., 35.

28. Ibid., 110.

29. This same paradox is evident in the "Observations de M. Diderot sur une brochure intitulée Garrick, ou les acteurs anglais," published in *Correspondence littéraire* on October 1 and November 15, 1770. The paradox

emerges on pages 137–38 of the section published October 1, 1770. As is well known, much of Diderot's text is in dialogue with David Garrick's theories of acting, which appeared in Paris as the pamphlet *Garrick, ou Les acteurs anglais* (translated by Antonio Fabio Sticotti) in 1769. See *Correspondance littéraire, philosophique et critique par Grimm, Diderot, Raynal, Meister, etc.*, ed. Maurice Tourneux, 16 vols. (Paris: Garnier Frères, 1877–82).

30. In his *Le comédien* of 1724, Pierre Remond de Sainte-Albine (1699–1778) defines *sentiment* in acting as a talent for experiencing the passions. He continues with this comparison: "Comme une cire molle, qui sous les doits d'un savant artiste devient alternativement un Medée ou un Sapho, il faut que l'esprit et le coeur d'une personne de théâtre soient propres à recevoir toutes les modifications que l'Auteur veut leur donner." *Le comédien* (Paris: Desaint & Saillant, 1747), 32. In Remond de Sainte-Albine's treatise, acting is presented as a matter of reproducing the signs of the passions, but at the same time the author argues that natural propensities make the imitations more or less perfect.

31. Du Bos, *Réflexions critiques sur la poésie et sur la peinture*, 141.

32. Ibid.

33. Diderot, *Paradoxe sur le comédien* (Paris: Bordas, 1991), 35.

34. Ibid.

35. Ibid., 32.

36. Ibid., 68.

37. Ibid.

38. Diderot, "Sur les femmes," in *Qu'est-ce qu'une femme?* with an intro. by Elisabeth Badinter (Paris: P.O.L., 1989), 167. For an insightful analysis of Diderot's literary strategies and their relation to issues of sexuality, see Marie Brisson, "Dire l'inconnu 'Sur les femmes' de Diderot," *L'Esprit Créateur* 39 (*fall*, 1989): 10–20.

39. Diderot, "Sur les femmes," 170–71.

40. Ibid.

41. Ibid., 171–72.

42. At first Guyon found favor at the French court and counted among her followers both Fénelon and Mme de Maintenon. At the urging of Louis XIV, however, Bishop Bossuet examined Guyon's beliefs in 1693 and found them heretical. She was imprisoned first at Vincennes (1695) and then at the Bastille (1698–1703), where she continued to write and publish. Margaret-Marie Alacoque was a nun belonging to the Order of Visitation. Her visions, ratified by Jesuit authorities, included not only the representation that would become central to the devotion—a radiant heart surmounted by a cross and encircled with a crown of thorns—but also the experience of a physical contact and union with Jesus, which she expressed in erotic language. See Raymond Jonas, *France and the Cult of the Sacred Heart* (Berkeley: University of California Press, 2000), 19. The cult of the Sacred Heart is also discussed in Christopher Johns, "That Aimiable Object of Adoration: Pompeo Battoni and the Sacred Heart," *Gazette des Beaux-Arts* 132 (1998): 19–28.

43. Jeanne Guyon, *An Autobiography* (New Kensington, PA: Whitaker House, 1997), 45.

44. Ibid.

45. Ibid.

46. Pierre-Joseph Boudier de Villemert, *Le nouvel ami des femmes; ou, La philosophie du sexe* (Paris: Monory, 1779), 209. This is a greatly enlarged version of his *L'ami des femmes* of 1758.

47. Boudier de Villemert, *Le nouvel ami des femmes*, 40–41.

48. Plato, *Phaedrus,* 25.

49. Guilia Sissa, *Greek Virginity,* trans. Arthur Goldhammer (Cambridge, MA: Harvard University Press, 1990), 21.

50. From *Contra celsum* as quoted in Sissa, *Greek Virginity,* 22.

51. Ibid., 23.

52. Heinrich Kramer and James Sprenger, *The Malleus Maleficarum of Heinrich Kramer and James Sprenger,* trans. and with an intro. by Reverend Montague Summers (New York: Dover, 1971), 44.

53. Ibid., 47. They add, "See Proverbs 30: There are three things that are never satisfied, yea, a fourth thing which says not, it is enough; that is, the mouth of the womb."

54. Michel Carmona, *Les diables de Loudun: Sorcellerie et politique sous Richelieu* (Paris: Fayard, 1988), 24.

55. Meric Casaubon, *A Treatise concerning Enthusiasm,* intro. Paul J. Korshin, facsimile reproduction of the 2d ed. of 1656 (Gainesville, FL: Scholars' Facsimiles and Reprints, 1970), 157.

56. Ibid., 2.

57. Ibid., 157–65.

58. Diderot repeatedly mentions the convulsions in his *Pensées philosophiques* of 1746, and his comments suggests that in the phenomenon all sorts of motives are at play.

59. The *convulsionnaires* entered modern French psychiatry in the work of Jean Martin Charcot (1867–1936), who in his studies of hysteria reinterprets the findings of eighteenth-century doctors. His *Iconographie photographique de Salpêtrière* includes an example drawn from the *secours* of the *convulsionnaires,* that of the crucifixion.

60. B. Robert Kreiser, *Miracles, Convulsions, and Ecclesiastical Politics in Early Eighteenth-Century Paris* (Princeton: Princeton University Press, 1978). The convulsions at Saint-Médard became part of the struggle over the papal bull *Unigenitus* (September 8, 1713), which demanded that Jansenist clergy conform to mainstream Roman Catholicism. Backed—indeed, sought—by Louis XIV, *Unigenitus* concerned both political and religious life. The king had long suspected Jansenists of disloyalty, especially since Jansenism embraced the seemingly "republican" idea that authority was vested not only in popes and bishops but also in the entire body of Church members. The persecutions continued in the eighteenth century, and a royal declaration of 24 March 1730 made *Unigenitus* a law of the state. In such circumstances, the events at Saint-Médard seemed miraculous to one side, and dangerous to the other.

61. Kreiser, *Miracles, Convulsions, and Ecclesiastical Politics,* 250n. 21.

62. One contemporary report estimated that of the 270 people seized with convulsions between August 1731 and December 1732, at least 200 of them were women. Another report stated that women comprised three-quarters of those who participated in the cult. Kreiser, *Miracles, Convulsions, and Ecclesiastical Politics,* 259, n. 47.

63. Ibid., 253–54. That women could achieve prominence led some commentators to believe that greed and vanity, combined with an inflamed imagination, motivated many of the *convulsionnaire*s. Indeed, simple fraud was the explanation the police favored. The idea that women would achieve some prominence in the movement provoked responses, for example, a play by Guillaume-Hyacinthe Bougeant, *La femme docteur; ou, La théologie tombée en quenouille* (1731).

64. "It is not necessary to be very knowledgeable in the affairs of the world

to know how many astonishing scenes have been presented to the public throughout all time by hysterical or vaporous girls or women whose enthusiastic operations have appeared so extraordinary that some have been attributed to God, others to the Devil. But even so, these creatures, often of mediocre virtue, have perpetuated a fraud, making considerable profit for themselves and others whom they have lured by their tricks even as they have satisfied their vanity in the world." As quoted in Lindsay Wilson, *Women and Medicine in the French Enlightenment* (Baltimore: Johns Hopkins University Press, 1993), 28.

65. As discussed by Jan Goldstein, "Enthusiasm or Imagination? Eighteenth-Century Smear Words in Comparative National Context," in *Enthusiasm and Enlightenment in Europe, 1650–1850* ed. Lawrence E. Klein and Anthony J. La Vopa (San Marino, CA: Huntington Library, 1998), 43.

66. On the *secours,* see Kreiser, *Miracles, Convulsions, and Ecclesiastical Politics,* 259–66.

67. The illustration of the *secours* comes from a text that defended the convulsionary movement and described the *secours* of Gabrielle in some detail. Far from showing any lasciviousness, the image of Gabrielle Moulère's *secours* emphasizes restraint. The young *convulsionnaire* is at the center of each scene in modest dress, and the spectators behave decorously without emotional excess. The text that accompanies the print offers a figurist interpretation for the *secours,* quoting from Exodus 3 in Latin and in French. It explains that these words are Moses' response to the miracle of the bush that burns without being consumed, a miracle that signaled deliverance for the children of Israel. In a similar way, the *secours* represents the miracle of a woman who is "destroyed," that is, beaten, crushed, and stabbed, without being destroyed, and hence the convulsions are the sign of the immediate coming of the Church's religious renewal. On the *convulsionnaire*'s use of figurist interpretation, see Kreiser, *Miracles, Convulsions, and Ecclesiastical Politics,* 246–49.

68. Voltaire, "Convulsions," in *Dictionnaire philosophique,* 208.

69. Ibid.

70. Voltaire, "Fanatisme," in *Dictionnaire philosophique,* 255.

71. *Suffrages en faveur des deux derniers tomes de M. de Montegeron* (Paris, 1749). As quoted in Catherine-Laurence Maire, *Les convulsionnaires de Saint-Médard: Miracles, convulsions et prophéties à Paris au XVIIIe siècle* (Paris: Gallimard/Julliard, 1985), 134.

72. Excerpted in Maire, *Les convulsionnaires de Saint-Médard,* 169.

73. Philippe Hecquet, *Lettre sur la convulsionnaire en extase; ou La vapoureuse en rêve* (Paris, s.d.), 28.

74. Ibid., 22. As Wilson has argued, Hecquet shared the attitudes of theologians who saw hysterical vapors as a disequilibrium of the moral, rather than the physical, constitution.

75. Diderot, *Sur les femmes,* 171.

76. Roussel, *Système physique et morale de la femme,* 46–47. Philippe Pinel, *Nosographie philosophique ou la méthode de l'analyse appliquée à la médecine,* 3 vols. (Paris: J. A. Brosson, 1813), 1: 103–4.

77. Page duBois, *Sowing the Body* (Chicago: University of Chicago Press, 1988), 175–76.

78. Ibid., 177.

79. Nicolas Boileau Despréaux, *Traité du sublime ou du merveilleux dans le discourse,* in *Oeuvres complètes,* with an intro. by Antoine Adam, annotated by Françoise Escal (Paris: Gallimard, 1966), 361.

80. In the standard English translations, "the Pythian priestess, on approaching the tripod where there is, they say, a rift in the earth, exhaling divine vapour, thereby becomes impregnated with the divine power and is at once inspired to utter oracles." Longinus, *On the Sublime,* trans. W. H. Fyfe, revised by Donald Russell, in *Aristotle's Poetics; Longinus on the Sublime; Demetrius on Style* (Cambridge, MA: Harvard University Press, 1999), 211. See also Longinus, *On Great Writing,* trans. G. M. A. Grube (Indianapolis: Bobbs-Merrill, 1957), 22. "She becomes impregnated with divine power." It should be noted, however, that Longinus did not give the explicit sexual reading that would occupy the Church Fathers, nor did he denigrate the Pythia or her relation with the god.

81. Étienne Falconet, *Oeuvres complètes,* 3 vols. (1808; reprint, Geneva: Slatkine), 1: 59.

82. Voltaire, "Enthousiasme," in *Dictionnaire philosophique,* 240.

83. Michel Dandré-Bardon, *Traité de peinture* (1765; reprint, Geneva: Minkoff, 1972), 169–70. Dandré-Bardon, like De Piles before him, overtly refers to Longinus in his text.

84. Boileau, *Traité du sublime,* 362.

85. DuBois, *Sowing the Body,* 170–83.

86. Boileau, *Traité du sublime,* 356.

87. Ibid., 356–57.

88. Batteux, *Les beaux-arts réduits,* 34.

89. Joan DeJean has argued that from the late seventeenth century Sappho "presides over a scenario in which woman's amorous passion and women's writing are synonymous: uncontrolled, spontaneous, excessive outpourings." Joan DeJean, *Fictions of Sappho, 1536–1937* (Chicago: University of Chicago Press, 1989), 24. She further argues that showing the Sapphic style to be "instinctive" was a prelude to a deprecation of all women's writing.

90. Abbé Jean-Jacques Barthélemy, *Travels of Anacharsis the Younger in Greece during the Middle of the Fourth Century before the Christian Era,* trans. William Beaumont, 5 vols. (London: G. G. and J. Robinson, 1796), 1: 275–76. Here Barthélemy footnotes Plutarch, among other ancient sources.

91. Ibid., 1: 276.

92. DeJean, *Fictions of Sappho,* 47.

93. Ibid., 96–110. It is not surprising, then, that a bust of Sappho appears in a 1725–26 illustration to Molière's *Les femmes savantes,* a play that mocks women's learning (on this play, see infra.). The engraving, made by François Joullain after Charles Coypel, shows the "learned ladies," Philaminte, Bélise, and Armande, listening to the pompous "bel esprit" Trissotin read his poetry. Two busts decorate the room: one of Aristotle and one of Sappho. For a discussion of this work, see Thierry Lefrançois, *Charles Coypel* (Paris: Arthena, 1994), 428–29.

94. Madeleine de Scudéry, *Les femmes illustrés, où Les harangues héroïques,* intro. by Claude Maignien (Paris: Côté-femmes Éditions, 1991), 155.

95. Ibid., 157.

96. The crown, of course, is the traditional sign of poetic genius; and the lyre, of lyric poetry, for which Sappho's art was the model. Playing over the sitter's dress, the musical notation likely refers to Plutarch's characterization of Sappho as the inventor of tragic or passionate lyrical music. The scroll recalls the famous depiction of Sappho—in Raphael's *Parnassus*—where she sits among the ancient poets holding both a scroll and lyre. On Sappho and music, see Christiane L. Joost-Gaugier, "Sappho, Apollo, Neopythagorean Theory and

Numine Afflatur in Raphael's Fresco of the *Parnassus*," *Gazette des Beaux-Arts* 122 (1993): 127–28.

97. On this point, see DeJean, *Fictions of Sappho*, chapter 2.

98. Jacques Ferrand, *A Treatise on Lovesickness*, trans. and ed. Donald Beecher and Massimo Ciavolella (Syracuse: Syracuse University Press, 1990), 229.

99. Ibid., 272.

100. Ibid., 231. Other commentators would cross one Sappho with another. For example, in his translation of Longinus, Boileau pushes the poet toward madness by making her seem more given to delirium in his French translations of her work. He also allows that her sexuality was not entirely directed toward men and classes her among the tribades. See DeJean, *Fictions of Sappho*, 84–86.

101. DeJean, *Fictions of Sappho*, 103–7.

102. Voltaire, *Dictionnaire Philosophique*, 240.

103. Barthélemy, *Travels of Anacharsis the Younger in Greece*, 1: 273.

104. Ibid., 1: 273–74.

105. Gill Perry, "'The British Sappho': Borrowed Identities and the Representation of Women Artists in Late Eighteenth-Century British Art," *Oxford Art Journal* 18 (1995): 56. For an excellent analysis of later nineteenth-century images of women as Sappho, see Janis Bergman-Carton, *The Woman of Ideas in French Art, 1830–1848* (New Haven: Yale University Press, 1995), 166–83.

106. In her *Souvenirs*, Vigée-Lebrun lists among those works made in Venice, "Mlle la comtesse de Fries, en Sapho, tenant une lyre et chantant, jusqu'à mi-jambes." Elisabeth Vigée-Lebrun, *Souvenirs*, 2 vols. (Paris: Des Femmes, 1984), 2: 347.

107. See Sheriff, *The Exceptional Woman*, 243–56.

108. DeJean, *Tender Geographies*, 168, 182–99.

109. D'Alembert, *Discours préliminaire de l'Encylopédie*, 68. On Boileau's continuing influence in the eighteenth century, see John R. Miller, *Boileau en France au dix-huitième siècle* (Baltimore: Johns Hopkins University Press, 1942).

110. DeJean, *Tender Geographies*, 177, 167–69.

111. Ibid., 192. DeJean here demonstrates the lasting influence of Batteux on the French literary tradition (189–92). Also by the same author, *Ancients against Moderns: Culture Wars and the Making of a Fin de Siècle* (Chicago: University of Chicago Press, 1997).

112. For an analysis of these works, see Sheriff, *The Exceptional Woman*, 43–53, 180–220.

113. *Le véridique au sallon* (1783), 16 (Deloynes Collection, vol. 13, no. 298).

114. *Apelle au sallon* (1783), 24 (Deloynes Collection, vol. 13, no. 288).

115. *L'ombre de Rubens au sallon* (Paris, 1787), 85 (Deloynes Collection, vol. 15, no. 371).

116. Ibid., 86.

117. Ibid.

118. Du Bos, *Réflexions critique sur la poésie et sur la peinture*, 1–14, esp. 9–12.

119. Diderot, "Salon de 1763," in *Oeuvres complètes*, 13: 341.

120. The first image of *Vertumnus and Pomona* by Boucher is a painting belonging to a set of overdoors made for the Château of La Muette (1749; fig. 13).

The overdoors depicted the four elements, with Vertumnus and Pomona representing Earth. The second image is a cartoon for a Beauvais tapestry from the series *Fragments d'opéra* (c. 1758; San Francisco: Fine Arts Museums of San Francisco). The third image is a design for a Gobelins tapestry (1763; Paris: Musée du Louvre).

121. Diderot, "Salon de 1765," in *Oeuvres complètes,* 14: 275–76.

122. Ibid., 14: 276.

123. This sort of expression Diderot connected to the sketch: "Dans les transports violents de la passion l'homme supprime les liaisons, commence une phrase sans la finir, laisse échapper un mot, pousse un cri et se tait; cependant j'ai tout entendu; c'est l'esquisse d'un discours. La passion ne fait que des esquisses." *Oeuvres complètes,* 16: 516.

124. Ibid.

125. Ibid.

126. Ibid.

127. Diderot, "Salon de 1767," in *Oeuvres complètes,* 16: 199–200.

128. Thierry Lefrançois dates the Coypel pastel portrait to about 1730–31. The portrait was engraved and copied in other media repeatedly. See the entry in his *Charles Coypel,* 237.

129. As quoted in Jack Richtman, *Adrienne Lecouvreur: The Actress and the Age* (Englewood Cliffs, N.J.: Prentice-Hall, 1971), 72. I thank Cathy Keller-Brown for this reference to Lecouvreur's performance.

130. There is only one brief mention of Lecouvreur in the *Paradoxe,* where her name is included in a list of tragic actresses whom Mlle Raucourt tries to outshine. Diderot, *Paradoxe sur le comédien,* 92.

CHAPTER 3

1. I do not imply that for these authorities only woman's imagination (as opposed to that of man) needed control. Rather, I suggest that woman's imagination needed a particular, and perhaps more stringent, form of control since it was widely believed that women had weaker powers of reason and stronger, less internally regulated powers of fantasy.

2. Barthélemy-Claude Graillard de Graville, *L'ami des filles* (Paris: Dufour, 1761), 127–31.

3. Pierre-Joseph Boudier de Villemert, *Le nouvel ami des femmes; ou, La philosophie du sexe* (Paris: Monory, 1779), 36–50. The conduct book claims the most important subject for women to study is men. Because men are their governors, women should know those to whom they must submit by law.

4. See, for example, Stéphanie Félicité, comtesse de Genlis, *Adelaide and Theodore, or Letters on Education,* 3 vols. (London: C. Bathurst, 1783), 2: 88. Much of this conservative treatise is indebted to Rousseau's *Émile.*

5. François de Salignac de La Mothe-Fénelon (1651–1715), *De l'éducation des filles* (Paris: Bassompierre, 1771; reprint, Imprimerie de Provence, 1983), 78.

6. My analysis here is indebted to Paula Radisich, "Louvisa Ulrike of Sweden, Patron of Chardin," paper presented at the College Art Association Meetings, Los Angeles, 1999; and to Dorothy Johnson, "Picturing Pedagogy: Education and the Child in the Paintings of Chardin," *Eighteenth-Century Studies* 24, no. 1 (1990): 47–68.

7. The Salon *livret* lists the work as follows: "Deux Tableaux Pendans, sous le même No: l'un représente un Dessinateur d'après le Mercure de M. Pigalle, & l'autre une jeune Fille qui récite son Evangile." *Explication des peintures,*

sculptures et autres ouvrages de Messieurs de l'Académie Royale (Paris: J. J. E. Collombat, 1753), 17 (Deloynes Collection, vol. 5, no. 53).

8. *Jugement d'un amateur sur l'exposition des tableaux de l'an 1753* (Paris, 1753), 43 (Deloynes Collection, vol. 5, no. 59).

9. DeJean, *Tender Geographies,* 156–58.

10. See infra, 106–110.

11. Jean-Baptiste Drouet de Maupertuis, *La femme faible où l'on represénte aux femmes les dangers ausquels elles s'exposent, par un commerce fréquent et assidu avec les hommes* (Nancy, 1733), 116–17.

12. Graillard de Graville, *L'ami des filles,* 122–26.

13. Diderot, "Salon de 1765," in *Oeuvres complètes,* 14: 163.

14. Ibid., 14: 164.

15. Diderot, "Salon de 1767," in *Oeuvres complètes,* 16: 288.

16. Ibid.

17. Ibid.

18. Ibid., 16: 289.

19. Condillac, *Essai sur l'origine des connaissances humaines,* in *Oeuvres complètes,* 1: 94–95.

20. Ibid.

21. Teresa of Avila, *The Autobiography of St. Teresa of Avila,* trans. E. Allison Peers (New York: Doubleday, 1960), 68–69. For a discussion of Teresa's interest in chivalric romances, see Jodi Bilinkoff, *The Avila of Saint Teresa* (Ithaca: Cornell University Press, 1989), 110–11.

22. The depiction of Saint Teresa contrasts with that of Saint Cecilia, who was inspired by heavenly music. Cecilia is often shown in an ecstatic state with her eyes cast heavenward as she sits at a keyboard instrument (see, for example, Rubens's *St. Cecilia,* c. 1639; Berlin: Staatliche Museen). Her conventional representation, which shows the pose and expression of enthusiasm, became a model for depicting an inspired musician or composer, man or woman. See, for example, Vigée-Lebrun's portrait of the composer Giovanni Paisiello (Salon of 1791; Versailles: Musée du château) and that of the singer Angela Catalini (1806; private collection). A virgin-martyr of the second or third century, Cecilia was not a mystic but, rather, a woman who took a vow of chastity. On her wedding day, Cecilia heard the sound of celestial music, and as she listened she invoked God, asking Him to keep her free from sin in body and soul. Although she marries a Roman nobleman, she persuades him to practice sexual abstinence. Depicting an inspired woman at a keyboard as a recognizable Saint Cecilia did not, I believe, have the erotic charge of depicting a woman as Saint Teresa in ecstasy. Cecilia's auditory vision of God turns her away from sexuality, and she remains a virgin.

23. Jacques Lacan, "God and the Jouissance of ~~the~~ Woman," in *Feminine Sexuality,* ed. Julie Mitchell and Jacqueline Rose (New York: W. W. Norton: 1985), 147.

24. Vigée-Lebrun, *Souvenirs,* 1: 175.

25. Stendhal, *Promenades dans Rome,* in *Oeuvres complètes,* ed. Victor Del Litto and Ernest Abravanel, 50 vols. (Geneva and Paris: Slatkine, 1986), 7: 133.

26. Hecquet, *Lettre sur la convulsionnaire en extase ou la vapoureuse en rêve,* 19–22.

27. Several well-known texts of erotic literature focused on the activity of nuns, clerics, and devout women. These include the seventeenth-century *Vénus*

dans le cloître; ou, La religieuse en chemise, the anonymous *Le triomphe des religieuses; ou, Les nones babillardes* of 1748, and Diderot's *La religieuse,* written in 1760 and published in 1796. Each of these works takes place in a convent where spiritual and erotic exercises are mixed with both philosophical discussions and a political critique that decries the practice of shunting women off to nunneries where their natural inclinations are thwarted.

28. Robert Darnton, *The Forbidden Best-Sellers of Pre-Revolutionary France* (New York: W.W. Norton, 1996), 89–114. Although some contemporaries speculated that Diderot himself authored the text, many now attribute it to the marquis d'Argens. But this attribution is not secure. I am much indebted to Darnton's interpretation of the novel.

29. The names Eradice and Dirrag are anagrams for Marie-Catherine Cadière and her Jesuit confessor, Jean-Baptiste Girard, two protagonists caught up in a cause célèbre whose notoriety coincided with that of the *convulsionnaires.* In 1731, Cadière accused Girard of using his position to seduce her, and although he was acquitted in court, the case generated a variety of salacious pamphlets (Darnton, *The Forbidden Best-Sellers of Pre-Revolutionary France,* 91). Although the Cadière scandal amused Aix-en-Provence while that of the *convulsionnaires* rocked Paris, the two were nonetheless connected in the popular imagination. This little ditty circulating around Paris makes clear the association: Que Saint Pâris à ses malades/Fasse faire maintes gambades/Le beau miracle que voilà!/Croyons plutôt à la Cadière/Qui fait sauter un Loyola/De Sodome jusqu'à Cythère. As quoted in Maire, *Les convulsionnaires de Saint-Médard,* 19.

30. *Thérèse Philosophe,* in *Romans libertins du XVIIIe siècle,* ed. Raymond Trousson (Paris: Robert Laffont, 1993), 602. For a definition of the *Dévotes,* see Elizabeth Rapley, *Women and the Church in Seventeenth-Century France* (Montreal and Kingston: McGill-Queens University Press, 1990), 75.

31. *Thérèse Philosophe,* 593.

32. Darnton, *The Forbidden Best-Sellers of Pre-Revolutionary France,* 92–95.

33. For the erotic use of lap dogs, see Jean-Honoré Fragonard's painting, *Girl Making Her Dog Dance on Her Bed,* and also *The Ring Biscuit,* a lost painting by Fragonard in Georges Wildenstein, *The Paintings of Fragonard* (New York: Phaidon, 1960), plate nos. 280 and 281, respectively.

34. *Observations sur les arts et sur quelques morceaux de peinture & de sculpture exposés au Louvre en 1748* (Leyden: Elias Luzac Junior, 1748), 90 (Deloynes Collection, vol. 3, no. 34).

35. I have found no eighteenth-century observers thinking of love when a man is pictured reading an untitled book that from its size might be a novel or romance.

36. For a discussion of the exception, see Geneviève Fraisse, *La raison des femmes* (Paris: Plon, 1992), 53–54, and idem, *La muse de la raison* (Aix-en-Provence: Alinéa, 1989). See also Sheriff, *Exceptional Woman,* 1–7.

37. The circulation of prints like *Le midi* could make representations of less overtly erotic garden reading, such as Jean-Baptiste Hilaire's *Reading in a Park* (dated to the second half of the eighteenth century; Paris: Musée Nissim de Camondo), seem titillating or dangerous. Hilaire increases the suggestiveness of his work by showing the woman's bodice unlaced and including an overthrown flowerpot as a sign of disarray.

38. Philip Stewart discusses these works and other examples of women reading in *Engraven Desire: Eros, Image and Text in the French Eighteenth Century* (Durham, NC: Duke University Press, 1992), 94–102. For nineteenth-century

images, see Janis Bergman-Carton, *Woman of Ideas in French Art, 1830–1848* (New Haven: Yale University Press), 103–24.

39. The boudoir and garden are related as sites of sensual pleasure in architectural theory, as well. Nicolas Le Camus des Mézières advocated a boudoir décor that created an illusion of nature. See *The Genius of Architecture, or The Analogy of That Art with Our Sensations,* trans. David Britt, intro. Robin Middleton (Santa Monica, CA: Getty Center Publications, 1992), 116. In her house on Paris's Place Vendôme, Mme Dangé enjoyed a boudoir decorated with vignettes from La Fontaine situated in woodland settings. On the same square, Mme Baudard took her leisure in a boudoir whose ceiling seemed to open into the sky and that led to a bathing room in which painted trellises appeared to screen an open landscape. As discussed in Rochelle Ziskin, *The Place Vendôme: Architecture and Social Mobility in Eighteenth-Century Paris* (New York: Cambridge University Press, 1999), 151, 154.

40. As quoted in Paula Rea Radisich, *Hubert Robert: Painted Spaces of the Enlightenment* (London: Cambridge University Press, 1998), 22; on Geoffrin's Monday's, 22–26.

41. Ibid., 23.

42. Dena Goodman, *The Republic of Letters: A Cultural History of the French Enlightenment* (Ithaca: Cornell University Press, 1994), 89.

43. *Observations d'une société d'amateurs, sur les tableaux exposés au salon cette année* (Paris: 1761), 10–11 (Deloynes Collection, vol. 7, no. 94).

44. In Genlis's *Adelaide and Theodore,* the novel *Zayde* is one that girls at the age of thirteen are allowed to read with their mothers. At a later age, when their minds have been properly formed and not "turned by foolish Romances," they can read *Zayde* alone and "without danger" (3: 169, 172).

45. Elie Catherine Fréron, *L'année littéraire,* 16 vols. (Paris: Mériot, 1751–89), vol. 6 (1755): 71.

46. Denis Diderot, "Notice sur Carle van Loo," in *Oeuvres complètes,* 13: 476.

47. The work was originally published with Jean Regnauld de Segrais as its author and with a preface by Pierre-Daniel Huet. However, both Segrais and Huet admitted in their memoirs that Mme de La Fayette was the true author. The *Segraisiana* (Segrais's memoirs) was published in 1723, and an edition of his memoirs appeared in 1755. See DeJean, *Tender Geographies,* 169–70. Also, in an article devoted to the possible transformation of a scene from *Zayde* into a theatrical performance, the *Correspondence littéraire* noted in May 1755 (3: 28–31) that Mme de La Fayette authored the novel and that Segrais aided its composition.

48. DeJean, *Tender Geographies,* 173–74.

49. Pierre-Daniel Huet, *Traité des origine des romans* (1799; reprint, Geneva: Slatkine, 1970), 3.

50. Ibid., 127.

51. Goodman, *The Republic of Letters,* 76.

52. Radisich, *Hubert Robert: Painted Spaces of the Enlightenment,* 34–45.

53. Goodman, *The Republic of Letters,* 102.

54. Pierre-Daniel Huet, *Traité des origine des romans,* 122.

55. DeJean, *Tender Geographies,* 174.

56. As quoted in Goodman, *The Republic of Letters,* 89.

57. Mary Vidal, "Style as Subject in Watteau's Images of Conversation" in *The Cambridge Companion to Watteau,* ed. Mary D. Sheriff (forthcoming). For a more extended discussion of this topic, see Mary Vidal, *Watteau's Painted*

Conversations: Art, Literature and Talk in Seventeenth- and Eighteenth-Century France (New Haven: Yale University Press, 1992).

58. See, for example, Masaccio's *Expulsion from the Garden* (1426–27; Florence: Santa Maria del Carmine, Brancacci Chapel).

59. Jean Mainil, *Dans les règles du plaisir: Théorie de la différence dans le discours obscène, romanesque et médical de l'ancien régime* (Paris: Éditions Kimé, 1996), 50. Mainil outlines the ridicule and disapproval that met women interested in science and discusses women's response to attempts to keep them from this sort of learning.

60. Jacques Ferrand, *A Treatise on Lovesickness,* trans. and ed. Donald Beecher and Massimo Ciavolella (Syracuse: Syracuse University Press, 1990), 243.

61. Fénelon, *De l'éducation des filles,* 73.

62. Louise Florence Pétronille Tardieu d'Esclavelles, marquise de Lalive d'Epinay, *Les conversations d'Émilie* (Paris: Belin, 1782), 442–43.

63. Londa Schiebinger has an excellent account of women's scientific networks in *The Mind Has No Sex* (Cambridge, MA: Harvard University Press, 1989), 37–65. Popular scientific writings, for example, Bernard de Bouvier de Fontenelle's *Conversations on the Plurality of Worlds* (1686) addressed themselves to women. Physics and astronomy, moreover, were common aristocratic pastimes and entertainments. See Barbara Stafford, *Artful Science* (Cambridge, MA: MIT Press, 1994), 47–70. Moralists warned women particularly against the biological sciences, which raised issues of the body and sexuality. Women, however, were dissuaded from the study of any science if pursued too seriously or too abstractly.

64. Anne Thérèse Marguenat de Courcelles, marquise de Lambert, *Réflexions sur les femmes* (Paris, 1828), 106.

65. Molière, *Les femmes savantes* (Paris: Comédie-Française, 1978), 9.

66. See infra, 164. On the relation between the Pygmalion theme and materialism, see J. L. Carr, "Pygmalion and the Philosophes," *Journal of the Warburg and Courtauld Institutes* 23 (1960): 239–55; and Suzanne Pucci, "Metaphor and Metamorphosis in Diderot's *Le rêve de d'Alembert:* Pygmalion 'Materialized,'" *Symposium* 35 (1981–82): 325–40.

67. André-François Boureau-Deslandes, *Pigmalion; ou, La statue animée* (Berlin, 1753), 48.

68. Ibid., 50.

69. Ibid., 66–67.

70. Genlis even includes a discussion of hypocritical learned ladies in her *Adelaide and Theodore* of 1783, mentioning how Molière ridiculed the learned women of his age, but "at least they knew something." Her learned women think themselves wits and scholars; they respond to the reading of a play with "enthusiastic" and "passionate" gestures and piercing voices. Genlis goes on to compare learned women to devotees in their hypocrisy. Genlis, *Adelaide and Theodore,* 1: 157–63.

71. Roussel, *Système physique et morale de la femme,* 101–4. Genlis echoes this opinion but without the "medical" authority, noting in *Adelaide and Theodore* that it is dangerous to "inflame the minds of women, or raise them above themselves." She goes on to say that "a taste for learning makes them appear singular, and deprives them of that domestic simplicity and tenderness, and of that society of which they are so great an ornament" (1: 29). And later, "Do not imagine, Madame, that my intention is to make Adelaide learned; you know my sentiments in that respect, which are not at all changed" (3: 143).

72. See, for example, Martha Wolff, "An Early Painting by Greuze and Its Literary Associations," *Burlington Magazine* 138 (September 1996): 583.

73. Many have suggested that *La philosophie endormie* is a portrait of Mme Greuze, associating it with an image Greuze exhibited at the Salon of 1765. See, for example, John Goodman's translation of the "Salon of 1765" in *Diderot on Art. I* (New Haven: Yale University Press, 1995), 102, and fig. 29. Wolff has disputed this claim, pointing out that in describing the portrait of Mme Greuze exhibited in 1765, critics noted that the figure was smiling and teasing the dog. Wolff, "An Early Painting by Greuze and Its Literary Associations," 583.

74. We know from his correspondence that Diderot wrote his *Le rêve de d'Alembert* (*D'Alembert's Dream*) in 1769. At first, the work was known only to a small circle of close associates, and from there it seems to have circulated unpublished. It was not published until 1830.

75. Denis Diderot, *Le rêve de d'Alembert,* in *Oeuvres complètes,* 17: 127–28.

76. Diderot uses his contemporaries as characters in this dialogue. Julie de Lespinasse (1732–76) was one of the most important *salonnières* in Paris. She was the niece of Mme du Deffand, who hosted a celebrated salon. Later, Mme Geoffrin befriended her and made Lespinasse her protégé and successor. Lespinasse was also d'Alembert's companion. Dr. Bordeu is Théophile Bordeu (1722–76), a renowned doctor and a Montpellier Vitalist.

77. Diderot, *Le rêve de d'Alembert,* 17: 129.

78. Diderot, "Salon de 1767," in *Oeuvres complètes,* 16: 230.

79. Ibid., 16: 232.

80. Nicolas Le Camus de Mézières, *The Genius of Architecture,* 115.

81. Le Camus de Mézières also argues for a circular plan through this analogy: "Consider a beautiful woman. Her outlines are gentle and well rounded; the muscles are not pronounced; the whole is governed by a simple, natural sweetness, whose effect we recognize better than we can express it; this stems from a tender quality that is already apparent in the cradle" (117).

82. Ibid., 116.

83. Rochelle Ziskin, *The Place Vendôme: Architecture and Social Mobility in Eighteenth-Century Paris* (New York: Cambridge University Press, 1999), 151–52.

84. I am grateful to Cynthia Bland for this suggestion.

85. Joan DeJean, "Introduction to Prévost's *The Story of a Greek Woman,*" in *The Libertine Reader* (New York: Zone Books, 1997), 546.

86. Boudier de Villemert, *Le nouvel ami des femmes; ou, La philosophie du sexe,* 128.

87. Darnton notes that the title echoes a key work of the early Enlightenment, *Le philosophe,* which appeared anonymously in 1743. The *Encyclopédie* absorbed its text, and Voltaire later republished it. *Le philosophe* presents the ideal type of the freethinker who exposes everything, and especially church doctrines, to critical reason. Darnton, *The Forbidden Best-Sellers of Pre-Revolutionary France,* 107.

88. Ibid., 96–100.

89. *Thérèse Philosophe,* 601.

90. Ibid., 614. Erotic fiction, like erotic images, exalt the pleasures of masturbation, although some have claimed that pornographic books usually presented female masturbation not as an end, but as a substitute for or prelude to heterosexual intercourse. True as this may be, it is difficult to envision a scene of female masturbation that did not transgress prevailing moral norms, and

sometimes these scenes are played to travesty both sexual morality and aesthetic appreciation.

91. Ibid., 615.

92. Here I agree with Darnton's reading of the novel. Given the possibilities and strictures of the mid-eighteenth century, *Thérèse Philosophe* departs considerably from the general norms for sexual conduct.

93. *Thérèse Philosophe,* 656.

94. Ibid., 655.

95. Ibid., 655–56.

96. Darnton, *The Forbidden Best-Sellers of Pre-Revolutionary France,* 111. Mainil, in contrast, has argued not only that books like *Thérèse Philosophe* were read and enjoyed by women but also that they were intentionally aimed at readers of both sexes. Yet for Mainil, forbidden books offered the pleasures of illicit reading only to enforce an acceptable sexual regime. In the case of *Thérèse Philosophe,* he sees that regime as heterosexual. *Thérèse Philosophe,* therefore, can (must?) be read as an invitation to penetration, which the novel also paints as a great danger (Mainil, *Dans les règles du plaisir,* 172). His analysis privileges pliant readers over both resisting ones and those with decided (even deviant) tastes who select the works that satisfy them. It also overlooks how significant it is that the novel embraces *any* form of birth control. While the heterosexual imperative in *Thérèse Philosophe* is strong, and while the novel does not urge complete sexual freedom, it does raise transgressive possibilities. And if vaginal penetration by a man's penis is privileged because Thérèse embraces it in the end, vaginal penetration by a dildo or by an adept finger—be it her own or that of a partner—is also presented as a positive pleasure for women throughout the novel.

97. Darnton, *The Forbidden Best-Sellers of Pre-Revolutionary France,* 114.

98. Diderot, *Le rêve de d'Alembert,* 17: 200.

99. Ibid., 17: 201.

100. By all accounts, Mlle de Lespinasse was herself horrified when she learned in 1769 that Diderot had written a dialogue in which dangerous opinions were put into her mouth and that this dialogue was making the rounds of polite society. On behalf of Mlle de Lespinasse as well as in his own interests, d'Alembert asked Diderot to destroy the manuscript. Evidently Lespinasse felt that such a public representation, even in a work of fiction, was too damaging. The demand for "modesty" fell even on women who frequented elite and intellectual society, women who might think like Thérèse and even seek their sexual pleasures outside the marriage bed. And it is notable that real women who had some claim to the title *femme philosophe* were careful to show themselves, and have themselves depicted, as modest. Few had the power to flaunt their sexual or intellectual enthusiasms.

CHAPTER 4

I am greatly indebted to my colleague Eric Downing for his careful, insightful, and immensely helpful comments on this chapter.

1. La Mettrie, *Machine Man,* 29.

2. Samuel-Auguste-David Tissot, *L'onanisme: Dissertation sur les maladies produites par le masturbation,* 10th enlarged ed. (Toulouse: Laporte, 1775), 80.

3. "Manstupration ou Manustupration," in *Encyclopédie,* 10: 51.

4. Ibid.

5. "Fureur utérine, nymphomania, furor uterinus," in *Encyclopédie,* 7: 377.

6. Ibid., 7: 378.

7. Ibid., 7: 380.

8. Ibid., 7: 377.

9. It is also interesting to note that this moral code for women, which requires their modesty, the *Encyclopédie* attributes to woman's need to attract men, who like to overcome obstacles opposed to their desires.

10. "Satyriasis," in *Encyclopédie,* 14: 703.

11. Ibid.

12. Ibid.

13. "Mélancholie," in *Encyclopédie,* 10: 308.

14. "Fureur utérine," in *Encyclopédie,* 7: 378.

15. Bienville assumed a physiology slightly different from that which supported the account of nymphomania in the *Encyclopédie,* and he believed women did, in fact, release fluids when sexually aroused. It is interesting that this difference in physiology did not l ead Bienville to conclusions that diverged substantially from those in the *Encyclopédie.* On this difference, see Jean Marie Goulemot, "Prêtons le main de la nature. II. Fureurs utérines," *Dix-Huitième Siècle* 12 (1980): 103, 108–9.

16. D. T. Bienville, *La nymphomanie; ou, Traité de la fureur utérine* (Amsterdam: Marc-Michel Rey, 1778), xvi.

17. Ibid., 13–14.

18. Ibid., 14–17.

19. Ibid., 89.

20. Tissot, *L'onanisme,* 51–52.

21. Bienville, *La nymphomanie,* 144. According to Bienville, imagination has great force in love, and those with lively imaginations are more susceptible to nymphomania.

22. Tissot, *L'onanisme,* 47–48. Bienville outlines several case studies that show the terrible condition to which women are reduced in nymphomania. See especially the story of Eleanor, Mlle de *** in *La nymphomanie,* 105–16.

23. Bienville, *La nymphomanie,* 12.

24. Bienville mentions treating women who for a long time hid the disease even from their doctors. He recalls that one claimed that she had succeeded in fooling her physicians and imagined that she could do the same with him, telling him in advance that he would not succeed better than his predecessors in giving her relief. *La nymphomanie,* 60–61.

25. Diderot, "Salon de 1769," in *Oeuvres complètes,* 16: 582.

26. If Jeurat's convalescing woman shares a pose and expression with Baudouin's reader, her demeanor is decidedly different both from that of the man depicted in Herbert Gravelot and Pierre Choffard's engraving, *The Amusements of a Convalescent* (Bibliothèque Nationale de France) and from the new mother shown in Jeaurat's *Recovering after Childbirth* (1744; St. Petersburg: Hermitage). In the first example, we see a gentleman in his dressing gown seated at a desk that is set before a fireplace and bookshelf. His activity and pose suggest he is seriously concentrating on whatever he writes, and there is no hint of excitement or enthusiasm, sexual or otherwise. The cello and writing instruments near him and the books that neatly line the shelf behind (no *beau désordre* here) point to a quiet, contemplative life given over to the pleasures of one's own study. In the second example, a young woman sits bundled up before a fireplace holding her fan in both hands. She neither leans back voluptuously, nor expresses passion. In fact, she stares vacantly as if still dazed from her wrenching experience. A maid has entered the room and is pouring her a cup of what might be either water or

milk. The pitcher the maid holds is the sort of utensil used for such liquids, and clearly not a teapot, coffee urn, or *chocolatière.* There is no interaction between the two women; the maid watches her work as the lady stares off into space.

27. Laurinda Dixon, *Perilous Chastity: Women and Illness in Pre-Enlightenment Art and Medicine* (Ithaca: Cornell University Press, 1995).

28. Bienville, *La nymphomanie,* quotations on 14, 16, 55, 18, 65, 77, and 75.

29. Pierre Rosenberg, *The Age of Louis XV: French Painting, 1710–1774* (Toledo, OH: Toledo Museum of Art, 1975), 22.

30. For example, see Bertin's *Bacchus and Ariadne* (1710–15; Saint-Etienne: Musée d'Art et d'Industrie).

31. Denis Diderot, "Salon of 1765," in *Oeuvres complètes,* 14: 194.

32. For a fuller discussion of Watelet, see Mary Sheriff, *J. H. Fragonard: Art and Eroticism* (Chicago: University of Chicago Press, 1990), 147–48.

33. This work is illustrated in Jean-François Heim, Claire Béraud, and Philippe Heim, *Les salons de peinture de la Révolution française, 1789–1799* (Paris: C.A.C. Sarl, 1989), 137.

34. See infra 64–65, 69–70.

35. Diderot, "Salon de 1767," in *Oeuvres complètes,* 16: 358.

36. Ibid.

37. Ibid., 16: 358–59.

38. Ibid., 16: 359.

39. Cahusac, "Enthousiasme," in *Encyclopédie,* 5: 721.

40. Ovid (Publius Ovidius Naso), *Metamorphoses, Books 9–10,* trans. Frank Justus Miller (Harvard: Harvard University Press, 1984), 83.

41. Ibid.

42. On the relation between Pygmalion and Orpheus, see Simone Vairre, "Pygmalion et Orphée chez Ovide," *Revue des Études Latines* 46 (1965): 235–47.

43. Boureau-Deslandes, *Pigmalion; ou, La statue animé* (Paris: Belin, 1742), 15–16. David Freedberg, in *The Power of Images* (Chicago: University of Chicago Press, 1989), 317–44, records an entire tradition of what he calls "arousal by image."

44. The story from Pliny is translated in Étienne Falconet, "Traduction du trente-quatrième livre de Pline," in *Oeuvres complètes,* 1:174–75.

45. Vairre, "Pygmalion et Orphée chez Ovide," 237. Jean de Marconville repeats this interpretation of Venus in his 1564 *De la bonté et mauvaiseté des femmes* (1564; reprint, Paris: Côté-Femmes, 1991), 123.

46. Abbé Géraud de La Chau, *Dissertation sur les attributs de Vénus* (Paris: Imprimerie de Prault, 1776), 20.

47. There are many erotic and titillating works that play on (woman's) sexual involvement with statues. Take, for example, the engraving *Scrupulous Nymphs* after Nicolas Lavreince (c. 1780), the various painted and engraved versions of Jean Fréderic Schall's *The Comparison* (Paris: Musée du Louvre) or the anonymous *Hymn to Priapus* from *The Patriotic Brothel Instituted by the Queen of France for the Pleasures of the Deputies of the New Legislature* (1791).

48. Diderot, "Salon de 1767," in *Oeuvres complètes,* 16: 289–90.

49. For a discussion of this treatise and other works related to Ferrand, see the introductory material to Ferrand's treatise in Ferrand, *A Treatise on Lovesickness,* esp. 98–138.

50. Ibid., 375.

51. Ibid., 260. Attention to the statue lover persisted in the medical and

psychiatric literature into the nineteenth century. The psychiatrist Étienne Esquirol (1772–1840) included in his treatise on mental alienation an erotomania directed toward an inanimate object. As examples of those suffering from this erotomania, Esquirol cited Alkidias of Rhodes who was taken with an erotic delirium for the statue of Cupid of Praxiteles. *Des maladies mentales,* 2 vols. (1838; reprint, New York: Arno Press, 1976), 2: 47.

52. On Pygmalion's narcissism, see infra, 182–83.

53. Kenneth Gross, *The Dream of the Moving Statue* (Ithaca: Cornell University Press, 1992), 82.

54. Rameau, "Pigmalion, Acte de Ballet," in *Fragments représentés devant le roi à Fontainebleau le 12 octobre 1754* (Paris, 1754), 35; Boureau-Deslandes, *Pigmalion; ou, La statue animé,* vi; Sulpice Edme Gaubier de Barrault, *Brioché; ou, L'origine des marionettes* (Paris, 1753), 13–17.

55. Bienville, *La nymphomanie,* 18.

56. Antoine Houdar de La Motte, *Le triomphe des arts. Ballet en cinq entrées* (Paris, 1700), 303–4.

57. La Chau, *Dissertation sur les attributs de Vénus,* 57. Also of interest is Abbé Banier's prose translation of the opening lines of the story, which refer to the Propoetides: "[E]lle [Venus] allume dans leur coeur le feu de l'impudicité, & elles donnèrent à l'univers l'exemple d'un affreux débordement. Pygmalion témoin de déréglement de Propoétides conçut tant d'horreur pour un sexe qu'un malheureux penchant rend esclave de tant de foiblesses, qu'il résolut de vivre dans le célibat." In *Les metamorphoses d'Ovide en Latin et en François de la traduction M. l'Abbé Banier,* 4 vols. (Paris: Delalain, 1769), 3: 215.

58. Ovid, *Metamorphoses, Books 9–10,* 81–82.

59. Voltaire, "L'origine des métiers," in *Oeuvres complètes de Voltaire,* 10: 48–49.

60. For example, in Hesiod's *Work and Days* and *Theogony* it is Hephaestus who fashions Pandora according to Zeus's command, and it is Epimetheus, Prometheus's brother, who invites Pandora into his home as his wife.

61. Jean-Pierre Vernant, "At Man's Table: Hesiod's Foundation Myth of Sacrifice," in *The Cuisine of Sacrifice among the Greeks,* ed. Marcel Detienne and Jean-Pierre Vernant, trans. Paula Wissing (Chicago: University of Chicago Press, 1989), 62.

62. Ibid., 66.

63. Hesiod's view of women has an interesting resonance with eighteenth-century commentaries. In his *Réflexions sur l'amour* of 1780, the comte de M. points out that contact with women leads to the loss of vital force, unhealthy languor, and premature aging. Women, moreover, are gluttons who will take the food right out of a man's mouth. See Kay Wilkins, "Attitudes toward Women in Two Periodicals," *Studies in Eighteenth-Century Culture* 6 (1978): 398.

64. La Motte, *Le triomphe des arts,* 300.

65. "Fureur utérine," in *Encyclopédie,* 7: 380. The tale of Messalina was also repeated by Marconville, who notes that Messalina, wife of the emperor Claudius, outdid all other dishonest women throughout history in impudicity and dishonor. One day she went into a bordello and challenged the most renowned courtesan to a contest of debauchery. Messalina won, having endured the lubricious company of twenty-five ruffians more than this courtesan could endure. And the courtesan afterward withdrew from the bordello and avoided the company of men. Marconville, *De la bonté et mauvaiseté des femmes,* 124.

66. Tissot, *L'onanisme,* 88.

67. See below 175–79. Also, see La Fontaine's fable no. 6, "Le statuaire et la statue de Jupiter," in which he writes "Pygmalion becomes the lover/Of the Venus that he fathered."

68. Ferrand, *A Treatise on Lovesickness,* 260.

69. Stephen Owen, *Mi-Lou: Poetry and the Labyrinth of Desire* (Cambridge, MA: Harvard University Press, 1989), 72.

70. Friedrich Nietzsche, *The Genealogy of Morals,* trans. Horace B. Samuel, in *The Complete Works of Friedrich Nietzsche* (Edinburgh and London: T. N. Foulis, 1910), 13: 131. Many thanks to Eric Downing for bringing this quotation to my attention.

71. See, for example, J. Hillis Miller, *Versions of Pygmalion* (Cambridge, MA: Harvard University Press, 1990).

72. Wilhelm Jensen, *Gradiva* in Sigmund Freud, *Delusions and Dreams,* trans. Helen M. Downey (New York: Moffat, Yard and Company, 1917), 102.

73. Ibid., 108.

74. "A psychiatrist would perhaps place Norbert Hanold's delusion in the great group of 'paranoia' and possibly describe it as 'fetishistic erotomania,' because the most striking thing about it was his being in love with the piece of sculpture and because in the psychiatrist's view, with its tendency to coarsen everything, the young archaeologist's interest in feet and the postures of feet would be bound to suggest 'fetishism.' Nevertheless, all such systems of nomenclature and classification of the different kinds of delusion according to their subject-matter have something precarious and barren about them." Sigmund Freud, *Delusions and Dreams in Jensen's Gradiva (1907 [1906])* in *The Standard Edition of the Complete Psychological Works of Sigmund Freud,* trans. James Strachey in collaboration with Anna Freud, 24 vols. (London: Hogarth, 1953–74), 9: 45.

75. Ibid., 9: 31.

76. One of the most compelling studies of Freud's aesthetic is Sarah Kofman, *L'enfance de l'art* (Paris: Éditions Galilée, 1970).

77. Freud, *Delusions and Dreams,* 9.

78. Ibid., 92.

79. Ibid., 131.

80. Ibid.

81. "Neurotics live in a world apart." Sigmund Freud, *Totem and Taboo,* trans. James Strachey (New York: W.W. Norton, 1950), 86.

82. Ibid., 83.

83. Ibid., 86.

84. Ibid., 90.

85. Sigmund Freud, *Civilization and Its Discontents,* trans. James Strachey, with an intro. by Peter Gay (New York: W.W. Norton), 22–36.

86. Ibid., 59.

87. Sarah Kofman, *The Enigma of Woman,* trans. Catherine Porter (Ithaca: Cornell University Press, 1985), 220.

88. Sigmund Freud, "Essay on Femininity," in *New Introductory Lectures on Psychoanalysis,* trans. James Strachey (New York: W.W. Norton, 1964), 117.

89. Kofman, *Enigma,* 218–22.

90. This quotation from a review in the *San Francisco Chronicle* appears on the cover of the paperback edition of Barry Unsworth, *Stone Virgin* (New York:

W.W. Norton, 1995). Also on the cover we learn that Unsworth is a winner of the Booker Prize.

91. Ibid., 291.

92. Ibid., 229.

93. Litsov, too, meets a bad end in the novel, murdered by an unnamed hand. Suspicion falls on his wife, at least as an accomplice, but an art dealer who has made fraudulent use of Litsov's art seems the most likely perpetrator. While an art dealer has likely killed Litsov, a Venetian senator from a rich noble family—the aptly named Fornarini family—has framed the Renaissance sculptor for daring to possess sexually the model, Bianca, who was Federico Fornarini's "whore." Fornarini insures that the artist faces execution and thus engineers the artist's "murder." That Litsov's wife, Chiara, is both a descendent of the Fornarini family and her husband's model further ties together the Renaissance and modern plots. Another recent rewriting of the Pygmalion myth is Richard Powers's *Galatea 2.2* (1995), in which a cognitive neurologist creates a thinking machine called Galatea. The cover for the novel illustrates Raphael's portrait of his mistress, La Fornarina.

94. Unsworth, *Stone Virgin*, 290–91.

95. Ibid., 298.

CHAPTER 5

1. Anotine Houdar de La Motte, *Le triomphe des arts. Ballet en cinq entrées*, 302; and Rameau, "Pigmalion, acte de ballet," 36.

2. Ovid, *Metamorphoses, Books 9–10*, 85. Here is how Banier rendered the scene: "De retour chez lui, Pygmalion va voir sa chère statue, s'assied auprès d'elle, la baise, & il lui paroît qu'elle a quelque sentiment. Il la baise un second fois & il apperçoit que l'yvoire s'amollit, & que sa du reté se prête à la main qui la touche." Banier, *Les metamorphoses d'Ovide*, 3: 215.

3. As in most painted representations, the statue seems carved from white marble.

4. Descartes, *The Passions of the Soul*, 58.

5. Honoré Balzac, "Le chef-d'oeuvre inconnu," in *L'chef d'oeuvre inconnu, Gambara, Massimilla Doni* (Paris: Flammarion, 1981), 69.

6. The pertinent figure is the Medusa head that turns men to stone. The severed head at once raises the specter of castration and allays castration anxiety because it turns the body hard, a process Freud likens to having an erection.

7. See *Les peintres du roi, 1648–1793* (Paris: Réunion des Musées Nationaux, 2000), 136.

8. Thomas Christiensen has suggested that Rameau's opera *Pygmalion* demonstrates his theory of harmony, the *corps sonore*. For Christiensen, this observation does not imply the work was written primarily to exemplify a theory. Nevertheless, as Christiensen points out, Rameau often referred to the opera and used parts of it as examples in his later theoretical writings. Thomas Christensen, *Rameau and Musical Thought in the Enlightenment* (New York: Cambridge University Press, 1993), 218–31. The opera was an undeniable success, staged in Paris more than a hundred times between 1748 and 1781, with additional performances for Louis XV's court at Fontainebleau.

9. J. Van der Veen, *Le mélodrame musical de Rousseau au romantisme* (The Hague: Martinus Nijhoff, 1955), 5–7.

10. Ibid., 13–21.

11. Jean-Jacques Rousseau, "Récitatif obligé," in *Dictionnaire de musique*, in

Oeuvres complètes de J.-J. Rousseau mises dans un nouvel ordre, avec des notes historique et des éclaircissements, ed. Victor Donatien Musset-Pathay, 22 vols. (Paris: P. Dupont, 1823–26), 13: 128.

12. On the relation between the Pygmalion theme and materialism, see Carr, "Pygmalion and the Philosophes"; and Pucci, "Metaphor and Metamorphosis in Diderot's *Le rêve de d'Alembert,*" 325–40.

13. Boureau-Deslandes, *Pigmalion; ou, La statue animée,* iii.

14. Ibid., 35–36.

15. Ibid., 17.

16. For a parallel reading of Diderot's commentary on Falconet's sculpture, see Suzanne Pucci's important new study, *Sites of the Spectator: Emerging Literary and Cultural Practice in Eighteenth-Century France* (Oxford: Voltaire Foundation, 2001): 91–96. Pucci's analysis is especially impressive in relating Diderot's text to a structure of beholding that she interprets throughout his Salon criticism. Her analysis of Pygmalion develops her earlier essay, "Metaphor and Metamorphosis in Diderot's *Le rêve de d'Alembert.*"

17. There is a smaller version of this group in the Walters Art Gallery in Baltimore, which Louis Réau believed was the one that appeared in the Salon. Louis Réau, *Étienne-Maurice Falconet,* 2 vols. (Paris: Demotte, 1922), 1: 212–15.

18. Ovid, *Metamorphoses, Books 9–10,* 83. The Banier translation also stresses this aspect of Galatea as statue: "vous eussiez dit qu'elle étoit animée & qu'il n'y avoit que la pudeur & cet te retenue qui sied bien au sexe, que l'empêchassent de se mouvoir, tant l'art étoit finement caché & imitoit de près la nature." *Les metamorphoses d'Ovide,* 3: 215. And when Galatea does come to life, Pygmalion's transports are no longer "pour une statue, mais pour une belle fille, qui rougit & qui ouvrant pour la premiere fois des yeux timides, voit en même temps la lumiere & son amant (3: 218–19).

19. Denis Diderot, "Salon de 1763," in *Oeuvres complètes,* 13: 409.

20. Ibid.

21. Ibid., 13: 410.

22. Ibid.

23. Voltaire, *Pandore, opéra en cinq actes,* in *Oeuvres complètes de Voltaire* (Paris: Garnier Frères, 1877), 2: 571–600.

24. Ibid., 2: 579.

25. Diderot, "Salon de 1763," in *Oeuvres complètes,* 13: 410.

26. Ibid.

27. As Pucci points out, Grimm was not as taken with Falconet's work as his friend Diderot, and as editor of the *Correspondence littéraire* he inserted his own brief comment into Diderot's text. Following Lessing, Grimm emphasized that sculpture was restricted to a single temporal moment. Pucci, *Sites of the Spectator,* 93.

28. Diderot, "Salon de 1763," in *Oeuvres complètes,* 13: 411.

29. Ovid, *Metamorphoses, Books 9–10,* 85. In the Banier translation: "Étonné & interdit, il n'ose se livrer tout entier à la joie, & craint de se tromper." *Les metamorphoses d'Ovide,* 3: 217.

30. Diderot, "Salon de 1763," in *Oeuvres complètes,* 13: 411.

31. The similarities between these two works were noted by George Levitine, *The Sculpture of Falconet* (Greenwich, CT: New York Graphic Society, 1972), 34–35.

32. Diderot, "Salon de 1763," in *Oeuvres complètes,* 13: 409–10.

33. In contemporary sales catalogs, the work was alternately titled *Garde à vous* and *Soyez discret,* suggesting an essential ambiguity. Réau, *Étienne-Maurice Falconet,* 1: 183.

34. Fragonard represented Falconet's *Menacing Cupid* as functioning in just this way in *The Swing* (1767; London: Wallace Collection). There Cupid takes his place as an actor and as garden sculpture set into an erotic scene. Falconet's *Menacing Cupid* is also related to the many semi-animated statues that appeared in works throughout the eighteenth century, for example, in Watteau's *The Champs Elysées* (c. 1717–18; London: Wallace Collection) or Greuze's *Votive Offering to Cupid* (c. 1765–69; London: Wallace Collection).

35. Étienne Falconet, "Sur la sculpture," in *Oeuvres complètes,* 3: 25.

36. Ibid., 3: 3.

37. Ibid., 3: 4. Falconet's desire for a lifelike sculpture was hardly unique or new. We find it, for example, in Callistratus's *Descriptions,* a work Falconet cited as admirable. Dating to the latter part of third century A.D.E., the *Descriptions* are a collection of fourteen ekphrases on antique sculptures, and all of them play on the lifelikeness of the works. For example, in imagining Scopas's *Bacchante,* Callistratus suggests that the sculptor transforms a piece of Parian marble into a real Bacchante, whose face shows sense perception although no perception is truly present, whose body is both soft flesh and hard stone, and who can leap in Bacchic dance although she has no power to move (Callistratus, *Descriptions,* in *Philostratus Imagines, Callistratus Descriptions,* trans. Arthur Fairbanks [Cambridge, MA: Harvard University Press, 1960], 381). Callistratus particularly praises Scopas's ability to render different sorts of flesh from a single material (383). Echoing Callistratus, we find Diderot praising Falconet's group: "Le faire du groupe entier est admirable. C'est une matière une dont la statuaire a tiré trois sortes de chairs différentes." Diderot, "Salon de 1763," in *Oeuvres complètes,* 13: 246.

38. Falconet, "Sur la sculpture," in *Oeuvres complètes,* 3: 23.

39. Ibid., 3: 7.

40. Ibid., 3: 5.

41. Diderot, "Salon de 1763," in *Oeuvres complètes,* 13: 409.

42. *Mercure de France* (November 1763), 208.

43. Ibid., 209.

44. M. Guichard, "À M. Falconet sur son Groupe de Pigmalion exposé cette année au Louvre," *Mercure de France* (October 1763), 19.

45. As quoted in Réau, *Étienne-Maurice Falconet,* 2: 207.

46. See infra. 136–140.

47. Denis Diderot, *Second entretien sur le fils naturel,* in *Oeuvres complètes,* 10: 99.

48. As quoted in Marie-Hélène Huet, *Monstrous Imagination* (Cambridge, MA: Harvard University Press, 1993), 7.

49. François-Marie-Pompée Colonne, *Les principes de la nature ou de la generation des choses* (Paris: André Cailleau, 1731), 230.

50. Ibid., 231.

51. Barnabé-Firmin de Rosoi, *Pygmalion. Drame lyrique en un acte et en prose* (Paris: La Veuve Ballard et Fils, 1780), 16.

52. Denis Diderot, *Le pour et le contre,* in*Oeuvres complètes,* 15: 19. The entire section reads as follows: "Pourriez-vous bien me dire, mais là, en votre âme et conscience, comme si vous étiez devant Dieu, que la trompette sonnât, que nous l'entendissions tous deux et je pusse lire au fond de votre coeur, si tandis que

moi qui ne regretterais ni un louis, ni deux, ni trois, ni quatre (voilà mes moyens) pour rendre votre Pigmalion et plusieurs de vos ouvrages à jamais invulnérables par la main de temps, vous ne donneriez pas tant, vous qui en êtes le père et qui devez avoir des entrailles; un écu pour assurer la même prérogative à ces précieux enfants-là?"

53. Michel de Montaigne, "Of the Affection of Fathers for Their Children," in *The Complete Essays of Montaigne,* trans. Donald M. Frame (Stanford: Stanford University Press, 1958), 293. For a discussion of this text and its relation to the Pygmalion theme, see Patrick Henry, "Montaigne and Pygmalion," and Jerome Schwartz, "Narcisse et Pygmalion—deux moments dans la mythologie personnelle de Montaigne," in *Montaigne and the Gods,* ed. Daniel Martin (Amherst, MA: Hestia Press, 1993).

54. Montaigne, "Of the Affection of Fathers for Their Children," 291.

55. Ibid., 291.

56. Voltaire, *Pandore,* in *Oeuvres complètes de Voltaire,* 2: 575 and 577.

57. Voltaire, "Letters," in *Les oeuvres complètes de Voltaire,* ed. Theodore Besterman et. al., 135 vols. (Geneva: Institut et Musée Voltaire, 1970), 95: 151–56. For a further analysis of this correspondence, see Sheriff, *The Exceptional Woman,* 41.

58. Voltaire to the comte d'Argental, 4 September 1749, in *Les oeuvres complètes de Voltaire,* 95: 151.

59. Voltaire to the abbé de Voisenon, 4 September 1749, in *Les oeuvres complètes de Voltaire,* 95: 155.

60. Voltaire to the marquis d'Argenson, 4 September 1749, in *Les Oeuvres complètes de Voltaire,* 95: 151.

61. This is a central argument in her work. Huet, *Monstrous Imagination.*

62. Falconet to Diderot, 10 February 1766, in *Le pour et le contre* in *Oeuvres complètes,* 15: 23.

63. Ibid., 15: 22.

64. Diderot, "Salon de 1763," in *Oeuvres complètes,* 13: 411.

65. Diderot, "Salon de 1765," in *Oeuvres complètes,* 14: 280.

66. As quoted in Réau, *Étienne-Maurice Falconet,* 207.

67. *Correspondance littéraire, philosophique et critique par Grimm, Diderot, Raynal, Meister, etc.,* ed. Maurice Tourneux, 16 vols. (Paris: Garnier Frères, 1877–82), 11: 139–40.

68. Editor's note, *Oeuvres complètes de J.-J. Rousseau,* new ed. (1792), 18: s.p.

69. J.-J. Rousseau, *Pygmalion,* in *Oeuvres complètes,* ed. Bernard Gagnebin and Marcel Raymond, 4 vols. (Paris: Éditions Gallimard, 1959–69), 2: 1225. For important interpretations of the piece, see Paul de Man, *Allegories of Reading* (New Haven: Yale University Press, 1979), 160–87; Jean Starobinski, *Jean-Jacques Rousseau: Transparency and Obstruction,* trans. Arthur Goldhammer (Chicago: University of Chicago Press, 1988), 65–80; Louis Marin, "Le moi et les pouvoirs de l'image: Glose sur Pygmalion, scène lyrique (1772) de J.-J. Rousseau," *Modern Language Notes* 107 (1992): 659–72.

70. Rousseau, *Pygmalion,* in *Oeuvres complètes,* 2: 1224.

71. Ibid., 2: 1226.

72. Marin, "Le moi et les pouvoirs de l'image," 666–67.

73. Ibid. For a discussion of Pygmalion's "attack" on Galatea in an image by Francisco Goya, see the excellent article by John Ciafolo, "Unveiling Goya's Rape of Galatea," *Art History* 18 (1995): 477–98. See also de Man, 180–81.

74. Rousseau, *Pygmalion*, in *Oeuvres complètes*, 2: 1226.

75. Ibid., 2: 1227.

76. Ibid., 2: 1230–31. De Man in particular considers the meaning of this dialogue and the dialectic of self and other, *Allegories of Reading*, esp. 185 ff.

77. Condillac, *Traité des sensations*, in *Oeuvres completes*, 3: 88–89.

78. Rousseau, *Pygmalion*, in *Oeuvres complètes*, 2: 1226.

79. Ibid., 2: 1229.

80. Ibid., 2: 1228.

81. Ibid.

82. Diderot, *Le pour et le contre*, 15: 11.

83. Ibid., 15: 23.

84. Ibid.

85. See, for example, Leonard Barkin's perceptive analysis of Ovid's *Metamorphoses, The Gods Made Flesh: Metamorphosis and the Pursuit of Paganism* (New Haven: Yale University Press, 1986); and J. Hillis Miller's consideration of Pygmalion-like stories in *Versions of Pygmalion* (Cambridge, MA: Harvard University Press, 1990). Narcissus also eschewed real women, but he did not have the good sense to make one of his own, to freeze his ideal into a work of art.

86. For a reading of Narcissus's story as an allegory of painting's origin, see Leon Battista Alberti, *On Painting*, trans. and intro. John R. Spencer (New Haven: Yale University Press, 1966), 64.

87. Irigaray, *Speculum of the Other Woman.*

88. For example, in the opéra comique by Charles-François Panard (d. 1765) and Thomas L'Affichard, *Pigmalion; ou, La statue animée*, (Paris: Delormel, 1746), the statue (named Galantis) comes to life and Pygmalion's sister supervises her education. In learning how to make her toilette, Galantis becomes a coquette. She falls in love with her mirror, "which pleases her more than anything." Pygmalion asks Cupid to make his Galantis faithful, but not even the god of love has the power to fulfill this mission impossible. He tells Pygmalion that it's one thing to give Galantis feelings, and quite another to fix them. Much to Pygmalion's chagrin, his sister encourages this female vice, teaching Galantis that although a woman is allowed only one husband, "substitutes" are permissible. A good husband she defines as one who goes out often and makes a lot of noise in coming home. After such an education, Galantis is not true to Pygmalion.

89. Hubert Gravelot, Charles Nicholas Cochin, and Charles-Étienne Gaucher, *Iconologie par figures*, 4 vols. (1791; reprint, 4 vols. in 1, Geneva: Minkoff, 1972), 4: 81.

90. Falconet, "Sur la sculpture," in *Oeuvres complètes*, 3: 2.

91. Ibid., 3: 3.

92. Marc Furcy-Raynaud, "Correspondance du Comte d'Angiviller avec Pierre," *Nouvelles archives de l'art français. Receuil de documents inédits publiées par la Société de l'histoire de l'art français*, vol. 21 (1905; reprint, Paris: F. de Nobele, 1973), 80–81. On this project, see Francis H. Dowley, "D'Angiviller's Grands Hommes and the Significant Moment," *Art Bulletin* 39 (1957): 259–77; Andrew McClellan, "D'Angiviller's 'Great Men' of France and the Politics of the Parlements," *Art History* 13 (1990): 175–92. The full name of the comte d'Angiviller is Charles-Claude Flahaut, comte de la Billarderie d'Angiviller (1730–1810).

93. On this project, see Dena Goodman, "Pigalle's *Voltaire nu:* The Republic of Letters Represents Itself to the World," *Representations* 16 (1986): 86–110.

94. Cahusac, "Enthousiasme," in *Encyclopédie*, 5: 720.

95. Ibid., 5: 722.

96. In the *Phaedrus*, Plato gave true poetry a philosophical function that also opened onto social utility. "A third kind of possession or madness comes from the Muses. It takes hold upon a gentle virginal soul, awakens and inspires it to song and poetry and so, glorifying the innumerable deeds of our forefathers, educates posterity." Plato, *Phaedrus*, 26.

97. See infra, 50–52.

98. See infra, 144.

99. Diderot, "Salon de 1767," in *Oeuvres complètes*, 16: 290.

100. "Lettre à M. ***," *Mercure de France* (April 1734): 770–73. See also Émile Dacier, *Une danseuse de l'opéra sous Louis XV: Mlle Sallé, 1707–1756* (Paris, 1909; reprint, Geneva: Minkoff, 1972), esp. 141–72.

101. Sallé's contribution to dance history is brilliantly explicated in Susan Leigh Foster's work. See *Choreography and Narrative: Ballet's Staging of Story and Desire* (Bloomington: Indiana University Press, 1996), especially "Pygmalion's No-Body and the Body of Dance," 1–12, and "Dancing the Body Politic," in *From the Royal to the Republican Body: Incorporating the Political in Seventeenth- and Eighteenth-Century France*, ed. Sara E. Melzer and Kathryn Norberg (Berkeley: University of California Press, 1998), 162–81. Sarah Cohen also offers insightful analysis of Sallé and eighteenth-century dance in *Art, Dance, and the Body in French Culture of the Ancien Régime* (New York: Cambridge University Press, 2000).

102. "Lettre à M. ***," 772.

103. Foster analyzes Sallé's contribution in *Choreography and Narrative*, 1–12.

104. Foster, *Dancing the Body Politic*, 164.

105. "Lettre à M. ***," 771.

106. Ibid.

107. Cohen, *Art, Dance, and the Body in French Culture of the Ancien Régime*, 260.

108. Ibid.

109. Foster points out that eighteenth-century writers, such as Francesco Algarotti and Charles Compan, were apt to give Sallé credit for her invention, whereas contemporary dance history has largely ignored her. Foster, "Dancing the Body Politic," 180.

110. Cahusac, *La danse ancienne et moderne*, 3: 139.

111. Ibid., 1: 141.

112. Ibid., 3: 140–43.

113. Ibid., 3: 154.

114. Mlle Clairon, *Mémoires de Mlle Clairon* (Paris: Ponthieu, 1822; reprint, Geneva: Slatkine, 1968), 233–34.

115. Cohen, *Art, Dance, and the Body in French Culture of the Ancien Régime*, 261.

116. Ibid., 259–61.

117. Michel de Cubières-Palmézeaux, *Galatée, comédie* (Versailles: Blaizot, 1777).

118. For recent discussions of Françoise Raucourt, see Marie-Jo Bonnet, *Un choix sans équivoque* (Paris: Éditions Denoël, 1981), 107–65; and Lenard Berlanstein, "Women and Power in Eighteenth-Century France: Actresses at the Comédie Française," in *Visions and Revisions of Eighteenth-Century France*, ed.

Christine Adams, Jack R. Censer, and Lisa Jane Graham (University Park: Pennsylvania State University Press, 1997), 155–90.

119. *Correspondence littéraire,* 10: 138.

120. Ibid., 10: 140.

121. Ibid.

122. Ibid., 10: 141.

123. *Mémoires secrets pour servir à l'histoire de la République des Lettres en France depuis MDCCLXII jusqu'à nos jours ou Journal d'un observateur,* 36 vols. (London: J. Adamson, 1780–89), 7: 188.

124. *Correspondance littéraire,* 11: 80.

125. For consideration of Raucourt in the *Mémoires secrets,* see Bonnet, *Un choix sans équivoque,* 137–44.

126. *Mémoires secrets,* 8: 232.

127. *Correspondance littéraire,* 11: 141.

128. Ibid.

129. As quoted in Émile Gaboriau, *Les comédiennes adorées* (Paris: E. Dentu, 1843), 96.

130. *Correspondance littéraire,* 11: 159.

131. Rousseau, *Pygmalion,* in *Oeuvres complètes,* 2: 1230. In its review of the play, the *Correspondance littéraire* said only that Galatea approached a nearby statue.

132. See above, 113.

133. Jean-Jacques Rousseau, *Lettre à M. d'Alembert sur les spectacles* (Lille: Giard, 1948), 120–21. It is important to note that Rousseau also denigrated actors, and denigrated them precisely because in becoming actors they became effeminate, selling themselves in performance and losing the attributes of men.

134. *Correspondance littéraire,* 11: 274.

135. Réau, *Étienne-Maurice Falconet,* 2: 210–11.

136. "Lettre de Marmontel," *Nouvelles archives de l'art français. Receuil de documents inédits publiées par la Société de l'histoire de l'art français, année 1873* (1873; reprint, Paris: F. de Nobele, 1973), 386.

137. Ibid.

CHAPTER 6

1. Toward the end of the eighteenth century, French artists occasionally called on an ancient woman, Dibutadis, to perform as an allegory of painting's origin. See Sheriff, *The Exceptional Woman,* 73–74, 230–39.

2. Two books have brought our attention to Heloise. Charrier, *Héloïse dans l'histoire et dans la légende*; and Kamuf, *Fictions of Feminine Desire.* See also Bergman-Carton, *The Woman of Ideas in French Art, 1830–1848,* 126–29.

3. As quoted in P. Rosenberg and C. Bailey, "Not Greuze, but Bernard d'Agesci," *Burlington Magazine* (April 2001): 204. For the first discussion of this work as a Greuze, see Wolff, "An Early Painting by Greuze," 580–85. I am indebted to his essay for identifying the book as *L'art d'aimer.* See also Bernadette Fort, "Accessories of Desire," *Yale French Studies* 94 (1998): 146–62.

4. In dating the work to the late 1770s, Rosenberg and Bailey locate the work at an interesting moment in the history of the Heloise legend, which I discuss at length later in this chapter. By the 1770s, the Heloise presented in Colardeau's popular 1758 poetic recreation of the letters (a piece that reworks for a French audience Alexander Pope's condensation of the correspondence) had become

the standard. After Colardeau, many poets and amateurs took their turn at recreating the letters, with little variation in tone and mood. Although Rousseau's *Julie, ou La nouvelle Héloïse* (1761) was a roaring success by the time *A Lady Reading* was made, this painting makes clear that his novel did not eclipse Heloise's letters. Indeed, versions of her letters and legends appeared throughout the eighteenth century and continued into the nineteenth, as well.

5. Charles Le Brun, *L'expression des passions et autres conférences,* ed. Julien Philipe (Paris: Éditions Dédale, 1994), 72–73. Le Brun's articulation of the passions was a standard reference work for artists throughout the eighteenth century.

6. *Nouveau Petit Le Robert* (1875), s.v. "Ravissement."

7. All these works are illustrated in Rosenberg and Bailey, "Not Greuze, but Bernard d'Agesci," plate nos. 10, 17, 20. As a young artist, Bernard d'Agesci came to Paris and trained with Jean-Bernard Restout. In the registers of the Ecole des Beaux-Arts, he is described as "protected" by the academician Louis-Jean-François Lagrenée. "Not Greuze, but Bernard d'Agesci," 204. It is likely that even at this late date, training would include the standard academic formulae for the expressions. Lagrenée called on Le Brun's *ravissement* in his reception piece, *The Rape of Deianeira* (1755; Paris: Musée du Louvre).

8. Of all the works by Greuze, his nymphets have received the least attention, even though they were very popular, judging from the number he produced. Some paintings of this type are so weak in execution that one wonders if Greuze actually painted them. Showing that other artists copied the nymphets, however, would only further attest to their popularity.

9. Diderot, "Salon de 1765," in *Oeuvres complètes,* 14: 188. See also Wolff, "An Early Painting by Greuze and Its Literary Associations," 580–85.

10. I thank Professor Tomassini of the University of Iowa for pointing out how pearls invite touch.

11. On the meaning of pearls in relation to Cleopatra, housewives, and femininity, see Mary Hamer, *Signs of Cleopatra* (New York: Routledge, 1993), 37, 68–69. Pearls in eighteenth-century French painting appear on seductive goddesses, coquettes, odalisques, and elite women.

12. See, for example, Virginia Swain, "Hidden from View: French Women Authors and the Language of Rights, 1727–1792," in *Intimate Encounters: Love and Domesticity in Eighteenth-Century French Art* (Princeton: Princeton University Press, 1997), 27.

13. Diderot, "Salon de 1765," in *Oeuvres complètes,* 14: 179.

14. Ibid.

15. Ibid., 14: 180.

16. Kamuf, *Fictions of Feminine Desire,* 12–17. The interpretation that follows is indebted to Kamuf.

17. *The Letters of Abelard and Heloise,* trans. and with an intro. by Betty Radice (London: Penguin, 1974), 113.

18. Jean-Baptiste Guys, *Abailard et Héloïse. Pièce dramatique en vers et en 5 actes* (London, 1752), v–vi.

19. Virginia Swain, for example, argues this is the case. *Intimate Encounters,* 27.

20. As quoted in Charrier, *Héloïse dans l'histoire et dans la légende,* 473.

21. My wording here represents an eighteenth-century understanding of the outpouring of grief at Abelard's castration. See "La Vie d'Abeilard et d'Héloïse," in *Lettres et épitres amoureuses d'Héloïse avec les réponses d'Abeilard* (Paris, 1777),

22. Also, "Avertissement," by Mme and M. Guizot in J. H. Marchand, *Abaillard et Héloïse. Tragédie en cinq acte et en vers* (The Hague and Paris: Tabarie, 1768), 5.

22. Illustrators did not shrink from showing the event. Charles Eisen, for example, includes a rather graphic scene of Abelard's castration as a headpiece for Charles-Pierre Colardeau's *Lettre amoureuse d'Héloise à Abelard* (1766). We see four men come to mutilate the helpless Abelard in his bed. As two of them hold Abelard's arms and legs, a third uses a razor to sever his genitals. To increase the tension of the scene, the fourth man pulls aside the bed curtains and wields a torch to illuminate the action. There is more than a touch of theatricality about the illustration with its raised curtain, stage setting, and dramatic lighting. Nevertheless, in actual plays based on the story, Abelard's castration was not seen but reported in the manner of Greek tragedy. For an illustration of the engraving and a discussion of the work, see Stewart, *Engraven Desire: Eros, Image and Text in the French Eighteenth Century,* 60.

23. Claude-Joseph Dorat, "Épître d'Abelard à Héloïse," in *Lettres et épîtres amoureuses,* (Paris, 1777), 168.

24. Guys, *Abailard et Héloïse,* 101.

25. Marchand, *Abaillard et Héloïse,* 83.

26. Ibid., 84.

27. For a further discussion of the broken seal as a possible sign of castration, see Mary Sheriff, "A rebours. Le problème de l'histoire dans l'interprétation féministe," in *Où en est l'interprétation de l'oeuvre d'art?* ed. Régis Michel (Paris: École des Beaux-Arts and Réunion des Musées Nationaux, 2000), 228–29.

28. Dorat, "Épître d'Abelard à Héloïse," 167.

29. Charles-Pierre Colardeau, "Lettre d'Abeilard à Héloïse," in *Lettres et épitres amoureuses* (Paris, 1777), 107.

30. Ibid., 110 ff.

31. Kamuf, *Fictions of Feminine Desire,* 8, 22–23, 38–40.

32. *The Letters of Abelard and Heloise,* 148. My interpretation here follows Kamuf, *Fictions of Feminine Desire,* 39–40.

33. That idealized domain of kinship is governed by the law of the father, which separates the little boy from the pleasures of the maternal body by prohibiting incest with the mother. This law is enforced through the threat of castration.

34. Colardeau, "Lettre d'Abeilard à Héloïse," 115.

35. Charles-Pierre Colardeau, *Épîtres amoureuses d'Héloïse à Abailard et d'Armide à Renaud,* (Paris, 1758), 18. Colardeau's poem is itself a translation of Alexander Pope's *Epistle of Heloise* (1717), known in France through a 1751 edition of Pope's complete works. With the other French writers who followed Pope in condensing the correspondence into one letter/poem, Colardeau increases the sensuality of the letters, pushes Heloise closer to love madness, and adds pastoral refinements. For a comparison of the two works, see Charrier, *Héloïse dans l'histoire et dans la légende,* 457–62.

36. From a letter to Marie Bonaparte cited in Ernest Jones, *The Life and Work of Sigmund Freud,* 2 vols. (New York: Basic Books, 1955), 2: 421.

37. Shoshana Felman, *What Does a Woman Want? Reading and Sexual Difference* (Baltimore: Johns Hopkins University Press, 1993), 6.

38. Wolff, "An Early Painting by Greuze and Its Literary Associations," 580–85.

39. Ibid., 583–84.

40. Diderot, "Salon de 1765," in *Oeuvres complètes,* 14: 188.

41. "Critique des peintures et des sculptures des M. de l'Académie Royale l'an 1765" (Paris, 1765), 26 (Deloynes Collection, vol. 8, no. 107).

42. Diderot, "Salon de 1765," in *Oeuvres complètes,* 14: 188.

43. Ibid.

44. Ibid.

45. Ibid., 14: 194–95.

46. In his commentary, Diderot also seems to liken the father in *The Well-Beloved Mother* to Greuze, and not simply because Greuze's wife—rather than Mme Laborde—modeled for the woman's figure. Like the father in the image, Greuze has produced a "pretty swarm of brats" in the paintings he has brought to the Salon. Like the mother, Diderot seems suffocated by the charges Greuze has laid upon him: "Ah, I can breathe, I've finished with Greuze. The work he gives me is agreeable, but he gives me a lot of it." Diderot, "Salon de 1765," in *Oeuvres complètes,* 14: 202. Diderot, moreover, describes Greuze in terms that resonate with his description of the father in *The Well-Beloved Mother.* Like the father, he is somewhat naïve, somewhat vain, and he draws attention to his own work (14: 177).

47. *The Letters of Abelard and Heloise,* 113. Thus it was not only as a young woman that Heloise ignored patriarchal law. As the still passionate abbess, she insisted on mixing up the sexual and the religious in her letters to Abelard. On this point, see Kamuf, *Fictions of Feminine Desire,* 25.

48. Colardeau, *Épîtres amoureuses d'Héloïse à Abailard,* 21.

49. Duchesse d'Aiguillon, *Épître d'Héloïse à Abailard* (Geneva, 1758), 9.

50. Ibid., 12.

51. And, as Kamuf has argued, her nun's habit only simulates the religious order at other points in the story as well. Twice before her final entrance into the convent, Heloise dons the veil to disguise herself as she hides from her guardian. Kamuf, *Fictions of Feminine Desire,* 25–26.

52. *The Letters of Abelard and Heloise,* 132.

53. See, for example, Simon Vouet (1590–1649), *Crucifixion* (Paris: Musée du Louvre). The skull that lies near Christ's cross in images of the crucifixion becomes an attribute of the Magdalene. See, for example, Georges de La Tour's (1593–1652) painting of the Magdalene (Paris: Musée du Louvre) in which she is seated in a pose suggestive of melancholy with a skull on her lap. Books are piled on a table near her.

54. Jacques Alluis, *Histoire des Amours d'Abailard et d'Héloïse* (Amsterdam: Pierre Chayer, 1700), 297.

55. As quoted and translated in Elizabeth J. MacArthur, *Extravagant Narratives: Closure and Dynamics in the Epistolary Form* (Princeton: Princeton University Press, 1990), 73.

56. *Le philosophe amoureux, histoire galante, contenant une dissertation curieuse, sur la vie de Pierre Abaillard, & celle d'Héloïse, avec les intrigues amoureuses des mêmes personnes,* 2d ed. (Au Paraclet, 1697), 200.

57. "Mon Dieu m'appelle en vain du trône de sa gloire. Je cède à la nature une indigne victoire."

58. Colardeau, *Épîtres amoureuses d'Héloïse à Abailard,* 12.

59. Pierre Bayle, *Dictionnaire historique et critique,* 5th ed., 5 vols. (Amsterdam, 1740), 2: 714–15.

60. Esquirol, *Des maladies mentales,* 2: 47.

61. Here I am following Elizabeth MacArthur's interpretation of the *Lettres portugaises* in *Extravagant Narratives,* 78–116.

62. Aiguillon, *Épître d'Héloïse à Abailard,* 15.

63. In discussions of breast-feeding, the infant is often figured as the mother's lover. See Yvonne Knibiehler and Catherine Fouquet, *L'histoire des mères du moyen âge à nos jours* (Paris: Éditions Montalba, 1980), 86.

64. Rosenberg and Bailey suggest this is the case. See "Not Greuze, but Bernard d'Agesci," 210n.

65. There is also an oil version of the work signed and dated 1740. See Thierry Lefrançois, *Charles Coypel* (Paris: Arthena, 1994), 232–34.

66. Kamuf brilliantly analyzes Heloise's rhetorical strategies, *Fictions of Feminine Desire,* 1–43. Heloise cites other learned women in her letters to Abelard, mentioning, for example, the Greek courtesan Aspasia, who joined the philosophers in their discussions.

67. See, for example, the biography in *Lettres et épitres amoureuses d'Héloïse avec les réponses d'Abeilard,* 9–10. In his *Historia calamitatum,* Abelard describes Heloise as more learned than beautiful: "In looks she did not rank lowest, while in the extent of her learning she stood supreme. A gift for letters is so rare in women that it added greatly to her charm and had won her renown throughout the realm." *The Letters of Abelard and Heloise,* 66.

68. Aiguillon, *Épître d'Héloïse à Abailard,* viii.

69. Marchand, *Abaillard et Héloïse,* 42.

70. On Gentil-Bernard, see F. Fayolle, "Essai sur la vie et les ouvrages de Bernard," in *Oeuvres de Bernard* (Paris: F. Buisson: 1803).

71. Julien Offray de La Mettrie, "L'école de la volupté," in *De la volupté* (Paris: Éditions Desjonquères, 1996), 118.

72. As many others have shown, letter writing was an important part of culture during the seventeenth and eighteenth centuries. Many wrote letters expecting an audience beyond their correspondent. Letters were read at salons, circulated, admired, and even criticized. Letters were also essential to the "progress of love," and lovers copied them from collections of fictional love letters. Writing letters, moreover, was one of few literary endeavors women were thought capable of doing well.

73. Rousseau, *Lettre à M. d'Alembert sur les spectacles,* 138–39.

74. For this chronology, see the introduction to Jean-Jacques Rousseau, *Julie, or The New Heloise,* trans. and annotated by Phillip Stewart and Jean Vaché (Hanover, NH: University Press of New England, 1997), xii.

75. Ibid., 70.

76. Ibid., 10–11. Rousseau also notes that in true letters thoughts are commonplace, style is not familiar. "Love fashions for itself another universe, surrounds itself with objects that do not exist to which it alone has given being and as it renders all sentiments by images, its language is always figurative. But such figures lack precision and sequence; its eloquence is in its disorder; it convinces more when it reasons less."

77. For the identification of Diderot as the interlocutor of "R.," see *Julie, or The New Heloise,* 656.

78. See, for example, Wolff, "An Early Painting by Greuze and Its Literary Associations."

79. Kamuf, *Fictions of Feminine Desire,* 97–122, esp. 101.

80. Vila, *Enlightenment and Pathology,* 212.

81. Rousseau, *Julie, or The New Heloise,* 410.

82. MacArthur, *Extravagant Narratives,* 216–20.

83. For an excellent recent analysis of the *Confessions,* see Sarah Herbold, "Rousseau's Dance of Veils: The *Confessions* and the Imagined Woman Reader," *Eighteenth-Century Studies* 32 (spring 1999): 333–54. Starobinski explores the literary sources for *Julie* that Rousseau claims in *Jean-Jacques Rousseau,* 341–44.

84. Jean-Jacques Rousseau, *Les confessions,* in *Oeuvres complètes de J.-J. Rousseau mises dans un nouvel ordre, avec des notes historiques et des éclaircissements,* ed. Victor Donatien Musset-Pathay, 22 vols. (Paris: P. Dupont, 1823–26), 15: 245.

85. Ibid., 15: 246.

86. Ibid., 15: 251.

87. Ibid., 15: 252.

88. Ibid., 15: 257.

89. Ibid. He goes on to say that he is embarassed to contradict himself so openly and fully, since he has preached loud invectives "against books, which exuded nothing but effeminacy and love."

90. Ibid., 15: 264.

91. Ibid., 15: 275.

92. Ibid., 15: 300.

93. Rousseau, *Julie, or The New Heloise,* 11.

94. Rousseau, *Les confessions,* 15: 246. Also of interest here is Freud's comparison of Rousseau with Norbert Hanold. At one point in *Delusions and Dreams,* Freud likens the two because both repressed sexuality and found diversion in mathematics. See Freud, *Delusions and Dreams,* 36.

95. Rousseau, *Les confessions,* 15: 416. I quote the entire passage: "Content d'avoir grossièrement esquissé mon plan, je revins aux situations de détail que j'avais tracées; et de l'arrangement que je leur donnai, résultèrent les deux premières parties de la *Julie,* que je fis et mis au net durant cet hiver avec un plaisir inexprimable, employant pour cela le plus beau papier doré, de la poudre d'azur et d'argent pour sécher l'écriture, de la nonpareille bleue pour coudre mes cahiers; enfin ne trouvant rien d'assez galant, rien d'assez mignon, pour les charmantes filles dont je raffolais comme un autre Pigmalion."

CONCLUSION

1. See above, 33.

2. For an extended analysis of the painting, see Sheriff, *J. H. Fragonard,* 30–57.

3. Ibid., 43.

BIBLIOGRAPHY

Aiguillon, Duchesse d.' *Épître d'Héloïse à Abailard.* Geneva, 1758.

Alberti, Leon Battista. *On Painting.* Translated and with an intro. by John R. Spencer. New Haven: Yale University Press, 1966.

Alembert, Jean Le Rond d.' *Discours préliminaire de l'Encyclopédie.* Paris: Éditions Gonthier, 1965.

Alluis, Jacques. *Histoire des amours d'Abailard et d'Héloïse.* Amsterdam: Pierre Chayer, 1700.

Amielle, Ghislaine. *Les traductions françaises des Metamorphoses d'Ovide.* Paris: Jean Touzot, 1989.

Apelle au sallon. Paris, 1783. Deloynes Collection, vol. 13, no. 288.

Aristotle. *Poetics.* Translated and edited by Stephen Halliwell. Cambridge, MA: Harvard University Press, 1995.

Bailey, Colin, ed. *Les amours des dieux: La peinture mythologique de Watteau à David.* Paris: Réunion des Musées Nationaux, 1991.

Balzac, Honoré. "Le chef-d'oeuvre inconnu." In *Le chef d'oeuvre inconnu, Gambara, Massimilla Doni.* Paris: Flammarion, 1981.

Barker, Emma. "Greuze and the Painting of Sentiment in French Art, 1755–1785." Ph.D. diss., Courtauld Institute of Art, 1994.

Barkin, Leonard. *The Gods Made Flesh: Metamorphosis and the Pursuit of Paganism.* New Haven: Yale University Press, 1986.

Barnabé-Firmin de Rosoi. *Pygmalion. Drame lyrique en un acte et en prose.* Paris: La Veuve Ballard et Fils, 1780.

Barthélemy, Jean-Jacques, Abbé. *Travels of Anacharsis the Younger in Greece during the Middle of the Fourth Century before the Christian Era.* Translated by William Beaumont. 5 vols. London: G. G. and J. Robinson, 1796.

Batteux, Charles, Abbé. *Les beaux-arts réduits à une même principe.* Paris, 1747. Reprint, New York: Johnson Reprint Corp., 1970.

Bayle, Pierre. *Dictionnaire historique et critique.* 5th ed. 5 vols. Amsterdam, 1740.

Beasley, Faith. "The Voices of Shadows: Layfayette's *Zaïde.*" In *Going Public: Women and Publishing in Early Modern France,* edited by Elizabeth Goldsmith and Dena Goodman. Ithaca, NY: Cornell University Press, 1995.

Bergman-Carton, Janis. *The Woman of Ideas in French Art, 1830–1848*. New Haven: Yale University Press, 1995.

Beauchêne, Edme Pierre Chavot de. *De l'influence des affections de l'âme dans les maladies nerveuses des femmes.* Montpellier: Méquignon, 1781.

Beauharnais, Fanny, comtesse de. *L'Abailard supposé; ou, Le sentiment à l'épreuve.* Amsterdam and Paris, 1780.

Becq, Annie. *Genése de l'esthétique française moderne, 1680–1814*. Paris: Albin Michel, 1994.

Berlanstein, Lenard. "Women and Power in Eighteenth-Century France: Actresses at the Comédie Française." In *Visions and Revisions of Eighteenth-Century France,* edited by Christine Adams, Jack R. Censer, and Lisa Jane Graham. University Park: Pennsylvania State University Press, 1997.

Bernard, Pierre-Joseph. *Oeuvres de Bernard.* Paris: F. Buisson: 1803.

Berquin, M. *Pygmalion, scène lyrique mis en vers par M. Berquin.* Paris, 1775.

Bienville, D. T. *La nymphomanie; ou, Traité de la fureur utérine.* Amsterdam: Marc-Michel Rey, 1778.

Bilinkoff, Jodi. *The Avila of Saint Teresa.* Ithaca, NY: Cornell University Press, 1989.

Boileau Despréaux, Nicolas. *Oeuvres complètes.* With an intro. by Antoine Adam. Annotated by Françoise Escal. Paris: Gallimard, 1966.

Bonnet, Charles. *Essai analytique sur les facultés de l'âme.* Copenhagen, 1760. Reprint, Hildesheim: Georg Olms, 1973.

Bonnet, Marie-Jo. *Un choix sans équivoque.* Paris: Éditions Denoël, 1981.

Boudier de Villemert, Pierre-Joseph. *Le nouvel ami des femmes; ou, La philosophie du sexe.* Paris: Monory, 1779.

Boureau-Deslandes, André-François. *Pigmalion; ou, La statue animée.* Paris: Belin, 1753.

Brewer, Daniel. *The Discourse of Enlightenment in Eighteenth-Century France: Diderot and the Art of Philosophizing.* Cambridge: Cambridge University Press, 1993.

Brice, Germain. *Description de la Ville de Paris.* 9th ed. Paris, 1752. Reprint, Geneva: Librairie Droz and Paris: Librairie Minard, 1971.

Brisson, Marie. "Dire l'inconnu 'Sur les femmes' de Diderot." *L'Esprit Créateur* 39 (1989): 10–20.

Brody, Jules. *Boileau and Longinus.* Geneva: Droz, 1958.

Brookner, Anita. *Greuze: The Rise and Fall of an Eighteenth-Century Phenomenon.* Greenwich, CT: New York Graphic Society, 1972.

Butler, Judith. *Bodies That Matter: On the Discursive Limits of "Sex."* New York: Routledge, 1993.

Cahusac, Louis de. *Épître sur les dangers de la poésie.* The Hague: Neaulme, 1739.

———. *La danse ancienne et moderne; ou, Traité historique de la danse.* The Hague, 1754. Reprint, Geneva: Slatkine, 1971.

Callistratus. *Descriptions.* Translated by Arthur Fairbanks. Cambridge, MA: Harvard University Press, 1960.

Carmona, Michel. *Les diables de Loudun: Sorcellerie et politique sous Richelieu.* Paris: Fayard, 1988.

Carr, J. L. "Pygmalion and the Philosophes." *Journal of the Warburg and Courtauld Institutes* 23 (1960): 239–55.

Casaubon, Meric. *A Treatise Concerning Enthusiasm.* Facsimile reproduction of the 2d. ed. of 1656 with an intro. by Paul J. Korshin. Gainesville, FL: Scholars' Facsimiles and Reprints, 1970.

Castle, Terry. *The Female Thermometer: Eighteenth-Century Culture and the Invention of the Uncanny.* New York: Oxford University Press, 1995.

Chambon de Montaux, M. (Nicolas). *Des maladies des femmes.* 2 vols. Paris: Hôtel Serpente, 1784.

Charrier, Charlotte. *Héloïse dans l'histoire et dans la légende.* Paris: Librairie Ancienne Honoré Champion, 1933.

Christensen, Thomas. *Rameau and Musical Thought in the Enlightenment.* Cambridge: Cambridge University Press, 1993.

Ciafolo, John. "Unveiling Goya's *Rape of Galatea.*" *Art History* 18 (1995): 477–98.

Clairon, Mlle (Claire-Hippolyte Léris). *Mémoires de Mlle Clairon.* Paris: Ponthieu, 1822. Reprint, Geneva: Slatkine, 1968.

Cohen, Sarah. *Art, Dance, and the Body in French Culture of the Ancien Régime.* New York: Cambridge University Press, 2000.

Coicy, Mme de. *Les femmes comme il convient de les voir ou Aperçu de ce que les femmes ont été de ce qu'elles sont, et de ce qu'elles pourroient être.* 2 vols. Paris and London: Bacot, 1785.

Colardeau, Charles-Pierre. *Épîtres amoureuses d'Héloïse à Abailard et d'Armide à Renaud.* Paris, 1758.

———. "Lettre d'Abeilard à Héloïse." In *Lettres et épitres amoureuses d'Héloïse avec les réponses d'Abeilard.* Paris, 1777.

Colonna, François-Marie-Pompée. *Les principes de la nature ou de la génération des choses.* Paris: André Cailleau, 1731.

Condillac, Étienne Bonnot de, Abbé. *Oeuvres complètes.* 16 vols. Paris, 1821–22. Reprint, Geneva: Slatkine, 1970.

Correspondance littéraire, philosophique et critique par Grimm, Diderot, Raynal, Meister, etc. Edited by Maurice Tourneux. 16 vols. Paris: Garnier Frères, 1877–82.

Coulet, Henri, ed. *Pygmalion des lumières.* Paris: Éditions Desjonquères, 1998.

"Critique des peintures et des sculptures de M. de l'Académie Royale l'an 1765." Paris, 1765.

Cubières-Palmézeaux, Michel de. *Galatée, Comédie.* Versailles and Fontainebleau: Blaizot, 1777.

Dacier, Émile. *Une danseuse de l'Opéra sous Louis XV: Mlle Sallé, 1707–1756.* Paris, 1909. Reprint, Geneva: Minkoff, 1972.

Dandré-Bardon, Michel François. *Traité de peinture: Suivi d'un essai sur la sculpture.* Paris, 1765. Reprint, Geneva: Minkoff, 1972.

Darnton, Robert. *The Forbidden Best-Sellers of Pre-Revolutionary France.* New York: W.W. Norton, 1996.

Daston, Lorraine, and Katharine Park. *Wonders and the Order of Nature, 1150–1750.* New York: Zone Books, 1998.

DeJean, Joan E. "Looking like a Woman: The Female Gaze in Sappho and Lafayette." *L'Esprit Créateur* 28 (1988): 34–45.

———. *Fictions of Sappho, 1536–1937.* Chicago: University of Chicago Press, 1989.

———. *Tender Geographies: Women and the Origins of the Novel in France.* New York: Columbia University Press, 1991.

———. *Ancients against Moderns: Culture Wars and the Making of a Fin de Siècle.* Chicago: University of Chicago Press, 1997.

———. Introduction to Prévost, *The Story of a Greek Woman.* In *The Libertine Reader.* New York: Zone Books, 1997.

Delatte, Armand. *Les conceptions de l'enthousiasme chez les philosophes présocratiques.* Paris: Société d'Édition Les Belles Lettres, 1934.

De Man, Paul. *Allegories of Reading.* New Haven: Yale University Press, 1979.

Descartes, René. *The Passions of the Soul.* Translated by Stephen H. Voss. Indianapolis: Hackett Publishing Co., 1989.

Diderot, Denis. "Sur les femmes." In *Qu'est-ce qu'une femme?* With an intro. by Elisabeth Badinter. Paris: P.O.L., 1989.

———. *Oeuvres complètes.* 25 vols. Paris: Hermann, 1990.

———. *Paradoxe sur le comédien.* Paris: Bordas, 1991.

Diderot, Denis, and Jean Le Rond d'Alembert. *Encyclopédie, ou Dictionnaire raisonné des sciences, des arts et des métiers, par une société des gens de lettres.* Microfiche facsimile of 1751–80 ed. 17 vols. Zug, Switzerland: Inter Documentation Co. Ag, 1979.

Disch, Lisa. "Claire Loves Julie: Reading the Story of Women's Friendship in *La nouvelle Héloïse.*" *Hypatia* 9 (1994): 17–45.

Dixon, Laurinda. *Perilous Chastity: Women and Illness in Pre-Enlightenment Art and Medicine.* Ithaca, NY: Cornell University Press, 1995.

Dorat, Claude-Joseph. "Épître d'Abelard à Héloïse" (1760). In *Lettres et épitres amoureuses d'Héloïse avec les réponses d'Abeilard.* Paris, 1777.

Dörrie, Heinrich. *Pygmalion. Ein Impuls Ovid und seine Wirkungen bis in die Gegenwart.* Düsseldorf: Westdeutscher, 1974.

Dowley, Francis H. "D'Angiviller's Grands Hommes and the Significant Moment." *Art Bulletin* 39 (1957): 259–77.

———. "Falconet's Attitude towards Antiquity and His Theory of Reliefs." *Art Quarterly* 31 (1968): 185–204.

Dragonette, Roger. "Pygmalion ou les pièges de la fiction dans *Le Roman de la rose.*" In *Orbis mediaevalis,* edited by Georges Güntert, Marc-René Jung, and Kurt Ringger. Berne: Éditions Francke, 1978.

Drouet de Maupertuis [Maupertuy], Jean-Baptiste. *La femme faible où l'on represénte aux femmes les dangers ausquels elles s'exposent, par un commerce fréquent et assidu avec les hommes.* Nancy, 1733.

DuBois, Page. *Sowing the Body: Psychoanalysis and Ancient Representations of Women.* Chicago: University of Chicago Press, 1988.

——— *Sappho Is Burning.* Chicago: University of Chicago Press, 1995.

Du Bos, Jean-Baptiste, Abbé. *Réflexions critiques sur la poésie et sur la peinture.* With an intro. by Dominique Désirat. Paris: École Nationale Supérieure des Beaux-Arts, 1993.

Ehrard, Antoinette, and Ehrard, Jean, eds. *Diderot et Greuze. Actes du colloque de Clermont-Ferrand.* Clermont-Ferrand: Adosa, 1986.

Épinay, Louise Florence Pétronille Tardieu d'Esclavelles, marquise de Lalive d'. *Les conversations d'Émilie.* Paris: Belin, 1782.

Esquirol, Étienne. *Des maladies mentales.* 2 vols. Paris: J. B. Baillière, 1838. Reprint, New York: Arno Press, 1976.

Explication des peintures, sculptures et autres ouvrages de Messieurs de l'Académie Royale. Paris: J. J. E. Collombat, 1753. Deloynes Collection, vol. 5, no. 53.

Falconet, Étienne. *Oeuvres complètes.* 3d ed. 3 vols. Paris, 1808. Reprint, Geneva: Slatkine, 1970.

Felman, Shoshana. *What Does a Woman Want? Reading and Sexual Difference.* Baltimore: Johns Hopkins University Press, 1993.

Fénelon, François de Salignac de La Mothe. *De l'éducation des filles.* Paris: Bassompierre, 1771. Reprint, Imprimerie de Provence, 1983.

Ferrand, Jacques. *A Treatise on Lovesickness.* Translated and edited by Donald Beecher and Massimo Ciavolella. Syracuse: Syracuse University Press, 1990.

Fleischmann, Hector. *Le cénacle libertin de Mademoiselle Raucourt.* Paris: Bibliothèque des Curieux, 1912.

Fontenelle, Bernard Le Bovier de. *The History of Oracles and the Cheats of the Pagan Priests.* Translated by Aphra Behn. London, 1688.

———. *Oeuvres de Fontenelle.* 11 vols. Paris: V. Brunet, 1761.

Fort, Bernadette. "Accessories of Desire." *Yale French Studies* 94 (1998): 146–62.

———. "Falconet contre Diderot: Le *Paragone* revisité." In *Les ennemis de Diderot,* edited by Anne-Marie Chouillet. Paris: Klincksieck, 1993.

Foster, Susan Leigh. *Choreography and Narrative: Ballet's Staging of Story and Desire.* Bloomington: Indiana University Press, 1996.

———. "Dancing the Body Politic." In *From the Royal to the Republican Body: Incorporating the Political in Seventeenth and Eighteenth-Century France,* edited by Sara E. Melzer and Kathryn Norberg. Berkeley: University of California Press, 1998.

Fraisse, Geneviève. *La muse de la raison.* Aix-en-Provence: Alinéa, 1989.

———. *La raison des femmes.* Paris: Plon, 1992.

Freedberg, David. *The Power of Images.* Chicago: University of Chicago Press, 1989.

Fréron, Elie Catherine. *L'année littéraire.* 16 vols. Paris: Mériot, 1751–89.

Freud, Sigmund. *Totem and Taboo.* Translated by James Strachey. New York: W.W. Norton, 1950.

———. *Delusions and Dreams in Jensen's Gradiva* (1907[1906]). In vol. 9 of *The Standard Edition of the Complete Psychological Works of Sigmund Freud.* Translated by James Strachey in collaboration with Anna Freud. 24 vols. London: Hogarth Press, 1953–74.

———. "On Narcissism: An Introduction." In vol. 14 of *The Standard Edition of the Complete Psychological Works of Sigmund Freud.* Translated by James Strachey in collaboration with Anna Freud. 24 vols. London: Hogarth Press, 1953–74.

———. "Essay on Femininity." In *New Introductory Lectures on Psychoanalysis.* Translated and edited by James Strachey. New York : W.W. Norton, 1964.

———. *Civilization and Its Discontents.* Translated and edited by James Strachey. With an intro. by Peter Gay. New York: W.W. Norton, 1989.

Fried, Michael. *Absorption and Theatricality: Painting and Beholder in the Age of Diderot.* Berkeley: University of California Press, 1980.

Furcy-Raynaud, Marc. "Correspondance du comte d'Angiviller avec Pierre." In *Année 1905* of *Nouvelles archives de l'art français. Receuil de documents inédits publiées par la Société de l'histoire de l'art français.* 34 vols. Reprint, Paris: F. de Nobele, 1973.

Gaboriau, Émile. *Les comédiennes adorées.* Paris: E. Dentu, 1843.

Gaubier de Barrault, Sulpice Edme. *Brioché; ou, L'origine des marionettes.* Paris, 1753.

Genlis, Stéphanie Félicité, comtesse de. *Adelaide and Theodore; or, Letters on Education.* 3 vols. London: C. Bathurst, 1783.

Goldberg, Ann. "The Eberbach Asylum and the Practice(s) of Nymphomania in Germany, 1815–1849." *Journal of Women's History* 9 (1998): 34–52.

Goldsmith, Elizabeth, and Dena Goodman, eds. *Going Public: Women and Publishing in Early Modern France.* Ithaca, NY: Cornell University Press, 1995.

Goldstein, Jan. *Console and Classify: The French Psychiatric Profession in the Nineteenth Century.* Cambridge: Cambridge University Press, 1987.

———. "Enthusiasm or Imagination? Eighteenth-Century Smear Words in Comparative National Context." In *Enthusiasm and Enlightenment in Europe, 1650–1850,* edited by Lawrence E. Klein and Anthony J. La Vopa. San Marino, CA: Huntington Library, 1998.

Goodman, Dena. "Pigalle's *Voltaire nu*: The Republic of Letters Represents Itself to the World." *Representations* 16 (1986): 86–110.

———. "Filial Rebellion in the Salon: Madame Geoffrin and Her Daughter." *French Historical Studies* 16 (1989): 27–47.

———. *The Republic of Letters: A Cultural History of the French Enlightenment.* Ithaca, NY: Cornell University Press, 1994.

Goulemot, Jean Marie. "Prêtons le main de la nature. II. Fureurs utérines." *Dix-Huitième Siècle* 12 (1980): 97–111.

———. *Forbidden Texts: Erotic Literature and Its Readers in Eighteenth-Century France.* Translated by James Simpson. Philadelphia: University of Pennsylvania Press, 1994.

Gravelot, Hubert François, Charles Nicolas Cochin, and Charles-Étienne Gaucher. *Iconologie par figures; ou, Traité complet des allégories, emblèmes, etc., à l'usage des artistes.* 4 vols. Paris: Le Pan, 1791. Reprint, Geneva: Minkoff, 1972.

Graville, Barthélemy-Claude Graillard de. *L'ami des filles.* Paris: Dufour, 1761.

Groneman, Carol. "Nymphomania: The Historical Construction of Female Sexuality." *Signs* 19 (1994): 337–67.

Gross, Kenneth. *The Dream of the Moving Statue.* Ithaca, NY: Cornell University Press, 1992.

Guichard, M. "À M. Falconet sur son Groupe de Pigmalion exposé cette année au Louvre." *Mercure de France* (October 1763): 19.

Guyon, Jeanne. *An Autobiography.* New Kensington, PA: Whitaker House, 1997.

Guys, Jean-Baptiste. *Abailard et Héloïse. Pièce dramatique en vers et en 5 actes.* London, 1752.

Halperin, David. "Why Is Diotima a Woman." In *One Hundred Years of Homosexuality: And Other Essays on Greek Love.* New York: Routledge, 1990.

Hamer, Mary. *Signs of Cleopatra: History, Politics, Representation.* London: Routledge, 1993.

Hart, Clive, and Kay Gilliland Stevenson. *Heaven and Flesh: Imagery of Desire from the Renaissance to the Rococo.* Cambridge: Cambridge University Press, 1995.

Hecquet, Philippe. *Lettre sur la convulsionnaire en extase; ou, La vapoureuse en rêve.* Paris, s.d.

Heim, Jean-Francois, et al. *Les salons de peinture de la révolution française, 1789–1799.* Paris: C.A.C. Sarl, 1989.

Henry, Patrick. "Montaigne and Pygmalion." In *Montaigne and the Gods,* edited by Daniel Martin. Amherst, MA: Hestia Press, 1993.

Herbold, Sarah. "Rousseau's Dance of Veils: The *Confessions* and the Imagined Woman Reader." *Eighteenth-Century Studies* 32 (1999): 333–54.

Heyd, Michael. *Be Sober and Reasonable: The Critique of Enthusiasm in the Seventeenth and Early Eighteenth Centuries.* Leiden: Brill, 1995.

Holmström, Kirsten Gram. *Monodrama, Attitudes, Tableaux Vivants: Studies on Some Trends of Theatrical Fashion, 1770–1815*. Stockholm: Almquise & Wiksell, 1967.

Houssaye, Arsène. *Princesses de comédie et déesses d'opéra.* Paris: L. Hachette, 1858.

Huet, Marie-Hélène. *Monstrous Imagination.* Cambridge, MA: Harvard University Press, 1993.

Huet, Pierre-Daniel. *Traité des origine des romans.* Paris, 1799. Reprint, Geneva: Slatkine, 1970.

Irigaray, Luce. *Speculum of the Other Woman.* Translated by Gillian Gill. Ithaca, NY: Cornell University Press, 1985.

Jensen, Wilhelm. *Gradiva.* In *Delusion and Dream.* Translated by Helen M. Downey. New York: Moffat, Yard and Company, 1917.

Johns, Christopher. "'That Amiable Object of Adoration': Pompeo Batoni and the Sacred Heart." *Gazette des Beaux-Arts* 132 (1998): 19–28.

Johnson, Dorothy. "Picturing Pedagogy: Education and the Child in the Paintings of Chardin." *Eighteenth-Century Studies* 24, no. 1 (1990): 47–68.

Jonas, Raymond. *France and the Cult of the Sacred Heart.* Berkeley: University of California Press, 2000.

Joost-Gaugier, Christiane L. "Sappho, Apollo, Neopythagorean Theory and *Numine Afflatur* in Raphael's Fresco of the *Parnassus.*" *Gazette des Beaux-Arts* 122 (1993): 127–28.

Jugement d'un amateur sur l'exposition des tableaux de l'an 1753. Paris, 1753. Deloynes Collection, vol. 5, no. 59.

Kamuf, Peggy. *Fictions of Feminine Desire: Disclosures of Heloise.* Lincoln: University of Nebraska Press, 1982.

Klibansky, Raymond, Erwin Panofsky, and Fritz Saxl. *Saturn and Melancholy: Studies in the History of Natural Philosophy, Religion, and Art.* London: Nelson, 1964.

Knibiehler, Yvonne, and Catherine Fouquet. *L'histoire des mères du moyen âge à nos jours.* Paris: Éditions Montalba, 1980.

Kofman, Sarah. *L'enfance de l'art.* Paris: Editions Galilée, 1970.

———. *The Enigma of Woman.* Translated by Catherine Porter. Ithaca, NY: Cornell University Press, 1985.

Kramer, Heinrich, and James Sprenger. *The Malleus Maleficarum of Heinrich Kramer and James Sprenger.* Translated and with an intro. by Reverend Montague Summers. New York: Dover, 1971.

Kreiser, B. Robert. *Miracles, Convulsions, and Ecclesiastical Politics in Early Eighteenth-Century Paris.* Princeton: Princeton University Press, 1978.

Lacan, Jacques. "God and the Jouissance of ~~The~~ Woman." In *Feminine Sexuality: Jacques Lacan and the École Freudienne,* edited by Juliet Mitchell and Jacqueline Rose. New York: W.W. Norton, 1985.

La Chau, Géraud de, Abbé. *Dissertation sur les attributs de Vénus.* Paris: Imprimerie de Prault, 1776.

Lafayette, Marie Madeleine Pioche de la Vergne, comtesse de. *Zayde. A Spanish History.* London: John Watts, 1729.

Lambert, Anne Thérèse Marguenat de Courcelles, marquise de. *Réflexions sur les femmes.* Paris, 1828.

La Mettrie, Julien Offray de. "L'école da la volupté." In *De la volupté*. Paris: Éditions Desjonquères, 1996.

———. *Machine Man*. In *Machine Man and Other Writings*. Translated and edited by Ann Thomson. New York: Cambridge University Press, 1996.

La Motte, Antoine Houdar de. *Le triomphe des arts. Ballet en cinq entrées*. Paris, 1700.

Le Brun, Charles. *L'expression des passions et autres conférences*. Edited by Julien Philipe. Paris: Éditions Dédale, 1994.

Le Camus de Mézières, Nicolas. *The Genius of Architecture; or, The Analogy of That Art with Our Sensations*. Translated by David Britt and with an intro. by Robin Middleton. Santa Monica, CA: Getty Center for the History of Art and the Humanities, 1992.

Le Doeuff, Michèle. *The Philosophical Imaginary*. Translated by Colin Gordon. Stanford: Stanford University Press, 1989.

Lefrançois, Thierry. *Charles Coypel: Peintre du roi (1694–1752)*. Paris: Arthena, 1994.

Letters of Abelard and Heloise. Translated and with an intro. by Betty Radice. London: Penguin Books, 1974.

"Lettre à M.***" *Mercure de France* (April 1734): 770–73.

"Lettre de Marmontel." In *Année 1873* of *Nouvelles archives de l'art français. Receuil de documents inédits publiées par la Société de l'histoire de l'art français*. 34 vols. Reprint, Paris: F. de Nobele, 1973.

Lettres et épitres amoureuses d'Héloïse avec les réponses d'Abeilard. Paris, 1777.

Levitine, George. *The Sculpture of Falconet*. Greenwich, CT: New York Graphic Society, 1972.

Lloyd, Genevieve. *The Man of Reason: "Male" and "Female" in Western Philosophy*. 2d ed. Minneapolis: University of Minnesota Press, 1993.

Longinus. *On the Sublime*. Translated by W. Hamilton Fyfe and revised by Donald Russell. Cambridge, MA: Harvard University Press, 1995.

MacArthur, Elizabeth J. *Extravagant Narratives: Closure and Dynamics in the Epistolary Form*. Princeton: Princeton University Press, 1990.

Mainil, Jean. *Dans les règles du plaisir . . . Théorie de la différence dans le discours obscène, romaneque et médical de l'ancien régime*. Paris: Éditions Kimé, 1996.

Maire, Catherine-Laurence.*Les convulsionnaires de Saint-Médard. Miracles, convulsions et prophéties à Paris au XVIIIe siècle*. Paris: Gallimard/Julliard, 1985.

Malebranche, Nicolas. *The Search after Truth*. Translated and edited by Thomas Lennon and Paul Olscamp. Cambridge: Cambridge University Press, 1997.

Marchand, Jean-Henri. *Abaillard et Héloïse. Tragédie en cinq acte et en vers*. The Hague and Paris: Tabarie, 1768.

Marconville, Jean de. *De la bonté et mauvaiseté des femmes*. Paris: Jean Dallier, 1564. Reprint, Paris: Côté-Femmes, 1991.

Marin, Louis. "Le moi et les pouvoirs de l'image: Glose sur Pygmalion, scène lyrique (1772) de J.-J. Rousseau." *Modern Language Notes* 107 (1992): 659–72.

Marshall, David. *The Surprising Effects of Sympathy*. Chicago: University of Chicago Press, 1998.

McClellan, Andrew. "D'Angiviller's 'Great Men' of France and the Politics of the Parlements." *Art History* 13 (1990): 175–92.

Mémoires secrets pour servir à l'histoire de la République des Lettres en France depuis MDCCLXII jusqu'à nos jours; ou, Journal d'un observateur. 36 vols. London: J. Adamson, 1780–89.

Metamorphoses d'Ovide en Latin et en françois de la traduction de M. l'Abbé Banier, 4 vols. Paris: Le Clerc, 1767–1771.

Meun, Jean de, and Guillaume de Lorris. *The Romance of the Rose*. Translated by Charles Dahlberg. Princeton: Princeton University Press, 1995.

Michel, Régis. "Diderot and Modernity." *Oxford Art Journal* 8 (1985): 36–51.

Miller, J. Hillis. *Versions of Pygmalion*. Cambridge MA: Harvard University Press, 1990.

Miller, John R. *Boileau en France au dix-huitième siècle*. Baltimore: Johns Hopkins Press, 1942.

Miller, Nancy. "Female Sexuality and Narrative Structure in *La Nouvelle Héloïse* and *Les Liaisons dangereuses*." *Signs* 1 (1976): 609–38.

———. "Arachnologies: The Woman, the Text, the Critic." In *The Poetics of Gender*, edited by Nancy K. Miller. New York: Columbia University Press, 1986.

Mitchell, W. T. J. *Iconology: Image, Text, Ideology*. Chicago: University of Chicago Press, 1986.

Molière. *Les femmes savantes*. Paris: Comédie Française, 1978.

Montaigne, Michel de. "Of the Affection of Fathers for Their Children." In *The Complete Essays of Montaigne*. Translated by Donald M. Frame. Stanford: Stanford University Press, 1958.

More, Henry. *Enthusiasmus Triumphatus*. Reprint of the 1662 ed. With an intro. by M. V. De Porte. Augustan Reprint Society, no. 118. Los Angeles: University of California William Andrews Clark Memorial Library, 1966.

Moscovici, Claudia. "Beyond the Particular and the Universal: D'Alembert's 'Discours préliminaire' to the *Encyclopédie*." *Eighteenth-Century Studies* 33 (spring 2000): 383–400.

Nicholson, Kathleen. "The Ideology of Feminine 'Virtue': The Vestal Virgin in French Eighteenth-Century Allegorical Portraiture." In *Portraiture: Facing the Subject*, edited by Joanna Woodall. Manchester: Manchester University Press, 1996.

Nietzsche, Friedrich. *The Genealogy of Morals*. Translated by Horace B. Samuel. In vol. 13 of *The Complete Works of Friedrich Nietzsche*. 18 vols. Edinburgh and London: T. N. Foulis, 1910.

Observations d'une société d'amateurs, sur les tableaux exposés au salon cette année. Paris: 1761. Deloynes Collection, vol. 7, no. 94.

Observations sur les arts et sur quelques morceaux de peinture & de sculpture exposés au Louvre en 1748. Leyden: Elias Luzac Junior, 1748. Deloynes Collection, vol. 3, no. 34.

Ombre de Rubens au Sallon. Paris, 1787. Deloynes Collection, vol. 15, no. 371.

Ovid. *Metamorphoses, Books 9–10*. Translated by Frank Justus Miller. Cambridge, MA: Harvard University Press, 1984.

Owen, Stephen. *Mi-Lou: Poetry and the Labyrinth of Desire*. Cambridge, MA: Harvard University Press, 1989.

Panard, Charles-François, and Thomas L'Affichard. *Pigmalion; ou, La statuë animée*. Paris: Delormel, 1746.

Paulson, Ronald. *Hogarth's Graphic Works*. 2 vols. New Haven: Yale University Press, 1965.

Peintres du roi, 1648–1793. Paris: Réunion des Musées Nationaux, 2000.

Perry, Gill. "'The British Sappho': Borrowed Identities and the Representation of Women Artists in Late Eighteenth-Century British Art." *Oxford Art Journal* 18 (1995): 44–57.

Le philosophe amoureux, histoire galante, contenant une dissertation curieuse, sur la vie de Pierre Abaillard, & celle d'Héloïse, avec les intrigues amoureuses des mêmes personnes. 2d rev. ed. Au Paraclet, 1697.

Pieper, Josef. *Enthusiasm and Divine Madness. On the Platonic Dialogue Phaedrus.* New York, 1962.

"Pigmalion, acte de Ballet." In *Fragments représentés devant le roi à Fontainebleau le 12 octobre 1754.* Paris, 1754.

Piles, Roger de. *Cours de peinture par principes.* With an intro. by Roger Puttfarken. Nîmes: Éditions Jacqueline Chambon, 1990.

Pinel, Philippe. *Nosographie philosophique; ou, La méthode de l'analyse appliquée à la médecine.* 3 vols. Paris: J. A. Brosson, 1813.

Pinto-Correia, Clara. *The Ovary of Eve: Egg and Sperm in Preformation.* Chicago: University of Chicago Press, 1997.

Plato. *Phaedrus.* Translated and with an intro. by W. C. Helmbold and W. G. Rabinowitz. Indianapolis: Bobbs-Merrill, 1956.

Pomme, Pierre. *Traité des affections vaporeuses des deux sexes.* Paris: Desaint et Saillent, 1760.

Poulain de La Barre, François. *The Woman as Good as the Man; or, The Equality of Both Sexes.* Translated by A. L. London: Nathaniel Brooks, 1677. Reprint, Detroit: Wayne State University Press, 1988.

Pucci, Suzanne. "Metaphor and Metamorphosis in Diderot's *Le Rêve de d'Alembert:* Pygmalion 'Materialized.'" *Symposium* 35 (1981–82): 325–40.

———. *Sites of the Spectator: Emerging Literary and Cultural Practice in Eighteenth-Century France.* Oxford: Voltaire Foundation, 2001.

Radisich, Paula Rea. *Hubert Robert: Painted Spaces of the Enlightenment.* New York: Cambridge University Press, 1998.

———. "Louvisa Ulrike of Sweden, Patron of Chardin." Paper presented at the College Art Association Meetings, Los Angeles, 1999.

Rand, Richard, ed. *Intimate Encounters. Love and Domesticity in Eighteenth-Century France.* Princeton: Princeton University Press, 1997.

Ravel, Jeffrey. "Actress to Activist: Mlle Clairon in the Public Sphere of the 1760s." *Theatre Survey* 35 (1994): 73–88.

Ray, William. "Reading Women: Fiction, Culture and Gender in Rousseau." *Eighteenth-Century Studies* (1994): 421–48.

Réau, Louis. *Étienne-Maurice Falconet.* 2 vols. Paris: Demotte, 1922.

Remond de Sainte-Albine, Pierre. *Le comédien.* Paris: Desaint & Saillant, 1747.

Reuilly, Jean de. *La Raucourt et ses amies.* Paris: Daragon, 1909.

Ris, L. Clément de. *Les amateurs d'autrefois.* Paris: Plon et Cie., 1877.

Roach, Joseph. *The Player's Passion. Studies in the Science of Acting.* Newark: University of Delaware Press, 1985.

Rosario, Vernon. *The Erotic Imagination: French Histories of Perversity.* New York: Oxford University Press, 1997.

Rosenberg, Pierre. *The Age of Louis XV. French Painting, 1710–1774.* Toledo, OH: Toledo Museum of Art, 1975.

Rosenberg, Pierre, and Colin Bailey. "Not Greuze, but Bernard d'Agesci." *Burlington Magazine* (2001): 204–11.

Rousseau, Jean-Jacques. *Les confessions.* Volume 15 of *Oeuvres complètes de J.-J. Rousseau mises dans un nouvel ordre, avec des notes historique et des éclaircissements.* Edited by Victor Donatien Musset-Pathay. 22 vols. Paris: P. Dupont, 1823–26.

———. "Récitatif obligé." In *Dictionnaire de musique.* In vol. 13 of *Oeuvres complètes de J.-J. Rousseau mises dans un nouvel ordre, avec des notes historique et des éclaircissements.* Edited by Victor Donatien Musset-Pathay. 22 vols. Paris: P. Dupont, 1823–26.

———. *Lettre à M. d'Alembert sur les spectacles.* Lille: Giard, 1948.

———. *Pygmalion.* In vol. 2 of *Oeuvres complètes.* Edited by Bernard Gagnebin and Marcel Raymond. 4 vols. Paris: Éditions Gallimard, 1959–69.

———. *Julie, or The New Heloise.* Translated and annotated by Phillip Stewart and Jean Vaché. Hanover, NH: University Press of New England, 1997.

Roussel, Pierre. *Système physique et morale de la femme.* Paris: Vincent: 1775.

Rubin, James. "'Pygmalion and Galatea': Girodet and Rousseau."*Burlington Magazine* 127 (Aug. 1985): 517–20.

Schiebinger, Londa. *The Mind Has No Sex?* Cambridge, MA: Harvard University Press, 1989.

Schneider, Mechthild. "Pygmalion—Mythos des schöpferischen Künstlers." *Pantheon* 45 (1985): 111–23.

Schwartz, Jerome. "Narcisse et Pygmalion—Deux moments dans la mythologie personnelle de Montaigne." In *Montaigne and the Gods,* edited by Daniel Martin. Amherst, MA: Hestia Press, 1993.

Scott, Barbara. "The Comtesse de Verrue. A Lover of Dutch and Flemish Art." *Apollo* 97 (1973): 20–24.

Scudéry, Madeleine de. *Les femmes illustrés; où, Les harangues héroïques.* With an intro. by Claude Maignien. Paris: Côté-Femmes, 1991.

Shaftesbury, Anthony Ashley Cooper, third earl of. *Characteristics of Men, Manners, Opinions, Times.* Edited by Lawrence E. Klein. Cambridge: Cambridge University Press, 1999.

Sheriff, Mary D. "On Fragonard's Enthusiasm." *The Eighteenth-Century. Theory and Interpretation* 28 (1987): 29–46.

———. "Reflecting on Chardin." *The Eighteenth Century. Theory and Interpretation* 29 (winter 1988): 19–45.

———. *J. H. Fragonard: Art and Eroticism.* Chicago: University of Chicago Press, 1990.

———. *The Exceptional Woman: Elisabeth Vigée-Lebrun and the Cultural Politics of Art.* Chicago: University of Chicago Press, 1996.

———. "Letters: Painted/Penned/Purloined." *Studies in Eighteenth-Century Culture* 26 (1996): 29–56.

———. "Reading Jupiter Otherwise, or Ovid's Women in Eighteenth-Century Art." In *Myth, Sexuality and Power: Images of Jupiter in Western Art.* Special issue of *Archeologia Transatlantica.* Edited by Frances Van Keuren. Providence, RI and Louvain-La-Neuve, Belgium: (1998): 79–98.

———. "Passionate Spectators: On Enthusiasm, Nymphomania, and the Imagined Tableau." Special issue of *Huntington Library Quarterly.* Edited by Lawrence Klein and Anthony La Vopa. 60: (1999): 51–83.

———. "À rebours. Le problème de l'histoire dans l'interprétation féministe." In *Où en est l'interprétation de l'oeuvre d'art?* edited by Régis Michel. Paris: École des Beaux-Arts and Réunion des Musée Nationaux. 2000.

Simowitz, Amy. *The Theory of Art in the Encyclopédie.* Ann Arbor: UMI Press, 1983.

Sissa, Guilia. *Greek Virginity.* Translated by Arthur Goldhammer. Cambridge, MA: Harvard University Press, 1990.

Stafford, Barbara. *Body Criticism: Imaging the Unseen in Enlightenment Art and Medicine.* Cambridge, MA: MIT Press, 1991.

———. *Artful Science.* Cambridge, MA: MIT Press, 1994.

Starobinski, Jean. *Jean-Jacques Rousseau: Transparency and Obstruction.* Translated by Arthur Goldhammer. Chicago: University of Chicago Press, 1988.

Stendhal, *Promenades dans Rome.* In vol. 7 of *Oeuvres complètes.* 50 vols. Edited by Victor Del Litto and Ernest Abravanel. Geneva and Paris: Slatkine, 1986.

Stewart, Philip. *Engraven Desire: Eros, Image and Text in the French Eighteenth Century.* Durham, NC: Duke University Press, 1992.

Swain, Virginia. "Hidden from View: French Women Authors and the Language of Rights, 1727–1792." In *Intimate Encounters. Love and Domesticity in Eighteenth-Century French Art,* edited by Richard Rand. Princeton: Princeton University Press, 1997.

Teresa of Avila. *The Autobiography of St. Teresa of Avila.* Translated by E. Allison Peers. New York: Doubleday, 1960.

"Testament de Madame de Verrue." *Gazette des Beaux-Arts* 16 (1864): 318–30.

Thérèse Philosophe. In *Romans libertins du XVIIIe siècle,* edited by Raymond Trousson. Paris: Robert Laffont, 1993.

Thomas, Antoine Léonard. "Essai sur le caractère, les moeurs et l'esprit des femmes dans les differents siècles." In *Qu'est-ce qu'une femme?* With an intro. by Elisabeth Badinter. Paris: P.O.L., 1989.

Tissot, Samuel-Auguste-David. *L'onanisme: Dissertation sur les maladies produites par le masturbation.* 10th ed., augmented. Toulouse: Laporte, 1775.

———. *Traité sur la santé des gens de lettres et des valetudinaires.* In *Oeuvres complètes de Tissot.* New ed.,vol. 3. Paris: Allut, 1809–13.

Triomphe des religieuses; ou, Les nones babillardes. 1748.

Tucker, Susie. *Enthusiasm. A Study in Semantic Change.* Cambridge: Cambridge Univesity Press, 1972.

Unsworth, Barry. *Stone Virgin.* New York: W.W. Norton, 1995.

Vairre, Simone. "Pygmalion et Orphée chez Ovide." *Revue des Études Latines* 46 (1965): 235–46.

Vanpée, Janie. "Jean-Baptiste Greuze: The Drama of Looking." *L'Esprit Créateur* 28 (winter 1988): 46–68.

Veen, Jan van der. *Le mélodrame musical de Rousseau au romantisme.* The Hague: Martinus Nijhoff, 1955.

Vénus dans le cloître; ou, La religieuse en chemise. Arles: Actes Sud, 1994.

Véridique au Sallon. Paris, 1783. Deloynes Collection, vol. 13, no. 298.

Vernant, Jean-Pierre. "At Man's Table: Hesiod's Foundation Myth of Sacrifice." In *The Cuisine of Sacrifice among the Greeks,* edited by Marcel Detienne and Jean-Pierre Vernant and translated by Paula Wissing. Chicago: University of Chicago Press, 1989.

Vidal, Mary. "*Watteau's Painted Conversations: Art, Literature and Talk in Seventeenth and Eighteenth-Century France.* New Haven: Yale University Press, 1992.

———. "Style as Subject in Watteau's Images of Conversation." In *The Cambridge Companion to Watteau,* edited by Mary Sheriff. Forthcoming.

Vigée-Lebrun, Elisabeth. *Souvenirs.* Edited by Claudine Herrmann. 2 vols. Paris: Des Femmes, 1984.

Vila, Anne. *Enlightenment and Pathology: Sensibility in the Literature and*

Medicine of Eighteenth-Century France. Baltimore: Johns Hopkins University Press, 1998.

Vincent, K. Steven. "Benjamin Constant, the French Revolution, and the Origins of French Romantic Liberalism." *French Historical Studies* 23 (fall 2000): 607–37.

Vincent-Buffault, Anne. *The History of Tears: Sensibility and Sentimentality in France.* Translated by Teresa Bridgeman. New York: St. Martin's, 1991.

Voltaire, François-Marie Arouet de. *Dictionnaire philosophique.* Edited with notes by Béatrice Didier. Paris: Imprimerie Nationale Éditions, 1994.

———. *Oeuvres complètes de Voltaire.* Paris: Garnier Frères, 1877. Reprint, Liechtenstein: Kraus, 1967.

Walter, Eric. "Le complexe d'Abélard ou le célibat des gens de lettres." *Dix-Huitième Siècle* 12 (1980): 127–52.

Weinshenker, Anne Betty. *Falconet: His Writings and His Friend Diderot.* Geneva: Librairie Droz, 1966.

Wellman, Kathleen. *La Mettrie: Medicine, Philosophy, and Enlightenment.* Durham, NC: Duke University Press, 1992.

Wildenstein, Georges. *The Paintings of Fragonard.* New York: Phaidon, 1960.

Wilkins, Kay. "Attitudes toward Women in Two Eighteenth-Century French Periodicals." *Studies in Eighteenth-Century Culture* 6 (1978): 393–406.

Williams, David. "The Fate of French Feminism: Boudier de Villement's *Ami des Femmes.*" *Eighteenth-Century Studies* 14 (1980–81): 37–55.

Wilson, Lindsay. *Women and Medicine in the French Enlightenment.* Baltimore: Johns Hopkins Press, 1993.

Wolff, Martha. "An Early Painting by Greuze and Its Literary Associations." *Burlington Magazine* 138 (1996): 580–85.

Zick, Gisela. "Amor Harpokrates. Zur Wirkungesgeschichte und Ikonographischen Herleitung einer Skulptur von Etienne Maurice Falconet." *Wallraf-Richartz Jahrbuch* 37 (1975): 215–46.

Ziskin, Rochelle. *The Place Vendôme: Architecture and Social Mobility in Eighteenth-Century Paris.* New York: Cambridge University Press, 1999.

INDEX

Page numbers in italics refer to figures.

Abelard, Pierre, 201, 203, 211–16, 219, 222–23, 225–30, 233, 239; as seen by Saint-Preux in *Julie, ou La nouvelle Héloïse,* 233; representation of his castration, 279n22

actresses, 5, 52–53. *See also* Arnoud, Sophie; Clairon, Clairon, Mlle (Claire-Hippolyte Léris); Lecouvreur, Adrienne; Raucourt, Mlle (Josèphe-Françoise Saucelle); Robinson, Mary

Adam, Lambert-Sigisbert, 143

Agesci, Bernard d', *A Lady Reading the Letters of Heloise and Abelard,* 11, 201–22, 227–28, 230–31, 234–36, 239–40, 242, *202*

Aiguillon, duchesse d', *Épître d'Héloïse à Abailard,* 223, 226–27, 229

Alacoque, Marguerite Marie, 54–55, 255n42

Alembert, Jean Le Rond d', 15, 104; as character in Diderot's *Rêve de d'Alembert,* 118–19; *Discours préliminaire de l'Encyclopédie,* 4, 15–19, 72, 248n3

Allius, Jacques, *Histoire des amours d'Abaillard et d'Héloïse,* 225

Angiviller, Charles Claude Flahaut, comte de la Billarderie d', 188

Apelle au sallon, 76–77

Apelles and Campaspe, 143–44. See also *Apelle au sallon*

Aristotle, 29, 34; *Poetics,* 31–32

Arnoud, Sophie, 196

ballet d'action, 190, 193. See also *danse en action*

Barnabé-Firman de Rosoi, *Pygmalion,* 177

Barthélemy, Jean-Jacques, Abbé, *Le voyage du jeune Anacharsis en Grèce,* 65, 70–71, 138

Batteux, Charles, Abbé, 9, 32, 64–65; *Cours de belles-lettres,* 74; *Les beaux-arts réduits à un même principe,* 21, 50, 74

Baudouin, Pierre-Antoine, 10; *The Cherry Picker,* 89–90, *90;* as criticized by Diderot, 89–91; *Noon,* 101–2, *101; Peasant Girl Quarreling with Her Mother,* 89–90; *Reading,* 95–97, 108, 115, 119–20, 131–33, 204, 209, 230, *95*

Bayle, Pierre, *Dictionnaire historique et critique,* 226

Beauchêne, Edme Pierre Chavot de, 9, 49; *De l'influence des affections de l'âme dans les maladies nerveuses des femmes,* 45

Benoist, Marie Guillemine, depiction of Sappho, 138

Bernard, Pierre-Joseph (called Gentil-Bernard), *L'art d'aimer,* 207–8, 221, 227–28, 230, 236

Bernini, Gianlorenzo: compared to Baudouin's *Reading,* 95–96; *Saint Teresa in Ecstasy,* 92–93, 204, *93*

Bertin, Nicolas, *Anacreon and Amour,* 136–38, *137*

Bienville, D. T., 209, 215, 237; difference from *Encyclopédie,* 267n15; *La nymphomanie; ou, Traité de la fureur utérine,* 128–30, 133, 147

Boileau Despréaux, Nicolas, 9, 108; *Dialogue des héros roman,* 74; *L'art poétique,* 72–74; *Satire on women,* 89; translation of Longinus, *Traité du sublime ou du merveilleux dans le discours,* 7, 21–22, 32, 61–64, 231
Bonnet, Charles, *Essai analytique sur les facultés de l'âme,* 44–45
Bordeu, Théophile, as character in Diderot's *Rêve de d'Alembert,* 118, 123, 265n76
Boucher, François: drawing of a young woman reading the letters of Heloise and Abelard, 221–223, *222; Toilet of Venus,* 208, *208; Vertumnus and Pomona,* 78, *80; The Woman Tying Her Garter,* 133, *134*
Boudier de Villemert, Pierre-Joseph, *Le nouvel ami des femmes; ou, La philosophie du sexe,* 55, 86, 120
boudoir: in *The Genius of Architecture* (Le Camus des Mézières), 119, 263n39; as a site for reading, 96, 101–4, 119–20. *See also* Maleuvre, Pierre
Boureau-Deslandes, André-François, *Pigmalion; ou, La statue animée,* 114–15, 143, 146, 165, 180, 230
Boulogne, Madeleine de, 68
Brioché; ou, L'origine des marionnettes, 146
Brosses, Charles de, as a character in Diderot's "Salon of 1767," 139–41
Buffon, Georges Louis Leclerc, comte de, as a character in Diderot's "Salon of 1767," 140–41
Butler, Judith, 40, 251–52n95–96

Cahusac, Louis de: *Enthusiasme,* 17–31, 38–41, 141–42, 188, 251n91; *La danse ancienne et moderne; ou, Traité historique de la danse,* 192–93, 252n98
Callistratus, *Descriptiones,* 175, 273n37
Casaubon, Merit, *A Treatise concerning Enthusiasm,* 56
castration, 213–215
Catherine II (empress of Russia), 107, 199–200
Chambon de Montaux, Nicolas, *Des maladies des femmes,* 37
Châtelet, Gabrielle Émilie Le Tonnelier de Breteuil, marquise du, 179, 230
Chardin, Jean-Baptiste, *Amusements of Private Life,* 97–99, *98; The Drawing Lesson,* 88, *88; The Good Education,* 86–89, *87*
Cheron, Elisabeth Sophie, *Portrait of a Woman as Sappho,* 68–69, *69*
chisel: as sign of sculpture, 163, 186, 190; as tool for sculpture and procreation, 177, 180–82, 184
Chrysostom, Saint John, on the Pythia, 56
Clairon, Mlle (Claire-Hippolyte Léris), 52–53, 83, 193, 244–45; *Réflexions sur la déclamation théâtrale,* 193
Clement of Alexandria, Saint, 144
Cohen, Sarah, 191, 193
Coicy, Mme de, *Les femmes comme il convient de les voir,* 254n20
Colardeau, Charles-Pierre, *Lettre d'Abeilard à Héloïse,* 213; *Lettre amoureuse d'Héloïse à Abelard,* 215, 223–226; as related to Alexander Pope, 277–78n4, 279n35
Colonna, François-Marie-Pompée, *Les principes de la nature ou de la génération des choses,* 177
Comédie Française, 82, 164, 182
Condillac, Étienne Bonnot de, Abbé, 15, 17, 24, 34, 38–39, 91–92, 107; *Essai sur l'origine des connaissances humaines,* 29–30; *Traité des sensations,* 26–27, 183
convulsionnaires, 57–61, 93–94, 130; influence on Charcot, 256n59; relation to French politics, 256n60; and the *secours,* 58–60. *See also* Moulère (or Moler), Gabrielle
Corneille, Michel: decoration for the Nobles' Room at Versailles, 67–68; *Sappho Performing Her Lyric Poetry, 67*
Coypel, Charles: illustration for Molière's *Les femmes savantes,* 258n93; *L'amour précepteur,* 228, *229; Portrait of Adrienne Lecouvreur,* 82–83, *83; Portrait of a Woman with a Lyre,* 71, *72*
Coypel, Noël Nicholas, *Rape of Europa,* 205–6, *205*
Cubières-Palmézeaux, Michel de, *Galatée, Comédie,* 194

Dandré-Bardon, Michel, *Traité de peinture,* 62
danse en action, 190–93
danse simple, 192
Darsant de Puisieux, Madeleine, *Conseils à une amie,* 89
Darnton, Robert, 94, 122–23
David, Jacques Louis, *Portrait of Madame Buron,* 100, *100*
DeJean, Joan, 6, 66, 71–74, 89, 108–10, 120
Descartes, Réne, *Les passions de l'âme,* 24–25, 30–31, 114, 249n33, 250n43. *See also* passions

Deshoulières, Antoinette, 74
Diderot, Denis, 17, 38, 46, 104, 123, 163, 178, 199, 250n46; correspondence with Étienne Falconet, 178–79, 184; correspondence with Sophie Volland, 212; dialogue with Rousseau, 234, 238; *Encyclopédie*, 15; *Essai sur la peinture*, 250n46; *La réligieuse*, 223, 226; *Le neveu de Rameau*, 33; *Notice sur la Carle Van Loo*, 108; *Paradoxe sur le comédien*, 33, 51–53, 83, 90–91, 193, 244; *Principes de la philosophie morale; ou, Essay de M S**** sur la mérite et la vertu Avec réflexions*, 7; *Rêve de d'Alembert*, 118–19, 123, 265n76, 266n100; "Salon de 1763," 168–73, 175, 181; "Salon de 1765," 78–81, 89–90, 130–31, 181, 206, 210–11, 217–20, 280n46; "Salon de 1767," 25–26, 34, 46, 52, 81–83, 90–91, 119, 189, 241; "Salon de 1769," 130; *Salons*, 11, 78, 83; *Second entretien sur le fils naturel*, 176–77; on the sketch, 260n123; *Sur les femmes*, 53, 60–61
Dorat, Claude-Joseph, "Épître d'Abelard à Héloïse," 212–13
Doyen, Gabriel-François, *Le miracle des Ardents* (*Miracle of St Anthony's Fire*), 34–35, 244, *35*
Drouet de Maupertuis, Jean-Baptiste, *La femme faible*, 89
Du Barry, Jean Bécu, comtesse, 220
Dubuisson, *Tableau de l'amour conjugal*, 177
Dumont, François, *Madame de Saint-Just d'Aucourt as Sappho*, 71, *73*
DuBois, Page, 6, 61–63
Du Bos, Jean-Baptiste, Abbé: on the difference between men and women actors, 51; *Réflexions critiques sur la poésie et sur la peinture*, 7, 20, 32–33, 35–36, 77–78, 82
Du Laurens, André, *De maladies mélancholiques et du moyen de les guérir*, 145

ecstasy: formulaic representations of, 206; of Heloise, 204, 215; of Rousseau, 237–38. *See also* Baudouin, Pierre-Antoine; Bernini, Gianlorenzo; passions; *ravissement*
Eisen, Charles, *Heloise in Her Cell*, 223–227, *223*
Encyclopédie, ou Dictionnaire raisonné des sciences, des arts et des métiers, par une société des gens de lettres, 15, 23, 28, 173; chart of the "Detailed System of Human Knowledge," 29, "Femme," 20, 47; "Mansturpration," 125–26; "Mélancholie (Médecine)," 36–37; "Nymphomanie, 126–28, 150, 267n15;" "Passion," 24; Prospectus, 18–19; "Raison," 28; "Satyriasis,"127. *See also* Alembert, Jean Le Rond d'; Cahusac, Louis de, *Enthusiasme*; Diderot, Denis; Fouquet, Henri, "sensibilité"; Saint-Lambert, Jean François, marquis de, "Genius" ("Génie"); Voltaire, "Imagination"
emulation, 22, 61–63, 66, 69, 74–77, 84, 168–69, 203, 231–32
enthusiasm, 6–11, 17–40, 50, 122, 192, 194, 241–45, 250n46; for the actress Raucourt, 194–95; confusion of sexual and poetic enthusiasm, 133–44, 159; confusion of sexual and religious enthusiasm, 94–97; for great men, 188; of Heloise, 201, 230–34; and male sexuality, 177–81; Pygmalion's enthusiasm, 175–77; religious enthusiasm, 56–66; as represented in *A Lady Reading the Letters of Heloise*, 203, 212; in Rousseau's writings, 181–84, 238–39; Sappho's enthusiasm, 70, 85. *See also* Cahusac, Louis de
Épinay, Louise Florence Pétronille Tardieu d'Esclavelles, marquise de Lalive d', *Les conversations d'Émilie*, 113
erotomania, 60, 145, 151, 153, 241, 244, 268–69n51
Esquirol, Étienne, 268–69n26; *Des maladies mentales*, 226

Falconet, Étienne: *Bather*, 170, 184–85, *171*; correspondence with Diderot, 179, 184; *Menacing Cupid*, 171–72, 273n34, *172; Pygmalion*, 166–78, 178, 184–94, 197–200, 242–43, *167*; *Réflexions sur la sculpture*, 34–35, 173–74, 186–89; translation of Pliny, 62. *See also* Guichard, M, "Sur son group de Pygmaliion exposé au Salon du Louvre"; Romilly fils, "Vers à M Falconet sur la statue de Pygmalion"; "Sur son group de Pygmalion exposé au Salon du Louvre"
Felman, Shoshona, 216, 240
femme philosophe, 120, 266n100
femme savante, 112–14
Fénelon, François de Salignac de La Mothe, *De l'education des filles*, 86, 113
Ferrand, Jacques, *A Treatise on Lovesickness*, 69, 113, 128–29, 145–46, 150, 152

fire as metaphor, 128, 133–38, 143, 149, 162, 169, 175–78, 182, 184, 188, 192, 195
Foster, Susan Leigh, 190
Fouquet, Henri, "Sensibilité," 44–45
Fragonard, Jean-Honoré, 4, 172; *Coresus Sacrificing Himself to Save Callirhoe,* 243–44, *243;* images of lapdogs, 262n33; *The Powder Keg,* 134, 137–38, *136; The Swing,* 172, 273n34
François de Pâris, 57, 59
Freud, Sigmund, 63, 151–56, 211, 213, 216; *Civilization and Its Discontents,* 155–56; *Delusions and Dreams,* 152–54; *Essay on Femininity,* 156; *Totem and Taboo,* 155
fureur pittoresque, 20–21. *See also* enthusiasm
fureur poétique, 20–21, 28. *See also* enthusiasm
fureur utérine, 126–28, 147–48, 150. *See also* nymphomania

Galatea, 5, 142–43, 146, 155, 180, 185–87, 242; as character in Cubières-Palmézeaux's *Galatée,* 194; as a character in La Motte's ballet, 147; as character in Boureau-Deslandes's *Pigmalion; ou, La statue animée,* 114–15, 165; in Falconet's *Pygmalion,* 166–71, 173–76, 181; in painting, 159–64; in Rousseau's *Pygmalion,* 181–84; women playing the part of, 11, 189–91, 193–94, 196–99
Galiani, Ferdinando, Abbé, 110
genius, 17–18, 20, 49, 62, 179, 192, 241, 244, 250n61; of Sappho, 65
Genlis, Stéphanie Félicité, comtesse de, *Adelaide and Theodore,* 263n44, 264n70–71
Geoffrin, Marie-Thérèse Rodet, Madame, 104–12
Gois, Étienne, *Statue of Chancellor de l'Hôpital,* 181
Goodman, Dena, 107, 109
Graville, Barthélemy-Claude Graillard de, *L'ami des filles,* 85–86, 89, 97
Grenaille, F. de, *Nouveau recueil de lettres des dames tant anciennes que moderne,* 225
Greuze, Jean-Baptiste, 10, 168; *The Broken Eggs,* 209–10, *210; The Dreamer,* 220, *221; The Lazy Italian Woman,* 117–18, *117; Philosophy Asleep,* 115–19, 265n73, *116;* in relation to *A Lady Reading the Letters of Heloise,* 203, 206, 228, 231, 239; *The Well-Beloved Mother,* 206, 217–19, 280n46, *219; A Young Girl Mourning Her Dead Bird,* 210, *211; A Young Woman Throwing a Kiss from Her Window,* 78–81, *81*
Grimm, Frédéric-Melchior, 181, 195
Gros, Antoine-Jean, *Sappho Leaping from the Rock of Leucatus,* 139, *140*
Gross, Kenneth, 146
Guichard, M, "Sur son group de Pygmaliion exposé au Salon du Louvre," 176
Guyon, Jeanne, 8, 54–55, 255n42
Guys, Jean Baptiste, *Abailard et Héloïse,* 212–13

Hanold, Norbert, as character in Jensen's *Gradiva,* 152–55
Heloise, 5–6, 8, 10–12, 201–39, 241–42, 245; as described by Abelard, 281n67
Hecquet, Philippe, 57–58; *Lettre sur la convulsionnaire en extase; ou, La vaporeuse en rêve,* 60, 93; *Le naturalisme des convulsions dans les maladies de l'epidemie convulsionnaire,* 60
Helman, Isidore Stanislas, *The Dangerous Novel,* etching after Nicolas Lavreince, 103–4, *103*
Hesiod: *Theogony,* 148–49; *Work and Days,* 148; writings related to *Réflexions sur l'amour,* 1780, 269n63
Homer, 61, 63
Huet, Marie-Héléne, 6, 179
Huet, Pierre-Daniel, *Traité de l'origine des romans,* 89, 109–11
hysteria, 54, 61, 155–56

imagination, 15–41, 43–55, 60, 64–65, 67, 83–89, 96–99, 104, 107, 115, 118, 120, 125–26, 129, 132, 139, 141–47, 153–56, 165, 182, 185, 192, 198, 250n46; active, 30–31; as analyzed by Malebranche, 249n34; combinatory, 17, 38–40; *imagination de détail et d'expression,* 31; *imagination d'invention,* 31, 250n61; passive imagination, 30–31, 39
inspiration, 20, 43, 58, 61–66, 71, 138, 143, 147, 175, 181, 182
instinct, 38–39
Irigaray, Luce, 40, 185, 251–52n95–96

Jeurat, Étienne: *Recovering after Childbirth,* 267n26; *Woman Convalescing,* 130–33, 267n26, *131*
Jensen, Wilhelm, *Gradiva,* 152–54
Julie, in Rousseau's *Julie, ou La nouvelle Héloïse,* 201, 232–33, 235–39

Kamuf, Peggy, 6, 211, 214, 235
Kauffman, Angelica, *Sappho,* 138, *139*
Kofman, Sarah, 156
Kramer, Heinrich, *Malleus maleficarum,* 56
Kreiser, B. Robert, 57

Lacan, Jacques, 92, 214
La Chau, Géraud de, Abbé, *Dissertation sur les attributs de Vénus,* 144, 148
Lafayette, Marie-Madeleine Pinoche de La Vergne, comtesse de, *Zayde,* 104, 108, 111, 263n44, 263n47
Labille-Guiard, Adelaïde, 4
Lambert, Anne Thérèse de Marguenat de Courcelles, marquise de, 113
La Motte, Antoine Houdar de, *Le triomphe des arts,* 143, 14, 149, 159
La Rive, 181, 190
La Mettrie, Julien Offray de, 125; *Machine Man,* 48–49
Le Brun, Charles: *L'expression des passions,* 204; *le ravissement,* 204–6, 231, *204*
Le Camus de Mézières, Nicolas, *The Genius of Architecture,* 119, 263n39, 265n81
Lecouvreur, Adrienne, 81–84; portrait of, *83*
Le Doueff, Michèle, 6
Lemoyne, François, *Pygmalion Seeing His Sculpture Come to Life,* 159–64, *161*
Lespinasse, Julie de, 122, 266n100
Leszczynska, Marie (queen of France), 78
Lettres portugaises, 223, 227, 232–33
Longinus, *On the Sublime,* 7, 21–22, 32, 61–66, 72, 231. *See also* Boileau Despréaux, Nicolas
love madness, 226, 237. *See also* erotomania
lovesickness, 127–28, 131, 145–47, 162, 175, 182, 191, 241

MacArthur, Elizabeth, 236
Mainil, Jean, 112, 266n96
Malebranche, Nicolas, *Recherche de la vérité,* 249n35, 252n1, 253n13–14
Maleuvre, Pierre, *The Boudoir* (print after Sigmund Freudenberger), 102–4, 119, *102*
Marchand, Jean-Henri, *Abaillard et Héloïse,* 213, 230
Marconville, Jean de, *De la bonté et mauvaiseté des femmes,* 268n45, 269n65
Marmontel, Jean François, 199–200
Mary Magdalene, Saint, 224–27
masturbation, 96, 120–21, 123, 125–26, 129, 131–33, 139, 265–66n90
melancholia, 8–9, 18, 34–37, 128–30, 145–46, 153, 182, 241; erotic melancholy, 127–28
memory, 15, 27, 29, 38
Messalina, 149–50, 269n65
Molière, 40; *Les femmes savantes,* 113–15, 230, 258n93, 264n70
monomanie érotique, 226. *See also* erotomania; love madness; lovesickness
Montaigne, Michel, "De l'affection des peres aux enfans," 178
Moulère (or Moler), Gabrielle, 58–60; illustrations of her *secours,* 257n67
Myrrah, 147, 150, 185, 189

Narcissus, 24, 178
narcissism, 163, 176, 177–78
neurotic, 154–56
Nietzsche, Frederich, *The Geneology of Morals,* 151
Noverre, Jean-Georges, 192–93; *Mysogyne,* 193
nymphomania, 10–11, 125–33, 147–50, 209, 226, 230, 238. See also *fureur utérine*

Origen, 56
Ovid, 70, 154; emulated by Gentil-Bernard, 228, 230; *Heroides,* 69; *Metamorphoses,* 142–43; Myrrah story, 150; Pygmalion story, 142–43, 146–49, 154, 159–60, 170, 178, 185, 187, 190, 198; story of Vertumnus and Pomona, 78. *See also* Pygmalion
Owen, Stephen, 151

Paillet, Antoine, paintings for the queen's rooms at Versailles, 68
Pandora, 148–49, 169, 185
pantomime, 165, 189, 190–91, 193
Pare, Ambroise, 227
Parrocel, Pierre, *Young Woman Reading before a Fireplace,* 133–34, *135*
passions, 19, 22, 24–30, 33–34, 36–37, 41, 43–47, 50–52, 57, 60, 64–65, 70, 77–79, 128, 133, 159, 162–63, 165, 173, 175, 176, 193, 199; astonishment, 25–26, 163, 168, 191, 194; desire, 17, 19, 21, 24, 26–28, 36, 40, 63, 74, 80–81, 83, 91, 94, 104, 115, 117, 120, 125–29, 136, 138, 141–45, 150–57, 159,165, 168, 175, 180, 183, 185, 187, 191, 200, 212–16, 225–27, 230–32, 235–37, 240, 250n43; *ravissement,* 93–94, 192, 205, 217, 227, 237, 239, 242; wonder, 24–26, 162, 166,

passions (*Continued*)
171, 181–82, 205, 249n33. *See also* Descartes, Réne, *Les passions de l'âme;* Malebranche, Nicolas, *Recherche de la vérité*
pearls, 203, 206–8
Perry, Gill, 71
Piles, Roger de, 20–25, 34; *Cour de peinture par principes,* 7, 20, 25
Philosophe amoureux, Histoire galante, 225
Pinel, Phillipe, *Nosographie philosophique; ou, La méthod de l'analyse appliquée à la médecine,* 36
Plato, 20–21, 40, 71; *Phaedrus,* 20, 56, 61–63, 277n96
Pliny, 62, 64, 144–45; *Natural History,* 144
Pomme, Pierre, *Traité des affections vaporeuses des deux sexes,* 37
Pompadour, Jeanne Antoinette Posson, marquise du, 171, 199
possession, 46, 57–58, 61–66, 74, 130, 231, 237
Poulain de La Barre, François, *De l'égalité des deux sexes,* 252–53n1
Prometheus, 148–49, 168–69, 176–79, 185, 199–200. *See also* Pandora; Voltaire
Propoetides, 142, 147–50, 189–90
prostitution, 141, 144–45, 148–50, 157–58, 186, 199
Pucci, Suzanne, 273n16
Pygmalion, 5, 10–12, 114, 141–52, 201, 239, 241, 245; in ballet, 189–94; enthusiasm of, 174–77; and Freud, 150–56; and Narcissus, 183–85; in *opera comique,* 275n88; in paintings, 159–64; as procreator, 176–81; as related to ethical aims of art, 185–89; and *Stone Virgin,* 156–58; in sculpture, 165–74; self-reference in representations of, 164–65. *See also* Boureau-Deslandes, André-François; Falconet, Étienne; Lemoyne, François; Raoux, Jean; Rousseau, Jean-Jacques
Pythia, 53–56, 61–66, 70, 74, 84

Radisich, Paula, 104, 109
Rameau, Jean Philippe, 146–47, 159, 271n8
Ranc, Jean, *Vertumnus and Pomona,* 78, *79*
Raoux, Jean, *Pygmalion,* 159–64, 187, *160*
Raucourt, Mlle (Joséphe-Françoise Saucelle), 194–99; in *Dido,* 194–95; in Rousseau's *Pygmalion,* 12, 194, 196–97, portrait of, *195*
reason, 15–30, 34, 38–41, 43, 47, 49–50, 59, 63, 67, 69, 84
Regnault de Segrais, Jean, 104, 263n47
Robert, Hubert, 109
Robinson, Mary, 71
Romance of the Rose, 146, 185, 212
Romilly fils, "Vers à M Falconet sur la statue de Pygmalion," 176
Rousseau, Jean-Jacques, assumed influence on painters, 234–35; compared by Freud to Norbert Hanold, 282n94; *Dictionnaire de musique,* 165; *Julie, ou la Nouvelle Héloïse,* 12, 201, 232–38; *Les Confessions,* 12, 237–39, 241; *Lettre à M. d'Alembert sur les spectacles,* 199, 232–34; *Oeuvres complètes,* 181–82; *Preface to the New Heloise or Conversation on Novels,* 233; *Pygmalion,* 12, 164–65, 181–84, 187, 189–90, 196–99. *See also* Julie
Roussel, Pierre, *Système physique et morale de la femme,* 9, 47, 49, 61, 115
Rubens, Peter Paul, 74–75, 77

Saint-Aubin, Gabriel de, *The Private Academy,* 133, *135*
Saint-Lambert, Jean François, marquis de, "Genius" ("Génie"), 17–18, 20
Sainte-Albine, Pierre Remond de, *Le comédien,* 255n30
Sallé, Marie, 11, 197; in *L'Europe galante,* 193; *Pigmalion,* 189–93
Sappho, 3, 5–6, 8–10, 61–74, 83, 129, 138–39, 201, 231, 232, 245, 258n96
satyriasis, 127
Scudéry, Madeleine de: as seen by Boileau, 72–74, 89; *Clélie,* 89; *Les femmes illustres,* 66–67; in Huet's preface, 108–9; in portraiture, 68–69; on Sappho, 66–70
sensibility, 23, 33, 39, 43–48, 51–55, 70–71, 82–83, 114, 138, 165, 235, 253n2, 253n14
Sévigné, Marie de Rabutin-Chantal, marquise de, 74
Sissa, Guilia, 6, 56
sketch, 137–43, 260n123
Sprenger, James, *Malleus Mallificarum,* 56
Shaftesbury, Anthony Ashley Cooper, third earl of, 7
Staël, Germaine de, 1–4; *Corinne or Italy,* 1–5, 71; on enthusiasm, 247n4
Steen, Jan, *The Doctor's Visit,* 132, *132*
Stendhal, *Promenades dans Rome,* 92–93
"Sur son group de Pygmalion exposé au Salon du Louvre," 176

Tasso, Torquato, 36, 91
Teresa of Avila, Saint, 54, 92–95, 118; representation contrasted to that of Saint Cecilia, 261n22

Therbusch, Mme (Anne Dorothea Lisiewska-Therbusch), 46
Thérèse philosophe, 10, 94, 120–23, 226, 230; the story of Eradice and Dirrag, 262n29, 266n96
Thomas, Antoine Léonard, *Essai sur le caractère, les moeurs et l'esprit des femmes deans les differents siècles*, 9, 49–51; on Descartes' valuing of women, 254n23
Tissot, Samuel, 37–38, 126, 129–30, 149–50, 209, 215, 236; *L'onanisme*, 126; *De la santé des gens de lettres*, 37
touch, 137–38, 143, 148, 152, 159–60, 168, 170, 177, 183, 197, 204, 206–8
tribade, 129, 138, 196, 199

Unsworth, Barry, *Stone Virgin*, 10, 156–57

Vallayer-Coster, Anne, 4, 75–76
Van Loo, Carle, *The Spanish Conversation*, 106, 110, *106; The Spanish Reading*, 104, 106–8, 110–11, *105; Saint Stephen Martyr*, 205
vapors, 45–46, 53, 60, 84
Venus, 159, 162, 164–65, 176, 184–89, 191, 196, 199
Venus with the Beautiful Buttocks, 145, 189
Vernant, Jean-Pierre, 149
Vernet, Joseph, 25, 119
Verrue, Jeanne d'Albert de Luynes, comtesse de, 220
Vidal, Mary, 110
Vigée-Lebrun, Elisabeth, 1–5, *Countess Fries as Sappho*, 71, *73; Self-Portrait*, 74, *75; Self-Portrait with Julie*, 74, *76*
Vignon, Claude, 68
Vila, Anne, 45, 236
Voltaire, 30–31, 38, 52–53, 57–62, 70, 169, 178–79, 188, 250n46; *Catelina*, 179; *Dictionnaire philosophique*, 58, 62; "Imagination," 30–31; "L'Origine des Métiers," 148; *Pandore*, 148, 169, 178–79

Watelet, Charles, 138
Watteau, Antoine, *Prelude to a Concert*, 110, *112; The Timid Lover*, 110, *111*
Weyer, Johann, 56
Wilson, Lindsay, 58
Wolff, Martha, 216–17

Zeuxis, 64–65, 142, 207
Ziskin, Rochelle, 119